Feminine Frequencies

**Social History, Popular Culture, and Politics in Germany**
Geoff Eley, Series Editor

*A History of Foreign Labor in Germany, 1880–1980: Seasonal Workers/Forced Laborers/Guest Workers*
  Ulrich Herbert, translated by William Templer

*Reshaping the German Right: Radical Nationalism and Political Change after Bismarck*
  Geoff Eley

*The Stigma of Names: Antisemitism in German Daily Life, 1812–1933*
  Dietz Bering

*Forbidden Laughter: Popular Humor and the Limits of Repression in Nineteenth-Century Prussia*
  Mary Lee Townsend

*From* Bundesrepublik *to* Deutschland: *German Politics after Unification*
  Michael G. Huelshoff, Andrei S. Markovits, and Simon Reich, editors

*The People Speak! Anti-Semitism and Emancipation in Nineteenth-Century Bavaria*
  James F. Harris

*The Origins of the Authoritarian Welfare State in Prussia: Conservatives, Bureaucracy, and the Social Question, 1815–70*
  Hermann Beck

*Technological Democracy: Bureaucracy and Citizenry in the German Energy Debate*
  Carol J. Hager

*Society, Culture, and the State in Germany, 1870–1930*
  Geoff Eley, editor

*Paradoxes of Peace: German Peace Movements since 1945*
  Alice Holmes Cooper

*Jews, Germans, Memory: Reconstruction of Jewish Life in Germany*
  Y. Michal Bodemann, editor

*Exclusive Revolutionaries: Liberal Politics, Social Experience, and National Identity in the Austrian Empire, 1848–1914*
  Pieter M. Judson

*Feminine Frequencies: Gender, German Radio, and the Public Sphere, 1923–1945*
  Kate Lacey

# Feminine Frequencies

Gender, German Radio,
and the Public Sphere, 1923–1945

Kate Lacey

*Ann Arbor*
THE UNIVERSITY OF MICHIGAN PRESS

Copyright © by the University of Michigan 1996
All rights reserved
Published in the United States of America by
The University of Michigan Press
Manufactured in the United States of America
⊗ Printed on acid-free paper

1999   1998   1997   1996      4   3   2   1

*A CIP catalog record for this book is available from the British Library*

Library of Congress Cataloging-in-Publication Data

Lacey, Kate, 1965–
    Feminine frequencies : gender, German radio, and the public
sphere, 1923–1945 / Kate Lacey.
        p.   cm. — (Social history, popular culture, and politics in
Germany)
    Includes bibliographical references (p.   ) and index.
    ISBN 0-472-09616-8 (cloth : acid-free paper). — ISBN
0-472-06616-1 (pbk. : acid-free paper)
    1. Broadcasting—Germany—Employees.   2. Mass media and women—
Germany.   3. Women in the mass media industry—Germany.   4. Radio
broadcasting—Germany—History.   I. Title.   II. Series.
HD8039.T382G356   1996
384.54'082—dc20                                                96-25344
                                                                    CIP

*For Mum and Dad*
*and in memory of my grandmother, Rose*

# Contents

Acknowledgments                                                          ix

Abbreviations                                                            xi

**Part 1: German Radio and Gendered Discourses**

1. Introduction                                                           3

2. Gender, Media, and Crisis:
   The Development of German Radio                                       17

**Part 2: Feminine Frequencies**

3. Let Women Speak to Women!
   On Women's Radio in Weimar Germany                                    57

4. Radio and the Maternal Spirit:
   On Women's Radio in Nazi Germany                                      97

5. Home Front / Front Line: Women, Radio, and War                       127

**Part 3: Experts on the Air**

6. The Mouthpiece of Modernity                                          149

7. All-Consuming Propaganda                                             173

8. Finding a Voice: Women's Radio and the
   Evolution of Broadcast Talk                                          193

9. Conclusion: Gender, German Radio, and the Public Sphere              221

Appendixes                                                              247

Bibliography                                                            261

Index                                                                   291

# Acknowledgments

I should like to thank first of all the various bodies that have funded my research—primarily the Research Development Fund of the University of Liverpool, whose three year studentship from the Centre for Interdisciplinary German Studies originally enabled me to embark on full time postgraduate study; also the German Historical Institute; the British Council; and the Conference of University Teachers of Great Britain and Northern Ireland, whose scholarships funded my research trips to Germany; and finally the German Academic Exchange Service, who enabled me to study for a year at the department of Geschichtswissenschaft at the Technische Universität Berlin where I benefited from the stimulating discussions of Karin Hausen, Karen Hagemann, and other members of the Colloquium historischer Frauenforschung. I should also like to acknowledge the help and advice I received from the staff of the various archives I visited while in Germany: the Bundesarchiv Koblenz, the Deutsches Filmmuseum, and the Deutsches Rundfunkarchiv in Frankfurt am Main; the Deutsches Film- und Fernseh Institut, Berlin; the Institut für Zeitgeschichte, Munich; the then Staatliches Filmarchiv der DDR, Berlin; and the Zentrales Staatsarchiv der DDR, now the Bundesarchiv in Potsdam. Grateful acknowledgment is also made to Sage Publications for permission to republish material from Kate Lacey, "From *Plauderei* to Propaganda: On Women's Radio in Germany, 1924–35," *Media, Culture and Society* 16, no. 4 (1994): 589–607.

Special thanks are also due to Eve Rosenhaft for her advice, faith, and patience as supervisor to the doctoral research on which this book is based; to Richard Bessell, Liz Harvey, and Paddy Scannell for their constructive comments on earlier drafts; to my colleagues in the Media Studies subject group and the School of European Studies at the University of Sussex for their encouragement; and to Geoff Eley and Susan Whitlock at the University of Michigan Press for their confidence and assistance. Last but not least, thanks to Esther Leslie, Diane Morgan, Lance Downie, and

Stephen Maddison for sharing the ups and downs, to Pat and Malcolm Lacey for their unfailing love and support, and to Chad Wollen for all this and more.

# Abbreviations

| | |
|---|---|
| ARBD | Arbeiterradiobund Deutschland e.V. (German Workers' Radio Federation) |
| ARK | *Arbeiterradioklubs* (workers' radio clubs) |
| BAK | Bundesarchiv Koblenz (Federal Archive, Koblenz) |
| BAP | Bundesarchiv Potsdam (Federal Archive, Potsdam) |
| BDF | Bund Deutscher Frauenvereine (League of German Women's Unions) |
| BDM | Bund deutscher Mädel (League of German Girls) |
| CH | Carola Hersel |
| DAF | Deutsche Arbeitsfront (German Labour Front) |
| DFF | Deutsche Frauenfront (German Women's Front) |
| DFW | Deutsches Frauenwerk (German Women's Bureau) |
| DKD | Deutscher Kulturdienst (German Cultural Agency) |
| DNB | Deutsches Nachrichtenbüro (German News Agency) |
| DNVP | Deutschnationale Volkspartei (German National People's Party) |
| DRA | Deutsches Rundfunkarchiv Frankfurt am Main (German Radio Archive) |
| Dradag | Drahtloser Dienst (Wireless News Service) |
| DS | Deutsche Stunde für drahtlose Belehrung und Unterhaltung (German Program for Wireless Instruction and Entertainment) |
| DW | Deutsche Welle GmbH (German Wavelength Company) |
| FRB | Freier Radiobund (Free Radio League) |
| FWK | Frauenwirtschaftskammer (Women's Chamber of Commerce) |
| HJ | Hitlerjugend (Hitler Youth) |
| IfZ | Institut für Zeitgeschichte, Munich (Institute for Contemporary History) |
| KPD | Kommunistische Partei Deutschlands (German Communist Party) |

| | |
|---|---|
| MadR | Meldungen aus dem Reich (SD Reports from the Reich) |
| Mirag | Mitteldeutsche Rundfunk AG (Mid-German Radio Company, Leipzig) |
| NH | Nachlaß Hersel (Carola Hersel's bequest of personal documents to the DRA) |
| Norag | Nordischer Rundfunk AG (North German Radio Company, Hamburg) |
| NSDAP | Nationalsozialistische Deutsche Arbeiter Partei (National Socialist German Workers' Party) |
| NSF | NS Frauenschaft (NS Women's Organization) |
| NSV | Nationalsozialistische Volkswohlstand (NS National Welfare Organization) |
| Orag | Ostmarken Rundfunk AG (East German Radio Company, Königsberg) |
| RAD | Reichsarbeitsdienst (National Labor Service) |
| RDH | Reichsverband Deutscher Hausfrauen (National Union of German Housewives) |
| RFF | Reichsfrauenführung (National Women's Leadership) |
| RFK | Reichsfilmkammer (National Chamber of Film) |
| RFJ | Reichsjugendführung (National Youth Leadership) |
| RKK | Reichskulturkammer (National Chamber of Culture) |
| RKW | Reichskuratorium für Wirtschaftlichkeit (National Advisory Board for Productivity) |
| RM | Reichsmark |
| RMD | Reichsmütterdienst (National Mothers Service of the DFW) |
| RMI | Reichsministerium des Innern (Ministry of the Interior) |
| RPL | Reichspropagandaleitung (National Propaganda headquarters) |
| RPM | Reichspostministerium (Ministry of Post) |
| RRG | Reichsrundfunkgesellschaft (National Radio Company) |
| RRK | Reichsrundfunkkammer (National Chamber of Radio) |
| RSL | Reichssendeleitung (National Broadcasting headquarters) |
| SD | Sicherheitsdienst (Security Service) |
| SPD | Sozialdemokratische Partei Deutschlands (Social Democratic Party of Germany) |
| Sürag | Süddeutscher Rundfunk AG (South German Radio Company, Stuttgart) |
| SWR | Südwestdeutscher Rundfunk (Southwest German Radio Company, Frankfurt) |
| USPD | Unabhängige Sozialdemokratische Partei Deutschlands (Independent Social Democratic Party of Germany) |
| V/H | Volkswirtschaft/Hauswirtschaft (national/home economics) |

| | |
|---|---|
| WDR | Westdeutscher Rundfunk (West German Radio) |
| Wefag | Westdeutsche Funkstunde AG (West German Broadcasting Company, Münster) |
| Werag | Westdeutscher Rundfunk AG (West German Radio Company, Cologne) |
| ZdH | Zentralstelle der deutschen Hausfrauenvereine (Central Office of German Housewives' Unions) |
| ZFL | Zentralfunkleitung (Central Broadcasting headquarters) |

# Part 1
# German Radio and
# Gendered Discourses

# CHAPTER 1

# Introduction

The years following the First World War saw the simultaneous emergence of radio as a public medium and the large-scale emergence of women into the public sphere of politics and production. The arrival of radio heralded the modern era of mass communication, while women's enfranchisement confirmed the onset of mass politics in the twentieth century. Both these processes have been widely documented and commented upon but generally in isolation of each other or with scant regard for their mutual implications. This book is concerned with identifying and analyzing the very real connections between these important developments and tracing the relationship between women and broadcasting in the years from its inception to the end of World War II.

The historical and theoretical implications of radio as a public medium penetrating the private domain in this period deserve critical attention primarily because of the various challenges to and negotiations of the boundaries between the public and private spheres, boundaries that also conventionally mark a gendered divide. Analyzing the discourses surrounding the relationships between women and radio highlights in some interesting ways the negotiation of women's political and symbolic entry into public life. It also focuses attention on an ongoing redefinition of the private sphere and offers new insights into the shaping of radio and a broadcast public sphere. In the recognition that the silencing of stories and voices is an exercise in oppression, it is also concerned with uncovering the neglected history of women's radio as a site where women found and exercised a public voice.

The inquiry into these relationships rests on and tests certain hypotheses—first, that the media can both reflect and influence change in society and ideology and that the study of the media can give indications of the framework within which particular meanings are composed and represented in a given social and political structure; further, that women's issues and gender ideology were symptomatic of the crises and ruptures in the continuity of this period in German history and that such issues serve and affect the symbolizing function of the mass media; and, finally, that the power of cultural products to define images can work toward the resolution of gender issues or at least highlight the processes of negotiation that are at work in a given social formation. The project that this book sets itself is therefore designed to assess the output of women's radio and radio for women not so much as a reflection of social reality but, rather, as an "indication of the boundaries within which particular meanings [were] constructed and represented" (Barrett 1985, 73).

Germany represents a useful setting for such a study. During the period under review Germany experienced enormous social and economic upheavals and underwent fundamental transformations in the nature of the state and in the level of state involvement in the media. It was also a period in which the succession of profound political and economic crises provoked a series of challenges to the conventional concept of gender roles and a period in which radio clearly came to play a meaningful and indispensable role in the lives of many women. While recognizing the pitfalls of generalization, taking Germany as an object of study seems to enable an examination of the processes of modernization in a country that offers not a *Sonderweg,* or "special path," but, perhaps, a "heightened version" of broader political, economic, cultural, and social processes in Europe during this period.[1] The particularities of German history therefore do not preclude more broadly applicable lessons being drawn; rather, the focus on Germany allows these processes to be followed through a history that lurched from one crisis to another, from democracy to fascism, from a troubled peace to total war, and illuminates a period in which the roles of women and of radio underwent continual redefinition and reinvention.

Crisis, the real or perceived disruption of social order, is proposed as a paradigm for investigating the relationship between continuity and change in Germany during this period. To define a moment as one of crisis is to identify a moment that is characterized by a threat or promise of radical change. Yet, paradoxically, in the present context it is possible to speak almost of a continuity of crisis pervading the discourses of the period. Some, such as the crises of the family or of morality or that of the threat of Americanization on German national culture, were continual themes; others, such as the hyperinflationary period or the years of depression, were specific moments of critical intensity. To define a moment as one of crisis is also to exercise a certain power. There has to be a distinction drawn between the crises perceived in contemporary (mediated) dis-

---

1. Fritzsche, for example, argues that Germany was remarkable in its confrontation with modernity only in having been a recently "self-made nation" and in its willingness to embrace catastrophe as an engine for change and reinvention (1994, 44–47).

courses and the crisis defined by the historian.[2] The social historian might find that the perception of a crisis of the family, which was so pervasive a notion in public debates of the period, was in fact more mythical than real, but in a discursive history these perceptions and mythologies, which helped define public discourse and the practice of politics, are objects of study in their own right and in the present case can illuminate the formation of media policies and the form of radio itself.

Political crisis was played out against a backdrop of social upheaval and cultural conflicts, which have been identified as the consequences of the internal contradictions of the "classical modernity" that reached some sort of apotheosis in Weimar Germany (Peukert 1991, 11–12). The whole period was characterized by a general sense of impermanence, experimentation, and instability.[3] The term *modernity* is a notoriously slippery one but is used here as a phrase which encompasses those economic, social, political, and cultural forms that characterize fully industrialized society in the twentieth century.[4] Some embraced the modern enthusiastically; others were anxious about the future and nostalgic about the past. No one was unaffected, and few could remain neutral. Modernity seemed to be in crisis because of the conflicts engendered in the processes of modernization—broadly, industrialization, urbanization, and a complex of social, technological, and cultural transformations—processes in which the notion of progress was supposed to inhere but that were widely experienced as unsettling dislocations. Anthony Giddens (1990, 18) has suggested that modernity is characterized by the separation of space and place, in that "modernity increasingly tears space away from place by fos-

---

2. The concept of discontinuity in historical analysis is fraught with many more theoretical difficulties than is that of continuity, although it is, paradoxically, both an instrument and an object of historical research. Michel Foucault addressed this problematic in his theory of history, *The Archaeology of Knowledge* (1972, 3–17).

3. For Benjamin (1984, 151) crisis was the very stuff of modernity: "Das es so weiter geht, *ist* die Katastrophe." See also Berman 1982, 15; and Harvey 1992, 10–12. If crisis becomes one of the very definitions of modernity, so Weimar becomes almost synonymous with the modern.

4. Detlef Peukert offered a succinct and useful definition: "In an economic sense, modernity is characterised by highly rationalized industrial production, complex technological infrastructures and a substantial degree of bureaucratized administrative and service activity; food production is carried out by an increasingly small, but productive, agricultural sector. Socially speaking, its typical features include the division of labour, wage and salary discipline, an urbanized environment, extensive educational opportunities and a demand for skills and training. As far as culture is concerned, media products dominate; continuity with traditional aesthetic principles . . . is replaced by unrestricted formal experimentation. In intellectual terms, modernity marks the triumph of western rationality, whether in social planning, the expansion of the sciences or the self-replicating dynamism of technology, although this optimism is accompanied by sceptical doubts from social thinkers and cultural critics" (1991, 82).

tering relations between 'absent' others, locationally distant from any given situation of face-to-face interaction." At the same time there is a compression of space and time with the intrusion of a collage of distant and disconnected stories into everyday consciousness and everyday life (Giddens 1991, 26–27). The development of broadcasting is clearly one of the key expressions of these modern processes and dislocations.

Radio as a cultural form was critically defined by these transformations, and yet it is not always readily associated with received images of Weimar modernity, in which cabarets, bicycle races, jazz, and the movies tend to take center stage. Yet here was a new technology with the ability to relay events as they happened, matching the speed and tempo of modernity and the metropolis but reaching into the deepest rural regions. Moreover, its disregard for physical and social boundaries and its easy accessibility was widely embraced in the prevailing mood of democratization and mass consumption. Unburdened by convention, radio potentially offered an ideal forum for experimentation and innovation in the arts, education, and entertainment, but, as Brecht argued in his "Radio Theory" of 1932, radio in Germany was encumbered by a parasitic dependency on already existing political and cultural forms and practices (1967, 127). Brecht also challenged the assumption that the system of unidirectional broadcasting as it had developed in Europe and the United States was either necessary or predetermined. True, radio was able to bring information and entertainment easily and efficiently into people's homes, and, if knowledge is power, then the chance to circulate knowledge to a limitless audience should have been good news for the infant democracy of the Weimar Republic. But the democratic development of radio would have demanded there being easy and general access to the reception *and* production of information.[5]

German broadcasting, however, developed along very different lines. There were obvious political advantages to be gained for the authorities from restricting the numbers of people sending messages through the air and from ensuring that radio remained a medium of distribution rather than a true medium of communication, a medium which reproduced the division between producer and consumer, between the elites and the masses, between the public and the private. It was not technical strategies that manacled radio's egalitarian, democratic potential, but legislative, bureaucratic, and economic ones. The decisions made during these early days of radio were of tremendous importance to the role it was to play for decades to come, but there was nothing inevitable about the way in which

---

5. In "Kulturindustrie. Aufklärung als Massenbetrug" Adorno and Horkheimer take up Brecht's theme in contrasting the "authoritarian" development of radio with the more genuinely "democratic" development of the telephone (1985, 109).

radio developed. The interest for this book, broadly speaking, lies in assessing the nature and extent of the impact of gender politics on these debates and on the development of German broadcasting.

The scope of the project both demands and, I think, benefits from an interdisciplinary approach that incorporates German historiography, media and cultural studies, feminist theory, and political philosophy. The variety of relevant contextual literature inevitably means that there are many moments that might deserve more sustained attention from the specialist, but I hope at least to map out some new territory in examining an area that has been almost entirely neglected. Despite the increasing volume of feminist work in German history and media studies, references to the relationship between gender and the rise of radio have to date been both scant and essentially anecdotal. Where women's histories engage with media history, there has been an emphasis on print media, for the obvious reason of its accessibility and variety. There has also been an attention to film, as the film stock is also still largely extant and reasonably accessible, and there is, moreover, an active tradition of feminist film theory on which to draw.[6] Radio is a much more ephemeral medium, and its history is more likely to be studied at an institutional than at a textual level. Yet even in these histories the story of separate programs for women, the *Frauenfunk,* is barely told.[7] Nevertheless, such fleeting references as there are triggered the search to find out more about these neglected programs as a way of approaching the questions arising about women's relationship to the medium in the early part of the century.

6. Moreover, in analyses of Nazi culture, in particular, the popular borrowing of Walter Benjamin's theorization of the fascist "aestheticisation of politics" and of Siegfried Kracauer's identification of the "mass ornament" has led to an analytical emphasis on the visual culture of the Third Reich—film, mass spectacle, and architecture (Benjamin 1970, 219–54; Kracauer 1975, 67–76).

7. In the authoritative five volume history of German radio edited by Hans Bausch, for example, there is only one explicit reference to the Frauenfunk, the separate departments of women's programming that were set up as early as 1924. The reference itself, which appears in the volume on audience research and refers to a survey of women listeners carried out in 1934, is typically dismissive of women's radio as a subject worthy of critical attention, suggesting that research on women and radio results in a "confirmation of the obvious"—that women use the radio more than men during the day (Bessler 1980, 30). Bessler is referring to an article by Lisa Peck in the critical radio journal *Rufer und Hörer* (1934). In fact, Peck's work yields some very interesting insights on closer analysis, such as the way in which women's relationship to the radio increasingly came to influence the nature of radio talk in general (see chaps. 4 and 8). Otherwise, the only significant reference to the Frauenfunk in any of the many radio histories listed in the bibliography appears in the study of the workers' radio movement in the Weimar Republic by Peter Dahl in which he cites criticisms of the middle-class bias of some of the programs produced for women (1978, 80). A group of feminist historians led by Adelheid von Saldern and Inge Marßolek are currently working on a project about gender relations in German radio of the Third Reich and the GDR in the 1950s (1995).

The initial response to my inquiries at the German Radio Archive in Frankfurt am Main was pessimistic about the chances of finding sufficient source material but alerted me to an unpublished dissertation on women's radio that had been written in 1942. In her introduction the author, Herta Kuhlmann, warned future historians of women's radio that "the chronicler of women's radio hunts in vain in the sound archives" (1942, 15). Kuhlmann's inquiries at each of the regional radio stations in the autumn of 1940 forced her to the conclusion that a study of women's radio could not rely solely on written documentary evidence and still less on recordings. Manuscripts were rarely filed away as a matter of course, and recordings were generally made only of the most important political speeches or events of national interest. Recording the "woman's hour" for posterity was low on the list of priorities, especially at a time when recording techniques were still primitive and cumbersome. In 1933 the thoroughness of the new National Socialist regime in sweeping the old system away meant almost all of what little material that had been filed by the radio stations was lost.

These were the problems facing Kuhlmann in 1942. The situation today for a historian of early women's radio is even more discouraging. Kuhlmann was able at least to assemble information by appealing directly to women who had contributed to the early development of radio and to conduct audience surveys of her own. The passage of time has taken its toll, and it has proven impossible to trace surviving pioneers of women's radio, whose recollections at best may well have been unreliable or simply anecdotal.[8] The ravages of war and the disruptions of occupation and the division into two Germanies further hampered the cataloging of manuscripts and policy documents. Incomplete as the surviving sources are, however, by drawing on fragmentary evidence in official government and other documents, information from personal files inherited by the German Radio Archive, and articles in contemporary newspapers, journals, and listing magazines, by sifting through the responses to Kuhlmann's questionnaires, analyzing the program schedules themselves, and using pub-

---

8. This was the conclusion I reached after inquiries at the Deutsches Rundfunkarchiv (hereafter DRA), where researchers advised me against the time-consuming search for individuals, details about whom were sixty years out of date. Their experience suggested that the quality of information it was possible to elicit in interviews was insufficient to warrant the time and effort involved. My inquiries at the Berlin Document Center (now Bundesarchiv Berlin Zehlendorf) for information on women who had worked in Nazi radio organizations proved similarly frustrating, given that the filing system there requires that the subject's date of birth be given, information that was impossible to find from the sources available. None of the regional radio archives I applied to could point me to any relevant material in their archives.

lished radio histories (albeit that none engage with the history of women in radio specifically), it has proven possible to piece together a useful picture of the early history of women's radio in Germany from its beginnings to the end of World War II.[9]

From as early as 1924 separate departments for women's programming were set up within the stations producing regular programs by and for women, an arrangement that continued throughout the "Third Reich" and beyond. Such a sustained and serious attention to the female audience is unusual, if not unique, although not enough research has been done to enable a proper international comparison. There was an early program for women on the British Broadcasting Company's London program from Savoy Hill, for example, but this was discontinued by 1924, and there was no regular service for women in Britain until "Woman's Hour" was reintroduced in 1946, though the idea was broached again in the 1930s (Lewis and Booth 1989, 60). There were programs for women in Australia, as Lesley Johnson has described, but it is not clear to what extent women were involved in their production (1988, 100—112). The history of women's programming in the fragmented radio landscape of the United States is more difficult to discern, but, although there were certainly programs aimed at housewives, an organized service comparable to the German Frauenfunk does not seem to have emerged (Cramer 1989, 214–16).

Recovering this history of women's programming at the level of institution, production, and reception is, then, an important part of the project, but it is not the sole aim of this book to perform this sort of "additive" history, filling in the gaps left by conventional histories of the radio of the period, nor is it intended as a "compensatory" exercise, acknowledging women's presence in program making and the definition of their own representations. This is a worthwhile descriptive exercise in its own right, which I hope contributes something to that body of feminist historiography that is characterized by a creative and sensitive analysis of detail and that focuses on what was once marginalized—part of a wider process of decentering the "grand narratives"—but also in part a pragmatic response to the fragmentary nature of the evidence of women's history that has been recorded and stored. Yet an analysis of the wider implications of the contemporaneous emergence of radio and women into the public sphere also implies a more discursive approach. An analysis of discourse in this Foucauldian sense is an analysis of power, of hierarchies, institutional rela-

---

9. The term *useful* is used here in the acknowledgment that no historical study, however abundant the primary sources, could ever claim completeness or even correctness but must, by its nature, be visional and partial and claim only a "verisimilitude rather than an objective truth" (Gottschalk 1950, 23). It can, nevertheless, be "useful" in terms of the academic production of new knowledge.

tions, modes of characterization, economic arrangements, and social processes expressed in language. Such an approach does not imply abandoning notions of subjectivity or agency but concentrates, instead, on the definition of "the positions and functions that the subject could occupy in the diversity of discourse" (Foucault 1972, 200).

It is an approach, therefore, that not only involves looking at women as individual agents, for they are often obscured or absent, but that foregrounds gender as an analytical category in the sense "not . . . of a universal statement but, as the Greek origin of the word suggests, in the sense of public objection and indictment, of debate, protest, process and trial" (Bock 1989, 11). In this sense, as Gisela Bock explains, gender is an analytic tool that allows neglected areas of history to be uncovered and challenges the sex blindness of traditional historiography. It is, significantly, "context-specific and context-dependent." It is not therefore used here as a synonym or replacement for the category "women," for it is important to recognize that women's experience historically *has* been different from men's and that experience should not simply be reconciled, resolved, or universalized. The new feminist historiography doesn't seek to replace old universalisms with new ones but rather recognizes that all perspectives, theories, and methodologies are partial. Gender, as Joan Scott has proposed, is therefore just "one of the recurrent references by which political power has been conceived, legitimated, and criticised" (1986, 1073). Recognizing that history, like literature, is a form of knowledge that creates its meanings through differentiation and in this way organizes knowledge about the world, Scott argued for a textual approach to history that would "disrupt the notion of fixity, to discover the nature of the debate or repression that leads to the appearance of timeless permanence in binary gender representation." Historians therefore need to examine not only the causes of the social construction of gender but also the *meanings* of gender, particularly its use as a metaphor and as a "primary signifier of power."

Certainly, gendered metaphors provided the frame of reference in the discourse about the new medium of radio. It was a public, "male" medium directed into the private "female" sphere, a process of dissemination and reception, of penetration and invasion, of expertise versus ignorance, activity versus passivity, power versus powerlessness, speech versus silence. But, as a major cultural medium, radio was also a site on which gender relationships were open to contest and redefinition, affirmation and reproduction. In this sense, following Teresa de Lauretis (1987), radio is one of the "technologies of gender," alongside institutional discourses, epistemologies, everyday life, critical practices, and other social technologies such as the cinema, producing gender as representation and as self-representation.[10] There is, then, a crucial dialectic at the center of this study in which gender ideology informs the definition and practice of broadcasting and in which broadcasting becomes one of the cultural modes in which gender is produced, reproduced, and transformed.

Of all the original sources available, then, the contemporary radio journals proved the most valuable, not simply as a quarry for program details but also as an indication of the discursive rules which informed the public perception and reception of radio in this early period. The representations of radio's integration into the social framework may not always be accurate reflections of "reality," but they do reveal the questions, assumptions, hopes, and fears reverberating in the public sphere about the place of radio in Germany and its relationship to gender issues.[11] Radio was a new and remarkable phenomenon that generated universal fascination and impassioned debate. Some of the radio magazines had circulation figures in their millions; others appealed to a more specialist audience, either intellectual or technical. Some were produced by the radio companies themselves; others took up a more openly critical stance.[12] Produced at a time when the definition of radio had not yet been firmly established and become entrenched, these various journals do not resemble the listing magazines of today but offer valuable reflections of the prevailing discourses around and within radio and how they were informed by gender.[13] This study is less concerned, therefore, with traditional audience research or with trying to assess the "impact" or immediate consequences of the programs it discusses—an activity that is fraught with theoretical difficul-

---

10. The term *technology of gender* is an adaptation of Foucault's theory of sexuality as a "technology of sex," the "set of effects produced in bodies, behaviours, and social relations" by the deployment of "a complex political technology" (Foucault 1980a, 127; cited in de Lauretis 1987, 2–3). See also Probyn 1993, 108–37.

11. It is because of the importance of the use of language that the main text is more heavily punctuated with quotations from the original sources than might otherwise have been the case. All translations are my own, unless otherwise stated.

12. In 1930 there were 61 radio publications, with a total circulation of 2,500,000, and approximately 500 books about radio in print ("Entwicklung des deutschen Rundfunks in Zahlen 1923–30," report published to mark five years of the RRG. BAK R55/1275, 54). See also Bauer 1993. Details about specific journals are given in the main text when relevant.

13. Lynn Spigel (1992) has employed a similar methodological approach in her work on the reception of the TV set in the American home of the 1950s. Robert E. Davis (1976) undertook a more general study of popular discourse surrounding the development of new media in American popular magazines from 1891 to 1955 in which he identifies a dual response to each new medium—as threat and as revivifier of traditional values.

ties even in studies of contemporary media[14]—hence, the audience is generally present here only insofar as it was constructed in the public discourses of the time.

The relationship between women and radio in these discourses is primarily an expression of a relationship between the public and private spheres, a relationship that was neither simple nor stable in the age of radio; it was in many ways throughout the period in a volatile state of negotiation and renegotiation. These questions seem important to the understanding of the development of the public sphere in the formative years of the age of mass politics and mass communication and the ways in which they came to acquire apparent fixity and normative status. If past constructions inform and illuminate the present, then the answers to these questions would seem to have contemporary significance. It is striking, for example, how much of the current debate about the Internet and the information superhighway echoes the hopes and concerns of the debate about radio in its early years, not least in its potential as a new democratic public sphere.

The book progresses both chronologically and thematically, approaching this gendered radio discourse from a variety of angles—institutional, ideological, biographical, and textual—and relating it where possible to the experience of real women as producers and consumers of radio programs. The chapter "Gender, Media, and Crisis: The Development of German Radio" is concerned with the implications of the emergence of radio as a medium in the public sphere entering the private domain and the institutional, legislative, and discursive responses formulated to understand and regulate them. Radio made the outside world more accessible to women traditionally alienated from the public sphere of politics and production. Coming only five years after the introduction of the vote for women, it had the potential to be a powerful medium for political education for a newly enfranchised section of society. But radio policy in the Weimar Republic was designed to keep the airwaves free of politics, a policy that was promoted in terms of defending the sanctity of the private home from the intrusion of politics. I argue that the history of radio in Weimar, and beyond, cannot properly be understood without reference to the gendered discourses that informed the debate about radio's function and future of radio.

Part 2, "Feminine Frequencies," focuses on the rationale, implementation, and development of programming for women, particularly house-

---

14. See the "state of the science" review of media effects research by Cumberbatch and Howitt (1989, 1–29); see also Morley 1989, 16–43. For an important theoretical account of the determining limits and possibilities of how messages are produced and disseminated, see Hall 1993, 90–103.

wives, as a distinct audience group. This section's first chapter, "Let Women Speak to Women! On Women's Radio in Weimar Germany," traces the influences, organization, and output of the various regional Frauenfunk departments and that of the national wavelength, the Deutsche Welle, demonstrating that this output was more complex and contested than has been assumed by those historians of radio who have either dismissed these programs in a few lines or ignored them altogether. The focus on programs explicitly aimed at women highlights radio's recognition and negotiation of its intrusion into the private sphere. The question of continuities and changes across the two periods is raised in the biographical excursus on Carola Hersel, whose career making programs for young women began in the Weimar Republic and carried over into the early years of the new regime.

In the history of women's relationship to radio in Germany the continuities between the Weimar Republic and the Third Reich are clear at both a discursive and a textual level, despite the ostensible rupture at the level of institution and state intervention, although changes are also in evidence. Chapter 4, "Radio and the Maternal Spirit: On Women's Radio in Nazi Germany," traces the negotiation of themes identified in the discussion of the earlier period: the structural relationships between women and radio, the gendered rhetoric of the discursive rules, the organization and production of programs for women, and the reception of and resistance to public discourse (and propaganda) in the private sphere. The following chapter, "Home Front / Front Line: Women, Radio, and War" explores the relationship of women after the outbreak of hostilities, when the discourse was very much about radio bridging the (gendered) divide between the home front and the front line. As the crisis deepened, the contradictions between Nazi ideology and practice became more evident, highlighted in this case by the efforts to mobilize the female labor force for war work. The question of women's broadcast resistance and resistance to broadcasts is also addressed.

The third part of the book, "Experts on the Air," continues the history of women's programming but with the focus on radio as an instrument that revolutionized women's domestic experience and acted as a channel of information, advice, and expertise. Chapter 6, "The Mouthpiece of Modernity," returns to the Weimar period and takes up these themes in an era of rationalization, consumerism, and technology. The programs of the Frauenfunk on the national wavelength, the Deutsche Welle, are the basis for examining the authoritative voice of the expert on air and the various ways in which women's experience of the contradictions of modernity were mediated. Moving on to the Nazi period, chapter 7, "All-Consuming Propaganda," describes how the private nature of radio reception dictated the terms in which radio, as the primary channel of public information and propaganda, was both understood and practiced. In particular, it is concerned with the way in which Nazi ideology, with its clear demarcation of separate realms of competence for men and women, informed the rhetoric about radio and influenced the production of programs for women. It concentrates on the radio propaganda aimed at women as consumers and women's complicity in that propaganda, looking in detail at the organization and output of a branch of propaganda which was intended to integrate women into the ideological construct that was the *Volksgemeinschaft,* or "national community." All of the chapters on Nazi radio hope to contribute to that "history of the everyday" which deepens our understanding of the operation and efficacy of fascism. They illustrate the politicization of the private sphere, the pervasiveness of the propaganda, its banality, its appeal, and its pernicious exclusions.

Chapter 8, "Finding a Voice: Woman's Radio and the Evolution of Broadcast Talk," synthesizes many of the preceding themes in an examination of what lies at the heart of radio: broadcast speech. It follows the story of women's voices on the air from the early days of broadcasting in the Weimar Republic through to the Nazi period and discusses the implications of the conditions of reception in the private sphere for the modes of public speech, examining the parallels between women finding their public voice and radio finding an institutional voice that could imitate private modes of speech. I argue that the development of a form of talk that is both intimate and public was vitally influenced by the relationship between women and the public sphere, as it surfaced in the discourses of the period, was first defined in the presentational style of women's radio and was of strategic importance to the propaganda of the Third Reich.[15]

The final chapter, "Gender, German Radio, and the Public Sphere," problematizes the concept of the public-private divide and explores the way in which public sphere theory is a useful framework for understanding the main arguments of the book. Although feminist critiques have been among the most productive encounters with Jürgen Habermas's model of the public sphere, they have tended, as Lisa McLaughlin (1993) has pointed out, to concentrate on the internal, oppositional function of counterpublics, to the neglect of a sustained analysis of the media, although the role of the media in democracy is recognized as a key consideration. On the other hand, feminist media studies has tended to concentrate on recuperating women's genres and consumption practices to the

---

15. A version of this chapter appeared as "From *Plauderei* to Propaganda: On Women's Radio in Germany, 1923–1945," *Media, Culture and Society* 16, no. 4: 589–608.

neglect of a consideration of the public sphere.[16] This book hopes to go some way toward bridging that gap. Yet, while the category of the public sphere as delineated by Habermas is clearly important here, there remain some uncomfortable compromises in the way in which his model has been reworked by feminist and media theorists. In confronting these compromises, what I want to suggest in this final chapter is that Hannah Arendt's conception of performative politics and an agonistic public sphere seems to offer a more productive way forward in a feminist analysis of the public sphere and the place of the media within it.

Throughout this period of recurrent crisis in Germany, then, radio was a crucial point of intersection for contesting definitions of the public sphere. It both mediated and recuperated challenges to the established delineation of the separate spheres while in itself constituting a radical extension of the public sphere and a redefinition of the private. These are tensions and contradictions that also seem to lie at the heart of how radio has become defined, and it is these tensions and contradictions that the present study seeks to reveal and explain.

---

16. Some work is already beginning to address this gap (e.g., van Zoonan, 1993). Nancy Fraser also recognizes the role of the media, particularly in her discussion of the coverage of the Anita Hill–Clarence Thomas hearings (1992), but an analysis of the way media practices structured the representation of the dispute is not Fraser's primary concern.

CHAPTER 2

# Gender, Media, and Crisis: The Development of German Radio

The child of crisis is nostalgia. The relentless crises that plagued postwar Germany were habitually translated nostalgically into crises of morality. A return to traditional values was reassuringly equated with a return to old prosperity and stability.[1] Home and family represented a safe haven from the instabilities characterizing public life.[2] Images of the "eternal feminine" were called upon to evoke a sense of predictability, calm, and composure.

It is tempting to characterize the Weimar Republic as a fourteen-year period of continual crisis, from its declaration amid the ruins of military defeat and the internal strife of revolution and unrest, via hyperinflation of 1923 and the onset of the Great Depression five years later, to its demise into fractional confrontation and the victory of fascism. Politics during this period was expressed in no small measure in terms of gender issues— the equality of representation and employment opportunities, population policy and sexual relations—issues which contested the apparent fixity of the gendered demarcation between the public and the private spheres. But beyond the level of everyday politics these issues carried a symbolic weight, the figure of woman in her various guises in the second decade of the twentieth century acting as mediatrix for a broader complex of issues. In this scenario women held the key to resolving the crises for which, at

1. Bessel (1993, 223) has argued that the postwar nostalgia for the pre-1914 world tended to romanticize and overestimate the moral stability of the imperial past.

2. The theorization of the private sphere in Western philosophy has time and again reproduced this version of the familial space as a retreat for the individual from the public realm of Reason, economy, politics, etc., though the masculine identity of the "universal" individual is rarely made explicit. (Lloyd 1993). As Turner has argued, classical social theory itself was born of a sense of social crisis and can be read as a nostalgic discourse concerned to account for the destruction of authentic communities by the advance of industrial capitalism (1992, 185).

least at a symbolic level, they were held responsible. As a result, women's images were manipulated and exaggerated to serve as pawns in some of the most crucial political and economic machinations of the time. The salient point here is that it was against this background of crisis that a new and soon very influential medium of communication, a new maker of images, was launched.[3]

But the term *crisis* has another inflection here by virtue of the particular relationship of the media to crisis. The media play a key part in the definition of crisis and, in so doing, exercise a real power. As John Keane puts it, they "ensure that a latent crisis becomes manifest by rendering collective the feeling of crisis among citizens, and by amplifying the claim of state officials that drastic action is required to remedy the crisis, which they have defined as such through the media" (1991, 96–97). In short, the media thrive on and yet are threatened by crisis, and they play a central role in its politics and management (Raboy and Daganais 1992, 1–15). Moreover, the emergence of a new medium more often than not itself seems to become linked to crisis in popular discourse, as it did when radio emerged as a public medium in Germany in the early 1920s, but, in order to understand how the relationship between women, radio, and crisis developed and was manipulated and how the institution of broadcasting affected and was affected by the position(ing) of women in Weimar society, it is sensible first with a few broad brush strokes to paint in the backdrop against which this relationship was played out.[4]

## The Position(ing) of Women in Weimar Society

World War I and its aftermath were decisive in splitting apart comfortable old notions about the structure of society and in generating the tensions and contradictions that were to plague the new republic and undermine the foundations on which the "most democratic Constitution in the world" so precariously rested. The *Burgfrieden,* or "party truce," declared

---

3. The term *image* is used here to encompass both materially constructed portrayals and imagined constructs, and also has connotations for women's "perceived reputation" (Williams 1976, 130–31).

4. Much of this account is concerned with tracing the contradictions of and contradictory attitudes toward the processes of modernization in this period which Kurt Sontheimer describes as "a political culture of contradictions" (1987, 458). At this stage terms such as *progressive* and *conservative* are employed with the caveat that they are helpful only in staking out broad positions and cannot account for the complexity, fluidity, and instability of the range of attitudes in society or public discourses. For more information on the Weimar Republic, see Stürmer 1967, 1980; Bessel and Feuchtwanger 1981; Kolb 1984; Winkler 1984, 1985, 1987; Bracher et al. 1987; Winkler 1984, 1985, 1987; Kershaw 1990; Peukert 1991; Heiber 1993. Further relevant texts are cited in the following notes and in the bibliography.

in the patriotic fervor that greeted the opening salvos of the war only delayed the inevitable explosion of conflicting interests which had been brewing during the Wilhelmine Empire. With the departure of so many men for the battlefields of Europe, the employment of hundreds of thousands of (mainly working-class) women in the munitions factories and other traditionally male occupations, together with the engagement of (mainly middle-class) women in relief and nursing organizations, brought women of all classes a new visibility in the public sphere, a new confidence in their ability to straddle both spheres (as their male counterparts did as a matter of course), and a valuable, albeit inconsistent and often begrudging, respect from the male half of the population. The influx of women into administrative, welfare, and educational work (deemed acceptable in terms of *soziale Mütterlichkeit,* or social motherliness) continued after the war, while their presence in heavy industry and transport was only a temporary phase; but the symbolic shock waves of women doing men's work rumbled on throughout the new republic.

The political organization of the Weimar Republic was a mixed bag for women, on the one hand enshrining the principle of equal rights and duties in the Constitution, which included universal adult suffrage for the first time, but retaining repressive legislation regarding abortion, birth control, marriage, and divorce.[5] The first national elections, held in January 1919, drew 78 percent of women to the polls and returned 47 women among the 423 delegates to the Reichstag, but this initial enthusiasm for political activity among the newly enfranchised female electorate waned considerably as politics in the Weimar Republic became ever more divisive and violent.[6] Moreover, women tended to vote conservatively, casting their votes for parties whose programs did not encompass the promotion of rights for women (Boak 1981, 157–67). The acceptance of the doctrine of the separate spheres of competence meant that suffrage could be assumed to mean different things for men and women, to reinforce the duality between power and morality (Elshtain 1974). Citizenship for women could, therefore, be regarded as an elaboration of their private duty, although the demand for the vote did undoubtedly "constitute a denial that women were naturally fit *only* for private life" (Pateman 1989, 128; following Dubois 1978, 46).

The extension of the vote to women ushered in the modern age of mass politics, although the focus on the mass in contemporary and retro-

5. The 1871 criminal code outlawed abortion and limited access to contraception; the 1900 civil code fell way short of guaranteeing equality in marital affairs. See Bridenthal et al 1984, 1–29; Frevert 1986, 180–99.

6. Figures from Arendt and Scholze 1983. See also Bridenthal and Koonz 1984, 35–44; Frevert 1986, 163–80.

spective accounts of the period "simultaneously insists on the femininity of the new public and obscures women's place in it" (Rosenhaft 1992, 163).[7] The explicit identification of modernity with processes of "massification" tends to disguise the "feminization" that was inherent in these processes, specifically the introduction of female suffrage and the institutionalization of conventionally private concerns in the form of the welfare state. Yet at the same time, since the "defeat" of the individual was analogous to the loss of (male) identity, so the suggestible, uncontrollable mass tended to be construed as female. Like a woman, the mass was at once a passive receptacle and its culture a source of decadence and corruption (Huyssen 1986).[8] Significantly, this was a conceptualization of the mass that was inherited by Hitler and Goebbels in their formulations of the theory of propaganda (Hitler 1938, 23; Kershaw 1991, 48–54).

Demobilization brought new tensions to the surface (Bessel, 1993). Returning soldiers expected to return to work, driving the female labor force into unemployment or lower-paid jobs (Bridenthal and Koonz 1984, 48). Women's assumption of male roles, particularly in heavy industry and transport, had been widely tolerated only as a matter of contingency. Resentment was running high between the sexes, for a return to prewar arrangements was no longer possible; their experience of war had been too sharply different. For many of those who had fought at the front, who had experienced the horrors and nightmares of the trenches, hopes of returning to the security and familiarity of the home they had left behind were bitterly dashed, for those homes were no longer the same (Brockmann 1994, 170–71). The shock waves of war reached way back beyond the front lines—something that the demobilized soldiers did not always appreciate. The camaraderie of the trenches, the esprit de corps, the intimacy of shared adventure and shared dangers, won new poignancy in the minds of many veterans who felt they had been betrayed by the home front, with scapegoats including the left wing, the Jews, and, as resentment grew, the women.

Returning to a country in chaos, it seemed to many veterans that women had defaulted in their duty to hold the fort at home while men had fallen for the Fatherland in their thousands. For some men this resentment

---

7. Craig Calhoun, for example, asserts that, "the gendered character of the early public sphere is . . . less clearly linked to the theme of transformation by 'massification' than is exclusion on class grounds" (1992, 3), although he accepts that "a key criterion for evaluating a public sphere" is the *extent* of participation "as an essential dimension of publicness." If voting rights are a criterion for modern citizenship, then we cannot fairly speak of mass participation in the public sphere before 1918 in Germany and the extension of voting rights to women.

8. By token of the same metaphor, modernism, with its pretension to artistic integrity and creative energy, was seen to exhibit obviously masculine characteristics.

took the form of a violent backlash against women, both physically and symbolically (witness the glut of portrayals of *Lustmörder* and prostitution in art, literature, and film).[9] For many of those women who had "manned" the home front, learning new skills, new independence, the longed-for return of a loved one often turned sour when newly explored horizons started to close in again. The divorce rate soared.[10] For others, of course, there was to be no reunion. The war left behind approximately 600,000 war widows (Hausen 1987,128). The "surplus" of widows, divorcees, and single women engendered fears of a falling population, with all the implications that entailed for interfering in Germany's recovery. For a society that had, in the words of Detlef Peukert, not yet "evolved new values and forms of behaviour in response to these new demographic patterns" (1991, 9), they also represented a veritable army of women whose need to support themselves and their families interfered with the reappropriation of prewar conditions.[11] Together with increases in the illegitimacy rate, juvenile crime, venereal disease, prostitution, and the availability of contraception, these demographic changes generated an acute moral panic about the crisis of the family (Usborne 1992, 81–85; Bessel 1993, 220–53).

Women who worked, voted, wore their hair and their skirts shorter, flaunted their independence and their sexuality, came to perform a central symbolic function for both the defenders and the detractors of the new republic. For the one side the "New Woman" was the embodiment of all

---

9. For example, G. W. Pabst's film *Die Büchse der Pandora,* the series of *Aufklärungsfilme* and paintings of sex murders by Georg Grosz (e.g., *Lustmord an der Ackerstraße* [1916], *Jack the Ripper* [1918]) and Otto Dix (e.g., *Lustmord* [1920]), etc. The prostitute was a particularly potent symbol of female sexuality in the Weimar period, with its anxiety about women's betrayals, the crisis of the family, women with careers, and the entry into the impersonal marketplace (Eberle 1985, 41; Lewis 1990, 111–40; Brockmann 1994, 173–74). See also Klaus Theweleit's (1989) extensive examination of the "neutralizations" of female eroticism in the language of the Freikorps and his assertion that sexual anxiety about women was central to fascism.

10. Bastowski et al. (1981, 2:112) speak of *eine wahre Scheidungsepidemie* (a real divorce epidemic), although the proportion of divorced women was still a tiny minority, around 0.6 percent, due in some small part to the high rate of remarriage (Frevert 1986, 188). The divorce rate peaked at almost 40,000 in 1921, more than double the prewar figure (Bessel 1993, 231).

11. Peukert summarizes the demographic structure in the Weimar Republic as follows: "rising life expectancy . . . a falling birthrate, a new ideal of the two-child family, a partial removal of the reproductive burden from women and a more pronounced segmentation in the age make-up of the overall population" (1991, 9). That women in work also found the changes difficult was suggested in 1932 by a contemporary psychologist, Alice Rühle-Gerstel, who in *Das Frauenproblem der Gegenwart: Eine psychologische Bilanz,* regarded the *Angestellte* as inhabiting a transitional social space, a proletarian according to her economic situation, a bourgeois according to her ideology, masculine according to her field of work, and feminine according to her outlook on work (cited in Frevert 1988, 26).

that was good in Weimar, the personification of youth, vigor, equality, a new beginning. She was progressive, enthusiastic, technological. For the other she was a threat to the established order; she undermined the sanctity of the German family and was responsible for male unemployment and myriad other ills that were befalling the nation. The Janus head of the New Woman looked forward to the modern technological age and back to the archaic world of symbolism and mystery. The move to find exegesis in the figure of Woman in time of crisis is part of a long-established tradition of transforming women into symbols and expressing power relations in gendered metaphors, making women at once central and marginal to the political and economic events of the (male) world (Warner 1985, 19–23; Mattelart 1986).Women's symbolic function in the Weimar period belied their "illusory responsibility in the face of their actual political impotence" (Bridenthal et al. 1984, 8). The New Woman represented the promise of liberation, but the experience of emancipation was all too often just a heavier load for women who went out to work but had to keep house too. She was a caricature rather than a portrait of even the young female white-collar workers who she was supposed to epitomize, but she was conceived and nurtured in the popular imagination, fed by the media, until she attained a sort of reality that was taken hostage and manipulated by both sides.

Fears of a breakdown of sexual standards and the family informed the rhetoric of both the moral Right and the political Left in the Weimar Republic as they attempted to discredit each other's policies for their different ends. For the one side they were a rallying point for the preservation of tradition and patriarchal structures; for the other they acted as a springboard for demands for social reform. The crisis of the family was a myth that articulated deep-set anxieties about political and social instability intrinsic to the crisis of modernity but which sought explanations in the private sphere. Yet the recognition of the "crisis of the family" as a social problem paradoxically situates the family in the social, public realm, not that of the private (Donzelot 1979). Examination of certain indices such as the popularity and resilience of marriage has shown that the crisis of the family was more a fabrication than an empirical phenomenon (Bridenthal et al. 1984, 1–29), but it was a myth of enormous cogency for the politics of Germany in the first half of the twentieth century. It was also a myth which shaped the discussion about the role of the new mass media.

By the time public radio was introduced onto the scene at the end of 1923, the young republic was reeling from yet another crisis that had its origins in the aftermath of war: inflation. Printing money to pay off the punishing reparations demanded by the victorious nations had driven a spiraling inflation rate, the effects of which tore at the very fabric of society.[12] Unemployment escalated, the middle classes lost their savings, pensioners on fixed incomes suffered, and no one could forget the images of shoppers with wheelbarrows of worthless paper money. Only debtors and big industry, buying up smaller concerns, concentrating wealth and power in ever fewer hands, and reaping in the profits of selling goods cheaply abroad, benefited from the chaos. But the social impact of the inflation cannot be measured in financial terms alone. The principle of deferred gratification, in both a financial and an ethical sense, became increasingly irrelevant as the chaos escalated. Inflation subverted traditional values both in economic terms (due to the futility of saving) and in moral terms (due to the weakening of sexual taboos). The decadence and depravity of Berlin, and especially the women who populated it, epitomized for many the devaluation in morality that seemed to accompany the loss in the value of money. Society in crisis once again sought its exegetic model in the figure of womanhood. The city itself was ascribed the body of a woman.[13] Respectable middle-class women found themselves forced into unaccustomed labor or even to seek their living on the streets. The latter image was a particularly potent one in cultural mediations of those turbulent months. The point is illustrated by a glance at the titles of the biggest films of 1923 (Brennicke and Hembus 1983, 250), many of which fell into the subgenre of *Straßenfilme* (street films)—for example, *Der Absturz (Downfall), Alles für Geld (Everything for Money), Dunkle Gassen (Dark Alleyways), Die Straße (The Street),* and *Tragödie der Liebe (Tragedy of Love).*

American money, currency reform, and a program of rationalization, heralded the "Golden Years" of the Weimar Republic, a period of five years that were by no means golden for everyone but which nevertheless represented a time of relative stability and prosperity. Rationalization processes—mechanization, standardization, Taylorization—had a particular resonance in the lives and images of women.[14] Assembly line work, fragmentary and repetitive, demanded few of the traditional skills that had long segregated the labor market. Women were able to move into these

12. Inflation characterized the whole decade from 1914, culminating in the crisis of 1923. Peukert identifies three main stages: war inflation from 1914–18, demobilization inflation from 1919–21, and hyperinflation from 1922–23 (1991, 61–66).

13. Petro discusses some of these invocations of Berlin as woman (1987, 117). She cites works by Carl Zuckmayer, Georg Grosz, Otto Dix, Bertolt Brecht, Erich Kästner, Walter Mehring, and also Walter Ruttmann's film, *Symfonie einer Großstadt* (1927). Linda Mizejewski's study of Isherwood's Sally Bowles character notes how, in each version of the story, her sexuality converges with "wild Weimar Berlin" to represent the threat (1992, 5).

14. Frederick Taylor publicized the introduction of scientific management to the production process; time and motion studies informed the creation of routinized series of tasks controlled by a central planning office, separating conception and execution as aspects of production. Henry Ford applied Taylor's ideas to mass production, significantly with the

low-skilled positions and to take on work in the expanding service industries, although the assumption, contemporary and retrospective, that they thereby took work away from men has been exposed as a particularly successful but nevertheless largely unsubstantiated myth.[15] Industries which employed women expanded, whereas the more traditional heavy industry that employed only men remained relatively static, and so the proportion of women in the work force increased without actually displacing men from existing jobs. Low-skilled work was also low-paid work and women were paid lower wages than men for the same work. In times of economic crisis their jobs were therefore marginally more secure than their male counterparts, so even their disadvantaged position was a cause for resentment. Acceptance of women in work at this time was still generally reserved for single or widowed women who had no alternative but to support themselves.

Most crucially, women's place in these new occupations, with their high media profile, highlighted the transformations happening in the sphere of production and in the circumference of female experience. But the reality for most women had not undergone such dramatic change. The vast majority of women in Weimar Germany were employed either in the home or in preindustrial concerns (agriculture, the service sector, and family businesses).[16] Moreover, even those who were integrated into the modern industrial process faced insecurity at both an economic and an ideological level, in terms of the swings in the economy and the hostility of many people toward working women. In times of crisis women were often the first to lose their jobs or were the ones who had to make up the shortfall when social services were curtailed. Added to the common experience of the "double burden" of wage labor and housework, this insecurity, as Patrice Petro (1989, 43–44) has argued, meant that even those women most integrated into the modern would have experienced modernity as a

introduction of the conveyor belt and the radical division of labor, with added refinements, such as the standardization of both tools of production and product and the reform of management-labor relations (Cooke 1990, 58–84). The conditions specific to the German case are examined more closely in chapter 6.

15. Bridenthal and Koonz detail some of the statistical delusions on which this myth was based; for example: "The first postwar census (1925) showed 35 percent of all women to be working, an increase of 5 percent over 1907. Less remarked upon was the increase in the proportion of men working: 6.6%, to include 68% of the total male population. . . . Before the war, women made up 34% of the working population; after the war, 36%, hardly a great leap forward" (1984, 44–45). See also Bajohr 1979.

16. In 1925, 55 percent of women worked in the home or on farms; there were almost 1.5 million *Angestellte,* 12.6 percent of all working women. Industrial workers accounted for 18.6 percent of the female labor force. Women made up 35.6 percent of waged labor in 1925 compared with 34.9 percent in 1907 (Frevert 1986, 171–72).

sharpening of traditional gender roles and responsibilities.[17] And yet the rights and wrongs of female employment was one of the central and most fiercely controversial debates of this period, a debate that was shaped by a host of other more deeply seated hopes and fears about the future of Germany. These hopes and fears were laid at women's feet by conservatives and progressives alike.

The precarious stability that had reigned in Germany since 1924 began to totter even before the Wall Street Crash of 1929, the effects of which hit Germany particularly hard. The agricultural sector was the first to suffer, followed primarily by heavy industry. Therefore, the women whose jobs were in the newer, more flexible industries were initially relatively secure, and they faced a tide of resentment swelled by latent prejudices against women in the workplace.[18] It was just one indication of a general shift to right-wing reaction, which eventually resulted in the accession to power of the National Socialist Party in 1933.

**Hopes and Fears for a Broadcast Public Sphere**

Radio in its infancy was conceived of as a means of communication sited squarely in the public sphere, with the art of listening defined by collective reception of broadcasts in public halls, much as the way film was introduced to the public. More than just a physical location, though, the cultural space in which early radio operated was a potential public sphere in the sense defined by Jürgen Habermas (1989), a historical concept referring to "opinion-publics" that develop outside the state to defend the general interest and to advocate, through open discussion, progressive changes in state policy (see chap. 9). The potential for radio to develop as a public space in this sense was all the greater given the return to civilian life of war veterans who had gained experience in transmission and reception and who represented a pool of technical expertise in the community.[19] This potential to develop as an autonomous site of exchange of interests and discourses featured large in early debates about the future of radio, but it was a potential ultimately foiled by the combined pressure of government and commercial interests. It quickly became clear to government

17. The *Gesetz über die Rechtsstellung der weiblichen Beamten,* passed in 1932, legalized the dismissal of "double earners" from public posts. The symbolic repercussions of this measure were more significant than its economic impact (Hahn 1981, 49–78; Frevert 1986, 193).

18. Women's share of the work force rose from 35.3 percent in 1928 to 36 percent in 1930 and 37.3 percent in 1931. The proportion of single, divorced, and widowed women in employment fell while that of married women rose by 13 percent, though 70 percent of all married women were housewives. Unemployment rates for women were less than for men, but they were harder hit by part-time work (Boak 1981, 163).

19. Some 185,000 men from the signals corps returned after the war (Lerg 1980, 43).

agencies, wireless manufacturers, and audiences alike that radio was destined to be much more than a passing technological fad; consequently, the state, the electronics industry, and individual consumers, for different reasons, all saw their interests best served by the provision of privately-owned sets situated in the family home. Instead of offering an incentive to an actively recharged *public,* radio's new constitution instituted the passive, objectified audience.[20] The arbitrary definition of the radio public as silent receivers of corporate messages was not only part of a wider historical process in which the state in capitalist societies has assumed a more active role in managing communicative activity (Golding and Murdoch 1991, 21); it also, crucially, coincided with the rise of mass, feminized politics.

The transition from communal to almost entirely individual reception has been a gradual but persistent one. The arrival of the first wireless in a street would inevitably be the cause of great curiosity and excitement, and proud owners would invite neighbors to share in, and envy, the wonders of the new machine. Radio was not only a social but a sociable phenomenon. Later, as more households could afford to join the radio-owning community, it was most often family or household groups who gathered round the set for an evening's entertainment. Later still, it became common for each member of the household to have his or her own personal radio: listening became an entirely individual affair. Radio became defined as a private experience, an immediate and intimate means of communication from one individual to another, and it is this which distinguishes it from most other modern media of communication. However, the previous reference to the cinema gives a vital clue to one of the incentives to that process, for the decisions about radio's future were made in the light of the cinema's recent past.[21]

Women's increasing public participation in politics had coincided with the rise of a medium (film) which constructed its public as a passive receptacle of its messages and of an institution (cinema) which deprived its public of any agency (Hansen 1983; 1991, 1–89; 1993; Kuhn 1988, 114–25). Miriam Hansen has argued that the efforts on the part of the establishment to deny the existence of a radically different public sphere imply that there was at least a very real potential for such a sphere to develop (1983, 147–84). There were those in Germany who faced this prospect with optimism, but for the most part the potential rise of an alter-

20. The term *passive receiver* is used advisedly only in this specific context. Elsewhere in the book the "activity" of the reader/listener is explicitly acknowledged.
21. Louise M. Benjamin has made a similar argument for the American case (1992, 87–101).

native public sphere was seen as a threat, an unruly phenomenon that needed to be legitimized and tamed. The question of morality dominated debates. Belief in and concern about the power of cinema to corrupt characterized the pronouncements from all sides (Arnheim 1979, 154–57; Wickham 1983, 336). Censorial measures were promoted, despite a refusal on the part of the legislators to grant cinema the status of a public proceeding because of the lack of a "public cause." Defined as entertainment, cinema was pronounced a private affair, though the laws passed to control it implied the opposite. In Germany the perceived threat this potential public sphere posed was, Hansen argues, constituted in terms not of class, as in the United States of America, but of gender.

Echoes of these debates about the threat (or promise) of a feminized public sphere resonate through the early period of radio's definition as a public medium. But there is another crucial parallel to be drawn between the new media. Film was finally granted the privileges and protections of a public medium with the lifting of all censorship three days after the declaration of the new republic, on 1 October 1918, but one of the results of this measure was the letting loose of a glut of the so-called *Aufklärungsfilme* (Enlightenment films), which had more to do with erotica than enlightenment. The flourishing of such provocative films ensured the question of censorship was soon back on the agenda, and, with the passing of the new *Lichtspielgesetz,* or cinema law, on 29 May 1920, it was back on the statute books. In a concession to the liberal spirit of the Constitution no film could be banned on political grounds alone, though the censor could intervene when "a film endangered public order and safety or Germany's international reputation" (Jason 1935–36, 23–24). Those who were frightened about the power of the cinema to undermine German culture and society argued that such a powerful medium should lie in the hands of the state to guarantee the moral standards of the nation.[22] For the time being cinema was destined to remain in private hands, but similar arguments surrounding the introduction of radio a few years later were to result in the decision to harness radio very closely in the interests of the state.[23]

While the similarities between radio and the press as disseminators of information had been recognized very early on, there was never any question of the constitutional freedom of the press being extended to cover

---

22. For example, "Zur Frage der Kommunalisierung des Kinos," *Denkschrift der Gesellschaft für Kulturforschung e.V.,* Berlin, June 1921, Bundesarchiv Koblenz (hereafter BAK) R32/64:269–71.

23. As early as 1892, the state had secured absolute sovereignty over the telegraph and telephone systems and assigned their regulation to the Reichspostamt, a monopoly that was "naturally" extended to radio.

broadcasting. Radio developed into a state monopoly partly because of technical restrictions but mainly because of military and political interests. The incentive to control output was heightened by the instantaneous and transitory nature of radio in the days before recording capabilities were widespread in order to quell the threat of spontaneous, improvised, reactive, and agitative radio. Every stage of program production had to be carried out with the advance approval of local censorship bodies, called *Überwachungsausschüsse,* though they had no formal legal powers.[24] Nonpolitical programs were overseen by the *Kulturbeiräte.*[25] As critics like Kurt Tucholsky insisted, flexibility and spontaneity were formally excluded from radio production in Weimar Germany, given the censorial powers of the *Überwachungsausschüsse* (Tucholsky 1994, 603–4). If radio was to exploit its greatest advantage over the press—its immediacy—the straitjacket of nonpolitical output would have to be thrown off.

Ideological, political, commercial, and consumer pressures all contributed to the public ownership and control of broadcasting and to the transition from communal to individual listening. Yet the general pattern of a transition from public to private reception does not ring true for a significant section of the historical audience, namely women in the home, for whom listening to the radio was from the outset a predominantly solitary experience and whose relationship to radio therefore developed in a unique way. It is necessary first of all, however, to place this discussion within the context of the institutional history of German radio. What follows is a synopsis of the decision-making process in the formative years of public broadcasting in Germany, which gave rise to a policy of political neutrality that in some important ways, I will argue, was critically determined by gendered discourses.[26]

---

24. Each body had two members delegated by the regional and one by the national governments. Most of those chosen (exclusively men), were senior civil servants or had some experience in radio. Party politics played an important part in the nomination of these members. The male domination of these boards seems not to have elicited much criticism (Bausch 1956, 122, 141).

25. The *Länder* dominated these bodies because of their constitutional right to determine regional cultural affairs. The officials were generally well-known artists, theater directors, musicians, or university professors. During the Weimar period only one woman was called to serve on them. Writing in *Rufer und Hörer,* Maria Buczkowska (1931–32) saw this lack as one of the reasons for schedules having failed to do women justice, although they made up the largest group of listeners. If women had been represented fairly on the boards which had ultimate control of decision making, perhaps women's programming would have been taken more seriously, given more airtime, or been less marginalized.

26. This account is drawn from both primary sources and a range of radio histories, including Pohle 1955; Diller 1957; Dahl 1978, 1983; Lerg 1980; Behrens 1986; Riedel 1987.

**Preparing to Open Pandora's Box**

The potential radio offered for a free flow of information in an authoritarian state already straining under class antagonisms and international tensions, was recognized in horror by the authorities, who were at first determined to restrict its usage to military and commercial purposes.[27] While radio's potential as a medium of public entertainment, information, and education was already being widely exploited in the United States (de Sola Pool 1983, 108–16; Benjamin 1992, 93), this sort of free enterprise was blocked in Germany, as in many European states, by the nervous deliberations of the authorities, who were afraid of opening a Pandora's box and letting loose such a powerful medium in the hands of political agitators and unlicensed entrepreneurs. Public debate about the future of radio at this stage was surprisingly muted; neither the press, the political parties, the unions, nor the general public seemed very much aware of the wheeling and dealing going on behind the scenes in various ministry buildings. The popular conception was that radio was just the latest plaything for the rich or a technical toy for radio hams. As such, it could either be ignored or resisted as an unwelcome disruption to the status quo. Long before politicians began waxing lyrical about the talent of radio to bring the nation together in one happy listening community, it was widely regarded as a positively divisive invention, just one more thing that would widen the gap between rich and poor (Schröter 1973, 16).

But the lack of public debate belied the bitter struggle for control of radio that was raging within the government and between various interested parties, none of whom made much effort to engage in open discussion. The Ministry of Post (RPM), with its monopoly of airwaves, and the Ministry of the Interior (RMI), with its responsibility for state security, were the main protagonists in this struggle. On the one side stood Hans Bredow, the responsible minister at the RPM who set up the new broadcasting department under his personal direction and who believed that public broadcasting should be entirely nonpolitical. His vision of radio was of a tool to distract the spirit (*Geist*) of the people away from the cares of everyday life and to refresh and renew their willingness to work (Bredow 1926; cited in Fischer 1957, 250). On the other side stood the representatives of the RMI, in particular the leader of the Social Democrats in the Prussian parliament, Ernst Heilmann, and his assistant secretary, Kurt

---

27. New technologies are often developed in the service of the armed forces. First used in 1898, radio came into its own during World War I. A second impetus came from commerce, where radio was used to develop a fast and efficient information service for exchange rates and trade figures, etc., which was valuable in helping to reestablish international trade relations after the war.

Haentzschel, who sought to exploit radio politically to strengthen support for the new republic and so wanted the state to be involved in the making of programs, "for the purpose of spreading propaganda for the neutral conception of the State and the awareness of national interests" (Heilman in Lerg 1980, 84). In practice their plans had less to do with strengthening democracy than denying access to all those who dissented from the mainstream opinion in the state. Of course, the defense of the state or even of the status quo is always already a political position, as Heilmann was aware in comparing the radio system to the civil service, in which loyalty to the state took precedence over partisan interests (Dahl 1978, 61). But this was particularly evident in the Weimar Republic, where large sections of the community, on the Left and on the Right, expressed challenges to the republic and its Constitution increasingly vocally and violently and withheld their support not only from the government but from the state itself. Under these conditions a state-run radio system could not properly hope to be either neutral or nonpolitical.

One of the key entrepreneurial players in these negotiations was Ernst Ludwig Voss. Having already set up the Eildienst GmbH, a commercial information service, he was eager to expand his radio interests into the potentially lucrative entertainment sector. In May 1922 he applied to the RPM for a license to broadcast radio programs to a fee-paying audience gathered in public halls, a system he called *Saalfunk*. An application for a broadcasting license was also submitted by the major electronics firms, Telefunken, Huth, and Lorenz, for a system modeled on the British Broadcasting Company in which programs were heard free of charge at the point of reception on private radio sets.[28] Neither proposal was accepted because the government, alive to radio's potential influence on public opinion, determined that radio should become an instrument of the state, closely controlled and supervised.

Eventually, a compromise was reached. An RMI-sponsored publishing house, the Drahtloser Dienst (Dradag), would be responsible for news and political programs, while Voss's new company, the Deutsche Stunde (DS), preferred by Bredow, would provide musical and literary ones. The electronics industry's bid was sidelined, but the license to supply transmitters and private radio sets was a lucrative enough concession, contributing to the greatest expansion in the electronics industry since the war. Although Bredow unwillingly had to concede a political content to some

---

28. The British Broadcasting Company was created by wireless manufacturers uniting to produce programs to boost sales of radio sets. It became a public corporation only in 1926, ostensibly because the government needed to control the distribution of airwaves; the real motivation was the fear of leaving such a powerful social and political weapon in private hands (Curran and Seaton 1981, 135–45).

of the programs, the deal assured the RPM full control of the technical side of operations, the production companies, and, crucially, the right to determine any future organizational restructuring of radio. His brief at the RPM did not officially encompass responsibility for program making, but his determination and powers of persuasion were such that his suggestions acted as unofficial guidelines, shaping the character of German radio in the crucial years up to 1926 before radio policy was codified.[29]

So, after months of interministerial wrangling, the die was cast for a system of public transmissions of privately produced programs. Responsibility for the transmission of these programs initially fell to a newly established broadcasting company, the Berliner Programmgesellschaft Radiostunde AG (later the Funkstunde), jointly owned by Dradag, the DS, and the RPM. Over the next twelve months a broadcasting network was built up to cover the whole of the Reich, transmitting from nine regional stations.[30] A national wavelength, the *Deutsche Welle,* began broadcasting in 1926. Private capital had a large stake in the new radio industry but never

---

29. Hörburger has argued that the enormous amount of criticism directed at the censorship laws applied to the film industry meant the government was eager to deflect further controversy by bypassing the legislative process (1975, 12).

30. Following closest on the heels of the Funkstunde was the Mitteldeutsche Rundfunk AG (Mirag), set up in Leipzig on 2 March 1924 with capital from the newspaper publishers Herfurth and the civic exhibitions office. The Schlesische Funkstunde AG was set up in Breslau on 26 March 1924 with money from the Darmstädter Nationalbank and various local manufacturers. In Bavaria negotiations for a radio station had begun between various financiers as early as 1922, and the Deutsche Stunde in Bayern GmbH was founded in Munich in September of that year, with backing to the tune of 50,000 marks from the Deutsche Bank. Voss was also involved until he was forced to resign under pressure from the RPM and the Bavarian state government. Broadcasts from Munich began on 30 March 1924. The DS not only made programs but also sold and rented wireless sets. Südwestdeutscher Rundfunk AG (SWR) was inaugurated in Frankfurt am Main on 1 April 1924. On the board of directors were Carl Schleussner and his son, owners of a photographic company; Fritz von Opel, the car manufacturer; a lawyer, Erst Boesebeck; Generalkonsul Karl Meyer; the city mayor, Ludwig Landmann; and the omnipresent Ernst Ludwig Voss. A month later, on 2 May 1924, what was to become one the most influential radio companies was founded in Hamburg, the Nordische Rundfunk-AG (Norag). Capital investments came from the grain company Blonck and the banker Peter Kruse. Southern Germany joined the network with the setting up of the Süddeutscher Rundfunk AG (Sürag) in Stuttgart on 12 May 1924 with shares held by local banks and industrialists, a concert agency, the RPM, DS, and Dradag. Ostmarken Rundfunk AG (Orag) started business in Königsberg on 14 June 1924, with finance from Walter Zabel, an electronic installations firm. It was later taken over by the Messeamt Königsberg in Preußen GmbH. Finally, the Westdeutsche Funkstunde AG (Wefag) was set up in Münster on 10 October 1924, with funds from the region's chambers of commerce and from the city of Münster. Cologne would have been the first choice as a base, but the Ruhr at this time was under French occupation. The company moved to Cologne in 1926 under the new name of Westdeutscher Rundfunk AG (Werag) (information from Dahl 1983, 33).

accounted for more than 49 percent of the shares in any station, and the RPM kept a monopoly of voting shares. The system was finally properly coordinated on a national level with the creation on 15 May 1925 of the national broadcasting company, the Reichsrundfunkgesellschaft (RRG), in which the RPM was the dominant financial and political mover.

On 29 October 1923 the first program was publicly broadcast from the attic of the Vox record company building in Berlin's Potsdamer Straße and was entirely devoted to classical music played both live in the studio and on Vox records. Barely two months later Bredow confidently predicted that it was likely that almost every home would be furnished with a radio set within the foreseeable future.[31] The figures were encouraging; by the beginning of December the number of licensed receivers stood at 467, a month later at 1,500, and a year later at 549,000. By 1926 the figure had reached more than a million (Fischer 1957, 14–37). Of course, the actual number of listeners was much higher, not only because of the practice of communal listening but also because of the thousands of unofficial home-made receivers. Promotional campaigns were launched to attract more listeners; the sight of vans advertising the advantages of radio with the slogan "Willst Du nicht mehr allein sein, lad' Dir die Welt in Dein Zuhause ein!" (If you don't want to be alone, invite the world into your home!) became a familiar one on German streets in 1923 and 1924 (Schröter 1973, 35). In a speech in 1926 Bredow described radio as an "indispensable means of connecting every household with the outside world" (cited in Pohle 1955, 60). It is clear that from the outset the companionate nature of radio, and its mission to bond the domestic world to the world outside, was central to its appeal and to the conception of its function.

Economically, the introduction of radio was badly timed, coming at the height of the inflation when 1 dollar was worth 2.2 billion German marks (Statistisches Reichsamt 1925, 6). Few people could afford such a luxury—the license alone cost 350 million paper marks at a time when the average cost of living was 657 million—so most of the early listeners were *Schwarzhörer,* running the risk of a hefty fine by tuning in "on the black" on homemade sets. The government introduced this penalty in an emergency decree passed on 4 April 1924, which also gave post office officials the same rights as police to make house searches for undeclared sets, a remarkable level of intrusion into the domestic sphere indicating the importance attached by the authorities to the control not only of the production but also the reception of broadcast material.[32] The government

---

31. Records of the Secretary of State in the RPM, Berlin, 11 January 1924, BAK R38/98:155.

32. *Notverordnung zum Schutze des Funkverkehrs* BAK R43/1999:203. The maximum fine was set at 100,000 gold marks (there was a short amnesty period). For more details, see Lerg 1970, 164–71. None of the histories or primary sources consulted indicate how rigorously the police pursued this policy.

also outlawed unauthorized tampering with wirelesses, in an attempt to prevent radio hams converting their receivers into transmitters. Only when the currency was stabilized, with the introduction of the Reichsmark and the license fee reduced from 60 to 2 marks a month, did the numbers of registered listeners increase substantially. Politically, however, the introduction of radio could not have come at a better time for the government, for it seemed to be a useful tool in curbing the unrest caused by the hardships created by the inflation. Haentzschel, for one, rued the fact that radio had not appeared on the scene earlier to help avoid the "unnecessary fighting and confusion" that followed the Kapp Putsch in 1920 and the various general strikes and uprisings that followed it (in Heydeck 1975, 134).

The parties at the extremes of the political spectrum at this time were in a strong position to attract support from the growing numbers of people disillusioned with the government, but the state monopoly of radio denied them what would have been a valuable means of organizing and coordinating their campaigns. The memory of the role radio technology had played in the German Revolution had not yet faded in government circles, and the fear of extraparliamentary groups using radio to unsettle the status quo was still fresh in their minds.[33] With violent nationalism and separatism shaking the very foundations of the republic, Germany was patently still in turmoil.[34] Nevertheless, Bredow maintained that it was only in 1923, once "political stability" had been secured, that there was a serious opportunity to introduce radio as a public service, even though the situation was sensitive enough to demand the airwaves be kept free of politically controversial statements. The play for neutrality ensured that music dominated the schedules almost entirely for the first year, which was a boost to radio's rapid acceptance and appeal. But, once the schedules expanded to incorporate nonmusical programs, the question of how to avoid political bias became paramount. In his memoirs Bredow defended the policy of nonpolitical radio in terms of the public interest: "At a time when one did not know if today's wages would pay for tomorrow, when battles between political parties were tearing the land asunder, when the

---

33. Throughout the Revolution radio proved a vital means of communication and coordination between the various soldiers' and workers' councils—the first time that radio had ever played a part in domestic politics. The councils often had the military radio stations (the only stations available) at their disposal, but, with the new regime, control of the airwaves was back in the hands of a conservative bureaucracy (Dahl 1978,13–18; Behrens 1986, 156–57).

34. On the very day public broadcasting began in Germany, the army, protected by paragraph 48 of the Constitution, removed elected left-wing officials from the government in Saxony, the government of the recently declared Rheinische Republik was announced in Aachen, the state of Bavaria and the cities of Trier, Köln, Düsseldorf, and Wiesbaden were threatening to secede, the Ruhr was still under French occupation, and a new wave of virulent nationalism was sweeping across the country. Hitler's "Beerhall Putsch" followed in Munich just a few days later.

audience's intolerance of politics had reached its limit and the Reich was faltering under internal and external pressure, the nation wanted to hear no more about politics and party quarrelling" (1960, 2:290).

The interests of the general public in this formulation were narrowly defined as to exclude what were considered marginal groups. Bredow believed the public mood to be defined by political fatigue, by which conclusion he judged all those who were so actively engaged in political action to be excluded from the general public. Politics, in such a worldview, was for outsiders, for others. Acceptance of the state and of the status quo granted entry into a more mystical and stable community founded on national rather than partisan ties. In a world that still defined the political sphere as male, the nonpolitical public was inevitably ascribed female characteristics in the withdrawal from the civic stage and the retreat to the autonomous regime of home and family. Precisely because of the postwar turmoil, society had become politicized down to its very roots. To turn a blind eye to politics was to admit its all-pervasiveness. To deprive radio of its political function as mediator of a plurality of opinion was to admit the victory of political intolerance.

The free-floating nature of radio crossing regional and social barriers, producing its goods at a unitary source for mass, simultaneous, if geographically discrete consumption, created a sense of its public being identical with the citizens of the nation-state, a sense which privileged the notion of the public good and which was used to justify government involvement, censorship, and claims to political neutrality. In the attempt not to offend any section of the national public at a time when the sense of nationhood itself was unstable, German radio missed its promise to act as a public forum for the exchange and development of ideas and opinions on the political affairs of the state. The consequences were as damaging for radio as for the infant democracy. The radio could not compete with the press as a source of political information and education, and, with the press becoming increasingly monopolized by right-wing proprietors, the chances of fostering an informed and balanced electorate were considerably hampered. The legislation passed in 1926 ruled that radio should serve no single party, that its entire production be nonpartisan, and that its news content be drawn only from officially sanctioned agencies. Instead of trying to achieve a careful balance of the various parties' views, Bredow insisted that political neutrality could be ensured only be keeping broadcasting altogether free of politics. In effect, the perceived dangers of a single political party unfairly dominating the airwaves was sidestepped by simply banning all party political discussion from the air and treating general political questions with a nervous caution that could lead only to the tamest and dullest of programs. The risk of vapid and colorless programming was one that Bredow and his staff were happy to take in the interests of not alienating any part of the audience (Bredow, cited in Fischer 1957, 250).

## A Class Act: The Workers' Radio Movement

Bredow was wrong to assume that entirely nonpolitical radio could ever become a reality in Weimar Germany. The recognition of the power of radio propaganda ensured that it could never be free of political influence and party-political intrigues. The influence of the RMI was also working to guarantee that the interests of the state were actively pursued on the air. For at least one section of the community, the organized working class, the essentially nondemocratic structure of radio was a major concern. Previously, the working class had always been able to provide itself with an alternative to the mainstream, middle-class cultural activities, such as theater and literature, but right from the start the state had enjoyed a complete monopoly on radio (Fritzsche 1990, 78; Guttsman 1990, 6–17). Nevertheless, soon after the first official transmissions in 1923, groups of workers came together in the cities to form *Arbeiterradioklubs* (ARK), which were to become among the most effective political organizations of the workers' movement.[35] The first issue of their journal, *Der Neue Rundfunk,* made clear the revolutionary impetus behind the movement, proclaiming that radio must become the mouthpiece of the proletariat in the realization of the historical destiny of the working class. The culture of an age being determined by class relations, so, it was argued, the class character of radio could only be overcome with the advent of a classless society. Echoing these sentiments, Brecht later argued that a system of free-flowing information would have been impossible to develop in the prevailing social structure; only with the end of monopoly capitalism and a more egalitarian system of production relations could radio become a true communicator, with generalized access to both the reception *and* the production of broadcasting (Brecht 1967, 129; Enzensberger 1970; Hood, 1979–80). In short, radio's technical potential was reached before the *content* or function of its communication was defined, or, as Brecht put it, "the public had not been waiting for radio; radio was waiting for its public" (1967, 127). For most contemporary commentators, however, the

---

35. There were also middle-class associations devoted for radio enthusiasts, but these lacked the theoretical political purpose and, more importantly, the emphasis on collective production and reception, the lack of which relegated their activity to the level of a technical hobby with little social impact. The first such radio club was set up in April 1923 with its journal, *Radio.*

truncated potential of democratic radio was of secondary interest to the range and variety of political content in the programs produced.

The initial impulse for the workers' radio clubs was twofold: first, to provide workers with the technical know-how to build their own radios, for commercial sets were beyond the means of the average worker's wage. Second, the clubs aimed to provide an alternative to the official bourgeois programs, ultimately broadcast by a worker-controlled transmitter (something that was achieved in Holland, Austria, and the United States with union-run stations but not in Germany). The union of workers' radio clubs was founded on 19 April 1924 to foster cooperation between the various groups, with the aim of bringing radio into the service of proletarian culture, spreading technical knowledge of radio among the working class, and influencing radio legislation and state-run broadcasting. The movement began with a membership of some three thousand, the vast majority of whom were men (Voigt 1929), though by 1927 there was some discussion in the journal about the possibility of integrating women more closely into the movement, a process that had already begun at grass roots level with introductory courses for women into radio technology.[36] While the organization could claim some success in its program of technical education, its broader aims would remain largely frustrated.[37] Programs aimed specifically at workers were broadcast from November 1926 by the *Deutsche Welle,* but this concession fell far short of what the clubs envisaged. It was just one of a variety of programs aimed at various target audiences, such as farmers, civil servants, doctors, dentists, even chess players.[38] Programs for women were also a mainstay of the schedules, and they, too, came in for their share of fierce criticism.

At first representatives of the Sozialdemokratische Partei Deutschlands (SPD) and Kommunistische Partei Deutschlands (KPD) had

36. See "Zur Integration der Frauen in der Arbeiterradiobewegung," *Der Neue Rundfunk* (February 1927): 1354; and "Bezirksgruppe Berlin/Kottbusser Tor: Einführungskurse für Frauen," *Mitteilungen des Arbeiterradioklubs* (February 1927): 1609. For a discussion of the relationship between the political working-class organizations, the working-class "movement" and the everyday lives of the working class in the period, see Wickham 1983.

37. In 1926 Bredow seemed to be entertaining the idea of realizing their demands, referring to a plan to build a transmitter for use by the clubs, but the fact that the plans never materialized and were so out of keeping with the otherwise solidly conservative minister's policies indicates that the announcement was a ploy to keep the clubs quiet, rather than a genuine intention to broaden the franchise for fear of their collaboration with the Soviet Union.

38. Thomas Childers has pointed out how political mobilization in its various forms (including that by the NSDAP), was addressed to the various occupations and that these occupational appeals were almost invariably expressed in the masculine form. Women were generally treated as a separate group or expected to identify with their husbands' occupations (1990, 339–40).

worked closely together, but this was not to last. Early in 1928 the ARK changed its name to the *Arbeiterradiobund Deutschland* (ARBD). By the end of the year all the posts had been filled by members of the SPD, led by Curt Baake, who introduced a spirit of reformism to the movement in keeping with the developments of the party as a whole. They even contemplated cooperating with the *Überwachungsausschüssen,* a move that was anathema to the Berlin branch of the ARBD, which soon broke away from the parent organization to form the more radical *Freier Radiobund* (FRB). It published its own journal, in opposition to the national organization, which was increasingly concentrating its efforts on purely technical considerations, maintaining that the construction of radio sets at home was a form of nonalienating production, which was more important than trying to change the content of the programs which these sets then received.[39] Until its prohibition by the Nazis in February 1933, the FRB undertook a wide variety of campaigns and activities, both legal and illegal, to try to establish a workers' radio station. A few illegal programs were broadcast from pirate transmitters on the lakes of Berlin, for example, but after the 1932 reforms its chief aim was in fighting the increasingly nationalistic and fascist character of radio and of society in general. A series of demonstrations were organized in 1932 protesting the gagging of socialist voices on the radio, attracting twenty thousand people in Leipzig, thirty thousand in Essen and Düsseldorf. The day-to-day activities of the FRB included organizing collective listening, where up to five hundred people would gather in a public hall to listen to the radio, encouraging critical discussion of the existing range of output. Hertha Maria Funck made an appeal in the pages of *Arbeiterfunk* for women to organize themselves into such groups: "There are workers' radio groups in most towns. Help them build up listening groups and invite working class women along. Delegate a comrade to lead the discussion about what was heard, write a short report about the proceedings and send a copy to the relevant party press and another to the head of the radio station" (1931, 1).

The groups for listening to women's, children's, and school programs were the most popular, although the rich potential for organizing housewives politically through these meetings was not fully realized. Other activities included helping the KPD during elections and encouraging people to tune in to Russian radio (on homemade receivers, as commercial sets were not powerful enough to pick up the signal), which broadcast reg-

---

39. The journal went through a series of names: *Der aktive Radiogenosse* (Active Radio Comrade), *Unser Sender* (Our Channel), and, finally, *Arbeitersender* (Workers' Channel), a monthly publication until February 1930 then published weekly until its forced cessation by the Nazis on 26 February 1933.

ularly in German. The government disapproved and tried to jam the Soviet signal. When the FRB was able to prove the interference was deliberately engineered by the government and not the result of atmospheric disturbances, as had been claimed, the government had to resort to transmitting anti-Soviet propaganda, warning, for example, that family life could be harmed by tuning in to Russian programs. In an article for the *Arbeitersender* in November 1932, the journalist Egon Erwin Kisch mocked the way the government was running around in circles trying to prevent the reception of Russian programs, while the papers were claiming all manner of deleterious effects on the unsuspecting population with "cautionary pictures of the destruction of marriages, the corruption of children, and the rebellion of domestic maids" (cited in Dahl 1978, 1964–65). But the impact of radio in the private sphere was also one of the concerns of the early workers' radio movement, although the fear here was that the bourgeois character of this most pervasive and persuasive means of communication would attack the working class at its roots, in the family home. Although the domestic ideal was a far cry from lived reality for much of the working class, the ideology of the respectable nuclear and domestic family was still prevalent within the working-class movement (Wickham 1983, 333). One of the flysheets distributed by the Cologne group in the early 1920s warned of the danger radio posed, although it is clear from its language that it was directing its warning only at the male population, whose members, once aware of the danger, could protect their wives and children: "With the radio, which infiltrates every town and village, every house and every family, the property-owning classes have a new biased means to influence and educate you, your wives and your children—in short, the broadest sections of the working population—into their way of thinking" (cited in Dahl 1978, 43).

But the new medium was not always demonized; it was also at turns welcomed as a potential stabilizing factor in the private sphere at a time of change and uncertainty or as a progressive force for social and political reform, not least in the lives of women. The rest of this chapter is concerned with tracing the way in which public discourse around the future of radio was defined and characterized by such gendered discourse and how the organization of radio negotiated the public-private divide in female experience.

**Gendered Discourses: The Conservatives' Disquiet**

The emphasis of the conservative disquiet was placed squarely on the supposed influence of an unwelcome intrusion into the sanctity of the private sphere, where contact with foreign ideas, with politics undiluted straight from the source, could turn women's heads and entice them away from their duties as wives, mothers, and servants. The bourgeois radio journals tended to regard the housewife as sovereign of her domestic domain who would simply treat any invasion of her territory from outside with suspicion and mistrust. As guardian of her children, she must therefore fear the unbridled influence of radio broadcasts which she could not censor before they reached the young and impressionable ears of her offspring, as the following passage from the journal of the RRG, *Rufer und Hörer,* illustrates: "There are some women who call on the inner riches of their home-making powers to keep the radio at bay from their homes because it seems to them that the outside world will push its way into the realm of their family life with a much too brutal force. . . . Others want to keep their homes free of the array of impressions that can stream in via the radio, for the sake of their children" (Buczkowska 1931–32).

Should these women's "inner riches of homemaking powers" fail to protect the home from the radio invasion, family life itself would be at risk, according to conservative critics, who identified mounting tension between family members as radio changed long-established habits. Perhaps in place of the "traditional" family evening spent in conversation or shared activities, they would now sit in communal silence with a set of headphones or paying attention to the sounds from the loudspeaker, rather than one another (Moores 1988, 26–31). Contemporary critics worried about *Bequemlichkeitserhöhung* (escalation of convenience), fearing that theaters and concert halls would be deprived of audiences, who found it more convenient to have their entertainment delivered directly to their living rooms (Flesch 1926, 24–27; Jolockwicz 1932, 32). For Mary Peakok, a critic writing in *Der deutsche Rundfunk* in 1926, this meant radio could be a cause of marital strife. She argued that, while women were just as fascinated by the new technology as were men, the men tended to spend much longer with it and go out less often than they had before. This was probably an indication of the lack of attention given to women as listeners as much as men traditionally having more leisure time in the home after work. Very few women were to be counted among the early radio hams, and, Peakok argued, wives often resented their husbands' new fad or their reluctance to leave the house in search of entertainment or even the attention devoted to radio artistes. In effect, the radio could become a rival for a man's attention: "Of course we're interested in his radio skills, but sometimes it just gets too much, and we wish that he would come back to us and listen only to what *we* have to say. But those days are probably over now. Not infrequently do we feel we've got a rival for his affections—the radio!" (1926, 3248).

According to Peakok and many of her contemporaries in the radio press, the invasion of the private sphere led to what felt like an occupation. The radio invited unknown experts into the home with advice on how best to care for one's family or educate one's children. The wife's privileged place in the home seemed to be under threat, a threat that could only be expressed in traditional terms of jealousy toward another woman, a jealousy so powerful that Peakok claimed it was not unknown for women to destroy the mistress machine, taking their anger and frustration out on the radio rather than their errant husbands. In the interest of domestic harmony she advised women to regard the radio as an ally, instead of as a competitor. (There was, of course, no discussion about the fragility of domestic relations, which could be so easily disturbed, why women might feel so insecure, or why their husbands saw fit to ignore them). The radio could be seen, rather, as a positive new attraction that kept men at home where once they might have gone out alone, and women should take advantage by cuddling up to their husbands to listen to the radio together, with the admonition that, "we can, when we want—and we want to quite often—seal our love with a kiss—our love for the radio."

**Gendered Discourses: The Conservatives' Embrace**

Peakok was not alone in coming to regard the new medium as a boon rather than a threat to traditional family life and as a tool to reestablish the stability of the separate spheres. In a lead article in *Die Sendung,* one of the biggest radio listings magazines, radio critic Ralph E. Zuar (1926), for example, began with the premise that the changes wrought by the women's movement had not fundamentally altered the division of the sexes, maintaining that women still belonged in the home and still wanted to belong in the home, despite their flirtations with the public sphere. The home, however, had changed, thanks to the innovation of radio, which, he claimed, was conquering women's hearts. Zuar saw in radio a chance to stem the tide of feminism, by bringing the outside world into the home and rendering women's need to break out of traditional domesticity redundant: "Radio has given the woman's home a new quality, a new meaning. If up to now she has been driven out of the home to recover from the burden and monotony of domestic activity, nowadays the radio brings all her heart's desires into the home. . . . There is no more thankless task than prophecy, but one can claim that, in all probability, thanks to radio, the home will once again become her world."

Conservatives since the war had been aware of the need to accord housework a new status if women were to accept again the tasks traditionally ascribed to them and which they threatened to desert under the influence of industrialization and political emancipation. An early party manifesto of the nationalist Deutschnationale Volkspartei (DNVP) declared that "the irreplaceable value created by the work of housewife and mother must be socially and economically recognised" (cited in Bridenthal and Koonz 1984, 43). Consequently, conservatives tuned in to the ideology of modernity, with its emphasis on change, technology, speed, progress. "Home economics" was promoted as a science, with courses and expert literature to impart a sense of worth and achievement to women who made housework their career. The methods of motherhood were mystified by self-appointed experts so that women turned to magazines and new products on the market in an effort to keep up with the latest opinion on what was best for baby. Instinct, initiative, and self-help were downgraded, replaced by anxiety and self-doubt cultivated in a market-orientated culture that stressed the supremacy of science and technology. But these projects were costly in terms of time and effort, and radio came as a boon to the reactionary lobby (see chap. 6). Now conservatives could admit that housework was a dull, monotonous, and soul-destroying occupation, without having to condone the exodus of women into the male domain. Radio eased the loneliness, ameliorated the monotony. Radio could impart a sense of *Lebens- und Gegenwartsverbundenheit* (attachment to life and the present) that would smother feelings of discontent in the home, especially among young wives who, having been working women, knew what it was they had given up on entering marriage (Schwarz 1929). Radio, too, came to play its part in advertising the latest labor-saving devices, devices which, with their aura of sophistication and modernity, also served to inspire respect for a long-since jaded occupation.

If radio could be exploited in such a way as to make the home a more attractive place for such women, some conservatives were ready to welcome it as some sort of savior, come to rescue Germany from degeneracy and demise. The language is particularly dramatic in the commentaries written during the economic crisis of the late 1920s, as in the following example: "Who can tell in how many cases the radio, an ever-ready, informative and entertaining "housefriend," has steered the imagination and lust for experience of women who are often left alone in such a direction as to strengthen a marriage and prevented them from going off in a direction which would bring only destruction and catastrophe?" (Schwarz, 1929, 437)

That such thinking was reflected in the official position of RRG itself is evidenced by the following extract, very similar in tone, from the company's yearbook of 1929:

[Radio] carries with it the possibility of binding together again that which is fettered and splintered. It can help [women] regain security in their place at the centre of the family. Domestic culture, which brings love and warmth to sons and daughters, husbands and friends, but which is endangered by the current crises and modern scepticism, can flourish again in the alliance between housewives and their radios.[40]

On an individual level the radio was for many women indeed a god-send. It provided distraction from the daily round of household chores; unlike the press, cinema, theater, music hall, or literature, radio could bring music and plays and countless other programs into the home in a form that did not have to interfere with the housework. It was a ready source of advice, stimulation, and entertainment and became a constant companion for many women working at home who were deprived of the chance to meet people at the workplace.

And yet the adoption of radio, with all the benefits it apparently offered, was not an entirely painless process. While the official statistics of the RPM indicate the rapid and persistent take-up of domestic radio in Germany,[41] there is also evidence of a certain reluctance or misgiving in the face of the new technology, not least among the female population, arising perhaps from a rejection of the unknown or a lack of faith in its durability. (There were, of course, others who were prohibited simply by the cost or complexity of the hardware.)[42] Moreover, the figures refer only to the licensing of radio sets, not to the pattern of listening. The installation of radio in a home was no guarantee of it being automatically accepted or understood by all members of the household. With such hopes invested in the capacity of radio either to (re)integrate women into the domestic sphere or to mobilize them politically, there was concern that women in particular did not always accept radio straightaway. A number of reasons for this reluctance were mooted. Some thought women were simply frightened off by the bewildering display of buttons and dials on the early radio sets, and certain technicians saw it as their proud duty to make the operating procedures simple enough for even women to work (E. S. 1930). Such a view, of course, says a lot more for the arrogance and chauvinism of the male technicians than for the inability of women to cope with technology, although women can and do internalize such prejudices and perpetuate the myth of inherent ineptitude. The radio journal *Funk* picked up on another rather more profound stereotype, putting women's

40. *Rundfunk-Jahrbuch 1929* (Berlin, RRG, 1929, 342–43).

41. "Geschäftsberichte" (1924–31), *Mitteilungen des RPM* (Berlin, RPM).

42. The cost of a set is difficult to gauge in a period in which so many wirelesses were homebuilt. The electronics industry only began to standardize its production in 1926. In 1928 sets ranged in price from RM39.50 for the Blaupunkt VII to RM280 for the Siemens Rfe 24 (Riedel 1987, 46–51).

reluctance to accept radio into the home down to their "inherent conservatism":

> The radio set will have been a marvel in the family during the first few days, a tremendous sensation—for the invariably conservative-minded housewife it was even perhaps an object of quiet fear from which some disaster or mischief could grow!—then it would gradually have become a toy, an enjoyable way to pass the time, a showpiece for visitors, until, finally, quite, quite slowly, it grew into something of more serious significance. ("Der Kurszettel . . ." 1924, 83)

Another reason radio was considered so attractive to housewives was the prospect that they would not have to rely so heavily on their husbands, fathers, or children for bringing interest and stimuli into the home. Housework, after all, with its constant round of repetitive monotony and deadening demands, does little to engage the mind. Though still tied to the sink, housewives would be able to experience at least something of the outside world through radio, if not at first hand, then at least independently of the more mobile members of the family. This was not, however, necessarily an emancipatory moment. It could be construed, as in the following passage from *Die Sendung,* as the acquisition of another social skill to keep husband happy; being *au fait* with current affairs was an attractive accomplishment, a method of keeping the spark in a marriage alive:

> On top of the housewife's loneliness comes the fear that domestic cares, fragmentation and trivia will increase the distance from outside life, that she will no longer be able to keep up with her husband, and that she'll vegetate and become estranged from him. . . . Then radio offers itself as a *vade mecum,* which in contrast to the printed word, has the great advantage of not taking up any of the housewife's time. (Schwarz 1929, 437)

There is nothing here about the possibility of so revolutionizing the female experience that fragmentation and alienation could be eliminated rather than just cosmetically powdered over. The enrichment that radio could bring to the woman cut off from the world is not celebrated as the potential for existential development of the individual woman but as a clever adornment for her husband to admire. What is more, her attractiveness to her partner can be increased without her efficiency as domestic servant being in any way reduced. Nevertheless, the ability to participate in conversations about current affairs and so on could bring a new sense of pride, militating against any sense of being cut off from the interests of the family outside the home (Jennings and Gill 1939, 24; Kuhlmann 1942, 9).

**Gendered Discourses: Feminist Voices**

The potential to inform women of their sisters' achievements, to inspire them to new experiences, to mobilize them in the direction of equality with men, was as clear to feminists as its potential to consolidate the status quo was desirable to conservatives. They argued that increasing women's access to information would be beneficial to society as a whole. Women had won the right to vote in the Constitution of 1919. For many women politics had always been alien to them, something that did not concern them or for which they had little interest, as they had little influence and fewer rights. But democracy is a political method that can only function if the electorate is able to make rational and informed decisions. Political education is therefore a necessary corollary to the right of suffrage. To this end there were calls to mobilize all channels of education and information in the cause of political enlightenment. The rise of radio as a public communicator followed close on the heels of the new constitution, and it was immediately recognized as being ideally suited to the task of providing its listeners with easy, direct access to the various political issues of the day. But the promise of radio as a great political educator could not be realized because of the policy of nonpolitical radio insisted upon by Hans Bredow, a policy that served to underscore the status quo. As the most recently enfranchised section of the community, women were arguably in greatest need of political education and therefore suffered most from the sterilization of broadcast opinion.

It was a common notion in the early heady days of broadcasting that transmissions from live events somehow offered the listener an immediate and unmediated version of reality (Scannell 1988, 17). This seemed to have special relevance to those women whose direct experience of life outside the domestic sphere was severely limited by the responsibilities of child rearing and housework and the social obstacles to full participation in the public sphere.[43] For women who worked at home, listening to the radio

43. Social obstacles included an understanding of what was deemed "respectable behavior," which, as Rosenhaft points out in an essay on the unemployed in Weimar Germany, involved "not only maintaining a clear distinction between public, private and work, but also avoiding appearances in public except in circumstances where one is unequivocally going about one's business or in highly structured situations like the Sunday promenade or organised procession. The breaching of these distinctions may be perceived as threatening in itself; those who habitually spend their time in public places open themselves to the suspicion of unreliability and even criminality" (1987, 205).

with a partner or anybody else was, for the majority of the day, a rarity. However, the knowledge that others in a similar situation were listening to the same programs at the same time, might have given rise to a feeling of collectivity with other anonymous, solitary women. For Alice Fliegel, a writer and presenter for Norag, one of the main values of radio for women was this opportunity, "to break through the barriers of the four walls and be united with their sisters" (1927a). The companionship of shared experience was underscored by the companionship of the radio artists themselves. In other words, it was the presence of a companionable "wall of sound" that was paramount in the listening experience. Radio's potential to bring together the isolated and lonely was particularly evident before the expansion of competing channels diluted the sense of common experience. Despite the generally private nature of the activity of listening or viewing, the sense of it being a shared activity is inescapable; it derives its wonder from the knowledge that the listenening experience is synchronized with that of innumerable, absent, and anonymous others, giving rise to a sense of "imagined community."[44]

The politician and radio activist Adele Schreiber was among those who persistently stressed the need for radio to fulfill its responsibility toward its female audience. Schreiber had been a prominent member of the Bund für Mutterschutz since 1907, a member of the SPD since 1918, and was elected to the Reichstag in 1920, where she was a member of its Population Policy Committee (Usborne 1992, 114). She wrote the following in an article in *Die Sendung* in her capacity as vice president of the Weltbund für Frauenstimmrecht und staatsbürgerliche Frauenarbeit:

> Beyond party politics, the point is to educate women to *think politically,* to develop their understanding of political events at home and abroad. Generally speaking, the level of interest of the newly enfranchised German citizen does not correspond to the responsibility which she has suddenly, and often without any preparatory schooling, received. Here, too, the radio can fulfil a great mission: the education of women to citizens of the state and their further education as citizens of the world. (1928, 131)

---

44. *Imagined community* is a term coined by Benedict Anderson in his book of the same name, which explores the concept of nationalism. Of particular relevance here is his revisiting of Hegel's observation of the mass secular "ceremony" of the daily newspaper: "Each communicant is well aware that the ceremony he performs is being replicated simultaneously by thousands (or millions) of others of whose existence he is confident, yet of whose identity he has not the slightest notion. Furthermore, this ceremony is incessantly repeated at daily or half-daily intervals throughout the calendar. What more vivid figure for the secular, historically-clocked, imagined community can be envisioned?" (1983, 39).

Schreiber argued that radio could help in the political education of its female listeners only if women were involved at all levels of the program-making process. Women who had found success in some area of public life should be heard regularly on the air and act as models for other women to emulate, for, she believed, it was only women who could carry further the banner of female emancipation. This was a project that could be achieved without transgressing the nonpolitical guidelines. It was believed by many that the insertion of "female characteristics" into the activities of the public domain would counterbalance the often divisive "male" attributes of aggression and ambition and deepen the understanding of social justice. The radio could help in amplifying the voices of such women. Schreiber also hoped that women's influence on politics would lead to the development of greater international understanding, presumably building on the common assumption of women's opposition to war and warlike machinations. But, in the end, the ultimate aim of even such lofty ideals as these was to save the institution of marriage and thereby ensure the stability of the state: "Our ambitious aim for the radio is that it should grow into a great people's college to kit people out for the battle of life, a spiritual fountain of youth—particularly for the woman tied to the home—protecting her from antagonism and atrophy, so that it might also become a source of eternal renewal for the institution of marriage" (Schreiber 1928, 131).

The liberal women's movement was a loud but by no means a lonely voice in the chorus of condemnation decrying the wasted opportunity to educate and inform the electorate. Katharina Kardorff-Oheimb, a moderate nationalist politician (DNVP), also saw benefits for women in the proper manipulation of radio. Writing in *Der Deutsche Rundfunk,* she proposed a two-headed approach that would see women's issues on the radio perform not just a passive educational function but that would act as an active political force in itself, mobilizing women and campaigning for paper promises finally to be translated into social change. Radio was important to women, "on the one hand, in every way to further our own education, and on the other to make the general public and above all the political parties hear how much there is still to do to realise the promises of equal rights for women which the constitution makes" (1929).

Worlds apart in almost every other respect, the socialist lobby, represented here by an article in *Der Neue Rundfunk,* sounds remarkably similar in its forthright denunciation of the all too precarious guarantee of women's rights and in its conviction that the radio had a part to play in securing those rights.

> Women need more. Their liberty still exists only in the paper constitution which can be torn up, and in the paper ballot which can still be

torn out of their hands again. They are still restricted in life. In the real life of society and family they are suppressed and handicapped. Therefore they must be taught that they have just as much right to independence as men. There is still a long way to go before their liberation is complete. But their freedom belongs to the inalienable human rights for which it is the highest human duty to fight. That and much more besides is what women want to hear on the radio. (J. B. 1927, 811)

*Der Neue Rundfunk* itself generally paid scant attention to the needs of women as a whole and, surprisingly, almost completely ignored the lot of the working woman, although by 1926 more than half the female population was occupied in some form of waged employment. Comment was mainly restricted to program reviews, which, although consistently critical of bourgeois bias, lacked the theoretical rigor that was applied to other areas. Women featured primarily simply as people who were confronted with the radio mania of their husbands, rather than as subjects in their own right (Willier 1977, 107–8).

Liberals and socialists alike argued that, no matter what the changes in legislation, the chance of effecting real change in society, in which ever direction that change was hoped for, would always be thwarted while the public remained uninformed. As the most immediate and accessible means of communication available, radio was an obvious weapon to wield in the crusade to raise political awareness. But the hopes of political activists of all shades were dashed by the unswerving adherence to the notion of political neutrality of the airwaves.

### The Politicization of the Airwaves

As radio became more popular and influential, the calls for a politicization of its output became louder and more urgent. By the late 1920s the politicization of radio was an issue often aired in the Reichstag. In 1928 the justice minister, Koch-Weser, for instance, described as intolerable the continued banishment from the airwaves of anything remotely "smelling of politics" (cited in Bausch 1980, 123). The debate was often characterized by the argument that radio listeners should be protected from political views with which they disagreed being beamed into their homes. In his speech to the RRG in Stuttgart in 1926, Bredow had passionately maintained that party politics and other such disputes belonged in the parliament and in the press. To introduce them to radio would be to abuse the spirit of radio, a spirit that was dedicated to the reconciliation of differences. The private home was not the place to disturb the peace (Bredow

1926; cited in Fischer 1957, 250). Opponents to this softly softly approach drew comparisons with the press. Just as the consumer could choose between various newspapers, so should the listener be offered a spectrum of opinion (Bausch 1980, 123–24). Radio should be as free as the press, on which no limits were set. Indeed, while radio could not and should not replace the press, it could take the task of political education further by giving airtime to the whole range of opinion, as opposed to papers, which openly displayed their political colors. Kardorff-Oheimb (1929) of the DNVP argued for politicization with the proviso that guidelines be drawn up to prevent "Beschimpfungen und Ausartungen, die gegen Gesetz und gute Sitte verstoßen" (slanderous and offensive language that infringes against the law and offends common decency). Hertha Maria Funck (1931), speaking for the workers' radio union, agreed that state radio should serve "die breiteste Oeffentlichkeit" (the widest public) and not one particular party. By the autumn of 1928 even Bredow had begun to question the advisability of completely nonpolitical radio. In a speech made during the festivities to celebrate five years of Norag, he explained why he had chosen the path of nonpolitical radio and why it was no longer viable. When public radio was launched, he had been convinced that radio had to accommodate the lack of political tolerance in German political culture. So great were the political antagonisms, so passionately and violently were they expressed, that the home had to be protected from such intrusions. But now he recognized that the banishment of all political discussion from the airwaves had resulted in what he called, "the peculiar situation where the most modern piece of news equipment is kept from dealing with contemporary problems, purely in order to protect the sensibilities of the intolerant listener."[45] He expressed the hope that the German people could safely be exposed to a variety of political opinions and that the radio could play a part in nurturing a culture of political tolerance.

Gradually, the idea took hold that political neutrality could be ensured as effectively by a balance of views as by a strict exclusion of all political opinion. The cause of political radio was encouraged by Carl Severing, the new minister of the interior in the Müller cabinet. He regarded it as a widely held misconception that the 1926 guidelines outlawed politics in every form; he argued that they spoke only of guaranteeing against political bias. He was eager to bring about change, announcing that he would gladly "chalk up the so-called politicization of radio on his balance sheet" (cited in Pohle 1955, 62). Under Severing's influence regular programs with a political content were launched, including a weekly press review, regular reports from the Reichstag, and a series called "Gedanken

---

45. *Das 5. Jahr der Norag,* 13–16, DRA.

zur Zeit," which dealt with controversial issues of the day such as electoral reform or censorship. The regions soon followed suit.[46] What the following chapter in its survey of women's programming will show, however, is that programs of a contemporary and political nature were already relatively common features within the schedules of the Frauenfunk, due partly to the impetus from the feminist movement to its establishment and partly to the politicization of the private sphere which a public medium of communication in a sense necessarily brought with it.

The year 1929 did mark some sort of watershed in the history of radio in Germany, but the concessions made to the politicization lobby did not go far enough. A year later very similar concerns were still being voiced, although the increasingly desperate economic and political climate made the sterility of political radio a matter of heightened urgency. The new interpretation of radio's function gained enough support that by 1930, when Wirth took over from Severing at the RMI, the debate was not so much about political neutrality as about the *Kampf um die Parität,* the battle for political balance. Even so, when airtime was increasingly offered to representatives of political parties, especially during the 1930 election campaigns, and even to foreign politicians, the communist and fascist parties were still denied access to the airwaves, as "enemies of the state." In a Reichstag debate of 17 June 1930 Wirth again argued in favor of protecting the family from the intrusion of political debate into the home, remarking that it was "impossible to expect families to go without radio simply if they don't want certain things to be heard in their family" (cited in Bausch 1980, 137). Crispien of the SPD replied that the label of nonpolitical radio was a mere cover for the fact that the radio system was thoroughly bourgeois and politically engaged against the socialist camp. The conservatives' notion of state radio serving the nation, he suggested, had less to do with equal representation of all interest groups than with a crude form of patriotism. The reforms which followed two years later proved the prescience of this critique. Until then, although there were no legislated amendments, the central stipulation about the nonpolitical nature of radio's output was interpreted ever more loosely as time went by. At the same time, the RMI became increasingly dissatisfied and frustrated with its limited sphere of influence. In 1931 its deputy director, Erich Scholz, drew up plans to deny private interests any role at all in radio. In an article for *Die Sendung* he made clear that he wanted both local and national

46. From October listeners in the Breslau area could tune into open, unscripted discussions. In Leipzig working men and women were given the chance to talk about their work in a series called "Aus dem Leben für das Leben." Hamburg and Cologne launched their own current affairs programs, "Aktuelle Stunde" and "Vom Tag" (Pohle 1955, 94).

radio to be more than "fleeting entertainment and superficial distraction" but, rather, "the bearer and transmitter of German culture and the German spirit," entirely owned and controlled by the state and operating "in the service of the German people" (cited in Dahl 1978, 75).

At first his plans met with little enthusiasm, but by June 1932 the Brüning government had been replaced by that of Franz von Papen, whose new minister of the interior, Wilhelm von Gayl, was much more receptive to Scholz's calls for reform. Listening figures had increased dramatically during the years of crisis, with people almost as hungry for news as they were for food (see app. 1). The government was now more eager than ever to seal its control of radio. Von Gayl set the administrative wheels in motion, despite opposition from the regional state governments and from shareholders in the radio stations. The workers' radio movement staged public demonstrations against the new developments but to no avail, and the reforms met with little opposition in the press. Moreover, Scholz had the invaluable support of Hans Bredow, who had expressed his belief that radio had a duty to support the state (Bredow 1930; cited in Dahl 1978, 30). On 15 June 1932 von Gayl introduced the first in a series of government programs broadcast nationwide every evening at six-thirty. His first broadcast for this *Stunde der Reichsregierung* declared the government's intention "from now on to speak directly to the German people so that they know what is happening, and because they have a *right* to hear us" (cited in Bausch 1956, 131). The chancellor was also empowered to use the radio to make intermittent government statements. Von Papen used this facility twelve times in six months. Radio increasingly came to be used by ambitious politicians to appeal directly to the public.

On 29 July 1932 the new reforms were introduced. Private capital was withdrawn from all radio concerns, giving the national and regional governments total financial control. The RRG became the central radio authority and was given new powers to pursue the interests of the state in broadcasting according to a new set of guidelines drawn up by the RMI. The only authorized national transmitter was the Deutschlandsender, and the only authorized news agency was the Drahtloser Dienst, a company directly associated with the RRG that came into being on 24 September 1932 with a brief to provide a daily news service according to the official guidelines and to broadcast any speeches or announcements that the government required. Supervision at the regional level was carried out by state officials, while two commissioners were appointed to take over the overall supervision of radio—one from the RPM with responsibility for technical, administrative, and economic affairs, the other from the RMI for the output of programs. Scholz himself was elected to the latter position on 10

August 1932. To give the impression of political independence in his new office, he resigned from the NSDAP but so offended the party in the process that he was forced out of his new post by the campaign it initiated against him.

The directives given to the program makers show how the government was concerned about the influence radio could have on the very fabric of society. They illustrate the central concern with the effects on family life and on Germany's international reputation. The very language also reflects the new nationalism coloring German radio policy. For that reason alone they are worth quoting in full, but they also clearly display the status and function intended for radio in the dying months of the Weimar Republic:

i.   The German radio serves the German people. Its programs unremittingly penetrate the German home and are heard throughout the world. This influence on nation and family and the effect abroad place the directors and employees under a particular obligation.

ii.  The radio participates in the life work of the German nation. The natural ordering of people in home and family, work and state is to be maintained and secured by the German radio. The radio does not therefore speak to the listener only as an individual, but also as a member of this natural national order.

iii. German radio adheres to Christian beliefs and behavior and respects the sincere convictions of dissenters. That which degrades the Christian faith or endangers the custom and culture of the German people is excluded from German radio.

iv.  Radio serves all Germans within and without the borders of the Reich. It binds Germans abroad with the Reich and permits Germans at home to share in the life and fate of Germans abroad. It is the duty of the German radio to cultivate the Idea of the Reich.

v.   Radio participates in the great task to educate the Germans as nation state and to form and strengthen the political thinking and will of the listener.

vi.  The admirable strengths and goods inherited from past generations of Germans and the German Reich are to be respected and increased in the work of the German radio. The radio must also develop and cultivate an understanding for the particular conditions and requirements of the present.

vii. It is the task of all stations to cultivate the collectivity and the entirety of the community of the German people. The regional stations will therefore begin with the particular characteristics of the people in their catchment area and to communicate the rich and varied lives of the German clans and regions.[47]

These guidelines represent a spectacular desertion of the previous policy of nonpolitical radio. Whereas before the emphasis had been placed on the avoidence of programs harmful to the equilibrium of the state, the new policy positively required the support of state and nation. The new policy was based on and justified in terms of a simplistic notion of direct effects on the audience, a stimulus-response model of media effects. It implies a listener who is entirely passive, vulnerable, and malleable and allows for a radio policy that both limits and directs the content of that which is transmitted. It dovetails with a conception of a violent and uncontrollable penetration of the private space and plays on prevailing notions of a threat to the sanctity of family life. It also, therefore, represents the further entrenchment of gendered discourse into the organization of radio in Germany. These reforms completed the nationalization and centralization of radio and made the RMI all powerful. When the Nazis came to power less than six months later, they found a system of radio already well suited to their needs.

To sum up, then, there was clearly a fundamental tension in the relationship between women and radio, a tension between form and content. The liberating potential of educative, cultural, and political programs was always destined to be limited by the structural function by which radio worked to integrate its female audience into the home, thereby maintaining the gendered division of labor. Daytime schedules aimed at women, or at least punctuated with moments which compensated for the tedium of domesticity and which echoed the daily timetable of the average housewife, performed a function which affirmed the legitimacy of the sociosexual spheres. This compensatory function, in Michèle Mattelart's words, "makes women's work legitimate, not as work, but as a duty that forms part of their natural function" (1986, 66). This process was at work, even when the airwaves carried a different message, when, instead of preaching the virtues of a life devoted to husband and home, the radio brought news of women's achievements in that other world of politics and work. The potential for political education or mobilization was equally evident but in Germany was thwarted by the strangulation of a policy which banished the political from the airwaves.

However, the realization that women had entered public life and were there to stay, that their support was essential to the stability of the state, was one of the central considerations in the debates which informed the history of radio in Weimar Germany up to and including the 1932 reforms,

47. Translated from the original text as reproduced in Fischer 1957, 85–89.

which prefigured the Nazi *Gleichschaltung* in spirit if not in name.[48] As the final extract from a conservative radio journal in 1931 shows, it was a realization that women's views and therefore women's radio now mattered after all. In the reactionary climate of late Weimar radio it was a realization that women, being impressionable creatures, could, if a suitably accessible format was devised, be readily influenced by a form of radio that spoke directly to them:

> It is precisely women's radio that offers one of the main educational opportunities in radio at the moment. It's an area still being fought over in the Weimar state today and will be in the future. Women have entered public life, objectively and subjectively. Radio is leading them ever further in. [A woman] listening alone to a broadcast speech or a good lecture quickly grasps the emotional values which are being relayed to her. . . . Radio offers the chance to bring her closer to history, nation, Germanness in a vivid, indeed in an entertaining way. Politically, radio could be a blessing for women and the family—if only it had the will.[49]

Social crises tend to engender the revitalization of philosophies of security, in which the family is often of central concern and the myth of femininity revived as a symbol of constancy, stability, and permanence. The public discourse around and within radio during the Weimar Republic expressed the tension between these philosophies and the ideology of modernity, which was one—on the surface at least—of constant change, dynamism, and progress. Radio itself was caught up in these contradictions, both as a site for their expression and in its own essential structural tension between revolutionary potential and stabilizing function. In the later period these contradictions were not resolved but repressed. Throughout the period women's images were manipulated and exaggerated to serve as exegetic figures, and the institutions of the mass media themselves became a crucial site on which the battle for and against women's emancipation from the private sphere was fought out. During the Weimar Republic it was a battle of attrition, with gradual advances for the conservative forces until the victory of national socialism, when the metaphor of battle itself became a driving force in radio imagery and imagining of women.

---

48. *Gleichschaltung* means "bringing into line"—that is, the Nazification of state institutions and policies (see chap. 4).

49. "Die Frau und der Rundfunk," *Der deutsche Sender: Wochenschrift des Reichsverbandes Deutscher Rundfunkteilnehmer für Kultur, Beruf und Volkstum,* 28 June 1931.

# Part 2
# Feminine Frequencies

# Let Women Speak to Women!
# On Women's Radio in
# Weimar Germany

Having explored in the previous chapter the ways in which gendered discourses influenced the development of radio as a medium bridging the public and private domains, it is useful now to consider in more detail the evolution of those programs that most clearly illustrate the practice of those discursive positions. Separate programs for women were introduced in Germany as early as the spring of 1924. Originally, the studios' support for regular features for women derived from the need to anchor the daytime audience of housewives and mothers; it had gradually become clear that regular targeted series could be one way of establishing a regular and committed audience that, once "hooked," could be drawn toward other regular features adjacent in the schedules (Moores 1988, 33–39). The schedules were designed to accompany the daily domestic rhythm, to weave themselves "unobtrusively into the fabric of daily life," and it was the imagined daily routine of a household with the woman at the center that provided the blueprint (Scannell 1984, 333; Paterson 1990). Constructing an audience by targeted scheduling has long been common practice, but it was these early attempts to focus programming for women that were the first experimental moves toward such a strategy.

There were three major influences on the development of separate programs for women in Germany that came from outside the radio system itself. The first was from the press, which already had a tradition of separate feuilleton pages for women. The second was from the middle-class housewives' unions, and the third was from commerce. This chapter traces the impact of each of these in the history of the Frauenfunk as a whole and

---

"Laßt Frauen zu Frauen sprechen!" (Herzog 1930, 127).

then goes on to explore the national and regional variations in scheduling and programming for women. In a final section the story of one woman's career in radio for young women serves as an introduction to the theme of continuity and change beyond 1933. The chapter begins, however, by setting the establishment of the Frauenfunk in the context of the discourses around gender and radio.

## The Politics of Programs for Women

For the women who became prominent in the production of women's programs, audience figures and commercial considerations took second place to an overtly political agenda. The women who were involved in Berlin's early Frauenfunk justified their activities by arguing that the media needed to recognize the special situation of women at a time when they were just beginning to be more prominent and active in the public sphere. The middle-class women's organizations wanted airtime allocated to women's issues and insisted it had to be left to women, and women in the (bourgeois) feminist movement in particular, to produce and present these programs, in order that women's vital interests might be "authentically" represented ("Frauen-fragen . . ." 1928). As the previous chapter showed, the opponents of feminism also saw benefits in establishing a Frauenfunk—only in this way could more women be lured to the wireless, there to be instructed in the "natural" order of things, to accept their place in the home. Support for separate women's programming also came, however reluctantly, from the workers' radio union, though there was little support for the actual output of the middle-class-dominated Frauenfunk. *Der Neue Rundfunk* argued that, if the male-dominated schedules were biased against women, then women had to appropriate a time when their concerns would be guaranteed an airing (J. B. 1927, 811). In the theoretical schema of the ARBD, women's radio would only truly benefit from a complete restructuring of the radio system, just as the "woman question" would only be resolved with the fundamental revolution of society, but, until the day when such demands were met, the concept of women's programming would survive. There were, therefore, never any calls for radical separatism, as an article by a member of the ARB, Anna Frankl-Hutterer, in *Arbeiterfunk* made clear, saying "women don't want special rights in radio; they don't want to be separated off from men, they just want the space they deserve to fight in their own way for a better present and better future" (1931, 455).

The early Frauenfunk, then, was overtly political at a time when German radio was overtly nonpolitical. The political content of broadcast subject matter might have been kept to a minimum, but the very presence of programs for women had an indisputable political edge. Moreover, some Frauenfunk departments managed to secure a degree of autonomy that enabled them to tackle overtly political questions, taking advantage of the complacent prejudices in the radio hierarchy that women's programs were uniquely involved with domestic concerns. But, despite the widespread, cross-party agreement that women needed to establish their own broadcasting space, the history of the Frauenfunk shows how difficult this proved to be. The downside of creating autonomous airtime was the tendency for women's programs to be given low priority, separated from the mainstream, so forfeiting the respect of producers and listeners alike. When the celebrations for the first five years of German broadcasting were held, for example, there was no mention of the programs for women, so low did these programs rate (Fliegel 1929). Another disadvantage in having a part of the day reserved for women's affairs, albeit often only a quarter of an hour or less, was that it tended to distract attention away from the need for a more genuine acknowledgment of women listeners in the rest of the schedules. The small but candid concession to women's interests effectively headed off protests that women were being ignored. On the other hand, there were complaints from some quarters (the following is from a speech by the head of the Deutsche Welle to the scheduling council of the combined radio companies in 1928) that, in the setting up of special departments to serve the needs of women and children, ordinary working or retired men were being left out in the cold:

> The radio has been attuned to the world of the housewife and mother, but no radio company, as far as I am aware, has considered, even at the close of the day, the men who, weary and worn and in need of relief from their physical and mental anxieties, make up a not insubstantial part of the audience.[1]

Complaints such as this were expressions of the wider process of locating leisure time increasingly in the home that characterized the shifting balance between the public and private spheres in this period and in which broadcasting played a key role (Morley and Silverstone 1990, 37). Insofar as such complaints implied calls for a *Männerfunk,* they proved ineffective because it was recognized that the existing range of programs already catered implicitly to such groups, or precisely because only those groups that could be defined in some way as "other" could be assigned such reservations in the daily schedules.

---

1. H. Schubotz, "Das Vortragswesen im Rundfunk" (paper given at the conference of the Program Committee of the German Broadcasting Companies, Wiesbaden, 7 June 1928, BAK R55/1281:144–55).

**Taking to the Airwaves**

The pressure for separate women's radio was translated into programs within a few months of German radio taking to the air. A major influence came from the press, particularly those metropolitan papers which had developed separate sections for women as a consequence of the growing influence of the bourgeois feminist movement. In the same way that early cinema drew inspiration from the music hall and the theater before it developed into an art form in its own right, it took time for the newborn radio to find a form of its own. At first output concentrated almost exclusively on musical programs because of the strict political restrictions on verbal output. When nonmusical programs were introduced more widely, they tended to be little more than "talking newspapers," literally the recitation of printed journalism. Until 1925 airtime was allocated to various major papers in Berlin, Munich, and Frankfurt, and so the women's pages of these organs became involved in preparing regular bulletins. The *Münchener Allgemeine Zeitung,* for example, produced the daily *Zehn Minuten für die Frau,* ten uncontroversial minutes of recipes, household tips, and fashion news. In contrast, when a program for women was introduced in Berlin a month later, in November 1924, a number of papers with different political allegiances were involved, with the consequence that political persuasions were clearly discernible even in an era of nonpolitical radio. When these newspaper-based programs were abandoned in 1925, many of the women who had worked on them continued as freelancers, providing continuity and experience and helping to safeguard a female input into women's programming.

It was members of the various housewives' unions, the *Hausfrauen-vereine,* who continued the work of the newspaper journalists or worked alongside them. The first stations to enlist their expertise were Breslau, Frankfurt am Main, and Münster.[2] The central aim of the Reichsverband Deutscher Hausfrauen (RDH), which had been set up in 1915 to mobilize women in the war effort, was the official and widespread recognition of housewifery as a career for which women needed to be trained, ideally in a state-run program of schools and colleges, in recognition of its importance to the well-being of the nation.[3] After the war it abandoned any nascent feminism it had once displayed and sided firmly with the counterrevolu-

---

2. *Neunter Jahresbericht des RDH,* 1925, Bundesarchiv Potsdam (hereafter BAP), 70Re2/8:240.

3. *Ziele und Arbeit des RDH;* BAP 70Re2/44:24. The RDH was an affiliated organization of the Bund Deutscher Frauenvereine (BDF), the middle-class Federation of German Women's Associations. For more information, see Evans 1976.

tionaries, insisting that domesticity was not only a real profession but that for women it was *the* profession (Bridenthal 1984, 153–73; Kramer 1987, 121). Part of the RDH's program was to insist on improved living conditions to encourage stable family life, to educate its members in contemporary economic and cultural questions, and to ameliorate housework through the modernization of methods and technology. The RDH tried to influence legislation concerning women and household affairs and to exert pressure on various economic corporations and school boards, etc., to promote its demands. Access to the airwaves gave the RDH an invaluable opportunity to address women directly in the home, cultivating a loyal and regular audience and spreading the unions' message to a much greater number of women than would have been possible by way of more conventional means. Some stations, like Berlin, drew on housewives' unions only occasionally; others, like Frankfurt, Breslau, and Königsberg, left production up to such organizations entirely.

The participation of middle-class housewives' unions did more than just restrict the content of the *Frauenstunden* to simple questions of useful household advice; it lent the programs a solidly middle-class ambience. In this respect women's programming was not out of place within the overall collection of programs. While radio was supposed to be a nonpolitical vehicle, one particular view of the world was continually portrayed as neutral and uncontentious. The status quo was taken as the norm from which all alternatives to the dominant conventions were mere deviations. For large sections of the audience, however, the existing broadcasts did not relate to anything within their own experience. For them the unspoken bias was all too obvious. The two groups most obviously disenfranchised by Weimar radio were the working class and women; working-class women were, of course, doubly cheated. In an interview in the *Der Neue Rundfunk* a representative of one of the housewives' unions, who was a member of the Frauenfunk committee in Leipzig, defended the existing output by saying that "the areas where the interests of the working woman diverge from those of the women's groups represented on the committee are areas which lie outside radio's area of competence" (J. B. 1927, 811). Her answer indicates how decisions about women's programs at this time were shaped by the uncritical assumption of gender as a category which transcended all other social divisions. It was part of an essentialist discourse which accepted women's domestic role as rooted in biology, innate and inescapable, and which therefore considered the rightful subject of women's radio to be the domestic, a subject that would interest and inspire women from all walks of life. The ARK did not find this answer satisfactory and disputed the notion that there were common interests which united women regardless of class or status:

Areas which lie outside radio's area of competence! Where might that be? These interests lie in that unconceptualised territory where the true meaning of radio lies. Is it so hard to recognise that the declination of interests begins exactly where the presumed point of common interests is defended?

Another commentator scornfully summed up the overall political tenor of these programs by saying that, "just as is fitting for good little women, all politics is excluded: but every so often some good soul or another can't resist showing evidence of her hearty black, white and red sympathies and that she expects at the very least the ills of the world to be cured by militarism" (Scherrel 1926, 891). Certainly, many of these programs seem to have differed very little from those that characterized the output of women's radio in the Third Reich.

The third major influence on the early Frauenfunk was advertising. With the introduction of *Unterhaltungsrundfunk,* or entertainment radio, the sale of wirelesses, and therefore the number of listeners, rose dramatically and more or less consistently for many years. From the outset commercial companies had been able to use airtime to promote their products. The very first broadcast, a Beethoven piano concerto, featured the first German radio commercial, informing the audience that the piano featured was a Steinway (Dahl 1978, 28). Time checks also featured the trade name of the clock. More substantial advertisements and commercial sponsorship began in mid-September 1924, though still only some twenty minutes or so a day. Guidelines on the form, duration, and content of advertisements were coordinated on a national level with the establishment of the RRG the following year (Fischer 1957, 13; Lerg 1970,195–208). Political and religious advertising was not allowed nor were advertisements for alcohol or places of entertainment. Moreover, advertisements had to be clearly distinguished from the rest of the output and so could not be expressed in the first person, to avoid the impression of a personal endorsement from the radio companies themselves. Lessons were learned from the commercially inspired experiments in the United States like the soap opera (see Nochimson 1992, 46–54), although the history of sponsorship in the German (and, indeed, European) context was rather different from the American experience. The most important insight borrowed from the States was to recognize a basic twofold function of a commercially orientated address to women, "to promote the sale of household products, and to integrate the housewife into her function and task by offering her romantic gratification" (Mattelart 1986, 64). In Leipzig, for example, the impetus for women's programming came from the sewing pattern firm, Beyer, which in July 1924 instigated and funded "Aus dem

Reiche der Frau" (From the Realm of Women), a weekly hour-long program dealing with issues considered to be of general interest to women and punctuated by dance music. Early program titles laid a stress on romance: "Liebe und Ehe" (Love and Marriage), "Die Dichterin" (The Poetess), and "Wie bleiben wir liebenswert?" (How Do We Stay Lovable?).[4] Reference to the sponsoring company did not intrude noticeably into the program, with just a mention in the introduction and in the closing credits, but it was still popularly nicknamed the Beyer Stunde, which no doubt pleased the company. Occasionally, its commercial interests gave rise to special programs like the fashion shows broadcast during the summer months. Such innovations did not shield it from scathing criticism from *Der Neue Rundfunk,* which dismissed it as "ein übler Bums, über den man besser schweigt" (a nasty thing that it's better to keep quiet about) (J. B. 1927, 811).

According to the guidelines of one commercial radio company, the Funkdienst GmbH, a subsidiary of the Berliner Funkstunde, there were three broad categories of advertisements: ten-minute slots made up of ten or more short contributions, fifteen-minute long "commercial lectures," and the sponsorship of concerts. The first category is of particular interest here. At an average cost of two hundred marks a minute, the Funkdienst ran a daily ten minute slot from 6.20 to 6.30 promoting household goods under the title "Ratschläge fürs Haus" (Tips for the House). Clearly, advertisers need to target their campaigns to reach those sections of the community most likely to be persuaded to switch to their client's product. Since it was women who were generally responsible for choosing among the various brands of consumer goods on offer, and since it was assumed that daytime radio audiences were made up primarily of women going about their household chores, the advertisers were eager to ensure a receptive audience by encouraging the extension of programs aimed specifically at women. Of course, housewives, still less women as a whole, do not form a homogeneous group. They are united only in their common function as the mainstay of the "support economy" (restoring the labor force by virtue of their unpaid—and undervalued—labor in the home and rearing the next generation of workers), but the female radio audience was constructed as a group unified in its function as consumers and courted by advertisers in the pursuit of profit. There was also an overt political dimension to programs addressing women as consumers, an aspect of women's radio that will be considered in more detail in chapter 7.

Not everybody welcomed the new commercial interest in radio; some listeners found the advertisements intrusive, and the radio companies

---

4. *Senderberichte zum ersten Jahr* (Leipzig: Mirag, [1925?]), DRA.

found that the income generated from advertising was barely covering their costs, but the loudest complaints came from the newspaper industry, which feared a loss in advertising revenue (Lerg 1970, 199–200). Those who resented the presence of commercial promotions on the airwaves were mollified somewhat in 1926, when, largely as a result of Bredow's opposition to radio advertising in all its forms as a threat to radio's cultural integrity, it was decided to restrict advertising to weekday mornings, the time when housewives were most likely to be listening. Complaints about the intrusion of advertising apparently all but disappeared as a result.[5] Commercials continued to feature in radio schedules until 1936, when it was decreed that the promotion of private interests was no longer compatible with a public medium designed to promote the interests of the National Socialist state.

There is also evidence that many women did nevertheless appreciate the extra attention paid to women's issues that such sponsorship ensured, and listening figures rose accordingly. At a special meeting of the board of Norag in Hamburg on 11 November 1927, the director of the station, Hans Bodenstedt, was able to report that the number of listeners had risen by some 124,000 in the year from December 1925, to around 188,000. In the discussion that followed it was reported that the woman's hour, "Stunde der Frau," had proven especially fertile ground for advertisers.[6] When Burnus advertised a free trial of its washing powder on the radio in 1931, nearly 400,000 people wrote off for samples, and even more must have heard the offer without being persuaded to take it up. At the time the national audience was just 4 million (Elly Heuß-Knapp 1931; cited in Kuhlmann 1942, 22). This popularity can partly be explained by the form that the new programs took. Many established programs lacked the imaginative presentation that was the stock in trade of the advertisers, who needed to catch and hold their audience's attention. Instead of the dry lecturing so widely favored, the advertisers used natural speech patterns with a spontaneous feel, dialogue, drama, rhyme, and rhythm. Lerg notes that such innovations were not universally appreciated, as sections of the press expressed familiar fears about a decline in standards and a lack of seriousness (1970, 202), but it was precisely these styles of presentation which were so important in the development of radio, as I argue in chapter 8. This chapter now continues with the history of the institution of women's radio as it was reflected in the regional schedules and on the national wavelength. Given the scarcity of available sources, the following account of Frauenfunk output does not claim to be exhaustive, but it can offer a his-

---

5. Bericht des Rundfunk-Kommissars des Reichspostministers über die Wirtschaftslage des deutschen Rundfunks am 31. Dezember 1930 (Berlin: RPM, 1931), 14.
6. Minutes of this meeting, in BAK, R78/603:180–91.

tory of its main characteristics and innovations and give at least a flavor of some of the programs that were produced. The journey begins in the capital.

## Programming in Practice: The Regions

The earliest attempt to cater specifically to Berlin's female audience was the *Hauswirtschafts-Rundfunk,* or "home economy radio." From January 1924, every weekday morning at ten o'clock, it broadcast the latest market prices of ordinary household goods and groceries to the ten thousand or so women who tuned in ("Der Rundfunk im Dienste . . ." 1925). Launched as an experiment to foster active listening, listeners were encouraged to buy special notepads into which over a period of one hundred days they could enter the latest prices as reported on the program as an aid to shopping. The success of the program, it was claimed by *Funk,* even made traders more likely to keep their prices low and competitive ("Der Kurszettel . . ." 1924). This sort of "service" broadcasting has remained a feature of German broadcasting ever since (Riedel 1987, 33). Generally, women's issues were not dealt with in any organized fashion by Berlin Radio during the first three years. There would be occasional items on child or health care, but these were often presented by men and not specifically targeted at women in the audience. While men could present programs on "women's issues," women could present little else. In a series entitled "Plaudereien zum Ernsthafteren" (Chatting about Serious Matters), for example, various men expounded their opinions on such matters of general import as the life and work of Henry Ford or the state of the national economy, while women were left to tell how they had decorated their homes or taught their daughters to cook.[7] The one regular slot that did target women was "Zehn Minuten für die Hausfrau" (Ten Minutes for the Housewife). That at least some of the targeted audience was antagonized by such short shrift was very evident. In 1925 *Funk* published the following letter from a listener disillusioned with both the content and the style of the latest offering for women:

> How nice of them to set aside a few special minutes of leisure for the never-resting housewife! Yes, but what's this? What sort of a homily is this?! Women aren't to have scientific talks, that's too boring for them, that won't interest them and they won't understand; but when there's music, they're right in there, that's nice, they can tap their little feet to that without getting tired![8]

---

7. *Drei Jahre Berliner Rundfunkdarbietungen. 1923–26.* DRA.
8. Hilde Boehmer, Berlin, 21 January 1925, "Briefe an den Funk," *Funk* 6 (1925): 76.

The paucity of output for women was eventually recognized, and, beginning in October 1926, the Funkstunde broadcast a serious program for women called "Frauenfragen und Frauensorgen" (Women's Questions and Women's Worries), at first twice weekly and later three times a week.[9] Alongside a regular fifteen-minute program for farmers, this was the most frequent of the regular discussion programs on the Berlin airwaves. While household tips and recipes still featured, the series was based on the premise that women's interests were more varied and wide-ranging than could be accommodated by housewifery alone. To the forefront of discussion topics was the bourgeois feminist movement, from whose ranks many of the speakers were recruited. One program traced the history of the movement and the changing relationship of women to the state; another challenged the rosy idyll of prevailing stereotypes of married life. Many programs were concerned with women's rights in marriage and other institutions or pondered the role of women in the workplace or in the caring services or even, occasionally, in trade unions. Education and training were popular topics, as was the comparison between women's lives in the city and on the land. Even the subject of female criminality was approached in a lecture by Detective Superintendant Bartsch of Berlin. The programs with the highest profile in 1927 were two cycles of lectures on "Bahnbrechende Frauen" (Pathbreaking Women), presented by the SPD politician Adele Schreiber (Schreiber 1927a–b).

Out of a total of 1,892 talks broadcast by the Funkstunde in 1927, 142 were devoted expressly to women's issues.[10] Even lectures on household affairs ventured onto more interesting ground than had often been the case before, with lectures like "Hauseinrichtung in England und bei uns" (Interior Decor in England and at Home), "Die enge Wohnung" (The Small Flat), and "Genie und Alltag: der schöpferische Mensch im Dienste der Hauswirtschaft" (Genius and the Everyday: Creativity in the Service of the Household Economy). Despite these more imaginative excursions, women who still had an appetite for more radio recipes continued to be catered for, thanks to monthly cookery installments by Anna Drewitz, deputy chair of the Zentralstelle der deutschen Hausfrauenvereine (ZdH). Yet, despite these efforts to broaden the scope of the Frauenfunk, most programs still managed to bypass the interests of ordinary working women. There was a prevailing assumption in early radio that its greatest potential was to offer a glimpse of lifestyles that were unattainable by the vast majority. Talks were given by and for women under the collective title of

9. BAK R55/1274:58–59.
10. *Das vierte Jahr. Berliner Rundfunkjahr 15.8.26 - 30.9.27:* 73, DRA.

"Gesellschaftsvorträge," or "society lectures," or the less formal "Gesell-schaftsplaudereien" or "society chitchats." The social niceties with which they were concerned became the target of bitter, patronizing criticism in the pages of *Der Neue Rundfunk:*

> Some ageing lady pops up and chats sentimentally about domestic cares and obligations and straightaway conjures up the atmosphere of loyal, German nationalist housewives unions around herself. Along-side such truly earth-shattering questions of importance to do with toiletry and society, they toy with chicly dressed-up problems. . . . Political allusions have no place here, one is too refined for that: one cannot say just how refined one is. This refinery is expressed in the recipes, too. . . . Money is, after all, the prerequisite for a discussible life. (Scherrel 1927, 891)

The following year, 1928, saw an increase in *Gesellschaftsplaudereien,* with their inclusion in the regular afternoon concert transmission. In general there was also a discernible shift, albeit a gradual one, in the sorts of issues aired by "Frauenfragen und Frauensorgen," back from the public to the intimate sphere. Margaret Caemmerer epitomized this development in her program, "Eine Stunde für das Alleinsein" (An Hour to Be Alone). Others dealt with the employment of housemaids, the economic importance of marriage, and the debate about marriage law reform. Dr. Herbert Rosenfeld gave a literary treatment of "the crisis of morals" in a talk entitled "Komödien und Tragödien der Ehe" (Comedies and Tragedies of Wedlock), but no topic was as popular as motherhood and child rearing. The Berlin radio approached such questions in programs such as "Wie helfen Stadt und Staat den werdenen Mütter?" (How Do City and State Help Expectant Mothers?) and "Der Arzt als Erzieher in Schule und Haus" (The Doctor as Educator in School and Home).

It is at this time that the controversy over the abortion law sharpened in public discussions. As the economy began its slide into depression, the position of women as bearers and socializers of the next generation, and therefore as legitimizers of the social and moral system, became an issue of critical importance. At the same time, the need for women to lessen "the burden of reproductive work" also grew with greater economic privations. Atina Grossman has described how there was a massive mobilization of press, intelligentsia, and culture in the campaigns over the abortion issue as the Depression deepened (1984a, 73). The radio, meanwhile, seems to have remained quite mute. Those groups that led the campaign against Paragraph 218 of the Constitution, which outlawed abortion, most notably the KPD, were denied free access to the airwaves. In May 1931 the

*Arbeitersender* printed a bitter satirical poem on the neglect of this issue in the Frauenfunk. This is from the last stanza:

> Während dieses Frauengespräch sich begab,
> Trug man eine proletarische Mutter zu Grab. . . .
> Wovon die Welt mit Entsetzen spricht:
> Den Frauenmord-Paragraph 218, den kennt der Rundfunk nicht![11]

Only in its increasing coverage of the practicalities and pleasures of motherhood does the impact of the abortion debate become evident. The politics of the nonpolitical radio system show up most clearly against its absences and silences.

The hastening retreat into privacy and domesticity was not absolute, however. The Frauenfunk in 1929 also offered such items as a treatment of the perennial debate about the relative benefits and disadvantages of provincial and city life, an analysis of personality in mass society, and a number of installments about women's contribution in various walks of life, including ten years of women's sport, forty years of women's social work, women and the pen, and the role of women in state and family life.[12] Some talks also reflected the changing economic climate and the ways women's lives were being affected by the world economic crisis, dealing with, for example, economic management in the home, the German woman and the world economy, issues of modern commerce, and the working woman's diet. The year 1930 brought few changes of consequence. In all there were 211 broadcasts by the Frauenfunk that year, not including the 48 put out for parents by the Elternfunk.[13] The usual subjects of motherhood and matrimony, fashions and kitchens, careers and childcare were aired, as were the more challenging questions of women's relationship to the state, their role in politics and academia, their contribution as artists, and their status under the law, and so on.

Programs for women in the regions generally displayed similar concerns to those in the capital, but their treatment was subject to variation. In Bavaria the emphasis was laid more squarely still on the role of women as wives and mothers, although the very first program put out by the Munich Frauenfunk was devoted to fashion. "Zehn Minuten für die Frau: Modeplaudereien" (Ten Minutes for the Woman: Chatting about Fash-

---

11. "While this women's conversation was going on / A proletarian mother was carried to her grave / What the world is talking about in horror / The women-murdering paragraph 218, the radio knows nothing about!" ("Das ist der Frauenfunk," *Arbeitersender,* 22 May 1931).

12. *Das sechste Berliner Rundfunkjahr 1.10.28 - 30.9.29,* 151–52.

13. *Das Berliner Rundfunkjahr* (1930): 4–5, DRA.

ion) was broadcast at five o'clock on 7 October 1924. The "chat" was supplied by Frau Dr. Elfriede Jäger-Jessen of the *Allgemeine Zeitung* and filled the interval in the afternoon concert. Household issues were not long neglected, though, as three days later she turned her attention to the kitchen in "Aus dem Reiche der Küche" (From the Empire of the Kitchen).[14] Hers became the best-known female voice during the early years of the station. Nevertheless, it was left to a man, *Onkel* Willner, to tackle the topic of childcare. Just as male chefs were considered more expert than female cooks and male fashion designers more esteemed than seamstresses, so it was that a man was given airtime to tell women how best to deal with their children, to educate them, occupy them, even how to talk to them, although storytelling was left to *Täntchen* Denera (the diminution is telling).

Munich differed from other regions in not leaving responsibility for the *Frauenstunden* in the hands of the largely middle-class women's organizations. There were still plenty of well-educated, middle-class presenters, but there were also more opportunities for fresh voices to be heard. Indeed, there were more opportunities for female voices to be heard altogether, for in no other region was so much airtime given to women's affairs. On Sundays there were fifteen minutes of "Die Praktische Frau" (The Practical Woman), while on Tuesdays and Fridays there was a full hour, though it still represented only a tiny proportion of total output. Moreover, most *Frauenstunden* were broadcast at a time of day inaccessible to working women, a fact one of the contributors, Ilse Weiß, claimed the male heads of the Frauenfunk were slow to grasp, in asking their employees to "bear in mind with all of your talks that 80 percent of your listeners are working," without stopping to think how few working women could listen to talks between two and three in the afternoon (Weiß 1930). The "Stunde der Hausfrau" (Housewife's Hour) differed little in style or content from similar programs of household tips elsewhere, but the Sunday afternoon slot did try something new. Instead of experts holding forth on the best methods to remove stains, pickle vegetables, or solve the other intractable problems of the day, listeners could write in with suggestions of their own that they thought worth sharing with fellow housewives. The large number of letters arriving each week indicated the popularity of such a service ("Frau und Kind . . ." 1926). Communication between the station and its audience was a particular feature of the Munich system. Every two to three months, for example, the Frauenfunk would invite listeners to afternoon tea in the broadcasting house, where suggestions and criticisms could be aired. Although it was a small group that was involved, it was an

---

14. *Senderberichte zum ersten Jahr* (Munich: n.p., [1925?]), DRA.

important experiment that not only led to a similar system being set up in Stuttgart but by 1930 had evolved into a *Frauenfunksprechstunde,* a surgery that provided a more permanent venue for such discussions. The director of the Frauen- und Jugendfunk (women's and young people's radio) from 1926 was Ewis Borkmann. She took the average listener to be "washerwomen, tram conductors' wives and shop assistants" and developed the "Stunde der Frau" accordingly:

> In these almost primitive listeners she tries to awaken something, leading their interest towards women in foreign lands, for example, or to modern women artists, to women in history or to the most basic marital problems. Then she plays a few songs sometimes or reads a simple story; sometimes she even tries Schiller. ("Die bayerische Frauenstunde" 1930, 35)

This is clearly a view of a public broadcaster in the Reithian mold, gently leading the passive listener into new and deeper cultural waters, rewarding her along the way with less demanding "entertainment." It is an elitist view but one that has at its heart a democratically inspired paternalism (or in this case, maternalism?). It was a philosophy which shaped the output of Berlin and Hamburg more than Munich, which, with its largely conservative Roman Catholic hinterland, generally concentrated to a greater extent on household and family issues. As Dr. P. Bauer put it in the *Bayerische Radiozeitung* (1931), radio in the Munich region was intended to be "Pfleger des Familiensinns, des Familiengeistes und der Familienliebe" (protector of the meaning of family, family spirit, and family love). Despite her innovations and her popularity, Borkmann had to give up her post at the beginning of 1931, because of growing pressure against the employment of married women ("Wechsel in der Leitung . . ." 1930, 202).

Western parts of Germany were initially served by a transmitter in Münster, since the first choice of location, Cologne, was ruled out by the French occupation of the Ruhr. Operations were transferred to the latter location in 1926. Although women's programming appeared somewhat later in the schedules than in other regions, it did offer regular evening installments six days a week when it began in mid-November 1924, though this apparent generosity with airtime falls into perspective when one learns that the slot was called "Fünf Minuten für die Hausfrau" (Five Minutes for the Housewife). This meager service was augmented the following March by a ten-minute commercially sponsored program called "Ratschläge für's Haus" (Tips for the House), which ran at 5:00 P.M. on Mondays, Wednesdays, and Fridays. These efforts could not be described as constituting a Frauenfunk proper. The programs limited themselves to dry household tips, forgoing any attempt to tap other interests, to educate, or even to entertain their listeners. Consequently, they faced sharp and cynical criticism, not least from Hertha Maria Funck in *Der Neue Rundfunk* (1927). First of all, the duration of the programs was ridiculed:

> My, how insignificant the majority of women are thought of these days! They are to listen for just five minutes—in other words: you can't focus your attention for any longer than that, your little brain could not grasp any more information. . . . Perhaps they also think that the working woman may not allow herself more than five minutes' rest on a chair in her hard day's work, more than enough for any beast of burden in human society.

But the most serious attack was reserved for the class bias of the programs. The vast majority of women, it was argued, were ignored or perhaps simply overlooked. Yet, rather than putting forward suggestions to redress the balance in the Frauenfunk, which was the normal practice of the journal, Funck proposed highlighting the existing prejudices of the service to raise women's awareness of the injustices in society:

> Perhaps we can make these five minutes useful in another form. We'll say to working women that every day they can learn that there are also women about who know nothing of life's battles, for whom anxiety is not a regular visitor. . . . From this point of view, the West German Radio can serve an educational function for proletarian women which won't please the radio or its bosses.

It is difficult to know how successful this strategy was. Many women certainly wrote letters to the stations expressing their dissatisfaction. Others, of course, wrote in thanking the program makers for doing such a good job. This does not mean that the right balance had been struck, but it does illustrate the perennial problem of trying to please all of the people all of the time. Looking at the choice of listening offered by the Frauenfunk, however, it is questionable if this was ever the intention. Moreover, it is difficult to ascertain the volume of listeners' letters on a regional basis, still less in response to particular programs, but there is some evidence that in 1930, for example, the radio stations across the country received some 15,500 letters a week.[15]

A new advice series was introduced in 1930 aimed at first-time moth-

15. "Entwicklung des deutschen Rundfunks in Zahlen 1923–30" (report published to mark five years of the RRG, BAK R55/1275:54).

ers. Broadcast between eight and nine on Wednesday mornings, it aimed to impart the latest expert advice on baby care in an informal and entertaining conversational style and to provide a platform for mothers to share their experiences of childcare with other women ("Mutter und Kind . . ." 1930). There was by this time, however, a broader range of programs being offered of specific interest to women. September, for example, brought a series of lectures on women's involvement in the international peace movement, which included a report on the women's congress in Geneva and women's efforts to outlaw chemical warfare. The following month saw a series of lectures on women's legal rights in the workplace and in the home ("Frauenstunden . . ." 1930a–b).

From August 1924 the Frankfurt station, Südwestfunk, transmitted "Drei Minuten für die Frau" (Three Minutes for the Woman) every evening just before the main news bulletin of the day. What the program lacked in length it almost made up for in having such a favorable transmission time, giving it one of the largest audiences of any woman's program. It was a slot eagerly exploited by firms promoting their latest products. Südwestfunk approached the Frankfurt housewives' union with the request for volunteers to produce regular afternoon programs for housewives in 1924. It appears to have been initially more enthusiastic than many of the other stations, which were generally far from generous in their allocation of airtime to women's issues. The resulting ninety-minute program, "Hausfrauen-Nachmittag" (Housewives' Afternoon), was first transmitted on 14 November 1924, in place of the afternoon concert.[16] It became a regular Friday feature at five-thirty on two different frequencies (one from Frankfurt, one from Kassel). A program for women lasting one and a half hours was a radical departure from the mostly meager allocation of airtime granted to a Frauenfunk department. Given the conservative nature of the unions and the limited aspirations of their political agenda, the programs were, not surprisingly, dominated by questions of cooking and cleaning, children and chores, but there were also occasional biographical features on union members and reports from the various conferences. Unusually, the Frauenfunk in Frankfurt was not opposed to using male contributors but nevertheless ensured that at least half the speakers in any one program were women.[17]

Women's programming was introduced only gradually into the schedules of Mirag, the company broadcasting to the mid-German region from Leipzig. The first item was a short spot on 17 July 1924, just four

16. *Senderberichte zum ersten Jahr* (Frankfurt: Südwestfunk, [1925?]), DRA.

17. "Hausfrauennachmittage im Rundfunk," *Jahresbericht von 1.1.–31.12.1924 des Frankfurter Hausfrauenvereins e.V.* Frankfurt a.M.: n.p., 1924), BAP 70 Re2/51, 190; and *Senderberichte zum ersten Jahr* (Frankfurt: Südwestfunk, [1925?]), DRA.

months after the station went on air, slotted in to the interval in the after-noon concert. Over the next few months this became a regular feature, and by the new year a fully fledged independent program was being broadcast each Tuesday and Friday evening at six o'clock. Generally, these pro-grams featured talks by one Frau von Bomersdorf, whose early programs covered such topics as "women's destinies" and women's role as compan-ions and mothers. The summer months brought Beyer-sponsored fashion shows. Some while later two new programs were introduced, "Frauen-funk: Billig, aber gut—der Küchenzettel der Woche" (Cheap but Good—Shopping List of the Week) and "Die kluge Hausfrau rät" (The Clever Housewife Gives Advice). Neither was particularly innovatory, but both indicate the main preoccupations of women's programming as a whole in this period, consumer advice and the rationalization of the home (which are examined more closely in pt. 3, "Experts on the Air").

Once a month legal matters encroaching on the world of housewifery were tackled, primarily the rules governing the employment of house ser-vants. A further ten minutes were given over to the Frauenfunk on Wednesdays for lectures on Weltanschauung and matters of practical psy-chology. On Fridays there was a twenty-minute slot for book reviews and literary items, and, lest the housewives of Leipzig run out of ideas for the family's meals, there was another new recipe program (using produce of the season) for Wednesdays, called "Markt und Küche" (Market and Kitchen). The aim of these programs was to contribute to the encourage-ment of socially—patriotically—responsible consumption.[18] By 1930 a trades union committee, representing three different unions, became closely involved in the program decision-making process and put pressure on the schedulers for an evening program for working women.

The Sürag transmitter in Stuttgart had introduced such a program as early as 1924. "Abend der Frau" (Women's Evening) went out every other Saturday evening at eight-thirty for six months. Described as a *Feierstunde mit Musik* (time off with music), it was also unusual for its emphasis on featuring eminent women artists and musicians past and present. But by 1925 "Abend der Frau" had been superseded by "Nachmittag der Frau" (Women's Afternoon), a program that featured items on health and home, fashion and food. Regular Frauenfunk programs began in March 1926, and thereafter a conservative thread ran through the lectures on Sürag (Sauter-Kindler 1928).

The one regional station that treated women's programming in a significantly different way was the Hamburg-based Norag company. The

---

18. "Interessante volkswirtschaftliche Hinweise sollen der Hausfrau zu richtiger Ein-stellung beim Einkauf verhelfen," *RRG Presse-Mitteilungen* 489 (Berlin: RRG, [1924?]), 8. See chapter 7 for a more detailed discussion of such programs.

notion of public service broadcasting in the tradition of the BBC was developed nowhere in Germany so much as in the Hamburg area, where in 1924 Norag introduced a "college of the airwaves" (Schott 1927, 10). The "Hans Bredow Schule" was designed to broadcast lectures in all subjects and disciplines. Those responsible for the scheme dreamed of making education truly *volkstümlich,* an optimism reflected in the school's motto, "Wer will, kann wissen!" (Whoever wants to, can learn!) The enthusiasm of the scheme's innovators is unmistakable:

> Imagine if every week, every year, all your life inspiration, advice and practical instruction which were directly relevant to you, wandered across the land. Wouldn't you might as well be dead if this miracle didn't move you as a living human being? Wouldn't you be stupid if you closed the door on this broadcaster that was serving you so selflessly? Your respect for radio is your respect for yourself! (Staepfele 1929)

A list of the subjects dealt with in the first series of talks alone illustrates the extraordinary breadth of interest catered to by the school: politics, current affairs, the occupation of the Ruhr, colonial politics, the state system, the police, the church, economics, international politics, ideology, career choices, youth, geography, technology, health, sports, and agriculture (Zobeltilz 1927, 209). Before long the "college" divided into a series of specialized schools. The first three were for languages, public health care, and North German affairs—the latter encompassing almost anything that didn't come under the rubric of the first two. Schools of economics and agriculture followed. Established to contradict the familiar tendency to make programs to appeal to the lowest common denominator, the "Hans Bredow Schule" was unashamedly elitist, believing in its mission to bring the best of German culture and knowledge to a wider audience than ever before. But, as with the Reithian ethos of public service broadcasting in Great Britain, the mainspring of this elitism was a conception of public responsibility that had more to do with democracy than authoritarianism and that found populism anathema. In other words, radio was seen as a means of sharing once privileged information and cultural goods with those sections of society that previously had been denied such access. The democratic function of radio was defined in terms of equalizing access to high culture rather than allowing popular cultures access to the airwaves.

Women, of course, made up a large percentage of Norag's audience. Initially, when women's issues came onto the agenda, they were incorporated into the curricula of existing faculties. The medical faculty, for example, offered advice on hygiene, home remedies, childcare, and nutrition, while the law faculty would occasionally venture into the world of marital or juvenile law. Yet it very soon became clear that the rapidly changing conditions in Germany, which were having such profound repercussions on women's lives, demanded that radio stations pay a closer and more sustained attention to women's issues.

The Hamburg station had been founded on 2 May 1924 and began its first series for women just two months later. "Funk für's Haus: Allerlei Wissenswertes für die Hausfrau" (Radio for the Home: Useful Things for the Housewife to Know) was followed in 1925 by "Das Haus der Frau Brigitt," a fifteen-part series, inspired by the new "soap operas" in America, in which a fictional character chatted about finding ways to cope with her house and family. The year 1925 also brought a series of talks called "Die schaffende Frau" (The Creative Woman), which provided the opportunity for leading women artists to discuss their work on the air.[19] It was the success of this series that inspired Frieda Radel to establish the Schule der Frau, the world's first women's college of the airwaves.

Twice weekly, at seven in the evening, a varied diet of half-hour programs was broadcast under this rubric to women wanting to broaden their horizons. The early evening slot was designed to enable as many working women as possible to have access to the programs, women who were so often neglected by Frauenfunk schedules. Reports on career opportunities in a wide variety of professions was another way in which the school recognized the interests of working women. It also sought to stimulate an interest in women's art and literature, not only by spotlighting established artists but also by giving completely unknown artists their first public exposure. Much airtime was also given over to reporting on the women's movement and the strides being made by women politicians. For director Frieda Radel the objectives of the school were to give women the opportunity to hear the important issues of the day discussed by women from all walks of life, to give practical advice, and to encourage women to get as much out of their lives as possible (1928, 4). In short, the Schule der Frau brought women who were breaking the traditional mold of male domination in every sphere into the limelight and held them up as examples to be emulated. Its format was so successful that, in its annual report in 1926, Norag referred to the Frauenfunk as a prime example of how to make good radio, with its weaving together of practical and cultural life across a broad range of subjects (Schott 1927, 10).

The school's first program explored marriage from a woman's point of view—the history of the institution, legal rights within marriage, the ethics of wedlock, and the possibilities of combining marriage with a

---

19. *Norag 3. Jahrbuch* (Hamburg: Rufu Verlag, 1927), 4, DRA.

career. The next few programs assessed the economic value of women's work as mothers and housewives to the national economy. The school provided a critical echo to the concerns of the established Frauenfunk. Realizing that women were facing all sorts of new challenges in the modern age, Radel explained why the school did not turn its back on these traditional areas:

> It is not only the professional and waged women who approach the demands of the modern day differently from former generations of women; the housewife and mother has also had to learn new things under the impact of economic relations, and many technological aids in the household. Not everyone has managed it without an inner battle, nor found it easy to overcome countless inner and outer reservations. . . . And running a marriage makes greater demands than ever on insight, understanding and improvisation since smaller flats and limited resources mean pressures from every side. (1928, 6)

The Schule der Frau nevertheless realized that women's interests now extended far beyond the four walls of the home. Eight years after the introduction of female suffrage it was imperative that women were educated as voters and as citizens with full and equal rights. There were regular updates on the activities of female representatives in the Reichstag and in regional and local politics as well as information on legislation concerning women specifically and social relations in general. News of women's issues on an international level was also a regular feature, with reports of developments in the League of Nations and foreign affairs. Early examples of such broadcasts include Dr. Else Matz on women's membership of political parties, Clara Mende on the female voter, and Dr. Marie Elisabeth Lüders on women in international politics. That the Schule der Frau, with its broadly social democratic orientation, represented a range of political opinion is suggested by the political biographies of these contributors: Matz was president of the Women's Committee of the right-wing Deutsche Volkspartei (DVP) and joined the Nazi Party in 1933. Mende, another DVP politician, was advisor in the Ministry of Economics from 1929 to 1932. Though she spoke out against the Nazi Party before 1933, she was a member of Guida Diehl's protofascist Deutscher Frauen-Kampfbund and eventually became a full member of the NSDAP in 1938 (Koonz 1988, 81). On the other hand, Lüders, director of women's work in World War I and a member of the Bund Deutscher Frauen (BDF), was imprisoned during World War II because of her undesirable publications, returning to politics as honorary president of the FDP and in 1953 becoming president of the Bundestag (see Stephenson 1981, 193).

   The need to inform women about the history of the women's movement and the possibilities of the future was too important for radio to be
left out of the campaign for as broad a base of information about women's
rights as possible. As Radel explained, the women's press could deal with
such issues more thoroughly and incisively than radio, but, since the spoken word would embed itself more firmly into the consciousness and
remain longer in the memory, and since radio was a medium intrinsically
better suited for the evangelical work of the women's movement, women
active in that movement could not afford to ignore the opportunity to
speak directly to new generations (Radel 1926, 51). The school's prosely-
tizing form failed, however, to win the support of the *Der Neue Rundfunk,*
which criticized what it saw as elitism (Grünbaum 1927, 374).

   Soon the Schule der Frau was able to build on its success, branching
out with a new department, Die Frau in der Kunst und in der Wissenschaft
(Women in Art and Science). Responsibility for this section fell to the poet,
Alice Fliegel, wife of Norag's director, Hans Bodenstedt. Picking up where
"Die schaffende Frau" had left off, the new department gave women
artists access to the microphone and to a new public. Indeed, such was its
success that public exhibitions inspired by the programs became regular
events. Staged in Hamburg for three weeks from 6 October 1927, the first
such exhibition, "Frauenschaffen des 20. Jahrhunderts" (Women's Creativity in the Twentieth Century), was designed to illustrate the creative
energy of German women across the spectrum of the arts and crafts, offering a comprehensive view of women's artistic achievements in northern
Germany ("Frauenschaffen . . ." 1927; Fliegel 1927b). Women's work had,
of course, been seen in public before, but it had so often been swamped by
works by men that it was an important departure to focus on women's art
in its own right. One of the objects of the exercise was to support women's
efforts to break into the commercial art market. Talk shows and interviews with the artists were broadcast from the exhibition.[20]

   At this time the two weekly installments of the Schule der Frau developed distinct identities. Tuesday broadcasts dealt with practical questions
concerning careers, housekeeping, and the like and legal matters concerning marriage, motherhood, education, and the position of women in the
home and at work. Tuesday topics included a Berlin police representative,
Dr. Martha Mosse, talking on the laws protecting the young in theaters
and cinemas, Dr. Marie Elisabeth Lüders on marital law reform, Dr.
Edith Jacoby-Oske on the art of homemaking, and Josephine Erkens, a
detective superintendent from Hamburg, on the city's housing shortage,

---

   20. Including contributions by Mirjam Horwitz, Käthe Kruse, Marianne von Allesch,
Maria Böhm, Gertrud Kraut, Irene von Garvens (*Geschäftsbericht des Jahres 1927 der
Norag,* 1927), DRA.

especially its impact on young people. Thursdays were devoted to women's art, science, and literature. Reforms in musical education, operatic heroines, and the pianist Theresa Carrono were among the first Thursday features. On the scientific front Frau Prof. Rhoda Erdmann assessed the hopes for a cure for cancer in the light of recent cell research, Germany's only female astronomer, Dr. Margarete Güssow, spoke about her work in Berlin, and there was a celebration of the work of the medieval natural scientist Hildegard von Bingen by Frau Dr. Margret Schimank.[21]

The year 1929 brought further changes to the Hans Bredow Schule. Listeners were now able to consolidate their aural study by reading relevant texts, which libraries in the region stocked specifically for this purpose. The school was winning recognition in the academic world and was allowed to send representatives to some academic conferences and meetings. It had already been granted the same status as other community educational institutions.[22] It also saw an acceleration of the move away from straightforward lectures, which had been evident for some while. More and more, programs were delivered in an easily accessible conversational, or *reportage,* style. A number of three- or four-part series (e.g., on the art of beauty or the history of women in the theater) were among the first programs to benefit from these stylistic changes.

In February 1930 women artists from all over Germany were invited by the director of Norag to a conference in Gandersheim, a small town in the Harz and birthplace of the medieval nun Roswitha, author of histories, plays, scientific essays, and discourses on eroticism and who, as the earliest known woman writer in the German speaking world, had became a symbol for women who sought to unearth a female artistic tradition denied them by the orthodox canon. In celebrating the thousand years since Roswitha's birth, they were not merely celebrating ten centuries of women's art but, more especially, the variety, quality, and newly found recognition of women's art in the twentieth century. Radio, the most modern art form, was placed at the center of this event and, by association, was designated as an inheritor of this female tradition ("Frau im Funk . . ." 1929, 78).

The proceedings of the Gandersheim conference were transmitted nationwide. Marta Große opened with an analysis of the Roswitha tradition. In another program Alma Rogge spoke of an era when literature had been the only space available for women to voice opinions, discontents, and opposition to the status quo, whereas the twentieth century was seeing the expansion of this space into politics, the workplace, the theater, and

---

21. *Geschäftsberichte für das Jahr 1928 der Norag* (1928): 50–51, DRA.
22. *Nordische Rundfunk A.G. Geschäftsbericht 1929* (1929): 48, DRA.

especially radio. Exploiting the full potential of radio for women was a central theme to many of the broadcasts from Gandersheim. Alice Fliegel, for example, insisted on the need to challenge women to listen to and consider new ideas; specifically, she stressed the potential of radio drama to break new ground, borrowing techniques, such as the informal sequence of scenes, from the other new medium, film. She described the highest form of this new art form as a "funkische Suite," whereby the dramatic form was infused with a musical structure. Another term for this is *melodrama,* an expressive cultural mode that privileges moments of excess, exaggerating emotions, gestures, and performance, which, in a realistic domestic setting, can serve to highlight the contradictions and frustrations of bourgeois ideology and give material representation to the unrepresented and the repressed. Patrice Petro (1989) has shown how the melodramatic was privileged in filmic and printed representations of women in Weimar Germany. Although women's radio texts from the period have largely disappeared where "women's films" have survived, there is a hint here that the melodramatic mode was at least in some measure translated into a broadcast form for women. Fliegel illustrated her new techniques in the adaptation of one of Roswitha's plays, *Thais,* for a modern radio audience.

The meeting at Gandersheim proved that there was a thriving interest in the relationship of women to radio, an interest that went far beyond the accepted notion that women just wanted to hear household tips and background music on their receivers and embraced experimentation with radio's aesthetic potential (L.Bd. 1930, 30). Despite the success of ventures like this, and despite its role as the vanguard of innovative and adventurous women's programming in Germany, the Schule der Frau was dissolved as an independent department late in 1931, and women's issues were once again dealt with by other faculties. It was one symptom among many of the increasingly reactionary atmosphere shaping the nature of German radio, epitomized in the series of reforms introduced the following year.

**Programming in Practice: The Deutsche Welle**

The final station to consider in order to complete the picture of women's radio in the Weimar Republic is the national wavelength, the Deutsche Welle. Set up on 7 January 1926, it had a remit to broadcast scientific and educational programs in a popular and comprehensible form, spreading the values of German education and culture to as wide an audience as possible. There were three main areas of activity: schools programs; specialist programs for various professions such as farmers, civil servants, lawyers and doctors; and, finally, educational programs for the general public ("Wie kommt . . ." 1927, 174). At first programs for women came under the rubric of "Stunde der Hausfrau und Mutter" and were limited to household matters, recipes, parental tips, and gossip, with one half-hour program aimed at rural women, another more specifically for the urban woman. They came under the auspices of the professional affairs department and were put together by the national association of agricultural housewives' unions and the central office of the housewives' unions of Greater Berlin (the Reichsverband landwirtschaftlichen Hausfrauenvereine and the Vertretung der städtischen Hausfrauen), under the direction of Anna Drewitz. Of the sixty-two women's programs listed in *D.W. Funk* for the last three months of 1926, twenty-seven dealt with women's role as housewife or consumer, the majority being devoted to advice on preserving foodstuffs but also three on the rationalization of housework, four on the latest results from domestic science laboratories, and two on the importance of women's position in the national economy. Seventeen programs were concerned with careers for women, although the examples were taken almost exclusively from the "caring professions" and other careers commensurate with prevailing notions about feminine nature. In the second year of broadcasting, 1927, programs for women accounted for the largest proportion of the nonschool schedule for the various professions.[23]

In 1928 programming for women was extended and reorganized with the establishment of a formal department for women's radio. The revamped Frauenfunk went on the air for the first time on 1 October. Programs were shortened by ten minutes but were broadcast daily from 3:40 to 4:00 P.M., with a different emphasis each day of the week. The intention was to address the "burdens and delights" of women in all their variety and to help in their "education and inner development." Housework continued to be discussed, but primarily as one career option among many ("Frauenfunk" 1928). The first program of the new *Frauenstunde* was an introduction to a regular Monday afternoon series called "Die Lebensgestaltung der Frau," in which Gerda Simons discussed the possibilities that allowed a woman to shape her own life, from the decision whether to

---

23. There were 1,887 individual items: 1,107 schools programs and languages, 172 for housewives, 141 for technicians, 90 on national economy, 88 for farmers, 49 each for lawyers, civil servants, and hygienists, 47 apiece on commerce and medicine, 25 for vets, and 23 for dentists. There were 968 programs in the category of "general education" (figures from Schubotz 1928, 2).

work outside the home to the potential for self-expression through interior decor. Tuesdays brought a series on motherhood, "Pflichten und Freuden der Mutterschaft," charting the responsibilities and pleasures women faced during pregnancy and the first years of motherhood. On Wednesdays the ZdH took over with programs on farming, gardening, housewifery, and reports from the housewives' unions. A miscellaneous selection was offered on Thursday afternoons, while Fridays brought William Wauer and Ursula Scherz and their "Künstlerische Handarbeit für Frauen und Mädchen," a sort of hobby program, or "Bastelstunde," which, recognizing that listeners carried out other activities while the radio was on, talked them through various simple decorative or money-saving handicrafts. These programs were especially popular during the Depression (Scherz 1932). Finally, the Saturday bulletin was devoted to women in the arts. All in all there was a marked break with the limited range of programs that had gone out before. In place of the endless tips on how to make pickles and preserves, even the Wednesday slot learned to venture out of the kitchen.

Although there was a certain subterranean political edge to these programs, it is clear from a close study of the output of the first year that the schedules at this time paid more attention to seasonal change than to changes in the political or social climate. (Monthly schedules were planned six to seven weeks in advance of transmission, with manuscripts ready at least five days before the date of the broadcast.) Programs reflected life from a safe, middle-class vantage point, where decisions about whether to work or not had less to do with financial imperative than personal fulfillment, where divorce or violence against women was not an issue, where households could afford to emulate the latest innovations from the United States, where unwanted pregnancies never happened, and where the ravages of recession never reached.

The new decade at first brought no significant changes to the schedules of the *Frauenstunde,* but by April 1930 there was suddenly a collection of programs which sought to address contemporary social problems, including a regular new feature, the "Volkswirtschaftliche Viertelstunde" (Quarter of an Hour on the National Economy), which over the next few months was used as a vehicle for impressing on women the part they had to play in dragging Germany out of the Great Depression, with items such as "Die Hausfrau als Verbraucherin deutscher Erzeugnisse" (The Housewife as Consumer of German Produce). But much of the agenda was still largely alienated from the experience of the average listener (with items, e.g., on cooking with venison, traveling through Guatemala, and landscape gardening). At this time women's affairs accounted for 6.8 percent of talk programs. Only educational, language, and agricultural programs accounted for a larger percentage of the airtime.[24]

By 1931 the Depression finally began to tell in the offices of the Frauenfunk. Among the 31 programs of "general interest" among the 144 *Frauenstunden* transmitted in total, there were half a dozen about facing the problems and pressures of everyday life in Depression-era Germany. Even the recipe department became aware of the hardships facing its listeners, devising cheap ideas for potato dishes, sandwich fillings etc. There was less emphasis on rationalization, and there was not one program on domestic technology or science, the emphasis being placed on making do and saving on bills. Nor was there so much talk about consumer power. Nineteen programs were devoted to rural concerns, with several dealing explicitly with how to weather the economic storm.[25] There were nine programs on mothering, concentrating on cheap ways to keep children amused and healthy, with one installment about the strain on young mothers' nerves. With the question of *Doppelverdiener* (double earners) raging in the face of massive male unemployment, programs dealing with marriage and careers accounted for twenty-eight *Frauenstunden*. These included a discussion on the legal status of married women, two programs on staying single, two on the threats to family life, two on the experience of war widows, one on being married to a man without work, another on how women without work could find help. There were programs on combining a career with marriage or with motherhood and an inquiry into the financial necessity of women working. Once again office jobs came under most frequent scrutiny, but there were also items on women architects, sculptors, social workers, press agents, managers, and blue-collar workers. In the political category the Depression was omnipresent, with advice on how to help the unemployed, especially on the land; the effect of the crisis on women's position in society; the economic struggles facing older women; and a whole series on how women could learn to help.

The DW *Frauenstunde* continued until the end of September 1932. During this last year the political content waned again. Of the twenty-four general interest programs three addressed the strains of modern-day liv-

---

24. School programs 15.6 percent, educational programs 12.5 percent, youth programs 12.5 percent, language programs 8.8 percent, and farmers' programs 7.7 percent. Other categories were: literature 5.8 percent, music 5.3 percent, workers' programs 4.3 percent, miscellaneous 3.8 percent, civic information 3.0 percent, history 2.7 percent, economy 2.4 percent, doctors' programs 1.8 percent, philosophy 1.7 percent, natural science 1.5 percent, civil servants' programs 1.3 percent, law 1.1 percent, programs for Germans abroad 0.8 percent, religion 0.7 percent (*Programmgliederung der "Deutschen Welle"* (Berlin: n.p., January–February 1930), BAK R55/1275:59.

25. For a discussion of the cycle of agrarian crises in the Weimar Republic, see Gessner 1981, 134–54.

ing; one of these was called, tellingly, "Kopf hoch, nicht klagen" (Chin Up, Don't Complain). The recipes were not quite so consciously cheap and cheerful, although still much less ostentatious than in earlier years. There were four programs on managing the family budget and seven on consumer power. As far as domestic technology was concerned, the emphasis, apart from two programs on electrification in the kitchen, was on the care and repair of old utensils. The economic crisis in the country-side also receded from the front line in the thirteen *Frauenstunden* on agri-cultural matters. Careers for women were discussed only six times. Moth-ering, on the other hand, accounted for eighteen programs that mostly dealt with baby food, although there were also three programs on how to cope with unemployed children, two on childlessness, and a further three on adoption, orphanages, and children's homes. As for "politics," there was one program on the definition of property, a report on a conference on social work, six "self-help" programs, and one on how to sustain a gen-erous spirit even through times of hardship.

Looking back over the first five years of women's programming on the Deutsche Welle, the trades union women's paper, the *Ge-werkschaftliche Frauenzeitung,* published monthly in Berlin by the Allge-meiner Deutscher Gewerkschaftsbund under the editorship of Gertrud Hanna, was able to report that there were a fair number of items that had been of interest to active trades unionists, such as discussions on women and politics, women in factories and in the office, women in law, etc., although these items were swamped by programs devoted to motherhood, marital questions, and other aspects of personal politics. There had been no opportunity, however, for women in the trades union movement to make their voices heard on the radio, no platform for them to describe their experiences and to lead the discussion about the future of women at the workplace, on the shop floor, as union officials. It was a consequence of the policy of nonpolitical radio and the unofficial policy which followed it of denying left-wing (and extreme right-wing) views airtime that union officials, who would have been an obvious source of expertise to draw on in the discussions about social and educational arrangements, were passed over in favor of more conservative organizations. Not only did this restrict the range of opinion aired in discussion; it also had implications for the range of subjects that were tackled. There was rarely any discussion about the problems facing working mothers or the lack of parity in pay with male colleagues, as Hanna's article went on to complain:

No matter how worthy these efforts might be, they do not offer the working woman in business and factory a complete replacement for a real women's hour which respects her experience with full understanding, which gives her inspiration, which speaks to her from a point of view which she particularly needs to hear, from a social point of view, from a knowledge of trade unionism. (1931, 7)

The journal urged its readers to become critical watchdogs of the Frauenfunk, writing letters of complaint or praise as they found fit to papers and journals, using, in fact, their power as consumers to influence the decisions of the program makers. Radio had to be an instrument of the times, progressive, an educator and leader of women in the modern state, it argued. Reactionary, sentimental, and nostalgic programs about women posed a positive danger in the eyes of the trades union movement. Since no one else was going to guard against these dangers, it was up to the enlightened workers in the unions to stand watch, to make sure that radio was used in the cause of women's liberation and equal rights. Judging by the content of the schedules for 1932, the campaign made little impact on the Deutsche Welle's programming policy. By the following year, with the Nazis' rise to power, all hopes of such reforms were completely dashed.

**Summary**

Despite the growth in women's programming, there was no attempt to coordinate the output of the different stations nor much interregional cooperation, even though such cooperation had been encouraged in other areas of broadcasting with the establishment of the RRG in 1925. Less surprising, perhaps, was the continued dictation of policy in this area by men. Despite participation in the production of programs by women in Frauenfunk departments, the final decisions on programs still lay with the management of the Vortragsdienst (Talks Department), in all known cases a post held by a man. Only Munich went some way toward reform; a department responsible for women's and children's radio was set up in 1930 under Ewis Borkmann. Otherwise, women only had the power to raise suggestions from a subdepartment (Buckowska 1931–32). The fact that it was the most conservative region in which women enjoyed most autonomy is only initially surprising. As with the organization of women's programming in Nazi Germany, such autonomy had little to do with notions of real equality. It was, rather, the privilege of a neglected and little respected branch of programming within an organization that hardly measured its prestige in terms of its output about household chores. Those companies that understood their responsibilities toward the female audience to include political education in its widest sense, such as the Berliner Funkstunde and Hamburg's Norag, tended to have a greater respect for the import and influence of the Frauenfunk and so, in the censorious climate of Weimar radio, perversely, could not afford to relinquish their governance of women's radio to the same degree.

Even such a cursory review as this of the types of programs transmitted by the various Frauenfunk departments illustrates the variety of responses to the central dilemma that was apparent from the start of public broadcasting, the negotiation of the challenge to the public-private divide. All the stations spoke to women as housewives and mothers, some, like Munich, almost exclusively so, while some, most notably Berlin and Hamburg, spoke to them also as citizens, voters, and even as intellects. All spoke to women as consumers, but, while Frankfurt, for example, whetted their appetites for new consumer goods, Leipzig encouraged their sense of patriotic duty as cogs in the wheels of the national economy. All spoke to women in a middle-class voice, although some acknowledged more than others the presence of other constituencies in the audience either by broadcasting during the evening, as Stuttgart and Leipzig did at first, or in adopting an express policy of opening up new avenues of culture and education to women whose circumstances otherwise deprived them of such opportunities, of which Hamburg is the prime example. All of them had to negotiate their role within the context of nonpolitical radio, the implications of which are explored more fully in the final chapter. The one thing they all had in common, whatever their complexion, was the conviction that broadcasting could change and improve women's experience in the transitional space between public and private life.

## A Biographical Excursus: Carola Hersel and Young Women's Radio

1928, and the Deutsche Welle has been broadcasting its curriculum of scientific and educational programs for two years. Its programs cater to a broad range of professional and special-interest groups, but one listener, a young woman of twenty-four, feels that she and others like her are being neglected. Determined to take the matter into her own hands, she writes a letter to the station director, suggesting the Deutsche Welle introduce a radio series for girls and offering her services in the production and presentation of such a program. To her great surprise, her suggestion is quickly accepted, and on 17 July 1928 Carola Hersel finds herself sitting behind the microphone in a studio at Königswusterhausen, broadcasting to the young women of Germany in the first such program of their own.

Hersel's involvement in the production of radio programs for young women and girls continued until the war, when she moved into women's magazines. Years later, in 1982, she donated her collection of documents from her radio days to the Deutsches Rundfunkarchiv in Frankfurt am Main, where they represent an unusual source material for a case study not only of youth radio for girls in the transitional period between the Weimar Republic and the Nazi period but also as a useful and rare insight into the biography of a woman who carved out a place for herself and her ideas in the schedules of national radio.[26]

One of the distinguishing features of the period was the higher visibility of young people in public life. In part this was due to demographic changes that had given rise to conflicts over the position of the younger generation in society, just as the role of women had been brought into the spotlight. Young people were increasingly conspicuous in the urban landscape of industry and politics, and yet with unemployment hitting hardest at the young, they often felt increasingly and frustratingly marginalized.[27] The experience of young women after the war was markedly different from that of their mothers, and the sense of a break with the past and a new beginning was profoundly important. Young women workers in Weimar were, for example, more likely to think about waged work as a long-term prospect rather than as a contingency measure in the few years before marriage; indeed, they were more likely even to conceive of a future without marriage at all. Even young middle-class women expected to have to work at some point in their lives. Indeed, it has been argued that, for women at least, the generation gap was a wider gulf than that between the classes (Grossmann 1986, 65). It has also been suggested that the new media and patterns of consumption tended to appeal particularly to young people, of whatever class. It was the young who most fervently embraced the trappings of modern American culture and who were among those who denounced its corrupting influence with most vigor, though, while they dominated the new leisure culture in organized, commercialized, and nonconformist activities, they rarely controlled these forms of leisure (Peukert 1991, 86–106). The contradictory and conflictual representations of youth in the Weimar Republic come to light in the attempts made to make radio more relevant to its younger audience.

The history of radio for the young, in particular for children, is also

---

26. Nachlaß Hersel, DRA Frankfurt (hereafter NH, DRA). The bequest consists of correspondence with the station, scripts, listeners' letters, and brief memoirs. See also *DRA-Informationen* 5, 30 May 1985.

27. There were more fourteen to twenty-five year olds than ever before in Germany in the 1920s, in absolute and relative terms (nine million, or 14.5 percent). The young found it most difficult to find work or apprenticeships in the crowded labor market after the war. The psychological and discursive impact outlived the relatively short-lived period of very high unemployment after the war. See Stachura 1989, 95–96.

the history of women's first breakthrough into the production side of broadcasting and the area of radio that women colonized most thoroughly during the Weimar Republic, outside the Frauenfunk itself. Since women were conventionally responsible for children's early education, it proved relatively straightforward to extend their influence in this respect to radio. No taboos had to be broken, no battles of principle fought. Girls' education on the Deutsche Welle was understood as a question of balancing girls' professional potential with their duties as future wives and mothers. Schools specializing in domestic science and childcare were given airtime alongside more academic institutions. Taking their cue from the former, there were three main strands to radio education for girls: the communication of practical domestic skills and techniques; the theoretical background to these skills in terms of national economic, health, population, and education policies; and, finally, the stimulation of "a sense of beauty in all things," particularly interior design, human relationships, and leisure pursuits (Albrecht 1926; Engelmann 1927).

When Carola Hersel sent her letter to the Deutsche Welle in 1928, there was already a well-established Jugendstunde, whose weekly programs were often implicitly orientated toward boys' interests, although the program makers claimed in their defense that modern girls were just as interested in the workings of the internal combustion engine, the latest aircraft technology, or news from the *Wandervögel* hiking groups as were boys. In this sense the programs reflected the situation in the youth culture as whole, in which girls participated in clubs and entertainment very much at a marginal level, lacking alternative forms of leisure independent of boys' activities. The possibility of girls being interested in masculine subjects was not denied by those who wanted to set up a girls' hour, but they did recognize that there were nevertheless particular questions facing these modern girls which were being neglected by the concentration on such traditionally boyish matters. When the lives of young women and girls *were* the subject of radio programs, the images that were broadcast bore little relation to the reality of a young person's life in 1920s Germany. Some commentators saw the neglect of young girls' interests at their most acute in the realm of personal and sexual relationships, as in the following extraordinary example (Kappstein 1930, 117), with its overblown metaphors and oblique reference to the recent hit song from *Der blaue Engel:*

What do girls want from the radio? Attention to their idiosyncracies! Even in those cases where it is not true that all they are interested in is falling in love from head to foot, their physical and mental moods should find release alongside the manifold corny jokes about the license to enter the erotic hunting ground.[28]

Radio as the most modern of media seemed to be dragging its heels in terms of the passionate debates on sexuality that were going on elsewhere in the public domain, not least between the sex reformers, feminists, and socialists on the one hand and the churches and conservative parties on the other (Usborne 1992, 99–101). Yet, precisely because of the gulf between the generations, some thought the radio could play a vital role as neutral counselor, sympathetic advisor, and source of information (W. J. 1930, 174), and it was the neglect of this particular constellation of needs experienced by women growing up in Weimar Germany and the failure of radio to act as a guide through the confusion of adolescence that Carola Hersel expressed in her letter to the Deutsche Welle (NH, DRA; Hersel 1930).

Hersel was fascinated by radio, reading all she could about it even before she had ever seen a wireless set for herself, let alone heard a broadcast. Her parents could not afford the sixty marks license fee, but her uncle, enthralled by her enthusiasm, decided to ignore the law and built her a small crystal set to which she listened avidly. But listening alone was not enough for the eighteen-year-old Hersel; she wanted to get involved on the other side of the microphone. Where most of her contemporaries dreamed of the glamour of the silver screen, and the most star-struck might have chanced their luck at the Babelsberg studios, Hersel's daydreams drew her to Königswusterhausen. This first hopeful trip from her home in the Berlin district of Karlshorst to the southern outskirts of the city did not result in the longed-for breakthrough into broadcasting, nor did her subsequent foray to the famous Voxhaus in the Potsdamer Strasse. Undaunted, she kept her dream of a career in radio alive by continuing to listen to as much radio as she could, writing regularly to radio stations and making a scrap album of newspaper cuttings. Meanwhile, she embarked on a training course in home economics. Her family was bemused by her fanatical interest in radio and made light of her ambitions for a radio career. When she wrote with her suggestion for a series for young girls to the Deutsche Welle in 1928, she asked for the reply to be sent to her hairdresser's address to avoid her family's ridicule in the event of another rejection. But the reply, when it came, was positive. Her persistence had

---

28. "Was begehrt denn das Jungmädchen vom Funk? Eingehen auf seine Eigenart! Ist es auch nicht in jedem Fall von Kopf bis Fuß auf Liebe eingestellt, so sollte, neben der reichlichen Kalauerei mit dem Freischein ins erotische Jagdrevier, die körperlich-seelische Stimmung der Jungmädchen zu ihrer Auslösung gelangen." The opening lines of Dietrich's (Lola-Lola's) famous song were: "Ich bin vom Kopf bis Fuß auf Liebe eingestellt/das ist meine Welt /und sonst gar nichts" (Walker 1984, 59).

finally paid off; she was invited to an informal interview, where she was offered a date for a pilot program on the spot.

Hersel's broadcasting career at the Deutsche Welle began with an informal chat (*Plauderei*) over the airwaves about how to throw a successful birthday party. She was paid fifty marks for the half-hour program. Over the next few months she broadcast a collection of similar programs on topics likely to be of interest to teenage girls—entertaining friends, travel plans, and beauty tips, etc. An example of one of these early programs was "Hilf zu Haus und bleibe schön" (Help at Home and Stay Beautiful.) Hersel devoted her twenty-seven minutes to arguing that housewifery was a modern career like any other, in which the wages were paid not in money but in love, and that it was as important to impress one's husband or family with a neat appearance as it would be to impress a colleague (Hersel 1928, 700). Of all the very real problems that faced young women in the Weimar Republic, keeping young and beautiful while doing the dishes was not, perhaps, such an inspired topic, but it was indicative of Hersel's contradictory stance toward her subject, at once recognizing the modern challenge to women's traditional roles, particularly as they faced the younger generation, while at the same time reproducing and reinforcing them. The attraction of employment to women was reduced to its most superficial form, the surface glamour of a modish uniform and the flirtatious respect of male colleagues, aspects that could easily be transferred back into the home, recuperating the threat to tradition by enlisting it to fight tradition's battle.

With programs like this, Carola Hersel was offered regular work. She took lessons at music college to train her voice for the microphone and to learn how to write for the radio. Hersel's ambition now was to see a regular program for young girls find its place in the schedules. Such a program was launched under the auspices of the women's hour, on the initiative of Elly Heuß-Knapp and Dr. Ilse Reicke, and, though Hersel felt aggrieved at being bypassed, she had to swallow her pride and join the Frauenfunk team.[29] The half-hour *Jungmädchenstunde* was broadcast every Friday afternoon at three o'clock. It formed part of the restructured weekly schedule, which concentrated daily on youth questions at the same hour. Mondays brought advice on child raising, Tuesdays the (boys') youth hour, Wednesdays the children's hour, and Sundays the parents' hour. An idea of the content can be gleaned from the titles of some of the early programs, which included "Sinn der Jugend" (Spirit of Youth), "Aus der Enge

---

29. Letters to Roeseler dated 27 December 1929 and 10 and 12 January 1930 (NH, DRA). Alongside Hersel other names associated with the program in its early days were Clara Bohm-Schuch, Käte Fröhbrodt, Hermine Scheibner, Grete Maria Markstein, Else Croner, and Franziska Jordan.

in die Welt" (Breaking Out into the World), "Das junge Mädchen und die große Stadt" (The Young Girl and the City), and "Altmodische Bescheidenheit" (Old-fashioned Modesty). Career opportunities were dealt with alongside questions of home economics and general "personal" affairs. The majority of topics were addressed from a strictly middle-class point of view, reflecting the existing class bias elsewhere in the schedules. Efforts were made to create an intimate atmosphere, a personal relationship between a girl and her radio, so as not to bore young listeners with lectures and homilies but to inspire them (Brix 1930b, 134). Despite the avowed good intentions, however, the station continued to receive complaints that the program makers still had little idea what young people were interested in, how they talked, or that they were likely to switch off if there was nothing but good advice and motherly counsel.

Two months after its launch Hersel was appointed "permanent freelance contributor" to the program and was granted some room to develop her ideas. One of her major concerns was that there was not yet enough understanding of the clearly heterogeneous nature of this listening group. She repeatedly urged listeners to the *Jungmädchenstunde* to write in with their comments about what they expected and wanted from their program. She spoke much more than was usual for the time in terms of a broadcast being just one side of a dialogue.

Radio in the 1920s was one of the most high-profile technological incursions into daily life. It was modern, pioneering, and laden with possibilities. Its potential appeal to the younger generation was clear, but the cautious development of the medium in Germany had failed to inspire much enthusiasm among the young. Carola Hersel was one of those who sought to give young people a sense of control over what they listened to (Hersel 1930, 101). Hersel's great hope was that, if girls could be inspired to get involved with the *Jungmädchenstunde,* they would continue to take an active interest in the radio in general in the future, and she echoed the optimism of the head of German radio, Hans Bredow, in asserting that the radio was a uniting factor in a divided society, a forum where girls of different backgrounds could share in entertainment and discussion.

In her first program for the new service Hersel talked about letter writing, which she regarded as an endangered art in the age of the telephone.[30] She wanted more from her listeners than passive consumption

---

30. It is interesting to note how the telephone predated and prefigured radio as a means of communication introduced into the domestic sphere, which worked to counter the isolation of female experience. When the telephone became more common in private homes, it very quickly became associated with women, who used it to extend the traditional neighborly chat over the garden fence. Of course, it was at first a luxury that only middle-class households could afford; indeed, by 1932 only 52 German citizens per 1,000 owned a telephone, compared to 165 in the United States (Peukert 1991, 174).

and encouraged her listeners to write in. Her office became something akin to a penfriend agency, with Hersel personally putting her correspondents in touch with one another. German girls living abroad were encouraged to exchange letters with girls at home, "who have a correspondingly Germanic sensibility," so that they would always "be aware that there are young girls in the Fatherland who know about you, who think about you, and who you got to know through the radio."[31] The audience response to this program, however, was to develop in a quite unexpected direction. The letters that Hersel received tended to deal with much broader issues born of the harsh experiences of life in Depression Germany—money problems, unemployment, hunger, and emotional strain. Such letters gave Hersel the idea of using her radio program as a clearing station for young women to offer practical help to one another. "Jugend hilft der Jugend" (Youth Helps Youth) developed into a monthly series that highlighted the plight of individual girls and called on its listeners to offer help to the individual featured and to others in similar straits.

The first installment told the story of a young woman who wanted to take up a voluntary post in Berlin but needed someone to offer her cheap accommodation in the capital; of a young tailor in Saxony who wanted to establish contact with someone with her finger on the pulse of the latest fashions in Berlin; of a trained sports teacher who had not been able to find a job but who was using her time to train unemployed teenagers; and of how a girl's schoolmates had raised money to pay for her to stay at school when her father lost his job. Hersel held out these and other examples to her listeners as ways in which the young people of Germany could help and support one another, arguing that no newspaper or leaflet could reach out to people as quickly and vividly as radio nor as indiscriminately of geography, occupation, or income. What had begun as a petition for penfriendship opened the floodgates to a deluge of appeals for help and offers of aid (Burger 1931, 312). Three programs broadcast in the autumn months of 1931 alone elicited 588 letters and 48 packets from listeners offering help to the *Winterhilfe* campaign. Hersel's office became a redistribution center for offers of old clothes, toys, and food supplies, the cost and time-consuming labor of which effort she took entirely upon herself. In 1931 twenty-nine young homeless men and women were found places to live. Unemployed youths were found work on farms. Schools began campaigns to collect money for the sick and the poor. People sent in books for students, instruments for musicians, money for children's homes. But of all her campaigns Hersel was most proud of the help she was able to direct toward Lemkenhagen, a fishing village of sixty families on the island of Fehmarn, which had been particularly hard hit by the Depression. Forty-

---

31. From the script to *Jugend hilft der Jugend,* 24 April 1931 (NH DRA): 8.

four volunteers provided and distributed food, clothes, and toys and laid on a party for the villagers (Hersel 1933).

The success of the program was seen by some as a shining example of "private welfare" and proof of the possibility of the *Volk* to pull itself out of the mire of economic depression; in August 1931 Else Steup promoted a similar program for adult women. (Steup 1931; "Zu dem Hilfswerk . . ." 1931, 842). Hersel's efforts were praised by the head of the station, Hermann Schubotz,[32] whose support helped her successfully fight plans lower down the organizational structure to take her program off the air in the spring of 1932, following accusations that she had exceeded the terms of her contract. She did, however, have to pledge to keep her talks more closely within the remit of the program, which, according to the board, was in danger of turning into a fully fledged institution for the alleviation of need and distress. Those who saw this process in a more positive light requested the program be moved to an evening slot for wider access, but this was firmly rejected by the board on the grounds that "the alleviation of social needs does not belong among radio's primary tasks." The board went on to warn her against continuing to organize her programs in the service of "an unlimited social welfare."[33]

One reason "Jugend hilft der Jugend" was so contentious was because of the sensitive clash of youth programming with what could be interpreted as a political agenda. Radio was conceived as a private, passive, nonpolitical medium. A program that had at its heart the search for a response to the economic crisis in the country was bound to rouse controversy. Some commentators regarded the main work of radio among the young to prepare them as voters in the new democracy not by introducing them to the policies of the various parties but, precisely, by offering a nonpartisan alternative to the strident political opinions found in the press. The debate came to the fore when a newspaper review was broadcast on the Berlin Jugendstunde, including reviews of political stories. There were those who thought politics had no place in youth radio, but the exclusion of open political discussion on the radio made vain the hope that radio could encourage reasoned and unprejudiced differentiation between the feuding parties (Mendzee 1930b, 14).

Hersel did not consider her programs to be political. While admitting that political persuasion and ideologies were factors that influenced every area of a young person's life, Hersel was more interested in concentrating on the similarities and commonalities between her listeners. She had claimed (1930) that political issues rarely came to the fore in the letters she received from her fourteen- to twenty-year-olds, but all shared the leitmo-

---

32. Letter from Schubotz dated 9 January 1932 (NH DRA).
33. Letter from the Deutsche Welle dated 15 June 1932 (NH DRA).

tif of "the eternal feminine which unites the moderns with the ancients." She was concerned, she said, with building bridges between girls of different backgrounds, ages, and worldviews. She was not interested in explaining the economic troubles facing Germany nor in discussing possible solutions, only in alleviating the symptoms. That this was one political stance among others apparently did not occur to her. Hersel was quite convinced of the positive role radio could play in creating a sense of community, on a broader and at the same time more intimate basis than had ever before been possible. Her motive was to win a loyal and participatory audience for the radio of the future and so to offer a public service.

In June 1932 the station was renamed the Deutschlandsender, following the sweeping reforms introduced by Erich Scholz. "Jugend hilft der Jugend" continued to be broadcast until April the following year, when it was taken off the air as part of the restructuring of the schedules. Hersel of course campaigned for its reintroduction, insisting that her listeners were still writing her dozens of letters.[34] A compromise was reached with a new version of the program called "Jugend regt Jugend an," in which the emphasis would lie on the exchange of ideas rather than of practical social help.[35]

Following the career of a single woman through the political revolution that affected radio highlights the way it was possible for individuals to make professional compromises in order to keep their jobs. In October 1932, for example, Carola Hersel had been invited by Norag to broadcast a lecture from Hamburg about the success of her program. She signed a contract in which she agreed to the principle of nonpartisan broadcasting. Just six months later, within three months of the Nazis' coming to power, Hersel was writing to the director of the Deutschlandsender, asking if she could integrate her program into the service of the new government or the Party organizations.[36] In particular, she wondered if she could offer her services and expertise in the propagation of Magda Goebbels's plans to provide holidays for needy children. Hersel certainly did not have any qualms about working with the new regime at this stage, even asking for the personal address of the "Frau Reichsminister" to facilitate a closer working relationship. Her inquiries were in the event redirected to Frau Fikentscher, head of the Nationalsozialistische Frauenschaft (NSF) in Berlin, just one of the Nazi organizations with which she corresponded; meanwhile, she received the assurance that her manuscripts would continue to be considered for inclusion in future schedules.[37]

---

34. Letter to Frl. Seeger dated 22 July 1933 (NH DRA).
35. Letter dated 8 September 1933 (NH DRA).
36. Letter to Dürre, director of the Deutschlandsender, dated 22 April 1933 (NH DRA).
37. Letter from Dürre dated 25 April 1933 (NH DRA).

In another letter to Herr Brodersen of the Deutschlandsender in 1934, she referred to her long-standing correspondence with the Bund deutscher Mädel (BDM) and other Nazi organizations during her six years of working with youth radio, a fact that she said had brought her verbal and written attacks from the Communist Party. She was writing to defend one of her manuscripts, which had had difficulty passing the censors, who judged it incompatible with BDM ideology. The interference of the censors obviously irritated her, if only for the reason that she had become accustomed to extemporizing from notes to achieve maximum spontaneity and intimacy. She was willing to provide finished manuscripts but warned that she would inevitably find herself writing more to please the critics of the board than her listeners. She defended the simplistic and direct form of address she favored by drawing attention to the size of her mailbag, complaining that the more sophisticated gentlemen censors who wanted her to change her style were not sensitive to the language and tastes of young female listeners.

The Nazification of radio production for young women was not a seamless process, although there was much in the programs of the late Weimar period on which the Nazi schedules could build. Hersel's program itself, with its emphasis on national community and self-help, is a case in point, as programs that concentrated on helping adolescents with existential problems tended to contradict the ideology which claimed to put community before individuality. Programs that appealed to listeners' social or charitable conscience loomed large in the schedules of the Third Reich, to underline the sense of *Volksgemeinschaft* and an artificially constructed national consensus that barely existed beyond the realms of the propaganda (Welch 1993, 1–15). The insistence that young people address their own problems independently also fitted in well with the development of youth organizations in the Third Reich, whose attraction lay not least in seeming to oppose traditional authority in the name of the Nazi social revolution (Peukert 1987, 173–74). Neither was it such an enormous break with tradition to concentrate on female youth as the mothers of the future.

The *Jungmädchenstunde* continued after 1934 under the new name, "Für's deutsche Mädel" (For the Little German Girl), with Hersel at first contributing to it rather safe items about Christmas preparations or handicrafts and then producing a series of more nationalistic, or *völkisch,* programs, such as "Mädel erzählen aus ihrer Heimat Sagen, Lieder, Sitten und Gebräuche" (Young Girls Tell of the Legends, Customs, and Traditions of Their Homeland) and "Auf Fahrt durch Brandenburg" (On a Journey through Brandenburg). Her scripts were also bought by various regional stations up to 1935. Most of these were concerned with domestic matters such as "Practical Christmas Gifts for the Housewife" (Norag, 2 December 1935), "One Dough, Three Cakes" (Reichssender Berlin, 30 April 1935), and the gripping "Let Your Children Lay the Table" (Norag,

16 April 1935). It is interesting to see how, in order to get even these sorts of topics accepted on the air, their author had to emphasize their ideological value as propaganda for women in the new order. In a letter dated June 1935 to the head of the Frauenfunk, Else Möbus, to sell an idea for a travel program, for example, she wrote, "I always have the impression that women especially could do more to promote the 'folk community.' Perhaps the enclosed manuscript 'Images and Experiences On the Move' could inspire women to think, and perhaps even to act."[38]

It is difficult to tell from the available sources, self-selected as many of them are, how much Hersel agreed with the new regime and how much she was just eager to go on working in radio. Certainly, the sort of programs that she had been primarily involved in during the latter years of the Weimar Republic were accommodated relatively easily into the new schedules. Defining herself as a "schaffender Rundfunkmensch" (a creative radio being), it seems that she, like many others, was quite happy to work with and for the new system, even though she did not join the Party or the women's organizations themselves. As a writer, she had to become a member of the Reichskulturkammer (RKK) to go on working at all, but, as a freelancer, it became increasingly difficult for her to get her work put on air, although it is not entirely certain what motivated the final departure from her beloved world of broadcasting. Since her early clashes with the censors, she had learned to provide the sort of material that was acceptable to the regime, emphasizing the traditional accomplishments of women in the home. There is no evidence of her ever having broadcast an openly anti-Semitic text nor of any blunt rallying cry around the swastika flag, but, as the following chapters show, propaganda for women worked on precisely this level of acceptability, banality, and familiarity.

Despite such ploys, Hersel found it increasingly difficult to get her programs on air. In one rejection letter the Deutschlandsender blamed "technical" reasons for cutbacks in the Frauenfunk,[39] but her declining acceptance rate probably had more to do with the replacement of freelance program making in favor of programs made by Party and state organizations, including the Hitlerjugend (HJ) and BDM (see chap. 4). In 1938 Hersel joined the Vobach-Verlag as an editor of women's magazines, returning to radio after the war as a freelance contributor to the Berliner Rundfunk and, from 1948, for RIAS Berlin. Finally, she returned to magazines and became editor of the Edeka consumer magazine *Die kluge Hausfrau,* harking back to her training as a housekeeper, which she had given up in the 1920s when she began her work with the Deutsche Welle.

38. Letter to Frau Möbus dated 17 June 1935 (NH DRA).
39. Letter from the Deutsche Welle dated 18 May 1936 (NH DRA).

CHAPTER 4

# Radio and the Maternal Spirit: On Women's Radio in Nazi Germany

Radio was regarded by the National Socialists as a comrade in arms, sharing a common history and a common destiny: both had burst onto the public stage in the autumn of 1923, both had reached maturity in the early 1930s, and neither could reach its full potential without the other (Dreyer 1934, 101–2; Hadamovsky 1934a, 12; Hagemann, 1948, 19). The sort of influence the NSDAP sought to wield could not be realized by control of printing and press alone; only radio offered the possibility of affecting the nation as a whole, proclaiming a unified message from a totalitarian regime.[1] But radio as it had existed throughout much of the Weimar Republic was of little use in such an ideological crusade, if its technological promise was not infused with the spirit of the cause and of the new era, as Ernst Dreyer of the *Reichskulturkammer* described:

> We know that the arrival of National Socialism was required in order to make sense of the invention of radio . . . to make use of it as a spiritual instrument. National Socialism and its means of communication, the radio, stand at the threshold of the era of National Socialism full of youth and optimism. (1934, 103)

The spirit which had imbued the radio of the Weimar Republic was considered to be the *Erkenntnisgeist,* the spirit of intellectualism (Peck 1933–34a, 243–47). The public service broadcasting ethos, the emphasis on education and information, on elites imparting wisdom to the masses, all that was held to have been a betrayal of radio's true spirit, which was

---

1. The lessons learned in World War I should not be underestimated in this regard. See Lasswell 1927; Kocka 1984.

defined in terms of the maternal spirit, the *Muttergeist.* Radio's location in
the home, its intimate address, its sensory appeal, grounded it firmly in the
female realm as it was understood in the essentialist ideology to which
National Socialism ascribed.[2] The key element of this avowedly antifemi-
nist ideology was the rigid distinction between the male public sphere of
the state and the female private sphere of the home and family based on
"natural" gender roles, which for women meant primarily family, domesticity, and childbearing. Emancipation for the National Socialist woman
was, in the words of ideologue Alfred Rosenberg, emancipation from
emancipation. Moreover, the antifeminism of Nazi theory and practice
was closely bound up with anti-Semitism and racist policy: pronatalist
energies were directed at the racially acceptable, while 200,000 other
women were forcibly sterilized as a precursor to a policy of genocide (Bock
1984, Kuhn 1990).

The terms *Erkenntnisgeist* and *Muttergeist* were borrowed from the
nationalist Leipzig philosopher Ernst Bergmann and defined the rational,
intellectual perception process assumed to inhere in the male and its opposite, the instinctual, intuitive, and sympathetic perception displayed in the
female.[3] According to this scheme of things, the history of radio had been
the history of a development away from intellectualism to maternalism. By
the 1930s the home was firmly established as the "natural" place of reception:

Radio takes people out of the public sphere and meets them again in
the familial circle. It gives the home a new centre around which to fix.
Certainly, there have been any number of attempts to reestablish the
old public sphere for the radio. Listening work shops were founded.

---

2. There are numerous accounts of the position of women in Nazi ideology, including:
Rabe 1932; Kirkpatrick 1938, 29–49; Gersdorff 1969, 39–43; Grunberger 1970, 251–66;
Stephenson 1975, 1981; Mason 1976; Rupp 1977; Scholtz-Klink 1978; Lück 1979, 29–49;
Klinsiek 1982, 20–24; Lehker 1984, 26–49; Thalmann 1984, 74–83; Tidl 1984; Koonz 1988,
175–220; Kuhn 1990, 39–50.

3. Bergmann's thesis, briefly put, was that patriarchy was a Judaic invention (patriarchal monotheism had deposed the goddesses of an original matriarchal order) that had led to
world historic decline and "degeneration." To this extent Bergmann turned on its head J .J.
Bachofen's influential characterization of history as progressing from a Dionysian matriarchal order to an Apollonian patriarchal order (in *Das Mutterrecht,* 1861). Redemption, in
Bergmann's schema, therefore lay in the glorification of motherhood and the maternal but
only for those women who met particular social and racial criteria, although the real outcasts
were those socially and racially acceptable women who repressed their natural instincts and
responsibilities by not bearing children (Bergmann 1933, 22–23). Here, again, he stands in
contrast to another highly influential anti-Semitic nationalist philosopher, Otto Weininger,
who in *Geschlecht und Charakter* (Vienna, 1903) sought redemption in the defeat of Judaism
and the feminine. See von Braun 1992, 6–28; Ziege 1995.

> But they can't change the fact that the natural community for the reception of radio is the family (Peck 1933–34a, 243).

The gradual move away from the "talking newspaper," from the dry, academic lecture toward dialogue, drama, and human interest that was traceable in the history of radio, was interpreted as evidence for the inevitable victory in all aspects of broadcasting of the *Muttergeist.* Similarly, for the Frauenfunk the invitation of public and political personalities into the home by the turn of the dial had opened up the world of politics to women who were "naturally" alienated by the world of debate, public meetings, and lengthy editorials. This, in the eyes of the new producers, was the direction in which radio must continue to progress. The contamination of women's radio with a misplaced *Erkenntnisgeist* needed to be urgently eradicated, the example of the high-brow program output of Norag's experimental Schule der Frau being castigated as the nadir of the pre-Nazi period. This "essential" character of radio demanded that all aspects of radio, but the Frauenfunk in particular, continue to be shaped by the *Muttergeist,* "inconspicuously to heed the awakening and strengthening maternal spirit" (Peck 1933–34a, 243).

Such was the rhetoric in the early days of the Third Reich. This chapter will examine the extent to which this rhetoric influenced the history of radio in the period and what it meant for the relationship between women and radio. It will look at the transitional period when the Nazis first came to power and the developments up to the outbreak of war. The following chapter will look at the output of women's radio in the war years, in particular the role radio played in women's lives as a source of information, a means of distraction, a channel of mobilization, and a bridge between the home front and the front line.

## Radio in Transition

The institutional history of radio in the Nazi period is well documented (Pohle 1955; Diller 1980; Wulf 1983), and it is not my intention here to give an exhaustive account of the history of German radio in this period, but it is necessary first of all to sketch in the prevailing attitudes toward radio and the plans for its future on the part of the new leaders and to understand the system of policy and program making of which women's radio was a part. As with so many institutions that came under Nazi control in 1933, the guiding principles behind reforms of the radio system were *Gleichschaltung* (coordination and centralization) and the *Führerprinzip* (leadership principle). As far as radio was concerned, the process was greatly facilitated by the reforms recently effected by the previous regime and the relative flexibility afforded by a medium still in its infancy, compared to the tradition-bound press.

The importance of effective propaganda had been recognized by the Nazis long before they came to power. Denied the right to broadcast its message via state radio during the Weimar period, the Nazi Party had learned to generate publicity very successfully in other ways—most notably via the public rally—but it eagerly grabbed the chance to add radio to its propaganda arsenal.[4] January 1930 had seen the launch of the journal *Funk und Bewegung* (Wireless and Movement), which was a clear signal of the Party's plans for the future (Fischer 1957, 24). The accelerating reforms in the Weimar radio system meant that by June 1932 Nazi politicians were granted limited access to the airwaves for the first time. The following month witnessed Joseph Goebbels's inauspicious radio debut, when his text was censored. Just six months later the Nazis' triumphant torchlit procession through the Brandenburg Gate on the night of the takeover was broadcast nationwide.[5]

Responsibility for radio in the new regime fell initially to Wilhelm Frick as head of the Ministry of the Interior (RMI), whose first imperative was to appoint men sympathetic to the new regime. Old faces had to make way for new. Hans Bredow, so long the champion of nonpolitical radio during the Weimar Republic, resigned in protest at the domination of radio by a single political party, as did the director of the Berliner Funk-Stunde, Carl Friedrich Duske, and lengthy, if ultimately abortive court proceedings were initiated against them. Many other officials and employees had the decision made for them, losing their jobs for having been members of left-wing political parties or for being Jewish. In an article in *NS-Funk* Horst Dreßler-Andreß, the new *Rundfunkkommissar,* stressed that all *volksfremde Elemente,* (elements foreign to the nation) both Jews and "half-castes," were to be removed from both administrative and creative aspects of radio. In June the radio press service reported that 98 managerial and 38 other employees had been dismissed out of a total staff of 2,115. Further dismissals followed.[6] All were replaced by supporters of the new government. Those that were left in positions of lesser responsibility kept their jobs by keeping quiet and falling into line, intimidated by threats of dismissal. In a speech to directors of the regional stations in May 1933

---

4. The mass rallies were only the most obvious incarnation of the "aestheticization of politics" that, Benjamin argued, granted the masses expression but in no way their rights (1992, 690). See also Labanyi 1989, 151–77.

5. The future Reichssendeleiter, Eugen Hadamovsky, who claimed his vision for the future of radio in Germany had come to him in a flash on the night of the Machtübernahme. Quoted in Aberle 1982, 3. See Diller 1980, 57, for further details.

6. Pressedienst der deutschen Sender am 5./8.6.33, BAK, R 78/780.

Goebbels made it clear: "If you can't or won't understand us, I think you should leave us. . . . Your job now is to . . . cleanse your radio stations, to clear out everything which doesn't belong" (cited in Diller 1980, 109).

Following the March elections, which had not been the overwhelming success the Nazis had hoped for, all the mass media were centralized under Goebbels's new Ministry for Popular Enlightenment and Propaganda, the *Reichsministerium für Volksaufklärung und Propaganda* (RMVP).[7] Goebbels acknowledged radio to be "the most modern and most important instrument to influence the masses, a true servant of the *Volk,* working to unite the German people in a common vision" (cited in Diller, 109). Radio offered the possibility of speaking to all Germans regardless of class, religious, or sectional loyalties and as such was perfectly in tune with what David Welch has identified as the central goal of Nazi propaganda—the replacement of such loyalties with a new awareness of a "national," or "people's," community, the *Volksgemeinschaft* (1993, 3).[8]

Centralization seemed unstoppable, although the ten regional *Reichssender* retained some sort of autonomy in programming matters until August 1939. All policy decisions emanated from Goebbels's office in Berlin. Every program was carefully monitored to ensure that all radio output conformed with Nazi ideology. News and current affairs programs were most tightly coordinated, but entertainment was also understood to perform an implicit political function and also came under close scrutiny. On 3 July 1933 the Nationalsozialistische Rundfunkkammer e.V. (National Socialist chamber of radio) was created within the RMVP as an umbrella organization incorporating all the various parts of the industry, from wireless manufacturers and program producers to amateur enthusiasts and radio critics. In September the radio chamber (RRK) became one of the seven departments in the newly established national chamber of culture, the Reichskulturkammer (RKK), the other departments representing the theater, film, music, the fine arts, press, and literature.

### The *Volksempfänger* and the Art of Listening

While the abandonment of the principle of nonpolitical radio helped make programming more relevant and topical, listeners began to complain as

---

7. At first, opposition to the government's total control of the nation's radio in the RMVP came from both the regional stations and from Göring (who wanted control over the news service and foreign propaganda), but, following Hitler's personal intervention, all opponents to Goebbels's supremacy over radio were silenced. Nevertheless, elements of the Weimar system remained intact, such as the investment of private capital and the copyright on regional programs.

8. Rosenhaft and Lee argue that Nazi policy aimed to replace conflict between class with conflict between "racial" groups, social divisions with gender divisions, and control over production with control over reproduction (1990, 4).

the schedules became increasingly dominated by reports of Party rallies, speeches by Party functionaries, and military music. Hagemann spoke of a veritable *Hörerstreik,* as listeners switched off their sets in disgust or tuned in illegally to foreign broadcasts (1935, 46). Goebbels became aware of the danger of driving people away with an excess of overt political propaganda and recognized that he had to strike a balance between banging the Party's drum and providing the sort of popular light entertainment that attracted people to tune in their millions (Kolb and Stiekmeier 1933, 11). From 1932 to 1937 the proportion of the schedules given over to music (apart from jazz, which was banned from 1935) increased by almost one-fifth, from 58 percent to 69 percent, a trend that accelerated during the war (Grunberger 1971, 402).

One of the most important contributions in the quest for effective mass propaganda was the ready provision of affordable radio sets. When the Nazis came to power, working-class households accounted for only 25.6 percent of radio owners, although they made up 43 percent of the population as a whole (Riedel 1987, 62). Under the motto "das Führers Wort in jeden Betrieb, in jedes Haus!" (The Führer's voice into every home and factory!), cheap radio sets called Volksempfänger 301 were mass produced and sold in vast numbers. At a cost of only RM 76 each, they were the cheapest radio sets in the world.[9] A special *Tag des deutschen Rundfunks,* or "German Radio Day," was declared on 11 February 1934 as the highlight of these efforts to achieve maximum saturation.

Listening figures began to rise again. By 1939 three million Volksempfänger had been sold, helping to bring the total number of sets in Germany to twelve and a half million, the highest figure in Europe (Riedel 1987, 64). The success of the Volksempfänger represented a further commodification of the family sphere and of leisure time and the increased isolation of individual listeners or family groups, which created a tension between the atomized experience of radio and the message of national community that it carried. In May 1935 a new tactic was introduced that could have offset this problematic tension—the erection of loudspeakers in public places so that "his master's voice" could be heard by still more of the population, willing or otherwise, in shops, cafés, or on the street. This was an important development in the history of radio—the penetration of both the private and the public spheres—a development that was unique

---

9. RM 76 at this time was approximately two weeks' average wage and roughly half the price of existing receivers on the market. Already by the opening of the first radio exhibition under the new regime, held in Berlin on 18 August 1933, some 100,000 sets had been sold, and the price was reduced further to RM 65 (Riedel 1987, 62). Another set, the portable Deutsche Olympiakoffer, was released to coincide with the Olympic Games in 1936, an event that was fully exploited to highlight the very latest developments in broadcasting technology.

to fascism.[10] Yet the vision of the perfect totalitarian distribution of monopolized information was never fully realized. The war put paid to a scheme to erect six thousand loudspeaker radios across the country (Grunberger 1971, 401). Meanwhile, special radio sets called Deutsche Arbeitsfrontempfänger 1011 were produced for use in factories, and in 1938 a modified version of the Volksempfänger, the Kleinempfänger DKE 38, helped boost radio sales still further.[11]

So successful were these various strategies that radio provision was nearing saturation point. It therefore became imperative not only to maximize the audience but also to ensure existing radio owners became regular and attentive listeners by offering what they wanted in a popular and accessible style and by enouraging selective listening strategies.[12] Housewives in particular were assumed to leave the radio on all day, listening indiscriminately and distractedly to a companionable wall of sound.[13] Where it had once been considered an advantage that listeners could be enthused or educated by the unexpected, it was now argued that different types of programs demanded different levels of attention. Ellen Rodt set down a list of guidelines for women in one of the journals of the Frauenschaft (1933, 924–25). Light entertainment programs were often specifically designed to accompany other activities, while only the most mechanical and undemanding tasks should be undertaken while listening to scientific and cultural programs. Political programs were too important to risk any distraction at all.

The refinement of a *Hörkultur,* however, had an ideological urgency as far as women were concerned, which again drew on radio's integrative function in the home. The more selectively women learned to use the

---

10. See Williams 1990, 24. For a discussion of the Italian case, see Richieri 1988, 49–56. Mass listening has been organized in other societies but as discrete events, not as a permanent fixture. See Pegg 1983, 173–94.

11. "German Labor Front receivers." The number 1011 was a reference to a speech Hitler broadcast from a Siemens factory on 10 November 1933, which had been massively promoted to the extent that every factory siren in the country was sounded before the broadcast, and all production came to a standstill while the Führer spoke. The speech was reprinted in newspapers and pamphlets. See Pohle 1955, 272; Fischer 1957, 31. The factory radio was also considered instrumental in providing distraction and relaxation with entertainment in rest periods. See *Handbuch des deutschen Rundfunks* (Heidelberg and Berlin, [RRG?], 1938), 16. The compact DKE (Deutscher Kleinempfänger) went on sale at a price of RM 35. It soon acquired the nickname "Goebbels-Schnauze" (Goebbels's gob).

12. *Deutscher Kulturdienst* (hereafter DKD), 10 March 1943, BAK R34/152: 58.

13. One of the concerns about such untamed consumption was to do with conserving precious energy resources, particularly with the advent of war, when the propagandists sought to convince listeners that a rationed and rational use of radio would have a discernible impact on the war economy. The language used was already familiar to women from wellestablished propaganda campaigns. See chapter 7.

radio, the more successfully they would be able to draw their families together to share in a common listening experience and sense of occasion. Radio, in short, became another tool women could use in forging closer family ties.

So, the potential for radio to strengthen the bond between women and the home was once again at the top of the agenda, but the promotion of efficient listening was only one side of the coin. The other side involved the efficient structuring of the schedules. Inasmuch as radio provided a background framework for housewives to work to, the programs they listened to had to have some sort of regularity and predictability, especially given the assumption that few women checked printed schedules to guide their listening. This was all the more important, it was argued, because the New Order in German politics had upset the usual rhythm of life for men, who now had new responsibilities and orders to answer to (F. M. 1934–35, 47). These men therefore were more than ever in need of a stable home life to compensate for the unpredictability outside. The radio had a part to play in helping women perform this stabilizing role, for "a woman tries to accommodate radio's offerings into the rhythm of her life. . . . The radio should organize itself around her. If she already has to accommodate the irregular activities of her husband, she ought at least be able to rely on regularity from her radio." It was also suggested that it helped men to know that their wives would be listening to certain programs at certain times. As well as instilling a sense of security, if the husband was able to tune in to the program too, the couple would be able to talk about it together in the evening, and it would become a shared experience, thus strengthening their relationship and ensuring a healthy family life.

Thus far these arguments did not differ greatly from the more conservative critiques produced in the Weimar period, which is significant in light of the fact that a "healthy" family life was also a prerequisite for the success of the NSDAP's racist program. Radio was recognized as being an important prop of these policies, by helping "to create a new family and children-friendly climate" and by representing "the process of marital-biological selection carried out by the racial-political office and the National Union of Large Families in programs of general interest" (Schmalfuß 1938, 9).

**Audience Research**

Audience research went hand in hand with promoting "the art of listening." Until the Nazis came to power there had been relatively little audience research, despite the political and commercial advantages to be gained from such knowledge. There is therefore more data available on women's listening habits during the Third Reich than during the earlier period (Hardt 1976; Bessler 1980). This was due partly to the developing academic discipline of audience research, partly to the refinement of market research techniques, and partly to the political necessity of knowing more about the listeners, the better to target the propaganda. Various agencies were engaged in assessing public opinion and public morale, including the Gestapo, the Sicherheitsdienst (SD), certain Party organizations (including women's organizations), local government authorities, and the judiciary, all of which were obliged to be sensitive to gender as one of the categories of their research.[14] Radio wardens were active throughout the period, checking that their neighbors were not tuning in to foreign stations, urging them to listen to propaganda programs, and making reports about their listening preferences (Bramsted 1965, 75).

If women's radio was to be as effective as possible, there had to be some feedback to the program makers from the audience. It was left largely to the official women's organizations to collect this information, although the SD also reported on the reception of propaganda among women from time to time from 1938 onward. From 1941, on the instructions of the national broadcasting headquarters, the Reichssendeleitung (RSL), the leadership of the national women's organization, the Reichsfrauenführung (RFF) also encouraged regional leaders to furnish monthly reports on women's comments about the radio service.[15] The findings of the RFF's regional surveys, under the title *Empfangsspiegel* (Mirror of the Listenership), were regularly passed on to the radio division of the Reichspropagandaleitung (RPL) in Berlin, but unfortunately they do not seem to have survived. Some indication of their content can be surmised, however, by examining the decisions made by Erika Fillies-Kirmsse, who was head of the Press/Propaganda Department at the Berlin office.[16] A common complaint seems to have been that scripts were too superficial. Occasionally, directives would be sent to the regional divisions of the RFF to pay especially close attention to a program that had received complaints or that did not seem to be completely in keeping with the principles of the

---

14. Hagemann 1935, 26. See also Steinert 1970, 43–44; also the survey of factory workers' listening, published in 1935 by Werner Hensel and Erich Kessler (cited in Bessler 1980, 31).

15. Memo (F 149/41) from the main departments culture/childrearing/education and press/propaganda (Pr/Prop Dept.) to all *Gaufrauenschaftleiterinnen,* dated Berlin, 13 December 1941, BAK NS44/36, in response to a central directive for all party organizations to start monitoring radio output.

16. Head Office, Pr/Prop, Radio Department, to Pr/Prop, *Gaufrauenschaftsleitung,* Silesia, 31 October 1942, BAP 62 Re1/6:187. (From October 1942 the decisions were again left to the regional departments of the RFF.)

organization.[17] Similarly, programs that were outstanding in any way could be recycled by other stations at the request of the central office, although the copyright remained in the hands of the original station.[18] While most manuscripts would pass the vetting procedure unaltered, others would have a key sentence or two amended, be rejected in their entirety, or be returned to the author for revision.[19] Requests for revision could be as minor as, for example, scrapping a suggestion of boiling eggs in onion water one Easter when onions were scarce (onion water turns the shells yellow) or replacing the word *butter* with *fat* in recipes.[20]

There is more to be learned about the makeup and habits of the female radio audience during the Third Reich from the questionnaire surveys carried out by Lisa Peck, a prolific critic of radio in the Third Reich for the journal *Rufer und Hörer* and herself a contributor to the Berlin Frauenfunk. One such survey was conducted in 1934 among five hundred women, divided equally among blue-collar workers, housewives, office workers, professionals, and rural women (Peck 1933–35a).[21] There was an almost unanimous preference across the board for musical programs, although the professionals tended to bemoan the lack of opera, while the blue-collar workers expressed a wish for more light music to relax to. Peck found that the response to political programs and current affairs seemed to be largely uniform across the five groups, noting that all shared a "similarly strong interest in politics, reports on national holidays and in the 'Hour of the Nation,'" which, she concluded, was evidence of women's activity in political life on a wider plane. Nevertheless, her survey also showed that interest was generated across the board by specialized women's programming, with its double focus on household tips and cultural magazines, leading Peck to conclude "that our working women and

17. See, for example, *Meldungen aus dem Reich* (hereafter MadR) IfZ MA 441/1 T175/R259, roll 752470, 30 September 1940; roll 754077–78, 19 June 1941. These records have been edited and published by Hans Boberach (1984), but the references given here are to the original unedited reports.

18. Erika Fillies-Kirmsse, RFF Pr/Prop Dept., Berlin, to the *Gaufrauenschaftsleitung,* Silesia Pr/Prop Dept., 17 January 1938: BAP 62 Re1/6:89.

19. A Saarpfalz program on a matter deemed to be of central importance to the party's ideological schema, "Die Schlüsselgewalt der Frau," was sent back for revision for maintaining that "the disposal of a married couple's income is a matter for the man" (Erika Fillies-Kirmsse, RFF Pr/Prop, Berlin, to the Pr/Prop Dept, *Gaufrauenschaftsleitung,* Silesia, 8 April 1938: BAP 62 Re1/6:76/83.

20. Erika Fillies-Kirmsse, RFF Pr/Prop Dept., Berlin, to the Pr/Prop Dept, *Gaufrauenschaftsleitung.* Silesia, 8 April 1938: BAP 62 Re1/6:76/83.

21. Fifty-three percent of professional women returned the questionnaire unanswered, saying they had no time to listen to the radio, much as they would like to. A greater proportion of the office workers and housewives replied, but the most enthusiastic listeners were undoubtedly rural women and blue-collar workers.

girls sitting in offices at this moment are in no way bluestockings, but want to become good and efficient housewives." Blue-collar workers listened almost exclusively to the bulletins on home economics, whereas with rural women it was the other way round. Isolated from the cultural heartbeat of the city, they were grateful to the radio for bringing them the art and culture of the metropolis and, Peck maintained, the ideas and ideologies from the political center. Housewives and white-collar workers listened to both weekly installments. Asked for ideas for improvement, blue-collar workers expressed a desire for more interviews and portraits of female celebrities, adventure stories, travel reports, political education programs, and German lessons. Rural women generally wanted more programs about exhibitions they couldn't themselves get to. Office workers complained that the most interesting programs for women were broadcast during the afternoon while they were still at work and joined the blue-collar workers in asking for more sports coverage. Professionals focused their discontent on the standard of presenters and announcers. Of all the women questioned housewives were the most satisfied with the existing output (note that the group "housewives" did not differentiate between women of different ages, classes, or regions). All groups wanted to relax to the radio but also to find stimulation and inspiration in its schedules, as long as it was not reduced to a purely educational apparatus. All groups also expressed a wish to see more programs for women.

Another source of information about audience preferences is the survey of 362 women from different backgrounds and of different ages Herta Kuhlmann conducted in the course of her doctoral research in 1940.[22] Her results showed age to be a more decisive factor in determining tastes among women than profession. In general, women under twenty and over fifty listened to more radio than those in the intervening age groups, and older women tended to be more disposed to listening to speech radio and preferred the classics and operetta to the military and dance music favored by younger women. The other main determining factor was location. Kuhlmann found distinct differences in listening patterns between urban and rural areas. The length of the listening day varied for different women. There was a sharp drop in the listening curve for all groups over three hours but with a sharp increase after five hours for housewives and blue-collar workers. Ninety-nine percent of women reported that they always or usually performed some other activity while listening to the radio. The

---

22. The study included 122 housewives, 78 commercial employees, 54 blue-collar workers, 51 intellectuals and artists (this group is overrepresented in relation to their number in society, but their tastes differed sufficiently greatly to justify a larger sample), 31 rural women, and 26 women in the caring professions (Kuhlmann 1942, 131).

pattern of the listening day also varied, though housewives were the only group whose listening was determined primarily by taste and not by opportunity. This ad hoc nature of listening distinguished radio from most other forms of entertainment and information, making it a much more powerful tool in the hands of the producers, who could rely on a core audience regardless of the effort put into promoting a particular program.

For most women radio's primary function was as a transmitter of music, though of all programs news and current affairs were the ones most regularly listened to, with at least 90 percent of all groups tuning into at least one news broadcast a day. The war had already begun by this point, of course, which may explain this high level of interest in current affairs. A large majority in almost every group by age and by profession said they were more influenced by what they heard on the radio than what they read in the press (on average 47 percent said radio, 13 percent newspapers). Only women in the intellectual and artistic category claimed to be more influenced by what they read, although 62 percent of all women supplemented the information they heard on the airwaves by reading a paper (the figure was considerably higher for housewives, at 79 percent, and lower for rural women, at 36 percent).

All but one of the women questioned were positive about the influence that radio played in their lives. It should be noted, however, that of 750 questionnaires sent out only 362 women replied, which may have skewed the results in favor of those who were more positively inclined toward the radio. Moreover, it may not have been expedient to have emphasized criticisms of the radio system in 1940, if those questioned indeed raised any. It is worth noting Kuhlmann's own ideological analysis of the statistics she collected: "Women's enthusiasm for radio is proof of radio's effect on the *Volk* as a whole, for women are more the *Volk* and will remain more the *Volk* than men" (1942, 179).

Ideological interpretations notwithstanding, it is difficult to draw meaningful conclusions from such statistics today. Listening figures alone cannot indicate the range of meanings that were made by the audiences in listening to the programs nor furnish details about the relationship between program makers and audience in terms of discursive practice. Such an analysis of the historical female audience would raise a plethora of methodological problems. It is undoubtedly an important part of the history of women's radio but one that goes beyond the concerns of the present project, in which the emphasis lies on the audience as it figures in contemporary discourses rather than as a sociological phenomenon. The audience figures here have been included simply in recognition of the fact that radio policy did not operate in a vacuum but created programs that were listened to, enjoyed, and criticized by real people and, more particularly, that women, in these surveys at least, did seem to invest a lot of interest in the programs of the Frauenfunk and in the experience of radio as a whole.

In conclusion, some of the typically positive responses to the questionnaire are illustrated by the following selection of quotations, beginning with a twenty-eight-year-old blue-collar worker from Heidelberg who said, "I can't think of another piece of equipment that could bring me more joy," and a fifty-year-old housewife from Wuppertal who said simply that she couldn't imagine daily life without it. The one exception that Kuhlmann cites was a woman who listened to more than five hours of radio a day and said it made her nervous. Women across the board cited the companionship radio afforded them as the main reason for their enthusiasm, as, for example, the thirty-two-year-old secretary from Wiesbaden who would always switch on her radio when she got in from work, "to have the feeling of company." Radio's ability to create an illusion of company is echoed by statements that anthropomorphosize the radio into a mechanical friend giving access to an otherwise exclusive world, as a twenty-six-year-old nursery teacher from Rostock put it—"the radio is a true friend bringing me news of events in the world and enhancing my existence"—or a twenty-four-year-old blue-collar worker from Heidelberg who claimed, "I couldn't live without radio because it lets me participate in everything faster and more directly than anyone else can." The radio was a friend from the outside world, from the world of politics and public affairs, of celebrities and causes, a friend who was as eagerly welcomed into the homes of women in paid labor as of women who worked in the home and on the land. A forty-two-year-old rural woman from Mittelfranken described how the radio let her participate in world events, a fifty-five-year-old housewife from North Germany relied on radio for her "spiritual sustenance," and a fifty-eight-year-old housewife from Wuppertal spoke for others like her when she said, "Radio broadens the horizons of housewives like me." The radio did not only create the illusion of taking women out into the "real" world of public affairs and cosmopolitan knowledge; it also offered them the illusion of escape from the constraints of real, everyday life. A thirty-two-year-old blue-collar worker from Berlin was not alone in describing how the radio "led her out beyond the everyday."

If radio was cherished as a means of information and escapism in peacetime, it was all the more valued as the war escalated, as the following chapter demonstrates. The rest of this chapter is concerned with outlining the broad philosophy of the Frauenfunk under the Nazis in the years following their assumption of power and to describe how this philosophy translated into programs for women in the years leading up to the Second World War.

## Radio as Recruit(er) in the Nazi Revolution

Women's relationship to radio was deemed to be of key ideological and practical importance in the Third Reich, a relationship which a revamped women's service hoped to bolster and utilize. Plans to establish a National Socialist women's radio service were laid well in advance of the Nazis coming to power, just as in other areas of propaganda. One of the early activists in this respect, Gerda von Bremen-Hirschkendt (1933b), talked about her membership in the NSDAP and the work she did for German radio in an interview with *Der Angriff* in April 1933. She had done radio work during the Weimar Republic, but, as a National Socialist, she felt that the constant demand for modernization and innovation was depriving the radio of the best of German culture and that she could no longer go on working in those conditions. She said it had become clear to her that she "neither could nor would broadcast such destructive, divisive intellectual products to the people." Back then she had been left with only one choice—"to leave the degenerate radio business and join the secret work preparing a form of radio rooted in the nation without compromise or concession."

During what became known as the *Kampfzeit* (time of struggle), von Bremen-Hirschkendt joined other women, mostly professionals and artists, in the NS Künstlerdienst des Reichsverbandes deutscher Rundfunkteilnehmer (NS Artists' Service of the National Union of German Radio Listeners). They practiced microphone techniques and prepared prototype transmissions, spurred on by the belief that one day they would be able to broadcast their programs for real. Bremen-Hirschkendt recalled how their efforts were scorned in the *Berliner Volkszeitung,* which had described how "finished manuscripts were delivered to the radio ladies, brown-house phrases offered up like warm bread rolls."[23] Now, three months into the new regime, the members of the Reichsverband felt they were having the last laugh; at last they were able to carry their message to the public across the airwaves, and their loyalty and bravery during the *Kampfzeit* were praised by the head of radio in Nazi Germany, Eugen Hadamovsky (cited in Aberle 1982, 3).

Women employed in radio were engaged in a campaign to alert other women to the National Socialist program and to recruit new members for the Nazi women's organizations.[24] The story of women's organization in

---

23. Koonz describes how before 1933 scorn and ridicule forged a unity among Nazi women, who often compared themselves to persecuted Christians (1984, 213).

24. In 1936, 27.5 percent of all radio employees were women, mostly engaged in programs for women and children, though there were a few journalists and program assistants in other areas (Marßolek et al. 1995, 22).

the Third Reich is a complex one that has been unraveled elsewhere, but the broad outline is as follows. A year after the NSDAP was founded, 10.5 percent of the members were women, but it declared itself engaged in a "masculine struggle" and announced that no women were to hold even minor office (Klinksiek 1982, 20). In 1931 the NS Frauenschaft had been declared the only official women's organization affiliated with the Party, achieving full party status in March 1933, under the leadership first of Gottfried Krummacher and then Gertrud Scholtz-Klink (Lück 1979, 102). It boasted two million members in 1936, although far from all its members were active (Stephenson 1981, 149–50). As an elite party organization, its primary task was the education of women as ideologically primed leaders for the Deutsches Frauenwerk (German Women's Bureau [DFW]), the umbrella organization that was set up in September 1933 to absorb the various women's organizations in a process of *Gleichschaltung*. The RFF was its central policy-making leadership. Left-wing and Jewish women's organizations were soon disbanded, along with the SPD, KPD, and the trade unions, and many socialists and feminists either went into exile or retreated from the public world of politics. The religious women's organizations, both Protestant and Catholic, broadly welcomed the new regime, although their willingness to integrate into the Nazi organizations varied. The BDF refused to undergo *Gleichschaltung* and disbanded, although its affiliated organizations continued to operate closely with the NSDAP, regarding the Nazi vision of separate but complementary spheres for men and women as a continuation of the ideas that had driven most of the civic, occupational, and religious women's organizations during the Weimar Republic.[25] The Deutsche Frauenfront (DFF), led by Lydia Gottschewski, and the National Federation, led by Paula Siber, were two organizations which attracted support in 1933–34 but were eventually incorporated into the DFW. As its base broadened and its political limitations became more clearly defined, the tenor of the Nazi women's movement changed from charismatic to bureaucratic. The firebrands of the *Kampfzeit* found themselves expelled or marginalized from their own organizations as more respectable women such as Scholtz-Klink took the helm. In July 1934 a woman's office was created within the German Labour Front, the Deutsche Arbeitsfront (DAF) again under the nominal leadership of Scholtz-Klink, thus contradicting Party doctrine by recognizing women in the workforce. Its role was to reconcile the industrial working class to the new regime through propaganda and social welfare (Stephenson 1981,

---

25. Indeed, much of Nazi propaganda was concerned with the reinforcement and sharpening of existing beliefs (Welch 1983, 2). Welch corrects two common misconceptions about propaganda: that it intends only to change ideas and that it consists only of falsehoods. It operates, rather, with many different levels of truth.

131). The Reichsmütterdienst (National Mothers' Service [RMD]) was set up on Mother's Day in 1934 by the RFF primarily to train young women as racially aware mothers in *Mütterschulen*. The other main section of the DFW was the home and national economics department based on the old Reichsverband Deutscher Hausfrauen (RDH), with the dual concerns of developing practical competence in housewifery and ensuring ideological commitment. Women were also organized within the welfare organization NS Volkswohlstand (NSV) and the Reichsnährstand (National Food Estate).

The women who filled new posts at the radio stations saw their work not as overt political propaganda but as gently touching a nerve in the nation's soul that would show their listeners the rectitude of the National Socialist path. For this reason Bremen-Hirschkendt believed a solid Party background was an essential qualification for all radio artists, because "whoever sees it as their job to work towards the self-determination and cultural ascendancy of our people, has to carry deep within themselves the experience of the National Socialist freedom movement in the battle for a new world view." The main aim of the Frauenfunk born of these practices, according to Bremen-Hirschkendt, was to inspire the women of the German nation to engage themselves in carrying forward the National Socialist revolution, so that "women of all classes who actively work together for the realization of vital national and social tasks will together experience a turning point, a new departure, a heightened intensity and a fusion of feminine energies towards a single goal: to work for the nation" (1933b, 119).

One woman with just such a solid Party background was Paula Siber, a district leader from Düsseldorf, whose speechmaking skills on behalf of the National Federation had brought her to the attention of Wilhelm Frick at the RMI. She became the consultant for women's affairs there, the only woman to hold a consultancy in any government ministry. She signed a contract with the Deutschlandsender, which gave her access to the national airwaves on a monthly basis, and for a while became the official and best known voice of women's politics in Germany. She represented the standard version of Nazi ideology in defending mothers' rights and advocating a return to the home and used the radio, alongside hundreds of speeches, dozens of articles and a book, to promote her vision of an educational system that would lead to a future Germany peopled by manly men and feminine women. After the takeover of power, she was the moderate female voice of Nazism, feminine and wifely, eloquent and inspirational, in contrast to and in competition with the leader of the DFF, Lydia Gottschewski.[26] She was keen to stress the allegiance of the DFW to the

---

26. Gottschewski published a book in 1934, *Männerbund und Frauenfrage,* outlining her vision of the spheres of influence between the sexes in the Nazi state.

state rather than the Party so as not to alienate the members of the former confessional women's organizations. Of all the early women leaders in the Party, she survived the longest, although she finally lost the battle with Scholtz-Klink to become *Reichsfrauenführerin* (national women's leader), for she was less willing to surrender her independence to the male leaders and fell prey to those who saw her political activities as neglecting her wifely duties.

In the first issue of *Die Deutsche Frauenfront,* the journal of the organization formed in March 1933 by Robert Ley and Gottschewski to integrate civic and religious women's organizations under the Party umbrella, a lengthy article was devoted to the challenges and changes facing women's radio in the National Socialist era (von Bremen Hirschkendt 1933a). Complaining that, despite women's "natural" interest in radio, programs had thus far failed to take an informed account of their audience's wishes, it was argued that the nature of the task facing the nation demanded fundamental changes in the structure of the Frauenfunk. When it came to questions of reshaping their way of life in the interests of the *Volk,* every "responsible German woman" should demand that the radio, as the "Voice of the Nation," could be relied upon to transmit "reliable" information. The way to ensure this was, as Bremen-Hirschkendt maintained, to organize and train women in the art of National Socialist radio. To this end the Rundfunkarbeitskreis der NS Frauen (NS Women's Radio Workshop) was founded as an affiliate of the DFF.[27] In keeping with Hadamovsky's directive that Nazi radio should be formed by a fusion of listeners, radio artists, and editors, the aim of the *Arbeitskreis* was to attract program contributions from women in all walks of life, to work closely together with the Party's women's organizations in the preparation of programs, and to train female presenters. It hoped to develop a close relationship between politically committed broadcasters and the public and organized listening groups to this end, though they proved a short-lived challenge to the inexorable trend toward listening in the familial, domestic sphere.

Nevertheless, the cooperation with the women's sections of the Party developed into a much closer working relationship. In 1935 the DFW was brought into the national broadcasting headquarters, the RSL, to oversee and influence the coverage of women's issues on the radio. The first appointment of a national consultant on women's radio, Frau Walendy, was made by Scholtz-Klink and Hadamovsky in March 1935 ("Frauenwerk . . ." 1935). The regional headquarters of the NSF were also involved

---

27. The "Radio Workshop of NS Women" drew its members from the only slightly older Rundfunkarbeitsgemeinschaft nationalsozialistischer Frauen (Radio Association of NS Women), an organization affiliated with the Reichsverband deutscher Rundfunkteilnehmer.

in producing women's radio in cooperation with the regional stations. The role of the NSF was not solely advisory. In special cases, as in the Mother's Day contributions, it made programs independently of the Frauenfunk.[28] The women's section of the DAF also had radio connections. From 1937, for example, the propaganda department was given access to submit regular short reports about its work and achievements for broadcast by the daily evening news service on the regional transmitters. Members of all the women's organizations were encouraged to listen out for these reports ("Frauenamt der DAF . . ." 1937, 61).

One consequence of the radio becoming more closely identified with the state was that the continuing advertising slots reserved for private firms became increasingly incongruous in the eyes of ideological purists. Comfort could be drawn from the fact that these advertisements were nowhere near as prolific as in the United States nor as intrusive into peak listening times as in Italy, but there could be no denying that the commercial plugs that remained did not correspond with "the lofty aims of a national broadcaster." From May 1935 advertising by private firms on the radio was abolished, with a complete ban on advertising coming into effect in October of the same year. No longer would private interests be able to speak with the "Voice of the Nation." They would have to go back to the old vehicles—newspapers, shop windows, posters, and pamphlets. Radio, as Hadamovsky had insisted the previous year, was not intended to be a glorified newspaper or news service. It was to be the voice of the *Volksgemeinschaft,* speaking in the public interest, advertising the policies and points of view of the government.[29]

As in other areas of public life in the "Hitler State," which was characterized by a complex of competing and overlapping institutions, the involvement of so many different organizations with their own internal hierarchies in the production of women's radio could lead to confusion and resentment (Broszat 1981). The lack of coordination between the various regional stations led not only to unnecessary duplications and inefficiencies but also promised to undermine the coherence of the central ideological message. It fell to the press and propaganda department of the RFF, under the leadership of Erika Fillies-Kirmsse, and to Gertrud Kappesser at the RSL to attempt some sort of coordination, encouraging all the regional editors to march in step toward a common goal (Peck 1934–35b).

---

28. The Pr/Prop Dept. in the RFF was also closely involved in the production of women's magazines, including the Party organ, *NS-Frauenwarte* (with a print run of 700,000), *Frauenkultur im Deutschen Frauenwerk, Deutsche Hauswirtschaft,* and *Mutter und Volk,* as well as coordinating the coverage of women's issues in the daily press.

29. "Rundfunk von Einzelwerbung befreit," *Der Angriff,* 20 March 1935.

Relatively few documents concerning the internal decision-making processes in women's radio have survived, but those that do present a picture of a network of women taking their duties very seriously who struggled for some degree of autonomy over the programs they produced in a system of competing claims to ultimate responsibility.[30] The creative autonomy they sought was, however, strictly curtailed—and they were willingly complicit in this restriction—by the delimitation of the areas of competence ascribed to the female sphere. The points of conflict were few and relatively benign, the result more of misunderstanding and the unwieldy nature of the organization than of important differences of opinion or belief.[31] There was no room for such divergence of opinion in the production of radio in the Third Reich. Further details about levels of cooperation and modes of delegation between the Party organizations and the Frauenfunk arise in chapter 7, which looks specifically at the campaigns that sought to influence women's patterns of consumption. At this point, however, it is more instructive to examine the output that was produced within this imperfect and tension-ridden structure.

**Continuity and Change in Programs for Women**

During the first two months following the takeover of power, the old system continued much as before, as changes could not be wrought overnight. However, even during this interim period, the number of programs for women broadcast on all stations increased almost twofold. In the week from 26 February twenty-five such programs were broadcast, while in the

---

30. The correspondence between the various offices working in connection with the Silesian Frauenfunk in 1936, which survives in the Federal Archives in Potsdam, serve as an illustration of the problems of resentment and antagonism that could arise. For example, see the series of acrimonious correspondence in 1936 between the Silesian radio representative of the NSF and the Berlin headquarters of the Reichsmütterdienst and the RSL. BAP 62 Re1/6:113–19.

31. The coordination procedure was not entirely watertight. "Erziehung zur Ehrfurcht" (Raising a Child to Respect), for example, was broadcast from Königsberg before Fillies-Kirmsse had vetted it, despite her subsequent assessment of it as vague, inaccurate, and misleading (RFF Head Office, Pr/Prop, Berlin, to the Pr/Prop Dept., *Gaufrauenschaftsleitung* Ostpreußen, Königsberg, 8 April 1941, BAP 62 Re1/6:195). This could suggest there was a tendency in the regions to regard the function of the central office as little more than a rubber stamp. Certainly, the regions were not afraid to contest decisions from above. One program about health care for children written by the women's consultant for racial politics in Saarpfalz, Frl. Dr. Mayer, for example, was rejected as superficial and dangerously misinformative by Gertrud Kappesser at the RSL. It was the tone of this rebuke, as much as the rebuke itself, that offended the regional NSF and caused it to lodge a complaint with Fillies-Kirmsse (*Gaufrauenschaftsleitung* Saarpfalz to Fillies-Kirmsse, 13 April 1940, BAP 62 Re1/6:181).

week from 19 March the number had risen to forty. This still represented a tiny proportion of the overall number of broadcasts, and, because of the concentration on short, instructional advice programs, there was only a marginal increase in the share of airtime, but it does indicate a solid dedication to the provision of women's radio nonetheless.

One of the consequences of *Gleichschaltung* was that differences between regional output became less marked. Regional traditions, costumes, and customs were given airplay in the name of *Volkspflege,* but the new traditions that radio helped to bolster, such as Mother's Day, were organized on a national, integrative level. Moreover, some programs were organized from the center with regional variations; for example, a recipe service could be simply tailored to the local availability of fresh and value-for-money produce. This again partly accounts for the increase in the number of women's programs offered by the various stations. Stuttgart, for example, increased its output of *Frauenstunden* from six to fifty-two between March and October 1933, Frankfurt from five to fifty-six, Hamburg from twenty-one to forty-three. Meanwhile, the nationwide service, the Deutschlandsender, had its own women's department, which, following a shake-up in 1935, also broadcast a relatively high proportion of material for women. This included a magazine program for rural women, "Die Landfrau schaltet sich ein" (Rural Women Tune In); a series of consumerist propaganda, "Hauswirtschaft–Volkswirtschaft" (Home Economy–National Economy); the "Mütterstunde" (Mothers' Hour) for questions of child education; and "Müttersorgen" (Mothers' Cares) for child health matters; together with intermittent programs for working women, women in the border territories, and German women living abroad.[32]

Even with *Gleichschaltung* some regional variation remained. Leipzig and Breslau, for example, gave least attention to women's matters, though their output increased in 1935 ("Neuregelung . . ." 1935), while Cologne offered only gymnastics and a short daily program called "Für die Frau." A twenty-minute program of the same name was broadcast daily at 8:10 A. M. by Hamburg, still one of the most prolific providers of women's programs. The legacy of the *Schule der Frau* is perhaps evident in the fact that, of all the stations, Hamburg was the only one to continue a program on legal affairs for women into the new regime.

In an article for *Der Deutsche Rundfunk* in 1935 Paula Knupffer, the head of the Berlin Frauenfunk—the first woman to head such a department—listed the various ideological functions that different types of programs within the women's programming were supposed to perform. Prac-

---

32. *Die Sendung,* 1 June 1935, 374.

tical programs sought to combine new nutritional science, national economic imperatives, and the traditions of German housewifery in times gone by. The magazine program "Allerlei der Woche" (Miscellany of the Week) highlighted the events and meetings that were recommended activities for the listeners' leisure time. Plays on the Frauenfunk were designed to increase women's sense of vitality and a feeling for the role that they were to play in the state and in the family, while musical and poetry programs thematized German virtue and beauty. But the most important service, she insisted, in keeping with the maternal spirit of broadcasting was the programming for mothers and children.

Gymnastics were also popular across the board, with most stations increasing their output during the first year of Nazified radio. The Deutschlandsender broadcast such a program six times a week, as did Königsberg, Cologne, Frankfurt, and Stuttgart; Munich and Breslau three times. One of the reasons for the popularity of these exercise programs was clearly that the Nazi conception of womanhood centered on the body, in that women were ascribed to the realm of Nature, and their biological function as mothers and protectors of the racially pure generations of Germans to come was given primacy over all other activity. Weak bodies, Jewish bodies, bodies which did not rightfully belong in the healthy body politic, were excluded with escalating extremism. The exercise programs on German radio were just one manifestation of the fascination with the aesthetic, ideological, and physical construct of a strong and athletic female form.

In terms of program content, however, the most striking difference between the *Frauenstunden* before and after *Gleichschaltung* was the stringent reduction in "cultural" items in favor of practical advice programs for the housewife and mother. In March 1933 the ratio had been 52:40 in favor of practical programs. By July of the same year it was 38:15. These figures also represent a reduction in the total number of programs, following the initial upsurge, although some of the shortfall can be accounted for by seasonal changes in programming. There was also a percentage reduction in programs of "general interest" on the Frauenfunk.

Although programs aimed at the housewife as consumer will be examined more closely in chapter 7, some examples are included here to give some flavor of the output. Frankfurt, for example, broadcast its "Küchenzettel" (Kitchen Notes) four times a week, Königsberg had a weekly program called "Die Frau mitten in der Volkswirtschaft" (Women at the Center of the National Economy), Breslau offered "Auch die Hausfrau kann sich erholen" (Even the Housewife Can Relax), and Cologne had "Hausputz als fröhliche Gymnastik" (Cleaning as Jolly Gymnastics). In a typical week in 1935 listeners to the twice-weekly "Stunde der Frau" in Munich heard an item on how to embroider a pearl collar, some fashion advice, a selection of traditional folk songs about women, and a promotion of the *Winterhilfe* campaign by Else Anlinger, in her guise as typical Munich character "Frau Schwinghammer." Affiliated to the station's "ideological department," the Munich Frauenfunk saw its part in "tending the language and the cultural heritage of the nation" (Jenssen 1935), although it also worked closely with the Reichsnährstand to try to influence patterns of consumption in line with government projections and with the NSF to make propaganda for the *Mütterschulen.*[33]

The rationale for the sharp reduction of artistic, literary, and political programs was that such programs were of interest to the whole community and no longer needed to be siphoned off into a separate sphere. German culture was indivisible in the eyes of the Nazi ideologues. But the effect of this policy was in fact to deprive radio of a female perspective on cultural affairs. The programs that survived were primarily of the sort that looked at the biographies of the women in famous men's lives or the female characters in literary and musical classics. The rest of the nonpractical schedules were made up of treatments of the feminine character—mainly pseudopsychological discussions such as "Das Ich im Spiegel" (My Self in the Mirror) or "Liebe läßt sich schwer verdienen" (Love Is Hard to Earn).

The reduction in cultural programs for women was additionally defended with the argument that a radio system imbued with the vital *Muttergeist* was no longer required to be an instrument of education and could therefore no longer sustain the provision of special-interest programs. This sounded the death knell of the sort of principles behind the erstwhile Schule der Frau in Hamburg and the more progressive parts of women's radio in Weimar Germany. Discussions about the ability of a woman to take a case to court without her husband, the division of property within a marriage, or a wife's right to make out an independent will, such as had filled the airwaves during the Weimar Republic, were now held up as indicative of the instability of the family and the institution of marriage during that time. Hitler's "unambiguous enunciation of the position of women in Nazi society" had rendered programs dealing with women's rights and related legal issues redundant (Peck 1933–34d, 361).

Not surprisingly, programs for the working woman were cut even further back than they had been in the Weimar period, in line with the prevailing ideology.[34] Career women no longer enjoyed such a high profile on

33. NSF Pr/Prop Dept., *Gauleitung* München-Oberbayern, to the RFF head office of Press and Propaganda, Berlin, 18 September 1942, BAP 62 Re1/6:105.

34. There was a discrepancy between ideology and practice regarding women's employment because of a variety of factors that saw the number of women working rise from 4.2 million in 1933 to 6 million by the end of 1937 (Lück 1979, 139). Already by 1935–36 the

the airwaves, and the careers discussed no longer covered such a broad range. Jobs in trade and industry took a back seat, while jobs in the fashion world, which had once been such a popular theme in Weimar, were cut out altogether. Only careers considered "useful to the nation" and befitting the maternal spirit, such as nursing, teaching, and domestic service, were given airtime (at least in the early years of the regime), and these tended to feature women recounting their personal experiences. Many programs were aimed at young girls, encouraging them to take up such work. One such was Berlin's weekly "Was soll meine Tochter werden?" (What Shall My Daughter Be When She Grows Up?), which ran for three years up to 1936. Two years later, in 1938, an intensive radio campaign called "Mädel, wir brauchen Euch" (Girls, We Need You) was launched by the RRF to encourage girls into domestic service. The compulsory year of agricultural, social, or domestic work introduced in 1938 for all unmarried girls or women under twenty-five, the *Pflichtjahr*, was given a high media profile.

No more programs aimed specifically at women were broadcast during the evening. There had been some limited concession to the daily routine of working women in Weimar radio, but now the evening hours were considered sacrosanct. Prime time was family time, and in theory the evening schedules were to have as broad an appeal as possible, across gender, age, class, and region. Back in the daytime schedules there was a corresponding increase in programs aimed at women as mothers. Early series included Berlin's "Die deutsche Frau im Kampf gegen den Geburtenrückgang" (The German Woman in the Battle against the Declining Birthrate), Breslau's "Die kinderlose Frau" (The Childless Woman), and Saarbrücken's "Die Frau als Trägerin von Erbgut und Rasse" (The Woman as Bearer of Heritage and Race). These programs were designed to promote the idea of motherhood as women's primary natural and political function. The official news agency for women's issues made much play of the creation of a listening community of mothers who could receive confirmation of their social importance and exchange information and experiences with others in the same situation.[35] To a certain extent these hopes were realized in that many of the programs did indeed take their inspiration for practical advice from tips suggested by listeners' letters—the source of such ideas always being expressly highlighted in order to strengthen the impression of an active and contented audience.

---

policies persuading women out of the work force were not pursued so vigorously (Klinksiek 1982, 101–10). Nevertheless, the proportion of women in regular work fell (Mason 1976, 7).

35. "Nachrichtendienst: Rundfunkstunden für die Frau," *Amtliche Frauenkorrespondenz*, 1 December 1933, 578

Other programs concentrated on children's health issues or on promoting the new body culture, with great emphasis put on child-rearing techniques as the center of a woman's role in life. These programs were often child centered, the advice given being primarily how to respond to a child's foibles, as in Berlin's "Mutter, mir ist langweilig" (Mother, I'm Bored), Saarbrücken's "Ist mein Kind musikalisch?" (Is My Child Musical?), or Munich's "Mutter, frag' mich nicht so aus!" (Mother, Don't Ask Me So Many Questions!). Bringing children up to be future citizens of the Nazi *Volksgemeinschaft* was an explicit part of the Frauenfunk curriculum, with programs like "Erziehung der Geschlechter untereinander und zur Volksgemeinschaft" (Raising the Sexes to Live Together and in the National Community), broadcast on the Deutschlandsender on 12 December 1933, or the series of plays commissioned in 1936 by the Berlin station, under the rubric of "Lenkung zu Kind und Familie" (Orientation to Child and Family). The year 1936 also saw the introduction of a regular feature in praise of large families. Called "Gruß der Jugend an die Kinderreichen" and broadcast in the interval of the popular midday concert, it involved children in the Hitler Youth and League of German Girls (BDM) offering their best wishes and congratulations to "healthy and prolific" German families at the birth of a new child and praising the rebirth of the German nation in song. Listeners were invited to inform their regional stations of women they knew who were having their sixth child or more, in particular if they were members of the Party or affiliated organizations ("Gruß an die Kinderreichen . . ." 1936). Programs such as this were the product of a careful agenda to produce suitable listening for the youth of the nation.

### On a Young Woman's Wavelength

The NSDAP was convinced that the future of the Party and of Nazi Germany lay in winning over the hearts and minds of the young people of the country. Radio was at the cutting edge of the propaganda aimed at the young, with the young people in the Party organizations taking an active role in the direction of that propaganda. Youth radio was divided into three areas—school radio, radio for ten- to fourteen-year-olds, and radio for the BDM and preschool children (the lumping together of which gives some indication of the lower priority given to girls' programming than boys').[36]

---

36. The main organization was for girls between fourteen and eighteen, with a subdivision, *Jungmädel im BDM,* for girls aged ten to fourteen. Younger children were encouraged to join the *Kükengruppen* (chick groups) run by the Frauenschaft, which was the organization girls were supposed to join on leaving the BDM at eighteen. See Klaus 1983.

Within a year of the takeover of power Reichsjugendführung (RJF) representatives were working at each of the regional radio stations and the RSL in Berlin. A specialist department for radio at the RJF, the Rundfunkamt, coordinated these activities and was responsible for all areas of radio propaganda for the RJF, including technical and financial matters, advertising to encourage wider radio ownership, the promotion of more effective ideological programs for young people, participation in program making by youth organizations, and the examination of existing youth broadcasts. Hilde Freytag, a representative from the BDM, was employed at the Rundfunkamt to coordinate state and media policies aimed at girls and young women (a similarly close arrangement was set up for the press). A BDM representative was also employed at each of the regional stations to cooperate in program production, and radio departments were set up within the administration of regional BDM headquarters (Freytag 1935, 39–42; Rüdiger 1983, 116–18). In 1934 a department for film and radio was also set up in the Reichsministerium für Wissenschaft, Erziehung und Volksbildung (the Ministry for Science, Schooling, and Popular Education), and soon the inclusion of certain radio programs in the weekly curriculum was decreed compulsory for children in the fourth grade and above.[37]

Beginning with one "Mädelfunk" broadcast a week, most stations were transmitting three or more such programs a week by 1935. For younger listeners, there were "Jungmädelstunden," which generally featured traditional stories, fairy tales, and folk songs. The flagship program was "Stunde der Jungen Nation" (Hour of the Young Nation), in which the movement's leaders reported on the month's events and gave advice and suggestions for the month ahead. Broadcast fortnightly from 1935, the HJ and BDM took it in turns to lead the proceedings. The regional stations produced their own programs, with the "borderland" programs being considered particularly important in the endeavor to create a community of listeners and sense of German-ness. For members of the BDM there were book reviews, handicraft tips, sports shows, agricultural programs, and, once a month, a singalong session, "Wir Mädel singen." Programs that reported on the activities of the BDM, describing the life and work within the movement, sometimes in the form of radio plays, were especially designed to attract those girls who had not yet grasped "their duty towards the community" (Freytag 1935, 40).

The year 1939 saw a nationwide campaign to attract new blood into

---

37. Between October 1937 and February 1942 this department was reintegrated into a department for general affairs, thereafter known as the Abteilung für allgemeine Angelegenheiten und für Film, Lichtbild, Funk und Schallplatte (Wulf 1983, 49).

the profession. The RJF, in collaboration with the head of German radio, published a brochure, with application form attached, to be circulated in the HJ and BDM, which was entitled, *Wie werde ich Rundfunksprecher?* Young artistic talent had long been channeled through the youth organizations to fill radio programs, but there was now a concerted effort to train the next generation of National Socialist radio presenters. Besides needing clear diction, applicants also needed "a clearly discernible respect for the truth, a strong will and a readiness to work, a sound general knowledge, but above all a firm grounding in National Socialist ideology."[38] They also needed to demonstrate their Aryan heritage. The propaganda work of the BDM was not restricted to radio, but radio was considered the most effective and relevant instrument for a young nationwide organization.[39]

The main problem for the programmers at the outset of the *Gleichschaltung* process was finding a way to present a public image of girls that would not be overshadowed by the very strong image of masculinity and heroism which defined the public image of young men in Nazi culture. The role of young male activists in the establishment of the new order was clear: they could take the message out into the streets and join the Party organizations. It was much harder to promote an active image for young girls to aspire to, when the only role ascribed to them was as mothers-in-waiting. The political turbulence of the Depression years had not left the young generation of women untouched, but nor had they been as strongly politicized or polarized as was the young male population. This led to the danger in broadcasting circles, however, of assuming that young women formed some sort of homogeneous group, which only increased the disaffection of the young female audience.

This was the basic premise of an article on the future of radio for young women published in *Rufer und Hörer* in February 1933 (Suhr 1933, 502), which suggested that, while it might be tempting not to give particular attention to young women in a transitional phase defined primarily in terms of active and masculine virtues, the importance of young girls who would one day be the mothers of a new generation would be underesti-

---

38. "Wer wird Rundfunksprecher?" *Reichsjugendpressedienst*, 28 July 1939: BAP 62.03/8213:5.

39. Baldur von Schirach, the *Reichsjugendführer*, for example, writing in 1934, ascribed his success in promoting the NSDAP youth organizations and the suppression of other youth groups to his regular access to the national airwaves (1934, 131). The movement also had specialists working with papers and journals for the young—for example, *Die HJ: Das junge Deutschland, Die Fanfare, Wille und Macht, Morgen,* and the BDM's own magazine, *Das deutsche Mädel.* Propaganda actions, such as the distribution of leaflets and posters, the holding of exhibitions, and cooperation with the production of *Wochenschauen,* were also part of the BDM's activities ([BDM-Hauptreferentin des Presse- und Propagandaamtes in der RJF] in Munske 1935, 43–45).

mated at the nation's peril. The author of the article, the broadcaster Werner Suhr, claimed the letters he received from his young female listeners expressed the desire for contemporary, heroic role models, or, as one twenty-three-year-old saleswoman put it, "thrilling portrayals of vivacious people and illustrious role models." There was indeed a concentration on the positive side of life to the exclusion of any but the most saccharine of social criticism. This was certainly the case in the programs broadcast in association with the BDM, which, as time went on, was given more responsibility in the production and censorship of programs for young women, although always working in close cooperation with relevant government departments and other party organizations, with the stated aim of creating an image of womanhood to which all young (Aryan) German girls should aspire.[40]

### The Politicization of the Private Sphere

Given the high priority attached to enlisting women in the services of the *Volk,* the Frauenfunk was one of the few special-interest radio departments to survive *Gleichschaltung.* The Weimar policy of targeting different interest groups with their own programs was abandoned in favor of a unified, totalitarian vision of radio.[41] Women's and children's programs were exceptions, justified by the separatist element in the ideological framework. Women were united in their maternal attributes; men were differentiated by a disparate number of professional and other social functions. Moreover, women's psychology was held to be more monolithic than men's, so human interest stories and fictional accounts, for example, were thought to be universally appreciated by women, which accounts for the high proportion of programs in the Frauenfunk that took a dramatic or conversational form. This was despite the recorded popularity of "hard" news and political programs among women at the time (Kuhlmann 1942, 138). Commentators referred not simply to the content of political radio programs but also to the fact that radio—and film—appealed directly to the senses, whereas traditional forms of political education and mobilization such as party membership, newspaper editorials, street demonstrations, and so on appealed to the masculine intellect and thirst for action. By bringing the voices of political leaders into the home, the radio made them into personalities who could then appeal to women on a personal level (Peck 1933–34a, 245).

The politicization of radio output represented a politicization of the

---

40. Hilde Freytag, "Mädelfunk - einmalig in der Welt," *Reichsjugendpresse* 272 (1935), Bundesarchiv Potsdam 62.03/6822:22.

41. See Goebbels's opening speech to the 1936 radio exhibition (Pohle 1955, 273).

private sphere, and yet the continuation of separate programming for women was an expression of a philosophy that insisted on the gendered separation of the public and the private spheres and the ostensible exclusion of politics from the schedules of the Frauenfunk. Yet the Nazi Frauenfunk was highly political. There were two main planks on which it operated: *Führung im Sinne der Bevölkerungspolitik, Volksgesundheit und Volkstumspflege* (leadership in terms of population policy, the health of the nation, and the protection of nationhood), and *Führung im Sinne des Vierjahresplans bzw. einer wirtschaftlichen Aufrüstung* (leadership in terms of the Four Year Plan and strengthening the economy / war economy). The first category included "nurturing the idea of motherhood and the family," advice on child rearing, promotion of gymnastics, the health of the nation, and the preservation of the national heritage. The second category, which was expanded to incorporate the demands of the war effort in later years, concentrated on influencing patterns of consumption and explaining and promoting the "rational" deployment of female labor power.

These interests represented an ongoing politicization of the domestic sphere. The contradiction that existed between the eulogizing of the family in National Socialist propaganda and the undermining of family integrity by the intrusion of the state into the private sphere is well recognized.[42] Claudia Koonz, for example, writes:

> True, publicity exalted the family as the "germ cell" of the nation, but social policy emptied the household of its members. Eugenic laws interfered with private choices related to marriage and children. The demand for total loyalty to the *Führer* undercut fathers' authority. As indoctrination supplanted education, youth leaders and teachers rivaled mothers for children's devotion. (1988, 178)

It seems that radio stood at the very fulcrum of this contradiction in providing both "familial cement" and in spearheading the public intrusion of the home. It offered an authoritarian voice that was both a substitute for and a reinforcement of the patriarchal voice in the home. Nazi ideology deemed that politics and women did not mix, and yet the political content of radio could not fail to bring the two together.

---

42. Stern noted that in the establishment of the BDM and the HJ inhered "precisely the dissolution of the traditional authoritarian structure of the German family" (1975, 172). Lück cites a contemporary joke about a family in which father was a member of the SS, mother in one of the women's organizations, son in the HJ, and daughter in the BDM, all of them so busy they only got together once a year—at the Party rally in Nuremberg (1979, 91). See also Mason 1976, 24; Welch 1983, 64–65.

The obstinate adherence to "traditional" women's issues is a useful indication of the ideological premise in the producers' minds that all women, regardless of age or financial or familial status, could be served by programs that centered on the home and family, and yet even these programs were highly politicized. Programs about cookery and child care might seem entirely innocuous in contrast to the most virulent fascist propaganda, yet their value to the regime should be measured not simply in terms of their content but also in terms of their structural function within the whole. The space that women had carved out within the broadcast public sphere became exclusively devoted to reinforcing women's exclusion from the public sphere in a broader sense. The recognition of a female space within the schedules facilitated the consolidation of the notion of separate and unequal spheres of competence. Whereas conservative media policy in the Weimar Republic had hoped to make the home a more attractive place for women by bringing the outside world and the air of modernity directly into the home, Nazi policy was to eulogize the moral and political duties of marriage and motherhood in a much more explicit way. The Nazis seized on the most modern apparatus of communication to advocate a return to a vision of womanhood expressed in terms of nature, spirit, instinct, and biology. Certainly in the transitional period between the two state systems, reforms were effected in conscious opposition to the intellectualizing of the traditional female role. The Weimar policy of nonpolitical radio was concerned with keeping public politics out of the private sphere, which in the years following the enfranchisement of women was in itself a political act. Nazi radio policy, on the other hand, was concerned with politicizing every aspect of the private sphere, while women's real political agency was suppressed.

The affirmation of the gendered separation of the public and private spheres coupled with a blurring of the traditional divide between public politics and the nonpolitical domestic sphere is a question whose importance is clear in light of the recent debate between two different approaches to the role of women in the Nazi state, as represented by Gisela Bock and Claudia Koonz. In Bock's view national socialism was particularly pernicious for women precisely because of the sexist and racist invasion of the private, maternal sphere. Koonz, on the other hand, regards women's defense of and retreat into a separate sphere, a separate *Lebensraum,* as having been fundamental to the maintenance of the Nazi state and has provided a wealth of evidence describing women's support for and active participation in that state.[43] An analysis of broadcasting in the period highlights these ambiguities.

43. Koonz (1984, 1986, 1988) traces the heritage of the rhetoric about women and the history of the term *Lebensraum.* She argues that "natural biological divisions by race and sex

While radio, lodged as it was in the domestic sphere, was the ideal medium for the mobilization of women within the terms of domesticity and motherhood allotted them, in terms of the relationship of women and radio propaganda, one cannot talk simply in terms of a public, male-directed medium penetrating women's sphere, for women both within and outside the Party organizations were actively involved with the production of propaganda aimed at women. The concentration within women's radio on traditional domestic and familial concerns promoted the impression of tradition, continuity, stability, and normality, which helped disguise the radical changes that were taking place. Women who willingly retreated into the separate women's *Lebensraum* remote from public politics and power, hiding behind aprons and a resurgent chauvinism, while maintaining a disarming semblance of participation in the public sphere, were vital to the easy acceptance of the Nazi regime and, by extension, to the success of racist and expansionist policies in pursuit of that wider *Lebensraum.*

With that in mind, there is a final caveat to add: in studying the propaganda of this period, there is a danger to some extent of reproducing the Nazi view of the world as it has come down to us in the propaganda images. Having restored women to the picture of radio history in the Third Reich, we must remember those women who were excluded in the banal propaganda of the everyday that has been described here, propaganda that was designed to integrate only racially and socially desirable women into the *Volksgemeinschaft.*

---

provided the framework within which Nazi leaders undermined independence, morality, and tradition. . . . Thus women became not leaders of their separate sphere, but raw material for the propaganda offensive that glossed evil with the healthy glow of motherly virtue" (1988, 228).

# CHAPTER 5

# Home Front / Front Line:
# Women, Radio, and War

With the outbreak of war the mass media took on a new importance in the lives of many women. Daily radio programs and the weekly *Wochenschau* gave the news from the front an immediacy that helped bridge the gap between friends and families split up by the demands of the war. Yet, despite women's evident interest in political bulletins and the concessions made acknowledging their presence in the audience, they were most commonly addressed only in terms of their relationship to men—as wives and mothers. During the war this was especially clear as the media took on the role of mediator between the home front and the front line, in effect a mediator between women and men. In a society that glorified "unmitigated masculinity" reference to men left at the home front was muted, and the divide between home and front was characterized as a gender divide.

Goebbels identified three major areas of propaganda: political propaganda explaining and justifying the aims of the war, propaganda aimed at control of consumption, and propaganda aimed at encouraging active participation in the war effort (Rupp 1978, 102). All three areas had particular resonances for the female population and are reflected in the radio propaganda aimed at women during the war years. This chapter looks at two of those areas (consumption propaganda is the subject of chap. 7), but it is also concerned with the relationship between women and radio more generally during the war. Underpinning this discussion is the recognition that a female public was addressed by a medium which was organized according to, and was designed to serve, ideological principles that sought to confine women to the private sphere but that were increasingly disregarded in the face of overturned by pragmatic considerations as the war turned against Germany. This chapter aims to document and discuss the resultant contradictions and tensions in media policy and practice. By concentrating on women's programming, it also serves to illustrate patterns of everyday wartime media production and reception, as opposed to reiterating the well-documented history of "high" propaganda.

## A Question of Morale

The jubilation that had greeted the declaration of war in Germany in 1914 was not matched in 1939, despite the long campaign that had been conducted via the radio and other media to prepare the nation psychologically for war and to stimulate a positive demand for military action (Behrens 1986, 214). Nevertheless, the swiftness and apparent ease of the initial victories, combined with the absence of an immediate threat to the (non-Jewish) civilian population at home, did at least mean that morale in the country was initially relatively buoyant. Two weeks into the war it was decreed that Jews could not own receivers, nor could anyone living with or married to a Jew. Their sets were requisitioned by the Wehrmacht (Boelcke 1966, 283).

Regular reports on public morale were filed by the head of the SS and chief of the German police, in a series called "Meldungen aus dem Reich." As early as 9 September 1939, it was reported that radio programs, the *Wochenschau* newsreels, and newspaper reports were already enjoying more favorable reception by the public than had been the case before the declaration of war a week earlier.[1] Eight months on, and the reports were still full of claims that the population was "extraordinarily satisfied" with both radio and film output.[2] The first cracks in the general support for the war came in the second winter of hostilities, 1940–41. By then it had become clear that the war would be a protracted one and that it could escalate into a second world war. The propagandists, however, were eager to dispel fears that the theater of war could not be contained. The SD reported that such fears were especially prevalent among women, apparently because of an increasing tendency to tune into foreign broadcasts.[3]

The mood became still more muted when the attack was launched on the Eastern front in 1942, especially because the propaganda about the atrocities committed by the "Bolsheviks" had been so effective. Once again the SD reported that the horror stories from the Eastern front made a particularly profound impact on women, especially if they had relations involved, and that one consequence was for them to believe the propaganda that the Jews were responsible, which led many to demand *eine radikale Behandlung,* "a radical treatment," of the Jewish population at

---

1. MadR IfZ MA441/1 T175R258, roll 750043, 9 October 1939.
2. MadR IfZ MA441/1 T175/R259, roll 751547, 20 May 1940.
3. MadR IfZ MA441/1 T175/R260, roll 752692, 4 November 1940.

home.[4] They also reported that women understood less of military matters and were more prone to panic if careful explanations, particularly in the press, did not accompany radio news flashes of important military maneuvers.[5] Moreover, as the war impinged more and more on women's daily lives on a personal level, they began to lose interest in trying to follow the minutiae of the campaign reports.[6]

A counteroffensive against the growing pessimism in the country was launched by the RMVP, in which radio entertainment was to be the key weapon. Goebbels did not enjoy undisputed control of the printed media, and the film industry did not offer him the flexibility of daily schedules, so radio took the lead in the new media campaign, under the leadership of Hans Hinkel. In order to facilitate these efforts to win listeners back, several of the more pedantic restrictions governing broadcasting were lifted. Guidelines designed to brighten up the schedules were distributed to radio stations by the RSL on 26 September 1941. Cooperation was sought from theater and cabaret directors, conductors, and composers. More humorous items and amusing announcers were introduced. Where the schedules had been "monolithic and dull," they were to become "very bright with lots of popular appeal."[7] Goebbels envisaged the radio as a "good friend and comrade through the dark days, a source of cheer and motivation, and a constant companion through the experiences of the war."[8]

A popular innovation was "Eine halbe Stunde Kabarett," broadcast for the first time on 9 August 1941. It marked a development away from the reliance on popular music alone to lighten the schedules, with features such as the banter between "Herr Schnick" and "Frau Schnack." These Berlin characters provided more than just comic relief; they also performed a propagandistic function, channeling information and opinions in a digestible form. The first program, for example, gently chided housewives for hoarding in times of scarcity, with later programs each treating some similar aspect of daily wartime experience.[9] Basing his judgment on listeners' letters, SD reports, and reports from propaganda departments, Hinkel deemed the changes he introduced to have been immediately successful (Klingler 1980, 57). By January, however, the new enthusiasm was

---

4. MadR MA141/1 T175/R261, roll 754252, 10 July 1941. Statements like this may say as much about the information gatherers as about the general atmosphere in the country but are interesting nevertheless because of the impact of these reports on policy decisions.

5. MadR MA141/1 T175/R261, roll 754846, 19 September 1941.

6. MadR MA141/1 T175/R263, roll 756658, 7 May 1942.

7. Programmrichtlinien, "vertraulich erfaßt" vom SD-Leitabschnitt München, 15 October 1941, BAK R58/1090, cited in Klingler 1980, 54.

8. Goebbels 1942; cited in Fritz Stege, "Das Ohr der Welt," *Leipziger Neueste Nachrichten,* 28 October 1943, n.p.

9. MadR MA141/1 T175/R261, roll 754558, 14 August 1941.

already beginning to wear thin, according to SD reports (58). Complaints that there was not enough variety in the schedules and not enough character to the individual programs began to plague the radio stations, and it became clear that a more thoroughgoing reform was needed. By mid-February plans to reshape the organization of radio were finalized. The decree effecting the necessary changes claimed that radio entertainment offering relaxation and relief at the front and at home was *kriegswichtig,* or "vital to the war effort."[10]

An editorial staff under the direct leadership of Goebbels and Hinkel was set up, dividing the light entertainment department into ten different sections. This division enabled a more differentiated program to be arranged and provided a more flexible framework for changing things that proved unpopular and for ensuring the schedules could provide programs that suited the popular mood at any particular time. There was also less emphasis on "local color" to stress the unity of the nation in the face of war.[11] The increase in light entertainment programs also brought with it the side effect, examined more closely in chapter 8, that women's voices were to be heard more frequently presenting programs despite the initial ideological reluctance to allow women such a prominent voice.

The RFF continued to work closely with the radio companies producing programs for women as before. Its department of press and propaganda now defined its most important task as "mediator between the leadership and the millions of women in the war effort," using all the means available to them to "make clear to them their responsibility and duty in the great events of the time" (Scholtz-Klink 1978, 83). The propaganda aimed at women to enlist their cooperation in the war effort in the first few months was deemed a success, and so the allocation of airtime for the Frauenfunk actually increased from 1939 to 1940.[12] In 1942 the RFF issued the following statement:

> The mood of the people can be influenced. We know how dangerously and skilfully it was ruined by Jewish propaganda in the Great War. . . .

---

10. "Anordnung zur *Neugestaltung* des Rundfunkprogramms vom 15.2.42," *Nachrichtenblatt des Reichspropagandaministeriums* 6, 28 February 1942, BAK R55/439. There were those who disagreed with such a policy—for example, Alfred Rosenberg, who argued that an authoritarian state should not bow to the dictates of popular taste (*Stichwort Protokoll über die Amtsleiterbesprechung mit dem Reichsleiter am 4.3.43,* National Archives Microcopy no. T-454, rolls 40, 54–60).

11. "Anordnung über die Verantwortlichkeit für die politisch-propagandistischen Sendungen des Großdeutschen Rundfunks vom 26.2.42," *Nachrichtendienst der RMVP* 6, 28 February 1942, BAK R55/439.

12. There were 2,277 programs equaling 24,890 minutes' airtime in 1939, compared to 2,348 programs, or 29,156 minutes, in 1940 (Scholtz-Klink 1978, 86).

The Nazi regime—in contrast to the Wilhelmine—knows its pernicious enemy and has largely stopped its little game, by creating in the press and propaganda, radio and film, powerful means to counter it effectively. But we still need to deal with enemy propaganda on the smaller scale of rumours and loose talk.[13]

The RMVP went to great lengths to impress on the nation's women, traditionally regarded as gossips and rumormongers, the need to guard their tongues. This had as much to do with curbing expressions of discontent about shortages and stringencies as a fear about careless talk on sensitive matters of national security or a fragile alliegance to the regime—for which there were already clear deterrents in place. The most pressing concern was that, if people were looking to other sources of information that they regarded as more reliable, such as letters from the front, "insider" information, foreign radio broadcasts, and rumors, then the widespread faith in the official version of events put out by the RMVP would crumble.[14]

### News from the Front

"What on earth did our poor mothers do in the 1914–18 World War—without the radio? It must have been a catastrophe." That was how one woman expressed her reliance on her radio as a source of information, propaganda, and diversion during the war in a letter she wrote to the Deutschlandsender.[15] In a war that was fought on the home front as well as at the front line, the radio offered a line of communication between them and the country's leaders.

Every day bulletins were recorded at the front and transmitted nationwide from Berlin within twenty-four hours. All sections of the community, especially veterans from World War I, were reported to be highly

---

13. A.v. S., "Verantwortlich für die Stimmung im Volk" *Nachrichtendienst der RFF* 7 (July 1942): BAP 62.03/6810:1. There were other measures, too; for example, a public information campaign was run to warn people—again, women in particular—against bruising morale among the forces by writing of the hardships at home in their letters to the front (MadR MA141/1 T175/R262, roll 755663–66, 21 January 1942).

14. It became a cause for concern for the propaganda department of the RFF, which feared listeners did not realize they were tuning in to enemy propaganda. The department chief, Gertrud Kappesser, pressed the head of the radio section of the Reichspropagandaleitung for a media campaign to enlighten the public about the importance of tuning in only to German civilian programs ("Durchsage kameradschaftlicher oder privater Nachrichten über verschiedene Sender," letter from the radio department, *Rundfunkkommandostelle* to *Abwehrbeauftragten Oberregierungsrat* Meyer, 10 January 1941, BAP 50.01/24:68).

15. Aenne Schilp aus Wiesbaden, o.J. BAK R55/1254: n.p.

interested in and motivated by these *Frontberichte,* but there are conflicting reports about just how popular the programs were with women. An
SD report in April 1940 noted that relatively few women in comparison to
men listened to them, particularly if they had relations at the front,
because they were too nervous about what they might hear.[16] Yet there are
other reports which record that the whole population was "literally hang-
ing on the radio's every word" and that radio had produced "a spiritual
bond between home and front as never before," thanks to the immediacy
of its news transmission.[17] Filmed reports came back only once a week,
although what they lacked in immediacy they gained in giving a clearer
overall impression of the week's events. Radio soon endeavored to match
this with a Sunday summary of the week's *Frontberichte,* which proved
particularly popular with the rural population, who appreciated the
opportunity to catch up on the week's events.[18]

Ninety percent of women questioned tuned in at least once a day to
the news and programs such as "Betrachtungen zur politischen Lage"
(Observations on the Political Situation) and "Zeitspiegel" (Mirror of the
Times). Hans Fritzsche's "Zeitungs- und Rundfunkschau" (Press and
Radio Review) attracted an especially loyal and enthusiastic female audience.[19] This large female audience was catered to specifically by the regular inclusion of interviews with women and reports about women's experiences carried out by the Frauenfunk. Collaboration of this sort between
the Frauenfunk and "mainstream" current affairs programs was introduced for the first time during the war as a way of keeping up morale on
the home front. Editors would run stories that emphasized efficient distribution of supplies or the safe return of German prisoners of war, for example, with their female listeners especially in mind. In 1943 *Gauleiter* Dr.
Jung of the Saar, confessed in the *Völkischer Beobachter* that through their
participation in the war effort women had earned the right to know what
was happening in the field (Tidl 1984, 42). Yet there were reports through-

16. MadR IfZ MA441/1 T175/R258, roll 751168, 3, April 1940.
17. MadR IfZ MA441/1 T175/R259, roll 751566, 23 May 1940.
18. BAK R34/273 121, 9 August 1941.
19. Hans Fritzsche of the DNVP had become the new head of the news agency, Der
drahtloser Dienst, in 1933, appointed to ensure that no news unfavorable to the government
ever reached the transmitters. On 1 May 1933 the Drahtloser Dienst was subsumed under the
press department of the RMVP. Fritzsche joined the NSDAP and became a valued propagandist. In 1938 he took charge of the press department and introduced his polemical radio
and press review on the radio. During the war he was one of the most well-known and popular voices on radio, with his almost daily reports about events at the front in his program, "Es
spricht Hans Fritzsche" (Hans Fritzsche Speaks). Goebbels recognized his talents and
appointed him head of radio in November 1942 and put him in charge of all political programming (Groth 1980, 42–50). See also DKD, 1 February 1940, BAP 50.01/16:26.

out the war of women complaining that the news was often cut short to make room for sports coverage and that there were too few interesting talks or advice programs broadcast on Sundays, the only day when most women really had time to devote to attentive listening.[20]

Interest in radio news in the early years of the war was generally proportional to the level of military activity in the field, until the war became so all pervasive that many people left their radios on constantly so as not to miss any important announcements, although, as the war dragged on and turned against Germany, the SD began to report that people were no longer as interested in news programs, often only tuning in for the headlines just to check that there were no major new developments.[21]

As early as the winter of 1941–42, however, there was evidence that one group of people was being driven away from radio—the bereaved. The dominance of light, cheerful music, designed to keep spirits up, was not balanced by any sort of program that honored the fallen or their families. The SD report urged that the radio "lead these mourners back into the active community."[22] The official Party magazine for women, the *NS Frauen-Warte,* turned its attention to this problem in an address to women who claimed they could no longer bear to hear news of the war since their loss. The author of the piece, Käte Reiners, tried to reassure her readers that she and the Party understood the pain of loss and desire to retreat from the war when the fanfares sounded for another report of German victory on some distant front:

> So you turn off your radio set, deeply affected by the war, which after all is often so alien to us women. You can't watch the newsreels any more, or read the papers, you don't want to hear any more about all of that. You live in the past, thinking that the present has nothing more to offer you. And nobody would chide you for that, you who have made the ultimate sacrifice. Or would they? (1942–43, 3)

But, in turning their backs on the war, Reiners argued, they were being disrespectful to the wishes of their dead loved ones:

> If your sons and husbands could still speak to you, they would demand of you: That which I died for, you must live for. For I fought

20. "Empfangsspiegel," report from Gertrud Kappesser, 2 May 1944, to the head radio office at the RPL: BAP 50.01/854:7. See also "Vertrauliche Information für die Presse," 7 May 1940; cited in von Gersdorff 1969, 129.

21. MadR IfZ MA441/1 T175/R259, roll 752117, 5 August 1940. This is a symptom of the withdrawal into inner life described by Schäfer 1981, 153–60.

22. MadR MA141/1 T175/R262, roll 755342–43, 27 November 1941.

for Germany, and to me you were Germany, you, dearest wife and you, my blossoming children. I fell, so that you could live, so that your home and hearth would not be destroyed by wild Russian hordes, because I knew that Germany will live on in our children. If you now do not live consciously and joyfully for Germany, my sacrifice will have been in vain.

Having put words into the mouths of the dead the author went on to invoke the mystical power of collective belief in the inevitable German victory. A woman's duty to listen to the radio despite the pain was compared to a soldier's duty to fight to the end in the field:

There are forces which we cannot measure or even conceive of, but which have their effect. Just as a mother can cure her sick baby by giving it all her caring and loving thoughts, invisible forces are generated by the joy and conviction which stream out of the nation when it listens to a special announcement, forces which don't just help our soldiers and the nation itself, but which also pulsate through our *Führer* and give him time and again this tremendous power and confidence in victory.

With time it became impossible to ignore the fate of bereaved mothers. It was, for example, the center point of the Mother's Day radio coverage in 1944, in particular, the speech given by Gertrud Scholtz-Klink (1944, 2), who drew a connection between the pain of childbirth and the pain of losing that child, in that all was suffered for the greater good of the Fatherland.

## Home Front / Front Line: Bridging the Divide

If people on the home front were hungry for news from the front line, those fighting wanted to be reminded of home, and some programs catered specifically to soldiers and medical teams serving at the front. One such was "Blinkfeuer Heimat" (Signal Homeland), a shortwave program that transmitted family greetings from Germany to men serving abroad; another, broadcast from Leipzig, was "Das sind Wir" (That's Us), a light entertainment program that represented the "inner front." Another mixture of messages and music from the home front, "Gruß aus der Heimat" (Greetings from the Homeland), was popular enough when it first appeared but, when rescheduled to an afternoon slot with a redesigned format, soon began attracting complaints, generally of the nature that it was too sentimental and coy. Its presenter, Grete Schmidt, was the target of a lot of criticism which found her too smug and prone to sentimentality.[23] A later program, "Über Land und Meer" (Over Land and Sea), put out twice weekly on Sunday and Wednesday evenings by the Deutschlandsender, tried to avoid such complaints by concentrating on descriptions of German landscape and culture and interviews with personalities from public life.[24] Sometimes the mere knowledge that a distant loved one would be listening to the same program was a source of comfort, as one woman explained in a letter to the RRG, praising the weekly "Deutsches Volkskonzert":

> We can hardly wait for the moment when those wonderful old songs sound in the "German National Concert." Thank you above all for "In Our Youth" which was sung so clearly and passionately. It is my husband's favourite song, and even though we can't hear it together as he is far away, the radio binds us together with this song. It's always nice to hear the song of the brave little soldier's wife, too.[25]

Many "brave little soldiers' wives" tuned in to the request program "Wunschkonzert," introduced by Heinz Goedecke and Edith Annuske, which was the most popular program of the war, billed as a *Zauberbrücke der Grüßen,* a magical bridge of greetings between home and front.[26] Other programs were designed to reunite families on the air, such as the 1942 series from Vienna, "Mein Sohn, ich möchte Dir sagen . . ." (My Son, I Want to Tell You . . . ), which gave women the opportunity to talk directly to their soldier sons. The first program featured ten women who could be held up as model mothers in the Nazi state: between them they had ninety-three children, sixty-two of whom were serving at the front.[27] There were similar relay broadcasts to mark special days in the Nazi calendar, including Mothers' Day,[28] but Christmas was the favorite time for such programs. "Die Weihnachtsringsendung" became an annual event which exchanged messages between women in the studio in Berlin and serving men all around the world. In his Christmas address to the nation in 1942

23. MadR IfZ MA441/1 T175/R260, roll 752796, 18 November 1940.
24. BAK R34/72 DKD 193, 21 August 1943.
25. "Stimmen zum Volkskonzert," DKD 105, 22 July 1941, BAK R34/272.
26. Much was made about a woman who claimed to have found the brother she thought had fallen at the front through the "Wunschkonzert" (DKD 137, 28 August 1941, BAK R34/274).
27. DKD 21 January 1942, BAK R34/567.
28. MadR IfZ MA441/1 T175/R261, roll 753921, 26 May 1941.

Goebbels sang the praises of the technology that fulfilled "the yearning of millions to speak through the ether to their loved ones abroad."[29]

One of the more unusual examples of these link-ups between women at home and men at the front was a number of marriages conducted over the airwaves. The "Kameradschaftsdienst" (Comrades Service) was a daily early morning program 5:00 to 6:00 A.M., which again relayed personal messages (vetted by the party for political and racial suitability) to servicemen in the field. To mark the five hundredth program, twelve brides, wearing wedding dresses and carrying bouquets of lilies, came to the Haus des Rundfunks in Berlin to be married, although the bridegrooms were still hundreds of miles away at the front. As the "beaming brides" and "courageous soldiers" said "I do" into the microphone, the listeners were reminded that everyone had their part to play in "this fateful battle" and that marriage, as "the living source of regeneration," was "a service to Germany in eternity."[30]

## Radio Warfare and Resistance

Radio was the most important weapon of psychological warfare, both at home and abroad. As countries were conquered, so the Germans appropriated their radio stations until the airwaves of most of Europe were under their control. Gradually, German language services were cut back as more priority was given to international propaganda (Soley 1989, 1–22). Even before the war there had been broadcasts to spread the fascist message throughout the world—as far afield as the Americas, Africa, and Asia. Women's programs for foreign consumption began on shortwave in 1938, designed for both German listeners living abroad and for non-German women. Monthly directives were issued from the RFF naming the topics to be covered on both national and international programs.[31] These latter programs came under the supervision of Eva Kuhn, the representative for women's and children's radio at the Deutsche Kurzwellensender. As with the domestic output, they concentrated on describing the work of the women's party organizations and the cooperation of German women in the war effort but were tailored according to the presumed tastes of the destination audience. In North America, for example, women could tune in once a week to "Jane and Janet's Weekly Chat" or "Through a

---

29. "Die allgegenwärtige Liebe: Die Weihnachtsringsendung des Großdeutschen Rundfunks!" DKD 299, 22 December 1942, BAK R34/297.

30. "Zum ersten Male: Eheschliessungen um 5 Uhr früh." The program was produced by a Frau von Clausbruch (DKD 87, 1 May 1941, BAK R34/271).

31. Letter from Gertrud Kappesser, head of the radio department in the press/propaganda office in the RFF, to Radio Head Office, RPL, Berlin, 2 May 1944, BAP 50.01/854:7.

Woman's Eyes." South Americans were offered "Plauderei von Ipina und Lina." Southeast Asia and the Far East also had special women's programs, but there was no such service for Africa. Once again the women's service was understood to strike right at the heart of the family, thus achieving disproportionate influence.

During the war those at home were kept informed about the victories of the German army (they were kept in the dark about the defeats, especially in the early stages of the fighting), about the "lies" of foreign propaganda, and were treated to morale-boosting entertainment. But, when distrust with domestically produced information set in, civilians began tuning in to alternatives, including the military stations, where the information was felt to be more reliable. There was also the option, albeit a risky one, of tuning into foreign stations. The Volksempfänger were deliberately limited in their receptive range so that people could not tune in to foreign broadcasts, although it was possible to add attachments to enhance their range, and radio magazines in Germany regularly printed foreign program details until 1939.[32] Although it became a criminal offense to listen to foreign broadcasts when the war broke out, there is evidence that many people still thought the risk worthwhile, especially after 1940, when cutbacks in regional transmissions encouraged listeners to find an alternative to the national program on their dials.[33]

The propaganda programs broadcast to Germany by the British Broadcasting Corporation (BBC) began four weeks into the war, on 27 September 1939. It was not a continual signal but, instead, an intermittent series of fifteen- to twenty-minute programs accounting for up to four hours in every twenty-four and aimed at different times at different social

---

32. The *Deutsche Radio-Illustrierte,* with its circulation in 1937 of over one million, carried the schedules from over thirty countries alongside the eleven German stations. The *Europa Stunde,* naturally enough, specialized in this service, with its listings for some sixty foreign stations, not to mention the frequencies for a further eighty. Blaupunkt unveiled a new receiver designed for picking up these foreign programs at the Radio Exhibition in 1937 (Übersee-Empfänger). In fact, almost all foreign newspapers and journals, with the exception of socialist and communist papers or individual issues containing anti-German sentiments, were available in at least the larger cities. Radio stations themselves also exchanged programs with their counterparts abroad, especially the United States (Schäfer 1981, 127).

33. Goebbels demanded the press give prominent coverage of offenders receiving harsh penalties and give no publicity to cases in which the sentence was less than four years (DKD, 11 January 1940, BAP 50.01/16: 8). Grunberger (1971, 113–14) cites a case in which a woman denounced her husband for listening to Radio Moscow and for refusing to father any more children, for which crimes he was fired from his job as a teacher and imprisoned. In another case a woman who thought she had lost her son on the Russian front was told by a neighbor who had heard his name read out on a POW list on Radio Moscow that he was still alive. The woman nevertheless denounced her well-meaning neighbor for tuning in to enemy broadcasts.

groups, including farmers, manual workers, the middle classes, the armed forces, and women. Alongside Allied reports about the fortunes of the war, accounts of life in Britain, and commentaries by German, American, and British luminaries, one of the most popular formats was the light-hearted character monologues, such as a long-running series featuring the patter of a Berlin waitress as performed by cabaret artist Annemarie Haase, or the fictional letters home of private Adolf Hinschal or the "over-heard converzations" of "Kurt and Willi," a small-time propaganda official and his schoolteacher friend, as they sat in a café on Potsdamer Platz and exchanged facetious antigovernment banter (Slattery 1992). Significantly, the BBC did not use information about the extermination camps nor call for armed resistance.

Radio was also a weapon in the hands of German antifascists, although the opportunities for effective oppositional radio were, of course, hugely restricted. The experience of the workers' radio movement was an important asset in the work of the left-wing resistance movement, training people in the use of Morse code, for example. One of the more successful operations was organized by some of the German socialists and communists who had gone into exile in the Soviet Union. German-language programs had been broadcast from Moscow since November 1929 but had first increased the intensity of their propaganda offensive during the Spanish Civil War, cooling off again for the duration of the Hitler-Stalin pact, when the two state radio companies even exchanged program material, and going on the offensive again thereafter.[34] Though reliable listening figures for resistance and enemy radio stations are obviously not available, it is clear, not least from the inclusion of programs which addressed them exclusively, that many of those who took the risk to tune in to these broadcasts in Germany were women. One such broadcast was "Nach der Kesselschlacht," transmitted twelve months after the battle of Stalingrad, which opened with the following words:

> Women and girls in the homeland, German mothers! I am a long way from you if we count the miles, but I feel with you and share your suffering, because we are concerned about one and the same thing—Germany. All the things that you can only suspect, that burdens your souls and keeps you awake at night, I learn about here undistorted by "propaganda," undiluted straight from the mouths of your sons, brothers, husbands, and fathers. What they have experienced at the

34. The first major German communist transmitter had begun broadcasting from the Deutscher Freiheitssender 29.8 just outside Madrid in January 1927. Franco's victory in 1939 forced it to transfer operations to Moscow, from where the Deutscher Volkssender began transmissions on 10 September 1941.

front is the utmost hellish suffering, the most terrible destruction, and utter horror. (Zinna 1975, 36–40)

While the message is different, there is a remarkable degree of similarity in style to the propaganda coming out of Germany, including the appeal to women as mothers, sisters, wives, rather than as individuals separate from their relationship to their men and the subordination of all other ideals to that of *Heimat,* of Germany. Though such patriotic language was, at least in part, a product of the wartime mentality of Germans in enforced exile, longing for a return to a homeland free of fascism, such an appeal is also born of the need to heighten the emotional impact and the need to talk to women in terms to which they were accustomed. To ask women to take on board a new assertion of their individual responsibility and political effectiveness at the same time as demanding they reject all the information that they had been fed by the government and its various agencies was to jeopardize the immediate aims of the exercise. Despite the similarities in terms of style and language, the exiles were, of course, concerned with ridiculing and challenging the domestic propaganda, with its distortion of events and the glorification of sacrifice for the Fatherland:

> "Proud to mourn"? What morbid mockery! What mother, what wife, what bride could feel pride seeing her loved one destroyed so senselessly and so needlessly? Senseless and needless, because Hitler's plundering war in which he has led the men of Germany into far flung territories is already lost. (38)

But the most important function was to encourage and activate opposition and resistance. The program concluded with the following call to the women of Germany:

> Listeners, you must help where you still can. You must save what can still be saved. Write to your husbands—if they love you, they will listen to you. Let them know that there is only one way left to save themselves and their family—to lay down their arms, to join "Free Germany," to fight against Hitler, to bring his defeat and the end of the war! (39–40)

There was more that women could do than just alert their menfolk to the realities of the situation or encourage them to join the opposition. If they had been brought in to work for the armaments industry, for example, they could be urged to go on a work slow or even to give up their positions for the greater good. Transmitters based in the Soviet Union often turned their attention to these women. One such broadcast went out from the Kuibyschev station on 6 May 1942:

> Women in the arms factories, listen to us! You stand day after day at the work bench, tired and exhausted by the demands of the slave-drivers. I know what goes on in your minds a hundred times a day, . . . that there has to be an end to all this misery! Have you ever thought that your loved ones might be torn limb from limb at the front? . . . Think about this, and remember the example of the German munitions workers in 1918. Consider how their actions and determination did so much to bring about an end to that war! (cited in Ostrogorski 1970, 76)

Again, the appeal is made to women on an emotional, personal level. Little time is wasted on explaining why the fascist war effort was so unjust or what the arguments were for supporting the Soviet alternative. Women are spoken to only in terms of their concern for the members of their family; the war is spoken of only in terms of the loss of their loved ones.

It is difficult to estimate the listening figures for such programs for obvious reasons—during the war listening to foreign broadcasts was by necessity a secret activity, and after the war everybody claimed to have committed this act of "resistance"—but reports by refugees, POWs, neutral diplomats, and the German section of the BBC's *Survey of European Audiences,* indicate that there was a not inconsiderable audience tuning in as regularly as possible to these programs. The intent of the broadcasts was to depress the enemy, to try to destroy social cohesion by setting one section of society against the other, to encourage sabotage and passive resistance, and to offer a vision of hope for the future. Again, the effects of these broadcasts is difficult to gauge, but, since the population was already depressed and divided and the call to resistance was falling on already converted ears, success most probably lay in providing a sense of solidarity with the outside world, although utopian visions of a better future probably sounded like so many optimistic but empty promises.

## Mobilization

The ideological confusion in relation to women was at its most obvious in the indecisiveness and contention surrounding the possible mobilization of the latent female labor force. The war effort required it, but the Party was against it in principle (Mason 1976, 15–24). Only by regarding war work as an extension of the duties of a mother to protect her family, of a wife to support her husband at the front, and of a National Socialist woman to be willing to make sacrifices for her country could the appeal to women as workers be made at all.

When the war first began, a directive had been issued to the media from the Labor Ministry urging restraint in the handling of the issue of women's work. This was despite the 1935 legislation that had decreed that every German man and, for the first time, every woman was duty bound to serve in the defense of the nation in time of war.[35] Nevertheless, at this time the seven million women already working in white- and blue-collar jobs constituted about a third of the labor force. Even then all information on women's work in armaments factories was to follow strict guidelines, stressing the voluntary nature of the work and that the work would not be overdemanding for the female frame. (While there is evidence to suggest that many women were overworked, there were also innovative efforts to improve working conditions in many workplaces because of the influx of women workers.)[36] While there was still a plentiful supply of male labor, no risks were to be taken in upsetting the propagandistic foundations laid by years of insisting on the primary role of women as being situated in the home.[37] However, despite the ideological rhetoric about the threat to the natural order and the purity of the race if women were to take on the work of men, the significant part of the reluctance on the part of ministers not directly involved with the military or industrial crisis was a fear about the potential for social discontent if women were faced with conscription into the work force. A directive was issued to the press in April 1940 to prohibit active promotion of women's war work until such time as it became absolutely necessary.[38] Meanwhile, the government relied on reforms to marriage loans, tax incentives, apprenticeships, and wage rates for women.

The change in emphasis came only when it became clear that, the early victories notwithstanding, there would not be an early end to the war. Despite the use of conscripted foreign labor from the occupied territories, by the time arms production was reaching its height in 1941, the shortage of women workers was becoming critical. Fritz Sauckel was appointed the new Plenipotentiary for Labor Conscription in March 1942, yet, even though he recognized the advantages of mobilizing the female

---

35. *Wehrgesetz,* 21 May 1935. For a detailed account of the mobilization of female labor in Germany, see Rupp 1978.

36. "Vertrauliche Information für die Presse," 7 May 1940; cited in von Gersdorff 1969, 129. See also SD-Bericht, Meldung 197, 26 June 1941; Sachse 1982, 218–41; Tröger 1984, 237–70.

37. "Anweisung an die Presse: Behandlung des Frauenarbeitseinsatzes, 21.9.39"; cited in von Gersdorff 1969, 297.

38. "Vertrauliche Information für die Presse. Behandlung des Frauenarbeitseinsatzes, *Geheim!*" 27 April 1940; cited in von Gersdorff 1969, 305.

work force, he dared not go against Hitler's explicit rejection of compulsory war service for women.[39] The one major campaign, "Frauen helfen siegen" (Women Help Win), was concerned with voluntary enlistment.

The first efforts to encourage women to help "man" the home front were made in mid-1940 by the various Party organizations. One of the initial moves in the turnabout was made within the walls of the Propaganda Ministry itself. The employment policy pursued by the RMVP was intended both as an experiment in mobilizing women for the war effort and as a propaganda event in its own right. It was a version in microcosm of what would happen in all sorts of concerns throughout the country.

At first the employment policy in government departments had clearly favored male workers.[40] This arrangement did not change significantly until 1942, when the RMVP began to replace a large part of its male work force with women to test the practicality of a policy that would release more men for the front and for the arms industry and to provide an example to other firms and organizations. Regulations that had prevented women from taking certain jobs, especially in political areas, were lifted. The men who gave up their jobs in this campaign, some 36 percent of the original work force, were guaranteed to return to their jobs in the ministry after the war, so many women's appointments and promotions were by temporary contract.[41] Altogether 264 male workers were replaced, leaving the ministry employing 450 men and 950 women.[42] The men who stayed on were mostly either too old or frail to be of use to the military or heavy industry, but 182 who were fit for military service remained in posts considered unsuitable for women.[43] Nevertheless,

---

39. "Mitteilungen des Beauftragten für den Vierjahresplan," 6–7; cited in von Gersdorff 1969, 54.

40. In 1935 the RRK had decided there was too high a proportion of female employees, and future posts were filled as far as possible by men; remaining female office workers were uniformly demoted to the position of shorthand secretaries. Letter from Schrieber to the RRK, 30 August 1935, BAK R56I 69:37–43.

41. Secretary of State Leopold Gutterer to Dr. Flügel, head of personnel, Berlin, 20 January 1942, BAK R55/18:112; also minutes of a meeting chaired by Gutterer on 16 January 1942, BAK R55/18:108, 271.

42. Before the war the RMVP had employed about 300 *Beamten,* 480 *Angestellten* (55 percent men), and 200 *ArbeiterInnen* (70 percent men). Increased propaganda activity in wartime led to an increase in the work force by some 40 percent, largely male *Angestellten,* engaged in monitoring services, secret radio transmissions, censorship, translation of enemy propaganda, etc. With the campaign to free men for the front, the proportion of male *Angestellten* fell from 90 percent to 20 percent, *Arbeiter* from 65 percent to 20 percent. The proportion of male *Beamte* remained little changed (BAK R55/18:8; also BAK R55/18:53–56. Director of propaganda to Flügel, 19 January 1942).

43. Flügel to Goebbels, 30 April 1942, BAK R55/18:209. Such posts included those that involved liaising with the military or passing on orders, for example, or those involving

women with suitable credentials could be engaged to do sensitive work such as monitoring foreign broadcasts, for example.[44] The posts were not advertised publicly in newspapers, appointments being made internally via regional party organizations, including the NSF. Women who were already employed elsewhere could not be considered, because one of the main objects of the exercise was the propaganda value of showing that the latent female labor force could be effectively mobilized.[45]

Heads of departments complained that finding suitable replacements was not as easy as the personnel department seemed to suppose.[46] Although there was a large reserve of potentially employable women, the policy that had long disadvantaged women in the employment market meant there was a lack of women with relevant experience. State support for the families of men serving at the front was generous enough for there not to be the same sort of financial imperative to work as there had been for many women during World War I. Moreover, attracting women into the work force after years of telling them their place was in the home was ideologically problematic. Representatives of the women's organizations in Berlin saw the solution in a propaganda campaign to persuade women of their patriotic duty and to advertise the "inner satisfaction" that employment could bring. Part-time work was also considered a practical solution, especially for women with families, though the campaign was not directed at mothers of children under fourteen years of age. At the same time, an education program was to be instigated by the army to deter soldiers from dissuading their wives to take up war work.[47]

Having put its own house in order, the main task of the RMVP was the organization of propaganda campaigns to attract women into war work nationwide. It was the heavy losses on the Eastern front in 1943 and the increasing toll of the bombing of German production centers that

---

censorship decisions, because of the prejudice that "even after training women are not capable of making political decisions" (head of the editorial staff to Flügel, 13 May 1942, BAK R55/18:98; see also BAK R55/18:53–56, 67, 101).

44. "Über den Fraueneinsatz im RMVP—eine Führerinformation vom Leiter Personal," 6 February 1942, BAK R55/18:141–42. See also BAK R55/18:107. The political and racial background of all new employees had to be vetted by the Party or by the Gestapo (a two- to four-month process) and on appointment were required to swear a vow of allegiance to the Führer and to sign an oath of confidentiality. Of some 700 women who declared themselves available for work through the Party organizations, only some 160 were deemed suitable for work in the Ministry ("Führerinformation," February 1942, BAK R55/18:159–60).

45. Gutterer to Flügel, 22 and 30 January 1942, BAK R55/18:113, 127.

46. Editorial Department to Flügel, 17 April 1942, BAK R55/18:96.

47. Minutes of a meeting between the head of the NSF Berlin, Rickentscher, the head of the women students' organization in Berlin, Trück, and a representative of the labor office, Gürteler (19 January 1942, BAK R55/18:110–11).

finally motivated a serious propaganda effort to draw women into the war effort. On 27 January 1943 it was decreed that all healthy women between the ages of seventeen and forty-five register their availability for the defense of the nation. Only mothers with one child under six or two under fourteen were exempted. In 1944 Goebbels, in his new capacity as Plenipotentiary for Total War, raised the upper age limit to fifty to cover the intensified call-up of civilians into the army, and the papers were full of advertisements urging women to perform their national duty. At first it was the hundreds of thousands of women who had been working before the war who were most easily attracted back into the work force. The women already working in the factories were there out of financial necessity. This new influx therefore hit the middle classes, which gave rise to increasingly bitter complaints that they were shouldering a disproportionate amount of the burden of war work, women from the "better classes" successfully finding convenient excuses to evade volunteering.[48]

The new policy, however, was not enforced with any vigor, nor was there a consistent or wholehearted propaganda campaign to back it up. Although the primary vehicle for this campain was a rather low-key affair run by the internal party organizations, the prevarication about mobilization policy is reflected in the radio schedules. There was no continuous, coherent, or comprehensive campaign to attract women into the factories even during the final years of the war, and there was a corresponding lack of recognition for the listening needs of those women who *were* employed outside the home. Of 101 current affairs programs broadcast in 1943, only 2 short series, broadcast in the autumn, were devoted exclusively to women's experience during the war—"Die deutsche Frau im Kriege" (The German Woman at War) and "Schaffende Frauen in Männerberufen" (Women in Men's Jobs); otherwise, output continued in much the same vein as before.[49] None of the strictly political programs were devoted to specifically female concerns, although there were occasionally interviews conducted under the auspices of the "Zeitspiegel," for example, with women who had volunteered to work in munitions factories or who were otherwise contributing to the war effort in paid employment.[50]

48. MadR MA141/1 T175/R262, roll 756160, 12 March 1942. For a discussion of the class differences in the mobilization propaganda in America, see Honey 1983, 672–87.

49. Performance report of the Broadcasting Office of the NSDAP in Radio Head Office for 1943, Berlin, 18 February 1944, BAK NS26/1178:111–25. (One innovation was a television play transmitted on Mother's Day, 17 May 1943, "Was Mutter schafft" [What Mother Does]).

50. "Der "Zeitspiegel" im Monat März" DKD 74, 29 March 1943, BAK R34/284. Some items raised objections from those sections of the audience who recognized and rejected the clash of ideological principle and pragmatism, as in the following extract from a listener's letter to the Deutschlandsender in 1943: "Yesterday evening in the propaganda pro-

Generally, though, the radio was used far more concertedly in direct-ing women as housewives as to their patriotic duty as housewives and con-sumers. Therefore, despite the increasing numbers of women working out-side the home, the radio schedules continued to reflect the dominant idea that women's programs should be broadcast during the morning and early afternoon and that evening programs need not take the presence of women expressly into account. On the other hand, there were many complaints that current affairs programs such as the "Frontberichte" and "Aus dem Zeitgeschehen" were broadcast at impossible times for workers both in factories and on farms. Among the letters sent to the head of radio in 1943 were several complaints about the transmission time of the popular cur-rent affairs program, "Zeitspiegel." Its early evening slot prevented many people, especially workers and parents of young children, from listening to it.[51] A fifteen-minute slot following the "Zeitspiegel" was indeed often given over to women's matters in 1944, but still the emphasis was on a woman's maternal role, with programs such as "Die gesundheitliche Betreuung der Kinder im Kriege" (Caring for Children's Health in Wartime) and "Brauchtum zwischen Mutter und Kind" (Traditions between Mother and Child).[52] In June of that year a new woman's hour, called "Der Frauenspiegel" (Mirror on Women), was introduced into the daytime schedules at 11:30 A.M.[53] By this time there were 14.5 million women working, three-fifths of the wartime labor force.

## Summary

There was obviously a discrepancy between the ideology of motherhood and the real-life experience of millions of women, which the propaganda patched over rather faint-heartedly in the contention that women's recruit-ment into the German labor force was no displacement from their rightful and natural place in the home, for Germany itself was their home: "The maxim 'a woman's place is in the home' is valid as long as 'the home' is understood to include all that which the maternal spirit encompasses. That

---

gram 'Women in the War Effort,' you informed your astonished listeners, male and female, that somewhere in Germany, a Frau Holsterkamp goes to work for nine hours a day, although she has a sick husband and three children at home! Do you not think that this woman would better serve her Fatherland if she did not neglect her family, but cared for her husband and three children? A woman who works despite all this belongs in the madhouse. You would achieve more respect for the working woman if you would use or make up more sensible examples. Heil Hitler!" (BAK R55/533:118).

51. See listeners' letters to the RMVP collected in BAK R55/532 and BAP 50.01/636:16–18.

52. DKD 63, 96, 107, 113, 1944, BAK R34/338.

53. DKD 128, 6 June 1944, BAK R34/293.

way, we women can rejoice in the recognition that our home is Germany, wherever we are needed!" (Köhler-Irrgang 1940, 235).

It was understood that after the war the boundaries of what constituted the home for women would once again be drawn much more tightly in. The experience of the workplace, indeed, would give wives an empathetic understanding of the strains and stresses of a hard day's work and make them want to treat their husbands all the more respectfully and tenderly, as the *Völkischer Beobachter* put it:

> A woman doesn't want to drive the worker from his job; when he comes back, she will return to his side and to her natural role; she will go back to being a housewife and mother, and when her husband returns home after a hard day's work, he will be received with loving understanding. She too, will have worked during hard times and will know that it is not always easy.[54]

But reality never conformed to the rhetorical visions of the propagandists. Broadly speaking, civil society, though galvanized by the consequences of a male-directed politics, had been feminized in its everyday reality in the absence of men, while women moved into traditionally male roles in the workplace and as heads of households. The clear gendered distinction between public and private was blurred by a total war, in which the home front increasingly became the front line. In war the fascist leaders would claim again and again that it was the essence of manhood to fight and the nature of womanhood to heal the fighters' wounds, but wartime brought with it contradictions and blurrings of this ideological divide. Military imagery was grafted onto the standard images of motherhood.[55] Women's struggles for the Fatherland were fought on the battleground of childbirth, where distinguished service was rewarded with the Motherhood Cross, refusal to bear offspring was considered desertion, and images of women as the givers and protectors of life recycled in the campaigns to persuade women to support a war that was killing people in the thousands.

---

54. "Der Weg vom Kochherd an die Drehbank," *Völkischer Beobachler* (VB), 2 August 1940; quoted in Tidl 1984, 71.

55. Hitler's speeches to women were loaded with such military imagery—for example, "Women have their own battlefield. With every child that she brings into the world for the nation, she fights her battle for the nation" ("Der Führer spricht zu den deutschen Frauen," *NS Frauen-Warte* 8 [1935–36]: 238).

# Part 3
# Experts on the Air

# CHAPTER 6

# The Mouthpiece of Modernity

Radio was one of a whole variety of new technological appliances that revolutionized women's experience in the home in the early twentieth century, and its persuasive powers were enlisted to attract women to the delights of other consumer goods.[1] Its programs encouraged the housewife to learn the principles of the market and the factory, the mother to listen to the advice of invisible experts. Both occupations were upgraded by reference to the terminology of modernization, rationalization, science, and technology. This chapter is concerned with the rise of the domestic expert in the early twentieth century and the exploitation of radio as a channel of mass communication for the effective propagation of prevailing wisdoms among housewives, mothers, and consumers during the Weimar Republic. The projects and implications of rationalization and domestic science in women's lives during this period have been well researched elsewhere. The purpose of the current chapter is to build on that work and to make the role of radio within these processes explicit. In particular it will examine the use of radio as a means of propagating the latest expert opinions about domestic science, the rationalization of home and body, consumerism, and consumption.[2] It will become clear in the discussion that follows just how political this apparently innocuous program matter was. Moreover, it will be seen how the concern of the program makers right from the start was

---

1. Radio as one of the technologies that transformed women's domestic environment is often absent from works on domestic technology. There is, for example, no discussion of the impact of radio on women's lives in the otherwise exhaustive account by Ruth Schwartz Cowan (1989), which nevertheless deals with other communication technologies such as the telephone and the automobile, alongside washing machines and electric stoves, etc.

2. The radio is rarely considered in this context. Nolan's examination of the discourse on the home and consumption is, for example, based on a study of the pamphlets and placards produced by the Home Economics group of the state-funded advisory board for productivity, the Reichskuratorium für Wirtschaftlichkeit (RKW), established in 1921 and the chief propagandist (1990, 549–77). My argument is that radio, too, played a not insignificant part alongside these more conventional media in channeling these ideas.

with women's negotiations of their contradictory experience of modern life.

In order to study the authoritative voice of the expert on women's radio in Weimar, this chapter will take its examples from programs broadcast by the sole national broadcasting company, the Deutsche Welle. Radio was clearly one of the forces of modernization that was leading to a greater cultural uniformity between the regions and between the city and the countryside, and the introduction of a nationwide program is the key expression of this trend. The Deutsche Welle was not simply a "clearing" station, taking the best of the regional programs for nationwide broadcast, though it did this after eight in the evening, but had a clear mandate to commission and produce programs to suit its position as a channel of public education.

The overtly pedagogic nature of the Deutsche Welle is a central reason for taking it as a case for study. The programs were of a serious but popularly accessible nature, designed to reflect and promote a representative sweep of German society and culture. Moreover, in addition to simple schedule listings, which are useful in terms of a quantitative analysis but limited when it comes to a qualitative analysis, detailed synopses of many of the programs were published in the station's weekly journal, *D. W. Funk* (published under this name from October 1926 to March 1928, when it became simply *Deutsche Welle*). The collection of journals, housed at the Deutsches Rundfunkarchiv in Frankfurt am Main, is a valuable source of information about Weimar radio, not least for the historian of women's radio, for many of the articles deal with programs addressing women's issues, a distinct advantage over many of the regional radio journals, in which such issues appeared only intermittently or the content of individual programs was not discussed.

**Radio in a Rationalized World**

Industrialization and the extension of market relations into the social sphere were processes attended by a long-term challenge to established gender relations, scoring a sharper division between the realms of production and reproduction and entrenching further the already established inequalities of patriarchal society (Gerhard 1978; Arnold and Burr 1985, 144–62; Ehrenreich and English 1988, 1–32). Old patterns had been rent asunder and gave birth to a vision of new opportunities—and new insecurities. Women's ambivalent relationship to modernity has been characterized by Joan Landes:

> On the one hand, woman, like nature, provided a moral antidote to the worst abuses of civilization. [Her] virtue could offer a justification

for her necessary privatization. How else could her spirituality, innocence or purity be preserved? . . . On the other hand, woman as nature inhibited the progressive side of society and its rational reconstruction. Insofar as woman represented a backward, traditional, irrational force, she had to be controlled, contended with and contained. (1984, 21)

The "Woman Question," so often part of the public discourse of this period, was the question of women's experience in the face of these contradictions posed by the modern world. One response to the question was the advocacy of women's assimilation into the challenging and prestigious public sphere of production. The alternative was to maintain the myth of essential differences between the sexes, which described women's natural place in a home that was a sanctuary from the trials and insecurities of the world outside, providing unpaid regenerative services for the family. It was these two opposing responses, broadly defined, that delineated the public discourse about women's place and function in society and whose language informed both the shape and the substance of radio for women in the 1920s.

The language of science also permeated these debates. Science, which since the Enlightenment had been elevated as the new secular arbiter of truth, and which had once acted as a liberating force in opening up all areas of life for objective, critical investigation, was increasingly used and abused to give credence to all manner of assumptions and attitudes. Biologists, psychologists, and philosophers sought "scientific" reasons for given gender differences and claimed to find them.[3] Central to this particular discussion, however, is the invention of a new "domestic science" and "scientific motherhood," which gave to the everyday chores of housewives and mothers the respectability that came with the rub of the outside rational world and infusion with the air of modernity.

In response to the plethora of professional advice for housewives, the radio sought to be an authority on expertise, offering a guide through the latest information available. The training and examinations of home economics schools (Bridenthal 1984, 155–57) were the subject of many an afternoon broadcast on the Deutsche Welle. Some innovations and insights were undeniably important—not least the recognition that pure water and a certain level of hygiene would reduce disease. But, as the trend caught on, the label "scientifically approved" justified an assortment of often erroneous advice. It was in the interests of domestic science always to be open to new developments in research, always to be able to define

---

3. For a useful discussion of the place of scientific discourse in the debates about women's rights, see Sayers 1987, 68–91.

new tasks or redefine old ones without limit. It is a familiar insight now that time saved by the introduction of "labor-saving" appliances does not necessarily become leisure time nor productive time but, rather, is swallowed up in the pursuit of endlessly rising standards in housework (Vanek 1974, 116–20; Bereano, Bose, and Arnold 1985, 172). Dust becomes less tolerable in the age of the vacuum cleaner, washing machines encourage a weekly, rather than a monthly, wash. This is the case even in homes that have not yet acquired the appliance in question, if the higher achievable standards become considered the desirable norm—all of which was in the interests of the manufacturers of household appliances and suited the purposes of making sure women never ran out of things to do in the home.[4] In July 1931 a lighthearted program about the danger of taking the housewifely virtues to an extreme was broadcast on the Deutsche Welle. In a backlash against the spiraling standards demanded by domestic science, Margarete Weinberg pleaded for a sense of proportion:

> Love of cleanliness is certainly a worthy characteristic. But when it becomes regarded as a general virtue, there is never an end to the cleaning. You only need to open a window onto a street, and the dust is blown in. You would have to set the vacuum cleaner behind the open window to catch the dust as it entered. (1931, 272)

A scientific legitimation of housework was attractive to women across the political spectrum for reasons both pragmatic and ideological. One expression of the Woman Question was a concern about women becoming dangerously idle now that many traditional female occupations had been translated into the public sphere. Where once cleaning and laundry had been minor and occasional occupations, they were now, along with cookery, elevated to activities designed to fill the day and fulfill the woman. In response to fears that the demise of the home as a manufacturing center had created a "domestic void," scientific "evidence" was enlisted to keep women busy maintaining ever-spiraling standards.[5] The domestic void was not only a matter of too much time but also of too little knowledge.

---

4. Note that other factors besides technology affect the amount of time spent on housework—the decline of domestic service, the changing participation rates of women in waged labor, the number of children, etc. Nor did domestic technology alter the gender specialization of housework. Studies have shown that making a task easier has the effect of making it actually less likely that men share the workload with women (note that women's relationship to technology is conventionally that of user, not of designer or repairer) (Bose et al. 1984, 53–82).

5. *Domestic void* is the term used by Ehrenreich and English (1988). Note that in Max Weber's account of the Protestant work ethic, wasting time was "the first, and in principle the deadliest of sins" (1930, 158).

The commercialization of food and textile manufacture and the spread of academic medical science encroached on areas of traditional female expertise and, it has been argued, created in place of productive, knowledgeable women a deskilled and undervalued domestic labor force. The disruption of time-honored, "natural" practices, together with the scientification of domestic and mothering tasks, undermined women's faith in their instinctive abilities and in the ways of their mothers and created a willing audience for the professional expert. Following the professionalization of medicine, education, social work, and a host of other activities, housework, too, came under pressure to be regarded more seriously as an alternative profession, albeit always an unpaid one. The appliance of science to housewifery, raising its challenge and its prestige, seemed to conservatives to offer a preventative measure against demoralization and disaffection in women and so safeguard traditional gender relations and ultimately the stability of the state, while trade unionists regarded it as part of the process of modernization and improved working conditions. Meanwhile, for many women on a personal level it simply offered the chance of coping with the double burden of waged labor and domestic duties (Grossmann 1984; 1986).

In the 1920s, when radio was taking its place as another of the new machines in many of the homes across Germany, the emphasis in domestic science was infected by the spirit of rationalization that was sweeping industry at the time.[6] The rationalization of housework was promoted by various quarters for various ends, from the visionary to the pragmatic. Mary Nolan has identified the promotion of these ideas from three main quarters: industrialists hoping for reduced labor costs and easier labor relations, bourgeois feminists hoping to raise the status of housework, and social democratic trade union leaders, who accepted it along with industrial rationalization as an inevitable and desirable part of modernization (1990, 565–71). It was also promoted on the radio. The latest innovations in rationalized living were relayed to the listeners of the Deutsche Welle's Frauenfunk from public exhibitions, such as the *Heim und Technik* exhibition held in Munich in September 1929 (Pelz-Langenscheidt 1928, 434–35). In twenty-one ideal flats the exhibition displayed the latest architectural designs, installation of amenities, and money-spinning, labor-saving technology. The remit of the exhibition and of the radio programs which it influenced was to bridge the gap perceived between the advanced state of the technological infrastructure of the world at large and the backward, unreformed state of most private homes:

6. One of the most influential manuals of the period was Erna Meyer's *Der neue Haushalt: Ein Wegweiser zur wissenschaftlichen Hausführung* (1926), reprinted thirty-six times between 1926 and 1929.

In an age in which technology, industry, trade, business and transport have been completely reformed, the smallest, and yet the most important community in the state, the home, has remained untouched and unchanged. Dated work methods and old-fashioned housekeeping are often out of step with the world outside.

The overriding message was that there was no part of women's experience that could not benefit from rationalization. Further programs on similar themes included a series broadcast in March 1929, in which the latest domestic technology, results from domestic science laboratories, and the relative advantages of training given at various schools and institutes were highlighted and explained (Rengier 1929, 211). While other topics were being given more airtime by 1931, there was still an interest in the rationalization of housework. In February, for example, a program about standardization in the home was broadcast that illustrated the benefits of mass-produced, uniform household goods. Not only were such goods easier to match, replace, repair, and afford, but they facilitated rational organization in the home, especially in the kitchen.

For all its success on factory production lines, Taylorism and Fordism when applied in the home did little to increase housewives' productivity. Not only were the potential savings in an individual home on such a small scale as to be insignificant, but, where the housewife combines in her person the functions of both scientific manager and labor force, the potential for saving time and energy actually translates into a creation of new superfluous tasks. Yet few argued for the rationalization of housework to be taken to its logical conclusion—for real savings in time and labor could only be made by deprivatization and the pooling of resources.[7] As long as housework was decentralized, labor intensive, and small scale, it remained inherently "inefficient," but the German rationalization movement as a whole rejected collectivization, seeing it as a contradiction of the "spirit" of the family household.[8] Moves to rationalize and modernize the home in Germany did not seem to question the basic role of women in the home but sought to combine factory efficiency with traditional femininity (Nolan 1990, 560–61).

On a practical level, while the methods of analyzing household tasks,

---

7. For example, Charlotte Perkins Gilman in the United States, Engels and Bebel in Germany, Alexandra Kollontai in the Soviet Union, who argued that collectivization of housework was a precondition of women's emancipation (Wajcman 1991, 81–109). Collectivization of housework was a matter of contention in the SPD, broadly regarded at best as a long-term aim (Hagemann 1990, 106–14).

8. Charlotte Mühsam-Werther at the 1927 International Congress of Scientific Management; cited in Nolan 1990, 564.

streamlining them, drawing up detailed rotas, and keeping meticulous and exhaustive records of everything from housekeeping finances to the exact location of each family member's underwear might have been adopted in their entirety only by the most enthusiastic converts, the basic tenets of time management, often learned directly from the factory floor, were enormously popular and influential (Koch 1988, 89–102). For those well-to-do women who could no longer afford to pay the sorts of wages to servants to compete with office or factory work, rationalization and mechanization seemed to offer a possible solution, as it did to increasing numbers of working women facing the "double burden" of waged labor and domestic labor in the postwar years, though the relationship of working-class women, whether working or not, to domestic rationalization was complicated, as Mary Nolan describes:

> Household rationalization was both alienating and appealing. . . . It provided one way to be modern even if that meant the modern management of a traditionally defined home and family. It enabled them to be new women, even if the rationalized housewife conveyed little of the glamour usually associated with the term. (1990, 573)

The propaganda for rationalization recognized these limitations and therefore placed a greater emphasis on education than on the advertisement of new appliances. The middle-class devotees of the new science saw it as their duty to bring word of its advances and advantages to the working classes, either by community visits, introducing domestic science education, or turning to the media. But their philanthropic mission was also a vehicle for the propagation of middle-class ideals and aspirations to the working-class women who were the target of these campaigns.[9] Nevertheless, their efforts were not necessarily received suspiciously as manipulation in the working-class constituencies that they visited but could be appropriated as the chance to improve the quality of home life, and so, while the workers' radio movement might demand a redress in the class balance of such reforming programs, *Der Neue Rundfunk* could also demand that there be still more serious dedication to questions of modernizing and rationalizing the home:

> The housewife doesn't need chitchats but information about affordable innovations in household technology, practical tips about light-

---

9. The audience and agents of these practices were working- class women, while the primary beneficiaries were "husbands and children, industry and the national economy, the political party and the state." This is in contrast to the U.S. model, which very much had a middle-class orientation (Nolan 1990, 552).

ening the workload of housekeeping that don't cost anything, about the best use of food according to the lastest scientific research, about *important* developments in the fixing of prices in the grocery and merchandise markets. (Grünbaum 1927, 374)

The trade unions and the SDP recognized the importance of the private sphere as a place of relaxation and recuperation for workers facing the stress and alienation of increasingly mechanized and rationalized working lives, and they vigorously promoted a modern (urban) housing policy as a bedrock for a program for social reform. The politicization of the domestic sphere, or political activity based in housing estates, was not, however, encouraged, for fear that it would be the KPD that would benefit. The SPD tended to be suspicious of the new distractions and temptations of mass culture and of the culture of consumption, although, as Adelheid von Saldern has shown, the democratizing potential of mass consumption of carefully chosen and functional products was embraced (1990, 333–54, 374). It was working-class women who had most direct experience of rationalization in the workplace and who would benefit most from the rationalization in the home as they tried to negotiate the dual demands of waged labor and the labor of love in the home, but it was middle-class women who dictated the terms in which household expertise was discussed on air. Housework was recognized as *work* across the board, but for working women that meant another form of labor, while for the women of the middle-class housewives' unions and of the Deutsche Welle it meant a whole profession.

The insight that new working conditions in the home required a rethinking of domestic space led individual women and housewives' organizations to lobby for a social building policy that took contemporary lifestyles into account.[10] Discussing these moves on the radio was part of the campaign to foster awareness of the matter among architects, planners, and housewives alike—not that there was a uniform conception of what constituted the perfect living space, however. Differences of opinion were especially contentious when it came to the kitchen, in terms of whether it should be designed purely in terms of allowing efficiency in cooking and washing or whether it should be incorporated into the living space of the flat to facilitate child minding and to integrate the housewife more closely into the life of the family. In 1930 the question of the built environment was given extensive coverage in a series of programs analyz-

10. Two and a half million flats were built between 1919 and 1932, and by 1930 nine million Germans lived in new flats, most of which were beyond the means of the working class (Saldern 1990, 334–36). For a discussion about the meaning of gendered space in home designs, see Wajcman 1991, 110–36.

ing the influence women could exert on architectural design and housing policy (F. R. 1930, 556). Kitchens in particular came under close scrutiny for maximizing efficiency. The fitted Frankfurter Küche, designed by Grete Schütte-Lihotzky in 1926, became a byword for the ultimate in functional domestic design, though it became a reality for relatively few. In fact, renovation schemes for older buildings in cities such as Hamburg were guided by more general principles of modernization and public health than of maximizing efficiency (Hagemann 1990, 101, 114–17; Lihotzky 1994). In these programs, however, the Frauenfunk declared that the smaller flats of the public housing developments of the early 1920s, built for reasons of economy, were now recognized as ideally suited to the demands of the modern-minded middle-class housewife, embedded in a nuclear family, who could no longer call on the support of domestic servants or whose time for domestic chores was restricted by other employment outside the home (Behme 1928, 405).

For most women the latest designs were unobtainable, so old methods had to be rationalized as best they could as women negotiated their lives around the prevailing ideology and the limits of the possible. Radio, too, was part of this new ordering of spatial relations, in the sense that, in offering entertainment and diversion within the haven of the home (whether or not the home was a Bauhaus design) and in providing a new familial focus, it was part of the general move "away from the collective occupation of exterior space towards a family grouping which had withdrawn to interior space" (Moores 1988, 25).

Although Berlin, the great modern metropolis, looms large in received images of Weimar modernity and the modernized home, the contradictions and challenges of modernization and rationalization reached far and wide, and this, again, was reflected in the schedules of the Deutsche Welle. The radio was seen as offering a solution to one of the expressions of the crisis of modernity, the antagonism between the city, especially Berlin, and the provinces. It was hoped that a direct form of communication such as radio, with its disregard for boundaries, physical or social, would help bridge the gap and ameliorate the sense of alienation of one from the other. Women were addressed specifically in this respect, in that the economic relation between city and farm was seen as one of the potential meeting points, namely in the relationship between the country women as producer and the city woman as consumer. Programs on the radio optimistically suggested that "the alienation between metropolitan and country women" could be ameliorated if "the one group had the chance to listen to the other" (Brix 1930b, 35). In reality, however, much of this communication was only one-way. There was a tendency among the program makers, based in the city, to believe the country folk hankered after the city and all it had to offer in the way of art and culture, excitement and intrigue, but also in know-how and authority. This attitude extended into women's affairs, as this passage from an article by Alice Fliegel shows:

> The artistic events which are a matter of course for us metropolitan women, are sorely missed by rural women. It represents an enormous enrichment of their lives that they can now partake of those events. . . . they have heard much of importance from the mouths of women who have gained a certain authority in questions of education and employment thanks to their life and work in the city. (1927b)

Despite the arrogance of some city-dwelling broadcasters, it is undeniable that radio provided a matchless opportunity to broaden people's horizons and enabled them to participate at some level in events and debates from which they would normally be excluded. It also provided women with the latest guidelines for economical and scientific housekeeping in rural households and was enlisted to help rationalize the activities of the farmer's wife, whose duties ranged beyond housework to milking, feeding, garden husbandry, and often also working in the fields (Theurer 1930, 648; Wendelmuth 1930, 545). In addition to broadcasting information programs, the radio was used to advertise courses and training opportunities organized either by relevant institutions or by women themselves. It is a coincidence, perhaps, but nonetheless worth noting that it was in the year public broadcasting began in Germany that women in rural occupations were given the opportunity to study for official qualifications in rural domestic science (legislation passed on 12 January 1923) and that the broadcasters' cooperation was enlisted to further public awareness of the new opportunities (Weigel 1926, 225–27; Delius 1927, 299–301).

Radio performed a function not only in the reorientation of domestic space and in disseminating information about working patterns but also in providing the rhythm for those practices. Women were exhorted to *rationalize* their listening in order to maximize its benefits (Honekamp 1930, 97). The division of the daily "flow" of broadcasting into discrete and specific segments was an important development in the history of radio and one that was an expression of a much wider historical process—the social organization of time (Adam 1990; Lash and Urry 1994, 223–36). Industrialization had brought with it a radical reorganization of time with the synchronization of labor in the factory process and the division of the day, week, and year into rhythms of work and leisure. Indeed, E. P. Thompson (1967), drawing on Marx, argued that the orientation to time, which superseded an orientation to task, was the key characteristic of industrial capitalist societies.

In addition to underscoring the social organization of time, the radio was involved in "the domestication of standard national time" (Moores 1988, 38). The constant time checks and the precise regularity and repetition of the daily and weekly schedules were more than an exercise in time keeping; they were bringing the precision and standardization of the modern industrial world into the home itself. Clocks and watches had started to become more common in the early nineteenth century, and it was among the upper classes that consciousness of time was first particularly marked with a strict routinization of the daily and annual social round. But capitalism itself, as Marx demonstrated, was founded upon the regulation and exploitation of labor time. It was the regularization of the working day and working week and the establishment of a new time discipline at the workplace, which spread a heightened consciousness of time to the industrial working class, that has lain at the heart of much social conflict in industrial capitalism (Thompson 1967; Thrift 1990, 109–26). The development of modern communication, including transportation systems, stimulated and reinforced the disembedding of clock time from social time.[11] In this process time, as Adam has argued, became a resource that could be spent, managed, saved, or wasted and something that in modern societies needs to be conceptualized in terms of power relations, "to the extent that clock time *as* time has become an independent, context-free value, a social and economic reality that structures, controls, disciplines, and provides norms for our social life" (1990, 120). Clock time, therefore, can be seen as having been the very organizing principle of modernity.[12]

Radio was multiply implicated in these modern redefinitions of space and time. At once simple and complex, concrete and abstract, the third of the mechanized arts (following the gramophone and film) was a powerful new invention whose potential was only gradually realized. As Raymond Williams argued in his essay "The Technology and the Society," technological innovation is not an accidental process operating hermetically at the margins of society, the products of which almost "naturally" then find their social application, but is part of "a crucial community of selected emphasis and intention" (1990, 26). Broadcasting offered one solution to

---

11. Durkheim argued that, while a concept of time is unique to humans, it is an abstract concept that is not natural or individual but socially organized—hence, time is a "social institution," an objectively given social category of thought produced within societies and therefore locally specific. Giddens (1990) developed the notion of how time and space are disembedded from social activities in modern societies. For a summary and critique of the sociology of time, from Durkheim to Giddens, see Lash and Urry 1994, 224–36.

12. The postmodern time frame is poised between the evolutionary time scale, realized by contemporary science, and the instantaneous, realized by computerized technology and communication. Both lie beyond the scope of human perception. See Rifkin 1987; Harvey 1989; Adam 1990; Lash and Urry 1994.

the crises in social perspective and social orientation engendered by the processes of industrialization and urbanization, as other media before it had offered responses to various particular needs of a new kind of society (the press for disseminating political information; photography to overcome distance in space and time as families dispersed; the cinema for entertainment and distraction; telegraphy and telephony for business information). Radio's place in society had to be defined within this context. Broadcasting was an entirely new social form of communication that was promoted as response to and incentive for those social and ideological transformations which Williams termed "mobile privatisation."

Mobile privatization refers to the two connected but in a way contradictory tendencies of modern urban, and specifically *suburban,* industrial living: increased mobility and an increasingly home-based way of life in which the home was becoming apparently more self-sufficient and well equipped but also in a sense cut off. Broadcasting to an extent could resolve the contradiction by serving this lifestyle that was both home based and mobile by seeming to overcome physical distances *and* to offer a mode of relaxation in the home that was becoming more rigidly defined as a place of leisure and recreation separate from the workplace, offering general access to forms of information and entertainment that had previously not been accessible to all, to provide a breadth of information speedily to a world that was shrinking and moving faster.

Chapter 3 showed how the daily schedule was devised to fit into the idealized daily routine of the woman in the home, but it is worth noting in the present context that the radio was also used in the rationalization of factory and office work, with workers' activities synchronized to the beat of radio music or their monotony simply alleviated by radio's distractions, as one machine worker testified in 1930: "One day the bosses set up a radio and loudspeakers in the machine rooms and straightaway it became quite lively. All 300 women, who all do nearly the same work as me, work with much more enthusiasm now."[13]

For most waged workers, however, radio listening was an activity enjoyed in leisure time. It was the labor of housework that was most widely addressed by and accompanied by the form and content of daytime radio. For the socialist radio movement the radio accompaniment to housework's repetitive chores (which had similarities to the repetitive work on the factory floor) could compensate for the housewife's lack of solidarity with coworkers (Bauer 1926, 80). For conservative critics there was a contradiction inherent in the translation of factory rhythms to the home and one that returns to the debates featured in chapter 2 about the

---

13. A factory worker in Breslau in *Schlesisches Funkkalender* (1930); cited in Bessler 1980, 25.

potential for radio to stabilize or disrupt the family home. The regimentation, segmentation, and acceleration of modern life as it was expressed in the modern technologized home seemed to threaten the serenity and calm of nostalgic versions of preindustrial domesticity.[14] And yet these reforms were embraced by the conservative Right as the only way of keeping the family from a descent into chaos (Grossmann 1986, 74). This tension between the romantic version of family life and its modern realities is one that was echoed in the contradictions of radio for women throughout the period.

**Sound Advice for the Modern Mother**

There was another element to the climate of rationalization that is relevant to the discussion about expertise on the radio—the rationalization of reproduction. The sex reform movement in Germany was concerned with the regulation and control of abortion, birth control, female sexuality, and childbirth. The debate about the politics of reproduction involved not only doctors and sex reformers but also nationalists, socialists, liberals, defenders of the moral order, and defenders of individual rights. Their concerns were informed by the prevailing anxieties about the falling birthrate and the threat to traditional family life perceived in women's, especially young women's, employment and attitudes toward marriage (Grossmann 1986, 62–70; Usborne 1992, 118–26). Cornelie Usborne (1992) has described the spirit of interventionism in reproduction as a new "politics of the body," in which the private became a matter high on the agenda of public politics.

The radio was used to spread information about government health campaigns, especially where there were signs of public mistrust, as was the case, for example, with the national immunization program in 1930. A popular format for this sort of propaganda was an informal dialogue between a mother and a medical or government expert (Gins and Gins 1930). While these dialogues were one of the positive ways in which women's private experience came to be heard in public, the distinction between private individuals and public representatives, with the concomitant distinction between experience and expertise, reinforced the hierarchy between public and private (Scannell 1989, 162). Official population policy was, of course, also reflected in the schedules of the Deutsche Welle, both by the Frauenfunk and by other departments. Family life was considered the keystone in the structure of the state, and a steady marriage was at the center of a stable family life. A new kind of counselor appeared to advise

---

14. For example, "Keeping to a certain rota is a good rule if not taken to extremes. As soon as it feels like a regulation it removes the original flexibility of domestic life and forces it into a corset which never suits any living organ" (Weinberg 1931, 272).

on marital matters in local authority marriage clinics, ostensibly guiding young people through the maze of puberty, helping them to find the right partner, and educating them about how to maintain a happy and productive marriage. These counselors, who broadcast regularly on the Deutsche Welle, drew on medical, biological, and psychological knowledge to assess the suitability of marriage partners in terms of the offspring they were likely to produce (Scheumann 1927, 654). Hindrances to marriage included the diagnosis of sexual disease and the possibility of passing on some sort of hereditary defect. Childlessness was considered a terrible psychological burden, especially for the woman, and such couples were actively encouraged to adopt. After consultation with the marriage counselor, clients who had been proven healthy were issued with a *Heiratszeugnis,* which declared that they had undertaken to conduct their future married lives with a sense of hygienic propriety and responsibility. These "wedding certificates" were the first step toward negative eugenics in Germany (Usborne 1992, 142–48). By the early 1930s, however, most of the clinics had become advisory centres on contraception. It was counseling that concentrated on smoothing over marital conflict that accounted for the greater proportion of these programs on the Deutsche Welle (F. R. 1929, 14–15; Simons 1929, 220–21).

Prevalent fears about the declining birthrate and its effect on a country that had already suffered the loss of two million young men on the battlefields of World War I were not frequently voiced on the airwaves. Statistical experts and politicians used the radio to argue the case for a population policy that would, for example, through financial and patriotic incentives, actively encourage all fertile couples to raise at least three children—in language that anticipates that more readily associated with the Nazi period. The following is taken from the notes to a program by a government official in 1927:

Marriages and families are the bearers of national renewal (*Volkserneuerung*). Families are the cells of the national body (*Volkskörper*). If the cells are healthy and strong, the body of the nation is healthy too. If they dwindle or die off on mass, the body of the nation is sick. Therefore a positive population policy must begin with the family. . . . The point must be reached where every healthy couple that is able and willing to procreate is economically in the position to bring up a sufficient number of children, i.e., between 3 and 4 on average.[15]

---

15. *Oberregierungsrat,* Burghöfer 1927, 654–56. See also Burghöfer 1928, 500–501; Heuß-Knapp 1931.

Paragraph 119 of the Constitution was regularly quoted in these programs, the paragraph which promised state support for mothers and aid for large families and which recognized marriage and family as the basis for the maintenance of the state. On Mother's Day in 1930 the discussion yet again centered on the decay of family life, but this time the blame was found not in the impersonal figures of population statistics nor in the effects of economic crisis but in the "family bolshevism" of the young generation, who thought themselves clever and important in rebelling against their parents and family life.

Mother's Day had been introduced into Germany as a day dedicated to the celebration of maternal selflessness, in 1923, the same year that public radio came on the scene (Hausen 1984a, 131–52; 1984b, 473–523). Imported from America, it was an idea initially promoted in Germany by the flower trade but it struck a chord among the conservative classes, the church, and the bourgeois feminist movement and rapidly became an established annual event. It also quickly became a fixed point in the radio calendar, with the first nationwide Mother's Day speech broadcast in May 1924 by the leader of the Union of German Florists, Dr. Rudolf Knauer (Hausen 1984a, 478). Its rapid acceptance into the radio schedules is all the more intriguing given the reluctance to embrace the "new tradition" by the national daily papers and even *Die Frau,* the journal of the BDF.[16] Paddy Scannell has shown how the evolution of the calendrical role of national broadcasting in Britain was part of the (re)invention of tradition in the modern age and argues that such broadcasts "unobtrusively stitched together the private and the public spheres in a whole new range of contexts" (1988, 17). The installation of Mother's Day in broadcast life clearly contributed to a wider process of reinventing a national tradition and a national identity.[17] The advertisements explicitly promoted the celebrations as a contribution to the *sittliche Wiedergeburt unseres Volkes,* the "moral regeneration of our nation," whereby women would be encouraged to resist the temptations of materialism, individualism, and hedonism, which threatened to draw them away from the family hearth. Mother's Day was conceived as *eine stille, treue Familienfeier,* "a quiet, intimate family celebration" (Hausen 1984a, 486). In other words, it was a public festival celebrated in individual homes and, as such, part of a conservative attempt to stem the perceived tide of women abandoning their domestic duties. The introduction of a *Muttertag* was Germany's great

---

16. For example, the *Vossische Zeitung* published its first Mother's Day poem in 1929; the *Berliner Tageblatt* waited until 1931 and the *Deutsche Allgemeine Zeitung* until 1933. Local papers gave the event more publicity (Hausen 1984a, 144–46).

17. "Wert der Familie . . ." (1930, n.p.). For a discussion about the need to (re)invent traditions in the modern period, see Hobsbawm and Ranger 1983.

hope for the future, that it might reawaken and nurture a belief in and respect for the family, though, as Hausen has demonstrated, there was a big gap between the propaganda and the practice in individual homes.

Motherhood in general was dealt with in two ways on the Deutsche Welle. First, there were the discursive talks on the *Frauenstunde* about the nature of motherhood, its satisfactions and its challenges, and there were practical advice programs. The prevailing wisdom as represented on the radio during the 1920s was that mothering had for too long been left to instinct and custom, and the all-encompassing abilities born of mother love, which, in their failure to curb infant mortality and prevent generational conflict, had proven inadequate. The insights and expertise of the scientists was needed to take over where instinctual female knowledge had failed. An editorial in the station's journal outlined the range of expert knowledge which women would have to learn to draw on—in language which fore-shadows the emphasis on biology and body culture and again anticipates that which dominated the discourse of femininity in the Third Reich:

> An understanding for racial hygiene and genetic science had to be awakened to let people grasp the importance of biological life forces. It was necessary to communicate pedagogical and psychological information. . . . The sort of practical experience that science and research and the newly awakened sense of social responsibility have demanded and achieved for motherhood and child rearing is not only available to help and guide every mother now, but also the next generation of young women. (F. R. 1928, 510)

Three years later, in December 1931, the message on the Deutsche Welle was stated more forthrightly still. Motherhood had become a science that "must be mastered before becoming a mother, because when you are a mother, there's no more time for complicated deliberations." (Fournier-Olden 1931).

Again, attention was also given to the particular problems faced by the agricultural community. The economic crisis on the land had posed a greater than usual burden on women, who were taking on more of the agricultural labor alongside their domestic chores, as farmsteads relied more and more on family labor. This extra workload was blamed for the relatively high levels of miscarriages and deaths in childbirth among women on the land. The scandal of this fact was seen not so much in the threat to women's lives but in the threat to the rural family as the most stable building block of the state. In a lecture broadcast in August 1929 the case was put for an intensification of training for rural women in the balancing of economic and familial duties (Sprengel 1929).

**Wireless and the Working Woman**

In general, although its afternoon place in the schedules made it difficult for most working women to tune in, the Frauenfunk at the Deutsche Welle was sympathetic to women who chose to work, but it was very much a defensive position against the intransigent belief in the editorial policy of the company that female nature tied women emotionally, if not physically, to hearth and home. It was not a campaigning stance—no pressure was ever put on nonworking housewives to make them think their lives could be enriched by work outside the home. The most that was attempted was to encourage a mutual understanding and acceptance of two different ways of life (Diel 1930, 229). The majority of programs looking at women and work concentrated on the basic question of whether to work at all and, if so, how best to combine it with the unavoidable feminine duties of marriage and motherhood. By the early 1930s, however, the reactionary backlash, with its scare stories about the economic and population cost to the nation of the increasing numbers of women in full-time work, did find expression in the editorial of the *Deutsche Welle:*

> The problem of waged labor and motherhood cannot remain a private matter for the families concerned, but must be recognised by everybody as a communal task of all national comrades and approached in a responsible manner. It is, and will remain, not only a problem for the national economy, but primarily a problem of national hygiene (*ein volkshygienisches Problem*), whose solution or intractibility will be of decisive importance to the future development of our nation's strength. (F. R. 1931, 556)

A few months later, in February 1932, a still more reactionary position was represented in which the declining birthrate and crisis in the family was blamed on women, who were not only taking jobs away from unemployed men and undermining the economy but were going against nature in taking on full-time employment in factories and offices. The problem as it was perceived by the author of the script, Dr. Else Möbus (1931), was not that mothers loved their children any less but that they simply did not have the time and energy after an eight-hour working day to devote to their offspring. More importantly, the intervention of reason and politics introduced a distance between a woman and her unborn children, her instinctual desire to procreate having been dulled by financial considerations and career ambitions.

There had, however, been other slightly less reactionary contributions which had looked, for example, at the prejudice women faced at the workplace. One such program, broadcast in December 1927, examined the play of sexual tension in the work experience of unskilled teenage girls in office and factory jobs.[18] It sought to analyze the impact of the conditions of work on the psychological development of these young girls. It looked at the tendency of uniform, repetitive, mechanical tasks to work against individualization and originality and argued that these effects were more profound for girls than for boys; it was also suggested that this sort of work acted to heighten these girls' sexual instincts. The argument went that, since women realized at an early age that promotion relied more on their appearance, youth, and erotic attraction than on their objective skills, young employees would seek to optimize their own positions at the expense of solidarity with other female workers. An alternative point of view was put by Erich Landsberg in a program billed as a historical survey of the lives of working women. He suggested that the financial rewards offered by professions most nearly suited to the feminine psyche were insufficient to prevent women from having to take work in offices and factories, where they had to strip themselves of all their femininity: "girls will be girls, which even the terms of contract cannot change" (1929, 174). By 1932, in a program called "Das berufstätige junge Mädchen und ihr männlicher Vorgesetzter" (The Young Career Girl and Her Male Superior), the position on sexual relations at work being represented at the Deutsche Welle was that, if a young girl found her male boss paying her friendlier than average attention, she had no one but herself to blame. Unusually, the editorial comment in the station's journal did not restrict itself to giving a synopsis of the program but decided to present the other, male, side of the case ( Burger 1931b, 481). In the program Dr. Anneliese Bretschneider had addressed the subject of sexual harassment from the girl's point of view, and the male editor sought to justify what he saw as perfectly natural relations between the sexes, relations that were not merely a matter of sex but were also given momentum by the fact that the male was the natural superior in the workplace and saw no threat of competition in his female colleagues. This freed him from the constraints of normal business protocol in his dealings with his female staff: "One doesn't have to watch oneself with a young girl. She simply doesn't have the ambition to unsaddle the boss, and is concerned only to make herself indispensable to him."

The editor's conclusion was that there was no need to talk about

---

18. For a discussion of youth employment in Weimar and the relatively worse conditions of young women, see Stachura 1989, 94–114; Grossmann 1984b, 190–94.

working relations between men and women because one could simply rely on common sense and everyday decency to prevail. Unfortunately, the program script has not survived, nor were the editor's views taken up in the letters columns of the *Deutsche Welle*. But it seems as though, in attempting to address a serious problem from a woman's point of view, the *Frauenstunde* had trodden on the toes of the prevailing ethos in the company.

The lack of female organization in the workplace referred to earlier was blamed on another reason in a program broadcast two years later ("Die Frau als Persönlichkeit . . ." 1929), namely the assumption on the part of middle-class working women in particular that their working lives were a temporary stage that would come to an end with the walk down the aisle. This lack of organization was the reason for the finding of the Allgemeiner Deutscher Gewerkschaftsbund (General Association of German Trade Unions) that even the highest wages of a skilled female worker fell below the minimum wage of an unskilled male worker, even though the rationalization and mechanization of labor meant women were equally productive in the work that they did. The programs of the Deutsche Welle increasingly concentrated on the reasons and remedies for the fact that legislative equality, even a spreading acceptance of working women, was no guarantee against unequal opportunities and rewards in the workplace.

Another program, broadcast in August 1928, considered the effects on women's health of industrial work caused by mechanization, hygienically inadequate working conditions, bad posture, and industrial poisons (Krüger 1928, 369). In advocating efforts to reduce the harmful effects of such conditions on the "frailer" feminine physique by a combination of work hygiene and sport for women, the primary aim in mind was to ensure their continued efficiency in their wifely, maternal, and domestic duties. The physical effects of carrying the double burden of waged and domestic labor were not cause for comment. When Dr. Karl Würzburger (1928, 474) addressed the question the following month, he came to the remarkable conclusion that in many ways holding down two jobs had actually made life easier for women. No longer did women have to work so hard at their domestic duties to win the respect of their husbands and children, for with waged labor came respect. Now the achievements of the working woman in the home could be regarded by the rest of her family as a gift made to them from the excess of her "infinite" and natural resources. In a similarly optimistic program broadcast in 1931 the argument was made that the work experience of women going into marriage had given them sufficient understanding of the ways of the world to make their decisions about the choice of partner based on rational and secure criteria and that the institution was safer than it had ever been in the days when partnerships had been based on dowries and the financial security a man could offer a woman (Drewitz 1931, 122).

The underlying point of view that a woman working was something that did not constitute the norm meant that female unemployment, even in the toughest days of the Depression, was not an issue on the Deutsche Welle. Although clear figures are difficult to ascertain, women workers were affected by the Depression, albeit less so than were men (Kramer 1987, 108–15). The question of unemployment generally only came up on the *Frauenstunde,* in terms of how a woman could continue to run the home while her husband was without work and how she could help to keep his spirits up while the search for a job went on (Franzen-Hellersberg 1927, 722–23).

The hobby programs, or *Bastelstunden,* illustrate this point. In the 1930s these programs were increasingly devoted to ideas for saving money and for stretching meager resources. The Depression meant there was a ready audience for tips on how to rejuvenate old household gadgets or to make old clothes fresh and fashionable again. With the unemployment rate soaring,[19] the programs began to attract many male listeners too, but, rather than expect the men to learn the skills of needlecraft and decoration, special items on carpentry and other traditional male crafts were introduced. Even in the depths of the Depression, as far as the public discourse on the airwaves was concerned, there had to be no danger of men who had lost their jobs being feminized by listening to daytime programs that were conventionally the domain of women. The traditional adherence to the notion of essential differences of being and function precluded any radical reappraisal of the place of men in society. Moreover, it would seem that indivdual women, particularly in the lower middle classes, would try to hang on to traditional divisions of labor in the home, despite the hardships and increased domestic workloads (Weiland 1933, 18; cited in Rosenhaft 1987, 219). The most the radio achieved was simply to register that daytime audiences could be expected to include many thousands of unemployed men.

### Radio as Consuming Passion

Radio did not speak to women only as rationalized workers, housewives, and mothers but also as consumers. In the words of the American historian of German rationalization Robert A. Brady, "mass production and mass consumption are the two inseparable halves of the rationalization

---

19. There were more than five million unemployed by the winter of 1930–31, rising to six million in the following year (Evans 1987, 6).

whole" (1933, 402). In many ways both the modern household and the modern woman became devoted to consumption, though clearly patterns of consumption remained static in neither personal nor political experience.[20] The devaluation of paper wealth in the great inflation fanned the desire for investment in consumer durables, which accordingly reinforced the logic of the mass production of industrial rationalization, although neither the take-up nor promotion of consumer durables was as rapid or straightforward as in the United States. Certainly, working-class women could rarely afford the new devices (Hagemann 1990, 90). Some of these changes can be shown statistically, such as the increased use of electrical fixtures in the home (per capita consumption of electrical fixtures increased by 127 percent from 1913 to 1928) or the shift away from traditional German cuisine to lighter and easier to prepare foods; other, structurally more important changes, such as the popularization of the notion of minimum standards of health and comfort, cannot be so easily represented empirically (Brady 1933, 405).

The crucial point here is that the female radio audience was understood to be an audience made up of consumers at a time that heralded the primacy of consumerism. The other new technological medium, film, was similarly implicated in the circulation of consumerism, with films functioning in some ways as shop windows that women could peruse for new ideas about fashion, furnishings, and femininity itself (Giese 1925, 63; Clark and Peiss 1989, 58–60). As Bowlby points out, while shopping belongs in a certain sense to women's "reproductive" role, it is, in contrast to the self-denial associated with motherhood, "also regarded as a field for the exercise of self-indulgent pleasures which are nonetheless taken to be 'feminine'" (1987, 186–87). Kracauer (1975) famously suggested the high-kicking chorus lines of the popular revue films echoed the uniformity and tempo of the Taylorized production lines.[21] Perhaps more importantly, female stars were packaged as screen goddesses, ideal types, models for the adoring fans. The image of woman was commodified in film, but, if film

20. Consumption lies at the heart of modern capitalism, or, in Lewis Mumford's words, "Industry [in the capitalist enterprise] was directed not merely to the multiplication of goods and to an increase in their variety: it was directed toward the multiplication of the desire for goods" (1962, 391). Although it is a commonplace that women became associated with shopping—the practice of consumption—it is a problem as much as a premise, as Rachel Bowlby argues, for, "while shopping is generally taken as an historical variable, women are thought to do it as part of their nature" (1987, 186).

21. Peter Wollen points out that Kracauer erroneously believed the Tiller Girls to be American, whereas coming from Lancashire they were in reality products of the Manchester rather than the Detroit era of manufacturing capitalism (1993, 54). See also Kracauer's 1931 essay, "Girls und Krise," first published in the *Frankfurter Zeitung,* republished in the 1977 collection *Ornament der Masse.* See also Witte 1981–82; Hake 1987; Hansen 1995.

was the medium of woman as commodity, then radio was the medium of woman as consumer par excellence.

Programs such as "Ratschläge fürs Haus" (Tips for the House) in Berlin and "Drei Minuten für die Frau" (Three Minutes for the Woman) in Frankfurt were vehicles for the promotion of new household goods, while programs such as Mirag's "Billig, aber gut—der Küchenzettel der Woche" (Cheap, but Good—Menu of the Week) constructed their listeners as patriotic guardians of the nation's purse strings (see chap.7). Increasingly, housewives were addressed by politicians, eager to make them aware of their contribution to the national economy, that they might be encouraged to tailor their consumption to a particular political/economic end and, as a bonus, feel themselves more fully integrated into the political public sphere. The egalitarian promise of mass production and mass marketing was sold as a promise of democratic agency in public and political life for women. Radio was sold as a consumer good and as good for consumers.

Of course, none of what was happening in Germany in terms of rationalization, consumerism, or modernization should be considered in isolation of the influence of the United States, either in terms of its intervention in the German economy or in terms of the fascination for the modern American way of life. That way of life could be invoked at different times by different parties as a promise or a threat. As far as a comparison is concerned, Nolan has written that the "New Woman" in Germany was to be:

> as efficient, as Taylorized, as her U.S. counterpart ostensibly was, but she was to enjoy neither new household technology nor the standard of consumption that prevailed in the United States. This was an austere vision of modernity, one in which the flamboyant consumerism of the American woman had been safely domesticated to the harsh material circumstances of post–World War I Germany. (1990, 550)

Attitudes at the Deutsche Welle to the American way of life were somewhat ambiguous, and in this seem to have reflected a more widespread ambiguity in society. American models of housework, family life, and femininity were "selective, eclectic, and undertaken with ambivalence," but those models "provided a language through which different countries and cultures could develop their own visions of modernity" (Nolan 1990, 552; 1994b). The life of the American career woman was described by a regular broadcaster on the subject, Louise Diel, alternately in tones of quiet envy and a certain condescension. In 1928 she painted a picture of a woman who had no trouble finding employment as and how she wanted, whose working conditions and wages were comfortable in comparison to Germany, whose leisure time was one social whirl of cinemas, jazz, and dining out, who was always young, always beautiful, and always happy (572–73). Self-service shopping came in for praise as a rationalized time and personnel-saving practice that had proven popular and effective in American supermarkets. All the American woman had to give up to have all this, Diel argued, was any claim to individual personality or characteristics that would set her apart from the crowd. Her apartment would be small but practically furnished. What were considered luxuries in Europe such as central heating and hot water were bare necessities in the States, whereas the basic *gemütliche* comforts of the German home, the pictures and personal momentos, the delicate ornaments and tasteful furnishings, were unknown in America. Domestic service was unknown there, for every woman considered herself a lady, and standards of housecleaning were consequently lower, for the independent woman had no time for such niceties. Her wardrobe was up to date with the latest Parisian fashions but made up of cheap copies that could be worn for six months and then replaced. Life for the working American woman as portrayed by Diel was fast-moving, transient, throwaway, fun: "Buy it, wear it, wear it some more, throw it away—next!" (1927, 589). Appearance was the bottom line, but Diel advocated a lenient judgment on the superficiality she had found, suggesting that there might be as much to be learned by German women about modern lifestyle as about modernized kitchens from the American example.

America was in vogue. American money and American ideas flooded into Germany in the 1920s. The rise of the mass media was both an expression of Americanization and a vehicle for its further dissemination. Radio filled the space for women between the American *Girl-Kultur*, which found its natural home in film and the pages of glossy magazines, and the Taylorized management of factory labor. This most modern of media was ideally suited to bridge these two related phenomena, which both had to do with the methods and moments of mass production. Radio breathed the fresh breath of American glamour into the home. It was modern, it was new, and the message it preached to women was infused with the contradictory spirit of modernity, the fusion of novelty and convention, the archaic and the modern.

Certainly, the programs for women at the Deutsche Welle were manifestations of the tension between the pull of the future and the hold of the past. Radio experts advertised the advantages of modernization in the home, the science of motherhood, the latest techniques and technology, and the lessons learned from the mechanization and rationalization on the factory floor. And all the while they were bolstering the traditional gendered division of labor and the unequal valorization of the public and private spheres. They spoke their message to women whose perception of their isolation from other women in the same position was heightened by the awareness of the creation of a mass public of women listening to individual radios in individual homes across the country—an awareness of artificial isolation that had to be created in the minds of women before it could be compensated for by the productive sense of solidarity with those similar, anonymous women. To reform domestic labor at the level of technology was implicitly to reinforce traditional ideology in a world of changing economic relations between the sexes. The rationalizing maternalist and domestic science programs of the Frauenfunk, for all their claim to modernity, ultimately, implicitly and explicitly, preached a continuation of the status quo. The imperative for constant innovation and improvement translated into a constant need to disguise the return of the always identical.

CHAPTER 7

# All-Consuming Propaganda

During the Weimar Republic radio had been used to integrate women into the modern consumer society by advertising new gadgets for the home and disseminating information and advice about the latest fashions in everything from home care to child care. It had presented itself as an expert guide through the contradictions of modernization, appealing to a sense of the modern while reinscribing the gender relations of the past. Throughout the Nazi period women continued to be interpellated as consumers in propaganda campaigns designed to integrate them into the national economy and the *Volksgemeinschaft,* by enlisting them in the drive for economic autarky and the preparation for war.

Long before war broke out the National Socialist regime had pursued policies to steer the country toward a war economy. Hjalmar Schacht, the minister responsible for economic affairs from July 1934, was charged with the economic preparation for war, to which everything else was to be subordinated.[1] There has been much debate about the extent to which rearmament and war preparation were realized by 1939, and the relative priority economic, foreign policy, or domestic imperatives had in leading Germany to war.[2] Certainly, there was no attempt to divert the economy

---

1. Text of secret Defense Law, 21 May 1935, in which Schacht was appointed plenipotentiary-general for the War Economy, ordering him to "begin his work already in peacetime" (*Nazi Conspiracy and Aggression* 4:638–39, Nuremberg document 2001-PS; cited in Shirer 1977, 259–60).

2. Early arguments that the economy was singly orientated toward massive rearmament (e.g., Taylor 1945; Namier 1952; Shirer, 1959–77) were revised and criticized by Burton Klein (1959), who demonstrated that the German economy was not geared for a major war in 1939 but, instead, a series of small-scale, relatively low-cost blitzkriegs. Alan Milward (1965) argued that Klein was basically right but that he had underestimated the preparations for the lightning wars and the preference for rearmament in breadth rather than depth. Bernice Carroll (1968) echoed this position in arguing that one cannot speak of a war economy in Germany until 1938, when 17 percent of GNP (i.e., 50 percent of public spending) was spent on arms. Histories written in the GDR and others following the Marxist-Leninist line

toward total war preparations until as late as 1943. The concentration of economic power and lowering of living standards inevitable in pursuit of such a course of action were avoided for fear of undermining the support for the regime. Nevertheless, in 1936 a second Four Year Plan was announced, the central aim of which was to make Germany as self-reliant on its own agricultural and manufacturing resources as possible within four years, largely by means of strict wage and price controls, reducing imports, and making synthetic materials out of domestic raw materials and therefore independent of strategic imports in the event of war. To this end the government manipulated the media to encourage women to help realize its ambitions for economic autarky. This chapter highlights and analyzes the role of radio in these consumer campaigns. It describes the aims and structure of these campaigns in general and examines the organization and language of individual campaigns, beginning with a brief discussion of the place of these campaigns within Nazi ideology as a whole.

**Consumption as Patriotic Duty**

The appeal of fascism was primarily an emotional one, stressing the political destiny of the *Volk,* rather than appealing to material interests of any particular group. And yet the contradictory visions of a utopian fascist future necessarily entailed some notion of either a reactionary economic revolution or industrial modernization and the promise of a solution to the economic problems that had plagued Weimar Germany. In the age of mass society in which the individual is swamped by massive and impersonal economic forces, the Nazis' anticapitalist/antisocialist stance to many people seemed to offer the hope of some degree of economic independence, freed from the impact of both big business and organized labor. Robbed of the right to organize, it was a vain hope, but it gave the Party the support it needed. It is possible to recognize these contradictions in the propaganda directed specifically at women during the Third Reich. In these *Verbrauchslenkung* and *Verbrauchserziehung* campaigns (direction of consumption and education in consumption) housewives were barraged with information about how, as customers and consumers, it lay in their power to have

---

laid down by the Third International in 1935 understood fascist economies as the imperial form predicted as the final stage of capitalism (e.g., Gossweiler 1971). Other writers stressed the anticapitalist strand in fascist propaganda, following it through into economic policy. More recently Richard Overy (1989) has argued that the blitzkriegs were the result of a mismatch between foreign and economic policy; the scale of rearmament and switchover to a war economy implies that Hitler had not intended the full-scale war to break out so soon.

a direct and profound influence on the German economy.[3] Women were reassured of their own personal economic agency in words that obscured the limitations of their function as economic actors. But, more than just alerting women to their potential power, the propaganda insisted it was their patriotic duty to ensure they acted in the best interests of the *Volk,* the welfare of which, as always, was to come before that of the individual or even of the family.

This involved more than simply promoting a "Buy German" movement. The New Plan of 1934 allowed the regulation of imports via bilateral trade agreements on political as well as economic grounds, with the intention of restructuring the geographical pattern of German trade, replacing manufactured imports from developed countries with raw material from underdeveloped southeastern European countries, which would then become dependent export markets for products manufactured in Germany. Germany would consequently realize what nationalists and National Socialists regarded as its "natural" role as the manufacturing heart of Europe, supplied by (racially) inferior peripheral states. A general boycott of foreign goods by individual consumers was therefore initially rejected on the grounds that, in a closely directed economy, such goods had been imported for the purpose of being sold.[4]

Nevertheless, housewives were still encouraged to opt where possible for homegrown farm produce and to use it as efficiently as possible in order to show solidarity with German farmers. It was simply an added bonus for the propagandists that, in all the information about preserving fresh produce with which women were bombarded, the favorite vision of an idyllic rural past could be evoked, epitomized by a return to the traditional housekeeping wisdoms lost in the process of urbanization and modernization. In general, the aim of the propagandists was, rather, to train women to understand the mechanics of their contribution to the economy and how to adjust their activity and behavior according to changing circumstances and in accordance with government policy. Shopping lists and recipe books, Germany's seventeen and a half million housewives were told, had to undergo *Gleichschaltung.*[5]

---

3. In announcing the second Four Year Plan, Göring declared women "trustees of the nation's wealth," as 60 to 80 percent of it passed through their hands (cited in Klinksiek 1982, 110).

4. "Verbrauchslenkung und Vorratswirtschaft notwendig: Darré [Reichsnährungsminister und Reichsbauernführer] an die Frauen," *Westfälische Landeszeitung* 35, 5 February 1936.

5. "Mitverantwortung für Deutschlands Nahrungsfreiheit," *Kurzberichte für die Frau,* 14, 2 April 1936.

These kinds of appeals did not come out of the blue. There had been a vociferous lobby to teach the housewife nationalist discipline in her expenditure and her housekeeping throughout the Weimar Republic, a lobby that came to a crescendo in the aftermath of the Wall Street Crash. As Edmund Kleinschmitt (1931) put it in the trade journal *Deutsche Handels Wacht,* housewives' combined purchasing power was "greater than the greatest company," which gave them "even more power than the government."[6] The journal urged women to use this power responsibly by refusing to buy foreign goods and by demanding lower prices in the shops. But that was the limit of their competence. In accordance with the emergency measures to lower prices and wages, women were encouraged to report to their husbands their impressions of those retailers who were cooperating and those who were being recalcitrant. Their husbands in turn could report to the local price watch committee, whose findings might eventually influence the decisions of the *Preiskommissar.* These arrangements indicate that the fine words about housewives' unlimited power were little more than empty rhetoric, the aim of which was simply to foster in the minds of German women a direct and emotional link between their decisions as consumers in the market place and the hungry families of unemployed men. By the same token, any failure of the economy to respond to the emergency measures could swiftly be laid at the feet of "irresponsible" women.

Radio had also propagated these ideas during the Weimar Republic. The ZdH, for example, was able to secure airtime with the Berlin Funkstunde and the Deutsche Welle to promote its aims to educate women in the connections between their household economy and the

---

6. See also, Potthoff 1928, 71; "Die Frau als Verbraucherin . . ." 1931; "Wirtschaftspolitik in der Küche" 1931. In a recent essay on consumption as "the vanguard of history" Daniel Miller (1995) invokes the housewife as an image of consumer decision making and consequently as the unrecognized fulcrum of modernity, going as far as to characterize the housewife as the aggregate "global dicatator." In so doing, he claims to highlight the contradictions of the modern First World consumer. Far from conforming to the consumer of economic theory who independently makes choices based on rational self-interest or the sterotype of the superficial status-seeking shopaholic, the "flesh and blood housewife emerges as one of the least individualistic of the social beings of the First World." Her own interests are subsumed by the interests generated by "the moral economy of the home," in which one of the housewife's key skills is thrift. At the same time, the exercise of power through consumption is not experienced as empowering, which Miller puts down to a historical contingency by which production-centered political movements superseded those based on consumption. The essay points to ways in which a shift in emphasis would be fruitful for consumption studies, but the similarities to the rhetoric discussed in this chapter are unsettling and raise doubts about the possibility of progressive political movements based on consumption.

economy at large.[7] Such programs appeared intermittently from 1926 on the Deutsche Welle, but in May 1930 a weekly installment, *Volks-wirtschaftliche Viertelstunde für die Hausfrau,* was introduced with the express aim of making women aware of their patriotic duty to help affect Germany's balance of trade so Germany could meet its international obligations. With the agricultural sector then in crisis, the emphasis was initially on appealing to women to buy homegrown produce (Prüfer 1930, 379). Later the campaign broadened to include manufactured goods. There were also renewed efforts to encourage women to join professional organizations that promised to be a far more efficient way of coordinating an effective consumer movement (Drewitz 1930, 511). The radio was also used to try to encourage more women to open national savings accounts, so the interest raised could be used for the welfare of all. Programs were aimed at women as it was reasoned that their maternal instinct made them more concerned about the future and the security of their children (Stern-berg 1931, 387). Nazi radio built on the foundations of these programs, recognizing that a concept of community was central to programs designed to alert housewives to their responsibilities and influence as con-sumers in the national economy. The Nazis also built on the rationalizing aspects of radio, using similar language and similar techniques as had already been established to encourage efficiency among German house-wives in the interests of the state. Moreover, beyond the propaganda potential of the broadcasts, the promotion of the Volksempfänger in itself represented the embrace of mass consumption, the stimulation of con-sumer demand, and the propagation of consumer values more readily associated with the 1920s or the 1950s (Schäfer 1983, 117).

**Driving the Message Home**

The earliest concerted campaigns targeted at women as consumers were left to the DFW and the NSF on behalf of individual ministries such as the Reichsnährstand. The Frauenfunk at the Reichssender Hamburg provided an early model, with its daily midday reports from the Frauenwirtschaft-skammer (FWK), Germany's first official civic chamber for women, which had been set up in May 1933 to act in association with the appropriate official bodies to channel women's economic, cultural, and social affairs in the best interests of the National Socialist state. "Markt und Küche" (Market and Kitchen) was a program designed to direct women to buy German produce in season and which gave the latest market prices with

---

7. "Tätigkeitsbericht der Zentrale der Hausfrauenvereine Groß-Berlin e.V.," 1 January 1925–1 May 1926, BAP 70 Re2/51:110.

tips on special offers and recipes. It was claimed that goods which were "advertised" in this way at midday were often sold out throughout the city by one o'clock ("Frauenwirtschaftskammer . . ." 1933; Meyer 1933). The developing cooperation between these organizations and the women's service of local and national radio stations was looked at more closely in chapter 4, but the broad aims of the NSF in terms of directing women's economic activity deserve to be spelled out again, here in the words of Gertrud Scholtz-Klink, broadcast on the Deutschlandsender in August 1934: "The main thing is that today women are conscious of their responsibilities in the life of the nation and know that their children's life, and therefore that of the German nation, hinges on their actions" (1934).

In recognition of women's consumer power, a series of major publicity campaigns were organized, often of several years' duration, deploying a staggering range of resources and costing millions of marks. A policy that called for self-sacrifice and belt-tightening so soon after the privations of the Depression was not easy to sell, and it has been argued that, for so much investment of time and money, the return was hardly impressive (Stephenson 1983, 119). Nevertheless, all the media were harnessed for this campaign, and each offered a different incentive. Much more than the fictional images portrayed at the movies, which worked at a subtle suggestive level, these campaigns were overtly designed to influence and change actual behavior and to leave women in no doubt about their function and status in Nazi society.[8] The following account of these campaigns is not intended to be exhaustive but to identify the distinctive role that radio played within them.[9] Again, the concern is less with the notion of "impact" than with the discursive and programming practices.

The Verbrauchslenkung campaigns not only exploited women's role as consumer but confirmed it. These were the two imperatives recognized by Dr. Else Vorwerck, the influential and prolific representative for national and household economics in the National Socialist women's organizations. Writing in the *Deutsche Allgemeine Zeitung* in June 1941, she claimed that the advent of National Socialist power in Germany had awakened a new understanding of the power of private household consumption on two fronts—first, on the part of the economy, which had to deal more closely with the household after the reorientation toward the domestic market after 1933, and, second, by recognizing the "natural divi-

---

8. Much has been written on Nazi film propaganda; for further information on the image of women in Nazi film and useful background information, see Albrecht 1969; Hull 1969; Leiser 1974; Belach 1979; Welch 1983; Balser 1986; Ellwanger 1989; Warth 1990.

9. Stephenson offers much useful information on the broad part played by the women's organizations in these campaigns but devotes only two paragraphs to radio (1983, 122).

sion of labor," which made the family household the primary site of women's contribution to the community.

Dr. Emmy Wagner, writing in the *Völkischer Beobachter* in February 1936, had added a third imperative, the need to organize the economy to realize racial ambitions, arguing that the housewife must learn to see the household economy in a "racial-political light." Only by pulling together in the national community could the "age of materialism be overcome." Wagner envisaged a time when town and country, workers and entrepreneurs, shopkeepers and consumers, would work together hand in hand, when it "would be a joy to make the economy in all its parts serve racial objectives."

Agitation for a boycott of Jewish traders necessarily had to concentrate on convincing non-Jewish German women of the justification of such action. Rhetoric against Jewish big business notwithstanding, the primary targets of anti-Jewish boycotts were small businesses. Brown-shirted SA men would stand guard outside Jewish-owned shops, and advertising columns would be plastered in posters urging passersby: "Deutsches Volk! Wehr Dich! Kauf nicht beim Juden!" (German People! Defend Yourselves! Don't Buy from Jews!). Slander campaigns and boycotts were only the beginning of a systematic catalog of measures to isolate and exclude the Jewish population from all aspects of German social, economic, and cultural life. Inasmuch as achieving widespread acceptance of the economic boycott was concerned, the propaganda failed in face of general public apathy (Carr 1987, 69–82). Until the notorious "Kristallnacht" of 9 November 1938 (the "night of broken glass," which left ninety-one Jews murdered, some twenty thousand arrested and detained in concentration camps, and thousands of shops and synagogues seriously vandalized) and the legislation that followed it to close all Jewish business establishments, economic measures against the Jews had been given relatively low priority in comparison to political measures to deprive them of civil and civic rights, for fear of disrupting the domestic economy and jeopardizing foreign trade (Hofer 1972, 271). The efforts to instigate boycotts at street level were, however, dangerously effective in cultivating an atmosphere tolerant of increasing levels of anti-Semitic propaganda and the enforced segregation of the community.[10]

---

10. A chilling account of all the measures taken to deprive the Jewish population of their rights is given in Rürup 1989, 111–23. Mommsen (1989) has argued convincingly how the passive acceptance of the exclusion of the Jewish population helped prepare the way for the Final Solution but as a necessary, not sufficient, enabling factor. More decisive than ideological factors and the effects of propaganda were the political and bureaucratic mechanisms that enabled the idea of mass extermination to become reality. Like Mommsen, Zygmunt Bauman (1989) makes the case persuasively that these mechanisms were not unique to Germany in the 1930s and 1940s but are integral to modern societies.

Clearly, there was a link between anti-Semitic propaganda and the propaganda attempts to direct or influence patterns of consumption. It was not a link that was made very explicit in the Verbrauchslenkung programs on women's radio, but it is a theme that is always there at a subtextual level when the exhortations to participate in the regeneration of the national community were clearly understood to exclude the Jewish population. The absence of explicit anti-Semitic propaganda from the programs on women's radio does not mean that the question of racism was removed from the concerns of the Frauenfunk; indeed, much of the rhetoric was constructed in terms of this exclusion, as the analysis of surviving scripts demonstrates in chapter 8. In terms of the present study it is important to make the racism of these absences explicit.

As the economy rose out of the Depression, bringing with it a rise in levels of consumption, so a need for a more broadly coordinated campaign structure was discerned. The result was the creation, in 1936, of the Reichsausschuß für Volkswirtschaftliche Aufklärung (National Committee for Popular Economic Enlightenment [RVA]).[11] This subdivision of the Werberat der deutschen Wirtschaft (German Business Advertising Consultancy) was a privately owned organization affiliated with the RMVP and was delegated responsibility for running Germany's national economic propaganda, both "selling" National Socialist economic policy to the people and getting the people to cooperate with the implementation of individual policy strategies. It considered its role as providing a link between the government, which planned, decreed, and headed economic measures, and the people, who had to see those measures through. It claimed to make life easier for both government and business by preparing the ground in public opinion.

A whole range of communications was available to the committee: fly sheets, posters, slide shows, newspaper articles and small ads, and window displays. Exhibitions were laid on and lecture tours made of schools, factories, and party organizations, covering as many of the smaller provincial towns as possible, until the constraints of the war made such extensive coverage a luxury they could not afford. Efforts were then concentrated instead on the large congress and exhibition centers, such as the autumn fair in Leipzig. There were even attempts to produce theater plays around "national economic" themes.

Radio was one of the most cost-effective media, much cheaper to organize than, for example, a nationwide leafleting campaign. Most importantly, it offered the chance to reach those women who were not attracted to either the party organizations, their exhibitions, or their courses (Stephenson 1983, 134). The regional stations would be strongly

---

11. "Das Aufgabengebiet des RVA" BAP 50.02/18, 30–34:35–41.

encouraged to use the material passed on to them by the RVA, but the style in which the propaganda was conveyed—indeed, whether it was conveyed at all—lay ultimately with the directors of the individual regional stations. Some stations preferred to receive manuscripts ready for broadcast, others, such as Stuttgart, defended their prerogative to shape their own output, arguing that the RVA's approach was too dogmatic.[12] Nevertheless, manuscripts were vetted by the RVA to guard against even the most minor deviations in content from the official line.[13]

There were three levels of advertising coordinated by the RVA: private businesses' own promotion, joint advertising of firms with similar targets, and public information. More money was spent on retail advertising than on all other sorts of commercial advertising put together.[14] Campaigns falling into this last category were not permitted to make mention of individual firms or products but were intended solely for "enlightenment and advice" in economic matters. The ideological content of all three levels of advertising had shown a marked increase ever since the takeover of power in 1933, but the onset of war boosted the trend still further. The public had to be persuaded of the needs for cutbacks and the preferred explanations for the shortages.

During the Four Year Plan, for example, great efforts were made to overcome the initial mistrust of new, artificial materials such as Plexiglas and spun rayon, which were being produced in an effort to replace traditional materials once imported from abroad.[15] It also provided an opportunity to sing the praises of German industry and technology and cajole

---

12. Letter from the RVA to the Reichssender Stuttgart, 31 January 1939, BAP 50.02/12:152.

13. For example, a manuscript was returned to the Leipzig station for revision of the suggestion women go out and buy secondhand clothes. Official policy was to encourage the repair and refreshening of garments already in the listeners' wardrobes (letter from the RVA to the Reichssender Leipzig, 20 September 1940, BAP 50.02/12:203). Another manuscript for the same station was returned for amendment for seeming to suggest that hand washing was in all cases preferable to machine washes. The RVA was anxious not to alienate the support of the washing machine industry and requested that the program emphasize the great technological advances made by German washing machine manufacturers in recent years (Aktennotiz an Herrn Salzmann, Reichssender Leipzig, 18 February 1939, BAP 50.02/26:151). Washing machines were just one of the modern consumer durables that were actively promoted among the middle classes during the Third Reich (see Schäfer 1983).

14. RM 543,000,000 by retailers, RM 350,000,000 by industry, RM 52,000,000 by wholesalers, and RM 15,000,000 by traders (*Handwerker*) in 1940, according to the figures of the advertising trade published in *Wirtschaftswerbung* 7, 3 July 1941, 1.

15. The domestic production of synthetics was, alongside rearmament and the manufacture of consumer durables, one of the main pillars of the economic recovery in the early years of the Third Reich. There was also a high level of government investment in heavy industry and construction, which were combined with policies to encourage saving and to redistribute income to those sections of the community less likely to spend on consumer goods (Overy 1982).

the public into doing its bit for the Fatherland. The public addressed in this case was, again, primarily female, the housewives and mothers who needed to be convinced of their patriotic duty to buy German goods, to preserve valuable resources, and to care efficiently for their husbands and families, with whom the future of Germany rested. It was a softer option than that of asking for civilian sacrifices in terms of reducing consumption levels or raising taxes to pay for deficit spending, sacrifices that the government avoided for fear of causing resentment in the population at large.

Depression and unemployment had left a legacy of insecurity and sense of vulnerability in the people, feelings that outlived the first signs of economic improvement. As in so many other areas of policy, the government information services walked a tightrope between conflicting messages. On the one hand, people were told how much better the economy was faring under Nazi control, on the other, how important it was for them to scrimp and save, to eat simple stews, and to donate to the *Winterhilfe* (Schäfer 1981, 166). There was at the same time a high level of government investment in heavy industry and construction, which was combined with policies to encourage saving and to redistribute income to those sections of the community less likely to spend on consumer goods—policies intended to restrain the increasing trend to consume.

The RVA worked closely with the women's organizations of the National Socialist Party, in particular the Volkswirtschaft/Hauswirtschaft (national/home economics [V/H]) department of the DFW, led by Else Vorwerck, and the women's office of the DAF, led by Frau Rohr. These organizations conducted preliminary consumer research and used all the means of persuasion at their disposal to ensure as effective a reception of the RVA's campaigns as possible. Courses in "German" home management and open demonstrations in "research stations" were arranged alongside slide shows, film evenings, and local radio programs. They also inspired individual large-scale campaigns, such as the fight against wastage, *Kampf dem Verderb,* although much of their work was conducted on the personal level of one committed National Socialist woman attempting to persuade another. From the summer of 1936 their Verbrauchslenkung work was to a large degree coordinated and centralized through the RVA. In return, the RVA provided funds to support connected projects initiated by the women's organizations themselves, such as Vorwerck's struggling publication of the *Volkswirtschaftlichen Mitteilungen* (National Economic Bulletins), and agreed to share the billing in the authorship of all pamphlets and brochures.[16] There were also cooperative

16. All such publications were to feature the words: "RVA bearbeitet vom DAF Abteilung V/H in Verbindung mit dem Frauenamt der DAF," as agreed at the meeting between the RVA and representatives of the relevant women's groups in Berlin, 19 June 1936, BAP 50.02/12:109–11.

channels of communication established between the Frauenstunden departments in the DFW and NSF at regional and national level, with the radio used to advertise and support these organizations' publications and initiatives.

Cooperation between all these different organizations was not always as smooth as the public image of a united front pretended, despite the high degree of overlap in personnel. One example of this constant, if restrained, rivalry is the accusation made by the DAF that the DFW was trying to monopolize responsiblity for organizing all RVA propaganda, by agitating for an end to lecture tours and demonstrations in factories, full responsibility for which had been delegated to the women's office by the leader of the DAF, Robert Ley. The RVA eventually backed the DFW in this matter.[17] If it came to a choice between the women's organizations and industry, however, it was likely the RVA would support the latter. This was the case, for example, in a dispute in 1942 over the content of a pamphlet about economy-conscious washing techniques. The advice contained came from the advertisers of the soap industry and contradicted the results of research carried out by the DFW laboratories in Leipzig. The RVA simply dismissed the DFW's calls for the pamphlets to be amended.[18]

It has been argued that propaganda left to the relatively unpowerful women's organizations was of low priority status (Rupp 1978, 105–6). The strict polarization of male and female spheres, however, meant women were left a degree of autonomy in the sphere allotted to them. It was for this reason that the official women's organizations were considered best suited for making the appeal to other women. And yet, just to make sure, the whole operation was orchestrated by a semipolitical, semicommercial committee, managed at the top level exclusively by men.[19] Moreover, the millions of marks channeled from central funds to run some of their campaigns indicates the importance attached to directing and maximizing women's purchasing power.

**Women, Radio, and the Four Year Plan**

The close coordination of all these different branches of public information can be illustrated by taking a closer look at one particular campaign,

---

17. February 1943, BAP 50.02/17:121.

18. Aktennotiz an die Geschäftsleitung, 12 November 1942, BAP 50.02/17:140:131.

19. The Reichsfachschaft Deutscher Werbefachleute reported in 1935 that it would like to see more women involved in advertising, although those women who were employed in the industry were among the most capable, ambitious, and well-trained in the business ("Aus dem weiblichen Berufsleben: Ist Werbung Frauenberuf?" *Berliner Lokal-Anzeiger* 48, 24 February 1935).

such as that organized in May 1937 to advertise women's duties in terms of the Four Year Plan. The RFF aimed to reach every woman in the country by way of the various propaganda channels within a two week period beginning on 9 May, Mother's Day. It was the first nationwide *Aktion* of its kind and was carefully coordinated from the center.[20] Rudolf Hess, for example, in his capacity as Hitler's representative, issued a directive to all party organizations insisting on cooperation with the DFW's campaign.[21] It was incumbent upon the various *Gaue* (administrative regions) to ensure that reports appeared in the local press outlining the practical ways in which women could help the country toward economic independence. A lengthy article about the campaign appeared in the May edition of *Die Deutsche Frau.* The radio campaign began with a Mother's Day speech by Gertrud Scholtz-Klink on the national wavelength. This was followed by daily items incorporated into the news bulletins and a radio version of the article in *Die Deutsche Frau* broadcast by all regional stations. The *Gaue* were also asked to prepare variety evenings with children's choirs and interviews with model women for regional transmission. Meanwhile, in all cinemas with seating for over two hundred, a series of slides produced by the DFW were shown during the week of 17 May. These activities were backed by the nationwide distribution to every household of centrally produced leaflets containing more detailed information about women's duties and by a nationwide poster campaign. Stencils of the same design were sent for reproduction to some two thousand eight hundred newspapers and one thousand eight hundred magazines.

The women's organizations certainly attached a great deal of importance to the initiatives, especially those inspired by the requirements of the Four Year Plan. It was a policy that seemed to put women somewhere near center stage. The small-scale efforts of women in the home were invested with national economic importance, and those efforts, be it saving energy or collecting old clothes, became political:

> The small scale is no different from the large scale. The state's campaigns in the service of the Four Year Plan . . . can only be realized with the participation and practical help of women; by getting involved and offering their services they express their political posi-

20. "Reichseinheitliche Aufklärungs- und Werbeaktion für das Deutsche Frauen-werk," *Nachrichtendienst der Reichsfrauenführung* 5 (May 1937): 132–34.

21. "Der Stellvertreter des Führers zur Werbeaktion des Deutschen Frauenwerkes: Rundschreiben 58/37 vom 11.5.37," *Nachrichtendienst der Reichsfrauenführung* 6 (June 1937): 153.

tion. . . . What women's work for the state might achieve can only be measured by the impact in the germ cells of the living community of a nation: in individual families. (Hessig 1938)

**Women's Radio and the War Effort**

The outbreak of war in 1939 caused momentary disruption to the propaganda schedules, although the message sent out to the nation's women was at first not so much changed in direction as in degree. In a report for the last quarter of that year the RVA described how the cooperation between the regional radio stations initially just fell apart, as programs and entire campaigns were abandoned until new directives were received from the central coordinating office of the RVA. Some stations did introduce new programs when war broke out, as in Leipzig, which began a series called "Wissenswertes kurz berichtet," weaving "hidden propaganda" in among the facts "every housewife ought to know." The Deutschlandsender also broadcast special programs as part of nationwide campaigns intended to ease the introduction of new measures such as clothing coupons. After a period of initial uncertainty, it was clear that the old campaigns could be safely brought down off the shelf again, dusted off, and, with a little touching up here and there, would serve the needs of the nation at war just as well as in peacetime. The prewar campaign, *Kampf dem Verderb,* for example, was promoted with new vigor early in 1940 and was one of the most important campaigns directed at women during the war years, advising women how to prevent decay and wastage.

While it is true that it was a long time before Germany really began to feel the effects of the war at home, it is surprising that there should have been so little output under the auspices of the Frauenfunk at this time to shore up morale and coax the population into readiness for the onset of trials to come. In part this was so as not to stir alarm, but it was also due to the widespread belief that the war would soon be over, long before any attack on German territory. What is more, the country as a whole, and the radio propaganda aimed at women along with it, had been geared toward preparing for war for years. When the time came, despite temporary confusion and hesitation, it was a question of just making a few adjustments in vocabulary, emphasizing a little louder the patriotic duty of following the government's directives, and of reiterating the wisdom of all the advice that had come before, rather than of announcing some sort of historical watershed. Meanwhile, in Britain there was an initial flurry of activity to get people to prepare for blackouts and bomb shelters in the expectation of imminent invasion. But the "phoney war" dragged on, and the press, including the women's magazines, was faced with the problem of keeping people's determination steady and keeping them "smiling through."[22]

## Soft Soaping the Nation

The wartime campaigns were more effective than those that ran in concert with the Four Year Plan in the mid-1930s, because of the greater incentives for thrift and patriotic purchasing. Private and public spheres merged in the propaganda for the home front as each measure to save resources was directly translated into resources freed for the war effort. One of the largest campaigns organized by the RVA during the war was *Sachgemäßes Waschen: Wasche Wäsche Weise* (Proper Washing: Wash Washing Wisely), launched early in 1940. A closer look at the strategies involved in a campaign of this sort illustrates exactly how radio was integrated into a broader propaganda machine. The campaign's aim was to educate women on how to do their laundry as efficiently as possible, protecting precious textile resources, and wasting minimum time, energy, and, above all, soap. With its high fat content, soap was a particularly sensitive issue in a country that was trying hard to achieve self-sufficiency in the production of fats and oils, the more so when imports in these goods were blocked. Washing techniques had to be brought up to date with the developments in technology and chemistry to protect both the machines and the new synthetics. There had been many complaints that these artificial fibers did not last as well as traditional materials, and the new campaign was driven primarily by the need to insist that any problems housewives found with increased wear and tear lay entirely with their own ignorance about how to handle unfamiliar fabrics.[23] The campaign ran for the duration of the war, spending as much as ten million marks a year. In December a special post was created in the DFW—the Reichsreferentin für Waschfragen (national consultant for laundry matters), but the mastermind behind the campaign was Hans Brose, whose advertising expertise was hired for a basic salary of RM 2,000 by the RVA.[24]

In 1939, on instructions from the manager of the Four Year Plan, Hermann Göring, and with cooperation from the textile industry, the RVA had issued unified guidelines on washing procedures, based on two

---

22. For example, Trevor Allen, "Smiling Through: Too Much to Do Is Hard—Nothing to Do Is Harder—But to Be Prepared Is Everyone's Job and It's Up to Us to Do It Cheerfully," *Women's Own;* reproduced in Waller and Vaughan-Rees 1987, 27.

23. Cf. letters from the RVA to various radio stations, dated 31 October 1938, BAP 50.02/26:196–200.

24. 50.02/17:419; RVA Letter from RVA to Brose, 24 February 1939 BAP 50.02/26:290.

years' research. A huge publicity campaign was organized to run through September and October, with the officially sanctioned washing instructions to be sewn into garments, displayed in shop windows, featured in public talks, and delivered in leaflet form to every household in the country.[25] But the war intervened, bringing with it the prompt introduction of textile rationing and the so-called *Einheitswaschmittel* (standard washing powder), with its lower fat content and lesser effectiveness, which made the carefully drawn up instructions largely irrelevant. Brand-name soap powders were withdrawn from the market, so it would have been counterproductive to have gone on distributing leaflets recommending the use of Persil and its competitors. Stockpiled by the million in shops throughout the country, they were optimistically stored away for use when the war was over. In their place a new brochure, *Schone Deine Wäsche!* (Protect Your Washing!), written by Elly Heuß-Knapp, was produced by the millions for urgent distribution to housewives via local shops throughout Germany— a service shopkeepers were expected to perform free of charge from a sense of national duty. A million copies were also printed in German and Czech for distribution in the protectorates of Bohemia and Moldavia. The twenty-five million copies of these *Kriegswaschfibel,* sold in stores and chemist shops at ten pfennigs a piece, were promoted and enlarged upon by radio talks, newspaper articles, exhibitions, synchronized shop window displays across the country, and advertisements placed by soap powder manufacturers in all magazines which had a predominantly female readership.[26]

Radio opened the campaign in mid-December, advertising the brochure with twelve short conversational programs broadcast nationwide on the women's hour and the current affairs program "Zeitgeschehen." This way the RVA was confident of reaching a high percentage of housewives in the first week of the campaign. Else Möbus of the Frauenfunk was charged with preparing programs for the nationwide frequency, but there was some difficulty in coordinating the interregional campaign, because the distribution of the brochures was introduced initially in eastern Prussia, Pommerania, and Berlin-Brandenburg, to be

25. *"Vereinheitlichte Waschvorschriften für das ganze Reichsgebiet:* RVA—Aufklärungs-Aktion des Waschmittel-Einzelhandels; Über das Thema *wasche Wäsche weise,"* BAP 50.02/18:155–59.

26. For example, *Beyer's für Alle* (with a circulation in 1939 of 72,000), *Hella* (75,000), *Deutsche Frauenzeitung* (100,000), *Deutsche Modenzeitung* (320,000), *Handarbeit und Wäsche* (130,000), *Mode für Alle* (230,000), and *Frauen-Kultur im Deutschen Frauenwerk* (17,000). RM 4,000,000 was paid out for similar ads in some four hundred daily papers in 1940, and there were some four hundred RVA-authored articles in 1940 alone. See also "Protokoll der Sitzung der NS Reichsfachschaft Deutscher Werbeleute," 14 April 1939, BAP 50.02/26:280; BAP 50.02/17:326.

extended in waves southward over the Reich. The RVA headquarters of the campaign sent a reprimand to the Reichssender Danzig for prematurely broadcasting a program about washing methods, which might have "disrupted the entire planning of the campaign."[27]

Following on the heels of the leafleting campaign, courses were provided by the NSF, and educational slide shows were given at DFW, DAF, and school meetings by some two hundred public relations representatives of the washing powder industry, who between them, it was hoped, would reach up to ten thousand housewives a day. Records were produced to accompany slide shows—often shown in cinemas before the main feature—with male voices singing jingles like: "Die Wäschefibel ist erschienen/Sie will im Krieg der Hausfrau dienen" (The washing brochure has appeared/to serve the housewife in the war). Film was in many ways less suited to these sorts of campaigns, as it was expensive and less flexible, but several propaganda films were made. For example, a short documentary film was commissioned by the RVA from the Color-Film-Gesellschaft to be scripted and part-directed by Elly Heuß-Knapp and funded by the sale of the brochures. Among other things it insisted that the new recommended washing techniques represented an advance over traditional methods, despite the fact that the standard wartime soap powder had a tendency to turn the washing gray.[28] A plan to recruit television to the campaign, broadcasting a series of still pictures with a "humorous" voice-over, was rejected by the RMVP because it was too expensive and the audience too small.[29] Finally, though less glamorous than film, less humorous than much of the radio output, and certainly less informative than brochures, perhaps one of the most effective means of publicizing the campaign was one of the simplest. From 1941 the soap ration cards themselves, produced in millions and passing through the hands of every washing man and woman, carried on the reverse side the words "Hausfrau! Verlange beim Seifeneinkauf die Kriegswaschfibel!" (Housewife! Demand the wartime washing brochure when you buy your soap!). Later still, an abbreviated version of the instructions were themselves to be publicized in this way.[30]

And yet, at the close of the first year of the campaign, the RVA had to admit that even this intense promotion had not yet achieved a sufficient reform in the nation's laundry habits. (This information was gathered at a

27. Aktennotiz vom 31.5.40, BAP 50.02/18:527.
28. Aktennotiz vom 4.1.41, BAP 50.02/18:408, including film treatment. The soap industry also made films of its own, and Ufa prepared a short propaganda film entitled *Ein Berg wird abgebaut* (A Mountain Is Dismantled) (BAP 50.02/31:67–74).
29. Exchange of letters, July 1940, BAP 50.02/17:480, 486.
30. RVA-Sachwerterhaltung 1941, 4; BAP 50.02/18:24.

local level by representatives of the Party's women's organizations). It was therefore proposed to repeat and intensify the campaign and "tirelessly to reach out to every housewife in the country."[31] This effort was also deemed necessary, not only to protect the *Volksgut* but also to counteract the grumbling discontent brewing in the country that the new standard powder was a second-grade ersatz designed to make the housewife spend longer at the sink. At the end of 1941 the RVA reported that their propaganda efforts were finally beginning to be effective in changing washing habits, and it was decided to keep the pressure up.[32] Part of the 1942 campaign included telling housewives that it was their own fault for the shortages of washing powder on the market and that they must be still more sparing, still more diligent in following all the public advice.[33] By 1943, however, questions began to be raised about the priority status of such a campaign, as the war effort was finally being stepped up into top gear. The previous year there had already been some changes made in radio scheduling, although the Verbrauchslenkung service had been spared. The stations which contributed to the prestigious national Doppelprogramm—Berlin, Breslau, Munich, Frankfurt, Vienna, Hamburg, and Königsberg—were scarcely affected by the cutbacks enforced in 1942 to release as many men for active service and the arms industry as possible. Meanwhile, the main service rendered by the remaining stations, apart from the special foreign language broadcasts from Luxembourg, were the women's radio programs designed to direct consumption and the agricultural service.[34]

The priority given to these campaigns can be gauged by some of the battles waged over female labor. The Armaments Commission of the Four Year Plan, for example, wanted to know if any of the large number of women engaged in the propaganda work for the RVA could be spared for the armaments industry. In its reply the RVA reiterated its view that enlightening the nation's women in matters of economy was just as essential to the war effort as producing arms and that the personnel carrying out this important work had already been pared down to the minimum.[35] These sentiments echoed the words of the national women's leader, Gertrud Scholtz-Klink: "Though our weapon in this area is only the ladle, its impact will be no less than those of other weapons" (cited in Rupp 1977, 372).

Similarly defending the importance of this work, the DAF official

---

31. Letter from the director of the RVA to the Schriftleitung, 10 January 1941, BAP 50.02/18:66.
32. BAP 50.02/17:47.
33. BAP 50.02/17:49–51.
34. Letter from the head of radio to Dr. Schmidt, 30 May 1942, BA R55/230:42.
35. Letter dated 8 June 1943, BAP 50.02/40:304.

responsible for organizing the RVA-inspired lecture tours of factories and workplaces, Johanna Schmidt, reported that, with the increasing scarcity of washing powder and textiles, the women she talked to were more grateful than ever for tips on how to eke out supplies. Curtailing the numbers of these peripatetic lecturers any further, she argued, would have serious consequences for the morale of the female workforce. Nor did she accept the argument that such lectures interrupted productivity at the workplace, for they always took place at times stipulated by the management and were usually integrated into other general political activities.[36] The RVA view won over that of the Armaments Commission, although the campaign budget for 1943, while still substantial, was considerably down from the RM 10 million spent the previous year, at RM 6,750,000.[37] To make up for this shortfall in funding, a new advertising angle was introduced. Posters and pamphlets now all featured the chirpy little *Dreckspatz,* the "mucky pup," or literally "Dirty Sparrow," whose function it was to liven up the message, which after three years was getting rather stale. He replaced the sketches of three elegant women doing their washing the wise way who had graced the posters since 1940, in the hope that a more humorous approach would do for the washing campaign what a similar cartoon figure had successfully done for a campaign to save coal.[38] By 1944 the RVA's publishing output was radically curtailed as part of measures to release labor for other work and to save paper, but the continued production of pamphlets for housewives, especially those dealing with nutrition and clothing, was staunchly defended to the end by the RVA, as being of irreplaceable value in keeping up morale and effectivity in the war effort on the home front.[39]

## Purchasing Power and Political Impotence

All this time money and effort was considered well spent since each year, so the propaganda insisted, textiles worth up to three or four hundred million Reichsmark had to be replaced, just for the want of a little more care or a little more know-how on the part of the nation's housewives. The campaign was therefore officially labeled *kriegswichtig,* vital to the war

---

36. Aktennotiz an die Geschäftsleitung, 11 February 1943, BAP 50.02/17:121.

37. Figures for the advertising campaign 1942–43, BAP 50.02/17:43, 1.

38. Aktennotiz der Geschäftsleitung, 4 June 1943, BAP 50.02/17:96. The year 1943 also saw three short movies on the subject of patriotic laundry management made for general cinema release, two produced by Ufa and the other by Tiller Film.

39. Letter from the Geschäftsführer of the RVA to the president of the Reichsschrifttumskammer, 19 August 1944, BAP 50.02/13:201–2 (e.g., the government's "Recipe Service" and the official publication *Die Landfrau* had both been withdrawn).

effort. If in times of textile shortages every garment or piece of bedding that had to be thrown away, and every malfunctioning washing machine that had to be replaced was a drain on the nation's resources, in times of war, according to the hyperbole of the propaganda, careless handling of laundry was not merely unpatriotic—it was practically treasonous.[40]

Within the context of the Third Reich the contradictions of reading political power off the practices of consumption become apparent. Purchasing power is by its nature inclined to be an emasculated power. The power to choose is limited by the choices being offered, while the power to decide what is offered lies elsewhere. An individual's recourse to affect those decisions is minimal. Collective action has more potential, but, when organized by the state, or by a body bridging both state and commerce as happened in the Third Reich, the notion of consumer power loses its meaning. Nazi propaganda, then, had nothing to fear in alerting the nation's women to the "power" they wielded with their shopping bags and their housewifely competence. It fitted in with the ideology of separate spheres divided by function but not by status, by telling women that there was a space for them to make decisions that could affect the life of the nation in which they were needed and would be respected.

That space, of course, was the home. Excluded from positions of any real power, they were fed the myth of an alternative power, one based on the permanent sacrifice of public and political agency. The law of nature was invoked to justify the decree that their economic power, however great, was ultimately defined in terms of maternal duty and that the willingness to perform that duty defined a woman's political position. Thus, a woman's reluctance to engage wholeheartedly in the state-run campaigns could be read, by the initiators of those campaigns, as an expression of dissent. Deprived of a vote or a voice in the political life of the nation, women were told that their political opinions were expressed by their behavior as housewives and mothers. They were expected to believe that their motherly devotion was an expression of devotion to the state. Leaving no room for resistance at this level—"withdrawal" of devotion to one's child was hardly a tenable political weapon—such an indicator of political opinion was always bound to be favorable to the government and drew the boundaries of political expression open to women still tighter in. Furthermore, no matter how energetically women chose to apply themselves to being good mothers and citizens, they were warned not to expect to see the fruits

---

40. E. Sch., "Vermeide Wäscheschäden!" RVA, BAP 50.02 /18:67–68. Note that radio manuscripts which mentioned the level of fat reduction in the new soap powder (from 45 percent to 10 percent) were withdrawn at the request of the body responsible, the Reichsstelle für industrielle Fettsorgung, with the admonition to speak in the future only of "lesser" amounts.

of their "political activity" until their sons and daughters were full grown. Women were exhorted to perform and conform in a system which described their great power but ensured that they were kept firmly in their place, and once again the radio was instrumental in channeling the renegotiations of the relationship between public and private politics.

CHAPTER 8

# Finding a Voice: Women's Radio and the Evolution of Broadcast Talk

It is clear that the central place of the family audience in the minds of the program makers was a major influence on their stylistic and scheduling decisions and that the conditions of reception in the private sphere have had important implications for the modes of broadcast public speech. The evolution of presentational style was profoundly influenced by the understanding that audiences generally consisted of families gathered around the hearth, seated harmoniously around the wireless, united in their new appreciation of the outside world. As radio matured, it became more familiar in its address, more populist in its appeal. The dry rhetoric of early lectures, the convention of experts talking to amateurs, the prevailing atmosphere of the public meeting, were gradually, but consciously, replaced by a studied informality befitting the familiar setting. The preferred tone came to be that of a supportive and trusted friend, the perfect family companion, a voice that would not intrude pompously into the sanctity of the family circle but one that people would be glad to welcome into their homes. In this chapter, however, I want to argue that, in Germany at least, the carefully scripted impression of a friendly fireside chat, which came to prominence in the "golden age" of radio, was an approach that was poineered in the realm of women's programming, in which from the outset many items came under the rubric of *Plauderei* (chitchat).

The firmer this resolution took hold in the radio schedules as a whole, the louder became the demands that women's voices become more prominent on the airwaves. In the early years women were heard infrequently outside the confines of the Frauenfunk. But even a proliferation of women as presenters of individual programs in prime-time radio would not suffice. It was the voice of the announcer that gave a station its characteristic signature, and it was as announcers that the measure of acceptance of women's voices on the radio can be tested, though with the caveat that on its own such a test simply reproduces the conventional hierarchies of the public-private divide (van Zoonan 1988, 1993; Holland 1989). This chapter, then, traces the history of women as announcers on German radio and the opposition they encountered. It also analyzes the presentational strategies devised by the Frauenfunk in recognition of the particular conditions of reception experienced by women and families in the home. Here the perceived characteristics of private female discourse—chitchat, gossip, and the heart-to-heart—were publicly manifested on the radio of the Weimar Republic and later came to be of strategic importance to the domestic propaganda of the Third Reich.

## Presentation Matters

Presentation is clearly not incidental to a program. Styles of address determine the mode of reception, the degree of attentiveness, the level of acceptance on the part of an audience. Different programs demand different styles, according to the seriousness of the material, the status of the contributors, the character of the target audience, the time of broadcast, and the intended function of the program—to inform, educate, or entertain. Choice of presenter and style of presentation are decisions of importance, and the outcome of these decisions can be a useful indication of overall broadcasting policies, as David Cardiff has argued about the evolution of radio talk in Britain before the war (1986, 228). The conventions of broadcasting style, he proposes, reflect not only the broad social outlook of the broadcasters but also a range of motivations specific to their occupation, such as maximizing the audience, targeting a particular section of the listening public, or accommodating the internal dynamics of the broadcasting organization and its relationship to the state. There is much, then, that can be learned by studying the history of radio presentation and in particular, I would argue, from the history of women on the radio. The prejudices that kept women off the air for so much of the day for so long shed light on some of the assumptions about radio's place in the public sphere. The presentational strategies employed by women in their own programs, moreover, mark the dawning realization, so vital to radio's future development, that, while radio talk is *public* discourse, the circumstances of reception are defined in the *private* sphere.

In 1928 *Der Deutsche Rundfunk* published an article by the actress Dora Dery, who spoke of her excitement at the prospect of working for the Berliner Funkstunde and of the different techniques she would be employing when she copresented the program "Die Frau von heute" (The Woman of Today) with Viktor Schwanneke. Though she loved the stage and all its trappings, she found the idea of speaking to countless listeners, capturing their attention "somehow intoxicating." Even the "loveliest words and the cleverest lectures" could fall flat if poorly spoken, so she was glad of the voice training she had received at drama school. She described the intentions of the program as follows:

> I want to portray a woman, a woman of today whose story unfolds in a series of dialogues, who experiences what all of us can experience these days: a relationship with a man, coming together, trouble with relations, the inevitable battles between the sexes, etc. And in the process, I want to touch on all the problems which interest us today, e.g., the loneliness of the independent woman; companionate marriage; to marry or stay single?; childlessness; child raising; social questions, etc. In short, everything which affects us today. And I also want to deal with everyday questions: cosmetics, sport, beauty, and fashion. And all in dialogues, to make it easier for the listener. Because I always find that it's very difficult to distinguish between more than two, at the very most, three voices on the radio. (3317)

This is exactly the sort of program deemed appropriate for the female touch, dealing with human relationships, social issues, and appearances and presented in a conversational style. And yet a man could copresent a program of this sort, a recognition of the universal interest in the "everyday" that was not matched by a recognition of women's interest in the universe of public affairs. For some commentators women's monopoly of the woman's hour became a matter of pride, as they ridiculed the editorial decisions to let men tackle women's affairs or even to read from works penned by a woman.[1] This was a position brought about in the face of real obstacles to the promotion of women's voices on the air at the time, but there were other commentators who argued against such separatism. One such critic was Meta Brix, who was afraid of the *Frauenstunden* losing touch with reality if they refused to entertain the male perspective at all. She argued, for example, that, in order to understand the mechanisms that controlled women's access to various social institutions, it was necessary to hear from the people, the men, who were in charge of those institutions. In that way, she suggested, the path toward equality would more easily be cleared and the understanding between the sexes enabled. Besides, it was simply refreshing to hear a man talk about things like cooking, either

---

1. Margret Mendzee was a particularly vociferous advocate of this position, writing a series of articles in the early 1930s on the subject. She also held the "gentle" arts such as fairy tales, romantic stories, and most forms of poetry to be the proper realm for women.

because of the humor of the situation, arising from the same sort of incongruity that was well rehearsed in the cross-dressing films of the period, or because of the critical distance created by a degree of alienation from the familiar (1931, 134). But Brix's was an unpopular position in the pages of the women's supplements to the radio journals, given that so little of the schedules was colonized by women, territory that was generally proudly defended against male incursion.

While women's voices might have been a rarity during the bulk of broadcast hours in Weimar Germany, the *Frauenstunden* were their almost exclusive domain. In women's radio the dominant form was either the apparently informal chat described by Dery or the staged interview between experts and a "representative" mother or housewife. The old formal style of presentation was preserved where it was deemed fitting either to the subject matter or to the standing of the presenter, but, increasingly, more intimate tones prevailed. To solve the dilemma of fitting an informal presentational style to subjects that seemed to demand a certain gravitas, individual talks increasingly gave way to debates, discussions, and interviews as ways of imparting difficult or controversial material in a more balanced, informative, and yet easily digestible form.

The dissemination of "expert opinion" via the radio to alter relations in the home is the subject of a separate chapter. Here the focus is on recognizing the significance of the evolution of these new styles of presentation. It is not always obvious that such familiar formats as the studio interview were once innovative strategies in response to a particular broadcasting problem. The task of the interviewer was to ensure that experts did not talk over listeners' heads and to make the information easier to absorb by promoting a lively dialogue. This particular mode of presentation was popular in the radio production of the late Weimar period precisely because of the way the inevitable relaxation of the strict nonpolitical line ran ahead of legislative reforms to monitor the output of political material. The notion of a disinterested third party moderating a discussion arose in the hope that the often unruly clash of opinions in radio debates could be tempered and channeled into more interesting radio by the mediation of a neutral chairperson, even if in practice the chair merely functioned to steer the speakers away from potentially controversial areas.[2]

The question of editorial style is of particular importance when considering the function and impact of censorship. To avoid controversy, overt political censorship could be camouflaged as a question of style. Station directors and program editors exercised a high degree of self-censorship and believed themselves to be operating in a relatively free space.

---

2. This was raised in an article in the *Berliner Tageblatt* in 1929; cited in Cardiff 1986, 235.

Ernst Hardt, the director of the Westdeutscher Rundfunk, insisted it was wrong to call the "editorial guidelines" censorship as they were not precisely formulated, leaving editorial decisions to "the political tact, the sensitivity and often the diplomatic abilities" of the individual station directors. He maintained that "you may say anything, you may express your opinions in full, but you must do it in such a way that people with another point of view do not feel insulted."[3] Hans Flesch, by 1930 director of the Berliner Funkstunde, was also quite adamant that there was minimal political interference in the decision-making process, saying that "nobody would seriously speak of censorship when to serve his purposes he seeks out something which suits the idiosyncratic laws of radio and leaves out that which does not. What influences the schedules is not radio censorship, but the director's sense of responsibility" (1930, 18).

These views were in accord with Bredow's conception of the radio professional as a servant of the state, whose personal politics played no part in professional decisions and who would take it as a slur should such an accusation be made (1929, 4). He suggested that the organizational structure was designed to bolster professional integrity, in that "every person in a position of authority in radio is his own watchdog and is constrained by the organizational set-up to work in such a way that his decisions are always made with the knowledge of his colleagues."[4] What this meant in practice was that radio schedules often reflected the personal whims of the men in charge. Professional responsibility in view of existing guidelines might have been of more importance than the decisions of the Überwachungsausschüsse or Kulturbeiräte on a day-to-day basis, but historians have uncovered examples of overt political interference not only by the bodies designed to oversee the neutrality of political broadcasts but also by various ministries, which thought their interests might be compromised by certain programs, and that the watchdog bodies did perform a censorial function, in the legal definition of the term (Fessmann 1973, 129; Hörburger 1975, 18–19).

Of course, censorship proper followed fast on the heels of the Nazi takeover. But in terms of presentation old lessons had to be learned afresh. Flush with success and ambitious for rapid acceptance of the new order, the Nazi program directors initially swamped the airwaves with bombastic music, live transmissions from Party events, and, most ineffectively, declamatory speeches and dogmatic hyperbole. The German radio was the "mouthpiece of the Führer," whose own voice, of course, regularly punc-

---

3. Ernst Hardt, minutes of the *Programmrat des deutschen Rundfunkgesellschaften,* in Bremen, 22 and 23 May 1929; cited in Pohle 1955, 70.

4. Hans Bredow, "Überparteilichkeit des Rundfunks," *Funk-Express: Rundfunk-Nachrichten-Schnelldienst* 96, 28 November 1929, 4.

tuated the airwaves The propaganda eulogized the impact of Hitler's voice, claiming that, "when men and women, boys and girls hear his voice sounding clear and masculine so that it beats in the heart like a divine understanding, then we can sense the living effect of the radio as the highest ordinance" (Varges 1941). But, despite such hyperbole, the public platform language of the demagogue did not in general transmit well on the radio, and listening figures plummeted. Before long the malaise was diagnosed and the remedy prescribed—namely, a return to a mixture of light music and intimate studio conversation. It was an approach that could apparently benefit from the female touch.[5]

**Prejudices Voiced**

From the beginning there was much discussion about which voices transmitted well over the airwaves. At first the choice was limited by the primitive level of the available technology, inasmuch as the electrical reproduction of a voice was still imperfect. Voices with a higher pitch suffered from distortion in the process of conversion of sound waves to electrical signals. This technical limitation was quickly translated into the maxim that women's voices were unsuitable for broadcasting. Prejudice against women announcers hid behind technological excuses long after the shortcomings of the hardware had been resolved. In Germany the excuse of technological limitation was still being used at least as late as 1941 to account for the dearth of women's voices on the air.[6]

The possibility of voice amplification offered by the invention of the loudspeaker and the microphone was important in giving to some women the confidence speak in public, but, given the strength of ideological opposition to women having a public voice of their own, the decisive factor in women winning access to channels of public communication was feminism. In her study of women's appropriation of the technology of amplification in the United States, Anne McKay came to the following conclusion, which is equally relevant to the German case:

> that when women used the new technology in support of the goals and activities of established institutions, they were applauded at best or ignored at worst. When they attempted to use it in ways that would lead to change in the traditional order and in women's customary roles, their right to use it at all was challenged. (1988, 187–88)

---

5. Gerard Eckert, "Männerstimmen-Frauenstimmen," DKD 123, 12 August 1941, BAK R 34/273.

6. Gerard Eckert, "Die Stimme, die jeder hört," DKD 225, 9 December 1941, BAK R 34/123.

As the technicians' expertise developed, so did the subtlety of the arguments about what type of voice listeners found most sympathetic to the ear. With regard to questions about the suitability of female announcers in early radio, these arguments often were less about what was sympathetic to the ear, than about what was most in sympathy with convention. At a time when women's public voices were still struggling to be heard, it was a major achievement when women became station announcers. As the voice of the station, an announcer carried a significant symbolic weight. The station's identity was intimately connected with the announcer's personality. On a national wavelength the announcer's voice was, by implication, the voice of the nation, so consequently few women announcers became well-known nationwide. It took almost ten years before the possibility of a woman speaking to and "for" the nation was seriously considered, and such an appointment aroused hostility.

The tendency to find the male voice more authoritative than the female has little to do with the physical characteristics that differentiate the voices of the sexes. Research suggests that acculturation is a more powerful determinant of gender-specific voice characteristics than is physique (Sachs, Liebermann, and Erikson 1973; Coates 1986; Macdonald 1995, 41–72). A deep voice has become a signal of authority simply because men have traditionally held the most prestigious positions in society, their voices being heard above the rest from pulpits and public platforms and so becoming associated with a higher degree of credibility. But women in Weimar radio tended to counter the claims that their voices were unsuitable on the same essentialist terms, citing the qualities in women's nature that would benefit the profession. Some claimed, for example, that women were better qualified as announcers than men thanks to their "natural" sense of duty and responsibility, their "instinct" to adapt sensitively to different situations, and their "essential" empathy (Mendzee 1930a–c, 1931). Others emphasized the personal tone of radio talk suggested by the domestic location of most radio reception or, in a similar vein, drew an analogy between the role of the annnouncer and that of a hostess, welcoming the listener into the broadcasting house (Brix 1932, 106). Even enthusiasts of women on the radio, though, had to admit that it would be a long time before there was general agreement that women should be heard as often as men on an equally broad range of subjects (H. R. 1931, 59).

The first female announcer to be heard in Germany was in fact not German but Italian. Luisa Buoncampagni's work introducing Radio Roma Napoli had made her voice famous all over Europe. German stations were slow to follow suit, only gradually overcoming their prejudices against women announcers and the concept of women dealing at any length with "serious" topics such as news and current affairs. In 1930 a number of newspaper articles dealt with the question to which many aspiring radio personalities wanted to know the answer: "How do I become a radio announcer?" ("Wie werde ich . . ." 1930). The advice the papers gave was to apply for a place at the new radio school in Berlin. Radio presentation was in the process of being professionalized. The problems a successful candidate might have if she were female, however, are illustrated by the controversy surrounding the appointment of the first female announcer (as distinct from presenter) to work for the Berliner Funk-Stunde, Gertrud van Eyseren.

Van Eyseren was an actress, who had already presented many language programs and children's hours for the Deutsche Welle. She took over the post of station announcer when Karl (Karlchen) Wessel, one of the station's earliest and most popular presenters, died in June 1932, though, because she was a woman, her contract did not encompass the whole range of announcing duties performed by her male predecessor, "a task which would hardly correspond with the narrow limits of the activities of a female announcer" (Brix 1932, 106). Almost a decade after broadcasting began in Germany, the appointment of a woman as a station announcer was still a contentious one. The press treated her appointment with skepticism and derision, some of which was directed at her proficiency in the job, much of which, however, was directed at her simply for the fact of her being a woman. The *Berliner Zeitung,* for example, poured scorn on the success of Luisa Buoncampagni in its caustic rejection of van Eyseren: "After Wessel's death, Witzleben [the Berlin transmitter] is searching for a new voice. The choice has fallen on a woman. They want to follow in the footsteps, no the waves of Trieste, and from now on let us get our information in dainty whispers."[7]

The *Deutsche Zeitung* on 23 July 1932 referred to public antipathy to the "experiment" in its attack. The journal *Funk* was less insulting than the daily press, albeit still cautious in its endorsement of a woman in such a prestigious position. Starting from the position that there could "naturally be no question of a female announcer being suitable for all programs," it welcomed the long-overdue introduction of a female presenter but wondered if van Eyseren's qualifications in the German language necessarily meant that she would have the required flair and flexibility in front of the microphone (Brix 1930a, 45). Part of the reason for this dubious reception was the timing of van Eyseren's arrival at a point of economic crisis. With male unemployment rocketing, any female appointment, especially in the public sphere, encountered hostility from those who saw male employment as a priority (Brix 1930b).

---

7. *Berliner Zeitung am Mittag,* 20 June 1932, n.p.

Berlin, for once, lagged behind the provinces. The first woman to hold such a position in Germany was Margarete Wolf, appointed in 1926 by Hans Flesch of Sürag, one of the more progressive station directors. Her appointment, which involved presenting financial reports, the news headlines, time checks, and the weather, was considered a most daring innovation. At first she was treated no differently than any other announcer and had similar responsibilities. She was, for example, the program anchor during the experimental broadcasts of the test flight of the Graf Zeppelin over Germany as it made radio contact with each of the regional stations.[8] But, gradually, women announcers were used increasingly for specialized introductions of programs that were considered more "suitable" for a woman, a state of affairs that did not change significantly throughout the whole period under consideration (Mendzee 1930c). Wolf was soon joined by Edith Scholz in Hamburg. Such was the novelty of a female voice on the radio that she was inundated with proposals of marriage from admiring listeners (H. R. 1931), yet her true love affair, she maintained, was with the microphone (Mendzee 1930d). Norag became the only station to employ two women announcers, when Maria Einödshofer was appointed to join her some time later. Nuremberg followed with the appointment of Toni Nebuschka, Leipzig with Martha-Elisabeth Teetzmann, and Stuttgart with the popular Ilse Kamnitzer, who went on to work on literary programs and to write her own radio play. All of these announcers had begun their careers on the stage. Maria Einödshofer, for example, had had a successful career at the Hebbel Theater in Berlin and elsewhere in Germany, Holland, and Scandinavia. Edith Scholz had worked at the Landestheater in Braunschweig and at other theaters in northern Germany before joining Norag. Actors were the preferred candidates for these posts because of their skills of projection and clear diction, although they were sometimes criticized for their very theatricality, which did not translate well to the more intimate medium.

The cultivation of the beauty of the spoken word and the development of spoken culture was something that was prominent in the minds of program makers, as the following extract from a 1930 board meeting of the RRG shows:

There are few people who know what a "voice" is and what it might mean. Germany does not yet have a spoken culture. . . . So we have to try to find speakers who can show us what a voice can mean. We must

8. Wolf said of this experience: "When the conversation, which had lasted about ten minutes, was over and sitting at the microphone I wished him well on his journey and thanked him for his call, I was frozen with excitement at the thought he was just then flying right overhead" (cited in Mendzee 1930c).

try to take up the culture of speaking as the foundation of a spoken culture and make elocution our business.[9]

In 1930 *Die Sendung* paid tribute to the talents of these women, particularly to those who fronted artistic and literary shows, maintaining that their talent had brought "the best of German culture" to a wider audience, "as far as the last Pommeranian village, and the fishing villages of the North and Baltic Seas" (Herzog 1930, 126). Radio clearly had its part to play in reinforcing a sense of national identity, of imagined community. But, if it is true that the vision of family listening was crucial in the development of radio, it is also true that the ideal image of the family home that program makers tended to have in mind, especially in the early days, was a specifically middle-class one. In this sense their decisions about both content and modes of address were based on an unrealistic, or at least an incomplete, understanding of the audience. The output was colored as much by an insensitivity to the diversity of interests in society at large as by a conscious determination to disseminate middle-class tastes and cultural values.

Shortly before the demise of the Weimar Republic *Der deutsche Rundfunk* published a review of the situation of women in radio. Its opening paragraph illustrates the progress made toward equality of airtime and opportunity with men but also the long road ahead:

> There is still no typical career for women in radio, no area of activity which they have mastered as such. But a few particularly competent representatives of the female sex have won positions for themselves at the stations and developed with such skill and success, that they have proved the professional possibilities and the suitability of the female character in this direction. (Tschauner 1932, 4)

Given that the prevailing prejudices worked primarily against women's involvement in politics and current affairs, there was, perversely, a disproportionately favorable opportunity for women to find work presenting programs during the period of "nonpolitical" radio. Ironically, under the Nazis those same prejudices worked to ensure women's voices continued to be heard as the amicable and intimate voice of radio. But the question of female announcers was still a contentious one, and Germany lagged behind many other European countries, including Britain, in accepting women at the microphone. If a mode of address were to be adopted in which the sense of community with the audience was promoted

---

9. Meeting of the RRG, 15 May 1930, MS [1930?]: 51, DRA, Bredow-Nachlaß; cited in Schiller-Lerg 1984, 61.

in contrast to the "hierarchical" structures that had gone before, then the "natural" coaxing, cajoling, caring skills associated with women should be put to good effect. It was in the realm of radio presentation that the concept of *Muttergeist* was called on most explicitly to refresh radio output.

There was, nevertheless, plenty of criticism of the women who had worked in radio in the old days. The prevailing tone of address adopted by women on radio had been, according to the *Deutsche Rundfunk,* alienating and ineffective—"of all radio personalities, the women speak the worst . . . so dry, patronising and dogmatic that it is no pleasure to listen to. You can hear the manuscripts rustling, the delivery is monotonous and it makes the listener feel uneasy" ("Unsere Meinung . . ." 1933, 2). Women listeners in particular would be put off by this, the article went on, because women, "expect a friendly voice from the speaker . . . simple, trustworthy and sympathetic." It criticized all the worthy advice programs that so dominated women's radio, arguing that it was terrible having "wisdom preached at you" and "information drummed into you. It makes you impatient, always to be shown the right way, and puts you in a bad mood." This article, written two months into the Third Reich, indicates that there was a recognition of the dangers of too simplistic an approach to propaganda on the airwaves. The problem, according to Werner Suhr, writing in *Die Sendung,* was the tendency to appoint former actresses, who tended to overdramatize even the simplest announcements and who did not therefore convey a sufficient sense of calm objectivity. They were seduced by the glamour of the responsibility, with the result that their sense of self interfered with the message they were trying to convey. The microphone amplified any such artistic pretensions, destroying the illusion of intimacy with the listener, and "the attentive and sensitive listener all too often misses the honesty of the feminine voice. The voices sound cramped and unnatural and above all: they don't sound private enough!" (1934, 299). The successful radio personality concentrated on speaking to a single listener, thereby winning over millions. Radio presentation went some way toward becoming professionalized during the Third Reich, with the introduction in 1935, for example, of a microphone test, the passing of which became a prerequisite for employment, along with proven Aryan status and, for artistes, membership in the relevant chamber of culture. There were also efforts were made to attract young apprentices into the profession, particularly through competitions (Kutsch 1985, 110–12; Marßolek et al. 1995, 20–23).[10]

---

10. There were also women who carved out careers for themselves in the technical side of radio, particularly in the later period, but they were few and far between, and a detailed investigation of their role goes beyond the scope of this study (see, e.g., "Über die Eignung der Frau als Rundfunktechnikerin," DKD 14.5.43:190; BAK R34/142.) For information on

*Funk* suggested a "cunning, feminine" compromise in a front-page article in its August 1933 edition—namely, to find women with "darker" voices who sounded sufficiently similar to their male counterparts as not to alienate the inherently conservative members of the audience:

> A dark voice has the advantage that it does not differ greatly from the male voice. (Note: a dark, not a deep, manly raw voice.) Despite its novelty, its arrival would not be a sensation in the schedules, but would be cautious, and win its place not with aggression, but with flattery. ("Das Problem . . ." 1933)

As always, the strict exclusion of women from the "important" matters of politics and the economy was defended unquestioningly. But the possibility of a woman becoming the "voice of the nation" was at least entertained. Women *were* heard on Nazi radio, but the prejudice that women were not suitable presenters of political programs was never likely to be overcome. The director of the Deutschlandsender, Götz Stoffregen, announced as early as May 1933 that the attempt to use women as announcers had failed.[11] It was not unusual to blame listeners, particularly women listeners, for resisting the idea of female presenters. Often, the simply ideological reasons for restricting women to light entertainment programs were tempered by reference to the prejudices of the audience, the essential qualities of the female voice, and limitations of technology. As Gerhard Eckert of the German news agency, the Deutsches Nachrichtenbüro, put it:

> Women's voices are less easily differentiated than men's. That creates difficulties for the radio play, but it does not mean women cannot be used as announcers. But there will be tasks which are not open to her, because the listener simply does not want to hear certain things from the mouth of a woman. News and politics remain a male preserve. But as the announcer of individual items during a concert, a woman has some potential.[12]

---

female technicians being employed by the RRG in 1943, see BAK R55/222:8, 110; and following directions from Himmler to Hinkel in 1943. As part of the scheme to train a new generation of radio professionals, forty young women and twelve wounded soldiers were trained in special classes for up to six months in the technical side of radio. Himmler suggested that one could indeed begin to speak of a new *Frauenberuf* (Himmler to Hinkel, n.d., BAK R55/1274:50).

11. Götz Stoffregen, "Der Hörer hat das Wort," *Berliner Börsen Courier,* 11 May 1933; cited in Marßolek et al. 1995, 21.

12. Gerard Eckert, "Männerstimmen-Frauenstimmen," DKD 123, 12 August 1941, BAK R34/273.

In the light of such thinking, and as women were taking over more responsibilities as men were called up to fight, the presentation of light entertainment gradually became the almost exclusive reserve of female announcers.[13] Output in the Third Reich was to be a seamless product, infused at every level with the breath of Nazi ideology. Radio as a site of national identity formation and shaper of public opinion could not afford any cracks in the facade. Ensuring the political allegiance of its staff was a prerequisite, but even the most enthusiastic Party member could not expect to work on news and current affairs programs if she were a woman.

Even with the existing restrictions, there were sometimes complaints about women handling affairs on the airwaves, which were the proper domain of men. During the war, particularly, there were a number of complaints from soldiers who objected to civilian announcers, especially women, referring to them as *Kameraden,* a term normally reserved for use by one soldier to another. The head of the armed forces wrote a letter to the radio section of the RMVP requesting that "the relevant authorities be informed that the appellation 'comrade' be used only in exceptional circumstances and only by those people who have earned the right to use it by virtue of fighting service at the front."[14] In a similar vein an *Oberleutnant* serving at the front complained to the RSL:

> We're happy to be spoken to by girls with delicate, whispery soprano voices or other young ladies, but don't you think it's a bit ridiculous when a (hopefully!) well-brought up, dainty little thing like that speaks to us rowdies as "comrades"; us, who she'd turn away from with a shy sidelong glance, if she was to see us in our tattered and filthy uniforms or realised how many daily "kills" we make (I'm referring to the lice!).[15]

While conceding to these sorts of complaints, it was decided at the highest level to continue to employ more women as announcers. The

---

13. During the war years women presented or copresented shows like "Tanz beim Kronewirt," an offering of folkloristic music with Anton Hofbauer and Helena Kraus, the series "Das Schatzkästlein," a mixture of poetry and music often presented by women, or one-off compilation shows with titles such as "Maidle, laß' Dir was erzählen" and "Hochzeit machen, das ist wunderschön."

14. Letter dated 10 August 1942, BAK R56 I/27:24.

15. The original colorful German is worth quoting here: "So lassen wir uns auch gern von Mädchen mit zärtlichem Flüstersopran (Weichsel) oder anderen Jungfrauen anreden. Aber sagen Sie doch selbst: ist es nicht zumindest lächerlich, wenn so ein (hoffentlich!) gutgewachsenes, zierliches Ding uns olle [*sic*] Rabauken mit "Kameraden" anredet, uns, von denen sie mit scheuem Seitenblick abrücken würde, wenn sie uns in unseren zerissenen, dreckigen Uniformen sehen oder die Zahl unserer täglichen "Abschüsse" (Läuse!) erfahren würde?!" (letter dated 1 August 1942, BAK R56 I/27:25).

increasing need for female announcers who would be taken seriously by the listening public was noted, for example, during one of the regular meetings held by Hans Hinkel, head of the chamber of culture, under the rubric "Force through more announcements by women!"[16]

### The Anonymous Voice in the Ether

For the most part radio announcers remained anonymous. Not all male announcers were well-known, but they had a greater chance of becoming radio personalities (e.g., Karl Wessel and Heinz Gödecke), if only because of their greater share of the airtime. The nameless, disembodied voice could become the site of fantasy in the intangible but intimate relationship between presenter and listener. Imagination could fill in all the details. Women presenters, in particular, were encouraged to "hold back" on personality, leaving the listener in almost total control of creating her persona in an interesting reversal of the general perception of the utter passivity of the radio listener. The woman presenter, in an editorial of the journal *Funk,* was described as "always merely an inconspicuous conveyor of information—her ego retreats right back in the constant service of the listener" ("Das Problem . . ." 1933, 125).

The story of the nameless female radio presenter was the stuff of film. *Die Stimme aus dem Äther* (The Voice in the Ether) was produced by Terra in 1939. Directed by Harald Paulsen, it starred Anneliese Uhlig, Mady Rahl, Ernst Waitzmann, and Ernst Waldow.[17] The film opens with the female lead defying her father, who does not approve of her ambitions to become an actress. Her mother weeps passively during this argument, which ends with the daughter leaving home to go to drama school. Her ambitions, though, are dashed when the examination piece involves a domestic scene that is too painful for her to reenact. But luck shines on her in the café, where she recounts her woes to a radio reporter from the Deutschlandsender, who says he might be able to help her. Via a swirling montage of radio magazines such as *Funk-Woche, Die Sendung,* and *NS Funk,* the scene shifts to the radio station, where one of the announcers is struggling with a sore throat. The station boss had been impressed by Brigitte's voice on the café interview and invites her to an audition. Showing her independent spirit once again, she only accepts the offer of work when she's guaranteed a decent wage, insisting that she cannot think about art until she knows how she is going to support herself.

16. "Noch mehr die Ansage durch Frauen forcieren!" (minutes of a meeting chaired by Hans Hinkel, head of the RKK, 21 January 1943, BAP 50.0 1/624:7).
17. I am grateful to the former Filmarchiv der DDR, Berlin, for enabling me to view this film.

Brigitte suggests a program called "Fünf Minuten unter uns" (Five Minutes to Ourselves), in which she intends to give each listener the impression that she is talking exclusively to them, an intimate *Zwiegespräch* (dialogue). The director approves and gives her a pile of scripts with possible themes. Her test is broadcast, unbeknown to her, and, as she talks to the listeners about how she'll be able to share in their problems and offer them a constant and faithful companion, a secret friend, she strays from the script. Fearing the repercussions, the editor sends her home, unpaid. But the audience likes her, and, in response to the volume of fan mail, she is rewarded with a regular program in the prime-time slot before the evening news. Her guide around the studios is also the filmviewer's guide behind the scenes of radio production, as she is taken around the special effects department and to a live musical recording and so on.

Meanwhile, romance is blossoming with a man who lives at the same guesthouse. Their day trips together incidentally work as propaganda by virtue of him taking her to see his work as director of engineering works on the new motorways. Hans is one of the program's biggest fans but does not guess that Brigitte is the "voice in the ether," and she enjoys the mystery. On air she begins to talk to the listeners like a lover. She says she can be whatever they want her to be, dark or blonde, and, no matter what, she will always be there for them, loving them. She begins to receive proposals of marriage from her listeners and starts to have misgivings about keeping Hans in the dark. She means to let the cat out of the bag on his birthday, by phoning him as "the voice" and promising to mention "mein lieber dummer Hans" on the show. She arranges to have the program prerecorded so she can be with him on a picnic when he tunes in on the portable set his colleagues gave him. But the plan backfires when he seems to lose all interest in her after the broadcast. Brigitte finds she is jealous of herself and plans a final trick. She asks her friend Erika to pose as the radio star and meet Hans at the Funkturm restaurant. He's disappointed at first at meeting his fantasy made flesh, but soon they're getting on famously. The film rushes to its happy end as Hans finds out the truth but stays with Erika, while Brigitte pairs off with a colleague from the radio station and finds fulfillment in launching her acting career in a tragic radio drama.

The film was not one of the really great box-office successes, but it was a popular film that dramatized certain current themes in radio and operated efficiently as a propaganda vehicle for the regime. It was granted the certificate *künstlerisch wertvoll* (of artistic value). A real-life version of the sort of program featured in *Die Stimme aus dem Äther* was the popular Monday morning show with Charlotte Köhn-Behrens. "Und wieder eine neue Woche" (Another New Week) was a short, ten-minute program cheerfully offering support and giving friendly advice about how to get through the difficult days of wartime. Köhn-Behrens's catchphrase was "Glück ist eine Leistung" (Happiness is an achievement). It had a good following and was especially popular with women, as listeners' letters held by the Bundesarchiv indicate.[18]

## A Good Talking To

Very few scripts from the Frauenfunk of this period survive in the archives, a consequence both of the disruption after the war and of the lack of prestige attached to these programs at the time. It is tempting, therefore, to ascribe those scripts that do survive a particular significance. Such is the case with the following script for a program broadcast from Königsberg on 15 March 1935, entitled "Mitarbeiterinnen des Frauen-funks plaudern miteinander: Bunter Nachmittag im Frauenfunk" (The Women's Radio Team Chat to Each Other: A Social Afternoon in the Women's Department).[19] This "social afternoon" took the form of a roundtable discussion between six of the presenters of the Königsberg Frauenfunk about their work. It therefore has a twofold relevance to the study in hand, furnishing further information about the workings of the Frauenfunk and the biographies of its staff while exemplifying the studied informality and the methods of propaganda in programs during this period.

This was no free-flowing, open-ended discussion program. The twenty-minute program was scripted carefully from beginning to end for maximum propagandistic effect, the multiple corrections and amendments of the editor's blue pencil throughout the typescript pages evidence that this is no simple transcription of an unscripted broadcast. Radio was still a live medium, and precensorship of broadcasts was essential in the closely controlled environment of Nazi propaganda.

The first thing worth noting is the labeling of the discussion as *Plauderei*. Women's talk about anything from baby care to employment policy was rarely dignified by the name *Diskussion* or even *Gespräch* (conversation). The same distinction is found in press, as Hannelore Kessler shows in her analysis of the women's pages of the *Völkischer Beobachter* (1981, 79). The leading participant in this case does refer to the program as a *Gespräch* in her final speech, however, which may imply that she was trying to recover a little more than its ascribed status. Public female discourse is never fully accepted as having broken out of the private sphere, and by the same token is signaled as being of inferior significance to other discourses (Spender 1980, 106–37; Spacks 1986, 3–46; Brown 1990, 183–200).

18. BAP 50.01/636; BAK R34/152.
19. Script for a program broadcast from Königsberg, 15 March 1935, DRA.

And yet, almost coincidentally, women's radio hit upon a presentational approach ideally suited to the medium of radio, whose listeners experience reception as individuals and not as members of a mass.

The discussion was led by Frieda Magnus-Unzer, who led the Frauenfunk department at Königsberg, with its staff of six, from 1930 to 1937. One of the most prolific activists in women's radio at this time, she claimed in an autobiographical essay written in 1935 that radio was her "destiny."[20] Coming to radio from a career in children's book publishing, her first contract, worth RM 276 a month, gave her responsibility for youth, women's, and schools radio. Officially, she was subordinate only to the station director, Herr Beyse, but she had to battle with the literary department for control of children's radio and with the director himself for control of the *Schulfunk*. Moreover, she claimed that many of the female staff resented having a female superior. She recalled how she had to fight *bis aufs Blut* (till blood was drawn) to get her program, "Praktische Winke" (Practical Tips), on the air four times a week. With so many obstacles in her path, she concentrated on writing, rather than producing. By 1935 she had broadcast over eighty-five programs of her own and since 1931 had written over twenty articles for the journal of the RRG, *Rufer und Hörer*. She welcomed the Nazi takeover and did everything to ensure that she kept her job, recalling, "when the new age came, the first thing I did was to prove my Aryan heritage, to counter any accusations of nepotism, and to prove that I was neither a double earner (small pension) nor well-off." *Gleichschaltung* finally gave her the responsibility she cherished. The two Jewish women at the station lost their posts. Magnus-Unzer described the women who remained as having had their "spirit" freed from the cynicism that had gone before.

The new station director, estimating that two-thirds of the audience were women, raised the number of programs for women and children to eleven a week. One of these was a Sunday program put together by the NSF called "Stunde für deutsche Frauen." It was designed to compensate those rural branch meetings neglected on the general lecture circuit. Members were encouraged to organize meetings to listen to the broadcasts communally. Magnus-Unzer planned the schedules three months in advance. Her stated objective was to win the women of Germany over to the National Socialist cause; her method was affability:

> The women who listen most to the radio are housewives with narrow horizons. No one else gets as close to them as I do with my radio. So I love them and I encourage them, telling them in "What can we

---

20. ". . . ich bin für den Rundfunk vorherbestimmt" (Frieda Magnus-Unzer, *Gedächtnisprotokolle* 1 DRA).

women do for our nation?" of the great duties in the state of the national community, and in "Tasks for women" of all the little tasks which one can ennoble. . . . But all in quite a warm and friendly manner.[21]

The particular script in question, "Bunter Nachmittag," was an installment of the flagship woman's hour, the longest running of all the programs, though its format was flexible. Magnus-Unzer would often announce Frauenfunk programs herself, but on this occasion it was left to the station announcer. The program was faded in, to give the impression that the listener was being allowed access to an internal meeting, to eavesdrop on a private conversation already in progress. In so doing, a tension was set up between the effect created and the reality of all broadcast talk, which is, by definition, public discourse. This is the "double articulation" of broadcast talk: the intercourse in the studio and the simultaneous communication of that intercourse to the absent listener (Scannell 1991, 1). Throughout the script there are at least two levels of meaning set up by this tension. The address to the listener was made explicit only in the summing up statement at the end of the program. As the discussion faded in, the listener heard Magnus-Unzer in mid-flow, suggesting that the Frauenfunk and the Kinderfunk benefited mutually from their close cooperation within the department. One of the longest-serving members of her staff, Frau Creutzberg, replied:

> Yes, dear Frau Magnus-Unzer, mother and child do belong together, and when we work for our children and family, it is the most natural thing in the world to talk about it. We have so many responsibilities in raising the younger generation. A child's first impressions remain with them all their lives, and they depend on our spiritual frame of mind. Thank God that we have so many listeners, many more than fit into a public hall, although as we sit alone at the microphone, we feel we are speaking to each of our sisters individually. We enter their most intimate environment, their homes. We hope that they welcome us into their hearts as we share fondly in their lives and in the life of their families. (Bunter Nachmittag, 1).

This first statement illustrates a whole range of presentational strate-

---

21. ". . . mythical signification . . . is never arbitrary. . . . Motivation is necessary to the very duplicity of myth. . . . What causes mythical speech to be uttered is perfectly explicit, but it is immediately frozen into something natural; it is not read as a motive, but as a reason" (Barthes 1973, 136, 140). Ian Kershaw writes, "success was guaranteed wherever it could identify Nazi aims with values which were unquestioned" (1983, 200).

gies, both in form and content. First of all, there is the address to "dear" Frau Magnus-Unzer, to create the impression of spontaneous and amicable discussion between colleagues, an impression without substance, for the rest of her speech is quite obviously addressed to the listeners, who by implication become honorary colleagues in the practice of the Frauenfunk. It is for the listeners' sake that Frau Creutzberg reiterates the official ideological position on women, that their place is with the children in the home. Repetition of the central tenets of that ideology lay at the heart of the propaganda aimed at women, to the effect that they seemed to become axiomatic, or rooted in the mythical wisdom of the *völkisch* past. Repetition of a concept through different forms is as precious to the propagandist as to the Barthesian mythologist (Barthes 1973, 129–30). With time, and with enough repetition, these ideological motifs would take on the functions of what Barthes referred to as realizations of the "cultural code," references to cultural knowledge acquired from common sense, popular science, etc., which are taken for granted (Barthes 1975). Much of the ideological propaganda aimed at women in this period was based on already established cultural codes—the ideology of motherhood is a case in point. Other positions, such as the duty toward Führer and *Volk* or the exigencies of racial hygiene, met with a greater degree of resistance. But the efforts to make the new ideas as familiar and axiomatic as the old were relentless.[22] All the output of the Frauenfunk was infused with overt reiterations of the ideological positions, to the extent that a cookery program, for example, gave not only tips for recipes and preparation but also spoke of national duty in buying German produce, maternal and racial duty in providing nourishing meals for their children as bearers of Germany's future, and the duty of a woman to be prepared to sacrifice herself to the needs of her family, *Volk,* and Führer.

The next presentational tactic to emerge is the insistence on the listener's personal responsibility in safeguarding the future of the nation. The effect is heightened by a sense of drama, in that but for the grace of God—and, by implication, of Hitler—a whole generation of children would be growing up without the benefit of a mother guided by the insights of National Socialist wisdom brought to her by the Königsberg radio. It is also interesting to note that in this early period references to Christianity were still fairly common, in the knowledge that the Nazi women's organizations had to be careful to maintain the support of the Christian women's associations from which they drew so much of their membership (Koonz 1987, 175–306). Gradually, overtly Christian allusions gave way to a pseudoreligiosity, in which the vocabulary of Chris-

---

22. Frieda Magnus-Unzer, *Gedächtnisprotokolle,* 1.

tianity was reappropriated in talk of the "resurrection" of Germany or the "spiritual regeneration" of the German people, as, in this instance, with the reference to the Nazi *seelische Einstellung* (spiritual frame of mind).[23]

One of the most important presentational strategies is the assurance given to the listener that she is not alone but, rather, is a part of a much larger listening community and, more than that, that she is an indispensable part. The tone is entirely reassuring. The activity of listening is legitimized by the notion of a listening community, while the women on the "other side" in the studio understand and respect the privilege of being invited into the private space of the home. In fact, it is that very understanding that enables them to do the job at all, but it is an understanding that implies a mutual responsibility, which brings us to the final strategy employed here, the imperative.[24] Couched in the vocabulary of warmth and sharing and expressed in terms of confident expectancy, this represents a thinly veiled instruction to put up no resistance to the presence of radio in the home or to the message it conveys.

The chat continues with reminiscences about how each of the contributors, aged between twenty-three and sixty, came to work for the radio. Most made their own approaches to the station, a confession that acts simultaneously as an invitation to the listener to get involved herself. Each contributor stressed how much pleasure their work brought them, because of their belief in the importance of what they were doing:

> *Frl. Woop:* I'm often aware that there is still a lot of work to be done in the education of women for our Fatherland. I wanted to help.
> *Fr. Magnus-Unzer:* And so you sent your first piece to the radio?
> *Frl. Woop:* Yes!
> *Frau Creutzberg:* Didn't you try to get something published in a newspaper before that, Fräulein Woop?
> *Frl. Woop:* No, Fräulein Creutzberg, it didn't even occur to me. I wanted to speak directly to my sisters, and feel a bond with them.
> *Frl. Königsegg:* I understand. When your heart is so full, you try to break down all the barriers.
>
> ("Bunter Nachmittag," 4)

---

23. Barthes identified one characteristic of myth as "language-robbery," though "speech which is restored is no longer quite that which was stolen" (Barthes 1973, 136).

24. "Myth has an imperative, buttonholing character: stemming from an historical concept, directly springing from contingency . . . it is *I* whom it has come to seek. It is turned towards me, I am subjected to its intentional force, it summons me to receive its expansive ambiguity" (Barthes 1973, 134).

Here the propagandistic aims are made quite explicit. The intention is to educate the listener to serve the Fatherland as understood by the National Socialist regime, driven not by a political agenda but by an altruism inherent in the female character. As in so much Nazi propaganda, there is a mystic element to the discourse. Fräulein Königsegg presented programs, which in the words of Frau Treike traversed "the reaches of inner thoughts, as is the way with sensitive women." This is how Frl. Königsegg herself described her work:

> It's so wonderful, the way everything comes together. People and their possessions issue from the past. We women care for the things that are passed down to us. Our children grow up with them. And so our cultural history becomes part of my own experience. How I found the way, I do not know. It comes from the inside, and leads in all directions. You don't know why, but you can't help it. It must be the same for you, Fräulein Treike. That's why all the practical things you talk about sound so convincing, because it is developed from the knowledge around the very essence of our people. ("Bunter Nachmittag," 6)

These are not women driven by ambitions for fame, fortune, or career. They represent the ideal selflessness and passivity of women so lauded by the Nazi ideologues. There is a deeper, more mystical force that determines the fate and the very knowledge of these women. The implication is that these women are in tune with the natural way of things, which imbues them with a natural and lawful authority and, further, that this sets them apart from and above the artificial morality of the Weimar period. A common feature of early Nazi propaganda in particular was the simple juxtaposition or opposition of black and white, which often was expressed in terms of a rejection of all that had gone before Hitler's assumption of power and a cheerful affirmation of everything that had happened since. Another feature particularly evident in the propaganda aimed at women was the prominence of emotional and highly personal language, often colored by high-flown metaphors and abstractions that mask the banality of much of what is being said. An appeal to the emotions was considered the most suitable approach, as women were not expected to respond critically or intellectually.

Part of the claim to naturalness was the retention, or adoption, of the natural speech patterns of the local dialect. Frau Treike, for example, mentioned how she also dreamed and prayed in the colloquial Low German dialect, *plattdeutsch,* suggesting that her radio talk was a similarly intimate experience deserving the honesty of unreconstructed language.[25] This confession "prompted" the following reply from Fräulein Woop, which also illustrates again the constant and arbitrary reintroduction of overt ideological statements:

> Yes, Frau Treike, if one tries to be so honest in work and prayer, one avoids hollow phrases, preferring the simple speech of one's homeland. I think, for now, I'll always have something to say. And though many say we women are restricted in the Third Reich, I find that it is only now that we can really make demands, because everybody knows what their duty is and everybody must devote themselves to their family and their people. ("Bunter Nachmittag," 6)

This overt denial of the increasing restrictions imposed on women in the Third Reich is fortified by many of the propagandistic strategies, including the prolific flattery of the listener and the glorification of the duties of women as mothers. By concentrating on their duties, achievements, and value as mothers, the aim was to distract from the fact that women were now esteemed almost solely on the single level of their reproductive function.

The purpose of this *Plauderei* was to act as an advertisement for the range of Frauenfunk programs offered for women, a schedule that Frau Horst described as having developed "organically." Each of the contributors took it in turn to explain what she found so satisfying about her work on each of the programs. It also provided the listener with background information about how the programs were put together. The following serves as an interesting example, especially as it touches on the question of mode of presentation:

> *Fr. Creutzberg:* It's a pleasure to work on "Working with young housewives." These programs feature members of the housewives' union, a sub-division of the Deutsches Frauenwerk. Many housewives in Königsberg have learned about working in radio in this way. And I find that they all have a natural speaking manner. My chats with a business woman and a mother of a large family were very true to life. These two brave women impressed me so much, that my own small part seemed quite strange and secondary to me.

---

25. Barthes refers to the honesty of "social speech" when he says, "Within a national norm such as French, forms of expression differ in different groups, and every man is a prisoner of his language: outside his class, the first word he speaks is a a sign which places him as a whole and proclaims his whole personal history" (1980, 81).

*Fr. Magnus-Unzer:* And yet you felt responsible for them. But the women mastered the situation completely. I notice time and again, that the people who fight the daily battle of life, have steady nerves even in front of the microphone.

*Fr. Horst:* Yes, we've all noticed that. And it is for this reason that their voices sound so free and natural.

("Bunter Nachmittag," 7)

This is a good example of another strategy that recurred frequently in the propaganda—flattery of the listener—although in this case it is a fragile line between emphasizing the natural flair of ordinary women on the radio and the professional skill of the station's employees. This is seen again in the exchange that followed, which dealt with the merits and otherwise of reading from a script:

*Frl. Woop:* Oh my heart beat so fast when I had my reading test!

*Fr. Magnus-Unzer:* It was alright in your case, but not everyone can read her own work. Few people recognise it, but a lot depends on the delivery. And it would do many people good to ask a practised female announcer to convey their thoughts to the listener. They'd get more from it that way.

("Bunter Nachmittag," 7)

This exchange represents a disarming admission that what the listener assumes to be natural dialogue is in fact scripted text. And yet no explicit reference is made to the fact that this *Plauderei,* too, is scripted. Perhaps this omission was intended to reinforce the deception of simulated honest discussion, to bolster the listeners' trust in the personalities fronting the Frauenfunk, as an investment in faith for the future. It is also a declaration calling for the ultimate identification of presenter and listener, the unity of thought and purpose for which the Frauenfunk strove. Magnus-Unzer summed up the discussion with an appeal to maintain the pressure for an even closer relationship between the Frauenfunk and its listeners:

We have over 100 people working for us in women's and children's radio. We get a lot of letters, and the prize competitions are very invigorating and give us a lot of ideas. And I hope that our current competition will be as stimulating for us and our listeners. We have asked all our listeners to listen to all the programs for women until March 31 and make notes about the content and their thoughts about them. All these notes should then be sent to the station and the best ones will get prizes. Our conversation [*Gespräch*] today is a part of this task. Write down all your thoughts about our women's radio, all you who are listening today. You are all our colleagues, after all. We six women wanted to involve you more closely in our work with our conversation today, and greet you with our hearts in the hope for inner comradeship. Heil Hitler! ("Bunter Nachmittag," 8)

It is seductive language. It appeals to a sense of common cause and sisterhood. It promises empowerment and reward. But there is much that it omits to say. The sisterhood is a select one. It excludes all those women whose work outside the home means they cannot listen to this nor the other programs of the Frauenfunk. And, if they could hear, and if they could suggest structural changes to the radio schedules or changes to the content of the programs to meet their needs, they would not win prizes. Nor does the sisterhood include those women in whose hearts the words "Heil Hitler" would inspire fear in place of adulation. The discourse is set up between "us" and "you" and becomes what turns out to be a sinister community defined against an unmentioned "other."

There were modifications in the techniques of the propagandists as time went on, particularly with the onset of war and the changing demands on women, but the changes were greater in terms of content than of style. The Verbrauchslenkung campaigns were obviously of very great importance in the overall output aimed at women on radio in the Third Reich, performing not only an information service but also reinforcing some central tenets of Nazi ideology with regard to women's role in society. The style of address in these programs in wartime was at turns intimate, jocular, pedagogic, and occasionally downright condescending. Taking two typical RVA scripts from 1943 as examples, one on rationing, the other on saving soap, it is possible to analyze these various techniques more closely.

The title itself gives away the tone of the first program, "Jetzt wird das Kochen erst zur Kunst! Der Hausfrau wird gut zugeredet" (Cookery Finally Becomes an Art! The Housewife Is Given a Good Talking To!).[26] It gives the impression that housewives have for too long been reneging on their culinary responsibilities and that official patience has finally run out. A hierarchy is already set up, as some higher authority is called on to bring the recalcitrant staff of the nation's family kitchens into line. It is an authority with superior knowledge, holding the secret of how to raise cookery from a chore to a craft. Gone is the faith in women's instinctual flair for homekeeping; they need expert direction, even bullying. The "expert" announcer (the script unfortunately does not specify the sex of

---

26. BAP 50.02/31:7–11.

the speaker, but the tenor of the piece implies that it was written for an authoritative voice) tries to give the impression that he or she can see into individual homes and is speaking exclusively to each individual listener: "There you are, sitting in your kitchen, sighing. . . . In front of you on the kitchen table are the pretty colored pieces of paper which you get given every four weeks: meat coupons, bread, fat and grocery coupons, cut up and stamped." More than that, he or she tries to give the impression that he or she could even tell what the listener was thinking: "My God, what a state of affairs! you think and *you really would like* normal conditions to return. Am I right? Well then."

In a totalitarian state in which "loose talk" could land you in prison or worse, in which your neighbor might report any sign of dissidence or nonconformity to the authorities under the Heimtücke-Gesetz of 1934, such stylistic tactics could well have touched nerves less sensitive in more open societies. Yet, in case the listener was thinking she didn't want to listen to yet another public information program—there were so many of these broadcast it must have been difficult to keep attention fixed—the speaker adopts the tone of a schoolteacher, telling any recalcitrant listeners to sit down, keep quiet, and listen: "Well that just doesn't help, and so I've got to give you a bit of a talking to. Wait! I know what you're thinking and I can see that you'd like to get up—you're practically standing up already: please, stay seated, don't turn off!"

It is an overbearing tone familiar on German radio at that time. The "good talking to" begins with a reiteration of the housewife's patriotic duty—this war is not only being fought at the front line and in the air but on the economic and psychological fronts, too—followed by a history lesson about the historical imperative for struggle dating back to 1914, which will end with a German victory bringing order, peace, cleanliness, and prosperity to all of Europe. The language is punchy and keeps urging the listener to recall her own memories of the hardships Germany had lived through over the last thirty years:

> You know, these days it's not a matter of what individuals want, wherever they are, they must do their duty. That's all. . . . It's a time of struggle again, no, that's not right, it's always been a time of struggle. . . . It's a matter of whether we fall prey again to the great thieves and oppressors, whether they suppress us again as they did in 1918— you remember that surely?

Again and again the listener is reminded of how vital her own contribution to the war effort will be and that, in so doing, she will be lightening the workload of the Führer himself. Her sense of responsibility, her sense of guilt and shame, are appealed to; she's not so much being persuaded as chided for her residual selfishness:

> For you should, indeed you must do your bit, courageously and gladly, with a strong soul and a hard will—your bit for victory. *You must now think only of victory. Is the Führer to do it all on his own?* Day by day, hour by hour. No longer think about vain little me. How you must be ashamed of yourself!

The tone switches briefly from admonition to instruction, to explain the "socialist" theory behind the introduction of rationing and the egalitarian distribution of resources according to need, but it returns again with a vengeance to ward off any potential interjection from the "little women" listening that no one could be expected to be able to stretch the rations available to feed a family adequately: "But you still can't manage. . . . What? That's the way it is? Hold on a minute little woman, make sure you don't fall off your chair, because I've got to make fun of you a bit now; you see, it is you who is to blame. *It is entirely your own fault.*"

Government calculations about the average family's requirements could hardly be wrong in the eyes of the propagandists, and so the blame for any hardships resulting from rationing clearly lay with the inability of the housewife to organize herself efficiently. The answer, according to the increasingly patronizing commentary, was to mirror the state-planned economy in the home. This would involve checking in the local paper at the beginning of the month what goods the family's ration cards would buy and working out in detail a kitchen plan for the next four weeks. But the endeavor to make the instructions amusing and easy to follow left the impression that the audience being addressed was made up of six-year-olds:

> You get a newspaper, don't you? Yes? Well, that's alright then. So, take a pencil or that delightful little fountain pen you got last Christmas or at Easter or for your last birthday. And then write on the first sheet of paper on the first line, nice and neatly: *Four Week Kitchen Plan.* Have you done that? Yes? Then let's proceed.

It is hard to imagine that such an approach would have appealed to women listening, although the writers as propagandists would not have used a style of approach that would obviously alienate the average listener. Without access to the *spoken* word, we are left with an incomplete relict, a *disembodied* voice. Julia Kristeva has suggested that every utterance has a dual relation between the "symbolic" moment, which names its referential function, situating the speaker in relation to an outside reality, and the "semiotic" moment, which names the unconscious, bodily condition of the utterance, such as rhythm, tone of voice, and gesture (1984, 124–47). Meaning is generated in the (shifting) relation between these moments. But, if meaning is constructed in part by the words, in part by the tone of voice, then it is also partly constructed in the activity of reception. To quote Paddy Scannell, "voice is the irreducible mark of the spoken, of its physical, embodied presence and, for radio in particular, is crucial for listeners' assessments of the character of speakers and their alignment (or otherwise) with their performances" (1991, 6). It is almost impossible to recreate the probable reactions of a group of listeners to a particular program almost fifty years ago, with so many parts of the equation missing, the more so when so few records of listeners' preferences or reactions were made and even fewer survive. Tastes and meanings are culturally specific, changing over time and differing from one individual to another, generally making the conclusions we can draw about the reception of a single program at best subjective, at worst unreliable—the more so when no recording has survived (Scannell 1989, 147–48). The value of such historical textual analysis therefore lies in offering an insight into the intentions and techniques of the propagandists and the nature of the audience inscribed in the text.

The script goes on to describe in painfully slow and pedantic detail how to ensure that on the last day of the four-week period there would still be the correct allocation of rationed food available. The women who were still listening at this point were assured that, despite the hardships, at least they were better off than the men who had lain besieged in the Alcazar—although the situation in Germany now was similar to that of a besieged fortress.

All the usual elements are here—the military metaphors, the hierarchical discourse, the assumption that it was women who represented the Achilles' heel of the German war effort—but there was another mode of address that was a more sisterly approach in which female presenters talked to the audience as equals, albeit less well informed equals. A sense of community was encouraged, promoting the idea that all women were in the same boat and had the same hardships and responsibilities to face. It was in no way a feminist approach, for the solidarity among women was not intended to be used as the basis for winning parity with men. It was, rather, an attempt to perfect the contribution women could make in the sphere allotted to them. As in the following extracts from a program called "Ein Kapitel zum Nachdenken" (A Story to Think About), the speaker would tend to use the first-person plural throughout.[27] Once again it is the vast wealth represented in textiles that is being reiterated, a wealth for which women were responsible: "And we, we housewives are, in a way, the bankers! *We* administer this huge fortune, *we* have to ensure that it remains intact, and we may not 'speculate' with it."

It was a favorite technique repeatedly to remind the women listening of their vital role in society, to keep reiterating that, while they might have lost status and function in the public sphere, in the sphere allotted to them they were really irreplaceable: "If it's up to the husband to earn the money, then it's up to the wife to spend it and look after her purchases properly."

Statistics were another common feature of these public information broadcasts. At times there was such a flood of facts and figures that it is questionable how much information the listeners would have taken in, but for the constant repetition of the cost to the nation of so many torn sheets, wasted soap powder, or inefficient use of energy should the misdemeanors of an average household to be multiplied by twenty million. Repetition on a theme was the main weapon in the propagandists' arsenal. Like a stuck record, the radio kept churning out two-minute programs here, five-minute playlets there, drumming the same message out again and again: that the war could be lost on the home front.[28] It was impossible to admit to potential cracks in the military's armor or in the country's weapons technology, but the home front, and that meant the women, could be accused of not pulling its weight, could be asked to tighten its belt, work harder, give more. Even when the propagandists had to do an about-turn when female employment was suddenly approved, it was alright to ask women to take on the extra burden of work outside the home, because they could always play the patriotic card. Until the blanket bombing of German cities began, women's complaints about rationing, shortages, longer hours, and loneliness were easily met by accusations of selfishness at a time when the menfolk were facing the ultimate sacrifice.

27. BAP 50.02/26:406–9.

28. Goebbels had graphically stressed the means and intended ends of this technique as early as 1934: "to saturate the people to the last fibre of their beings with this certainty and this frame of mind . . . to hammer and grind and squeeze the people until they succumb. That is the main task of the German radio" (speech to the staff of WDR in Cologne, 24 April 1933; cited in Aberle 1982, 3).

CHAPTER 9

# Conclusion: Gender, German Radio, and the Public Sphere

A gendered history of radio does more than just make women visible as audiences and program makers, although this is certainly an important part of the project. The previous chapters have shown that there was a distinctive history of women's role in early German broadcasting to be told, and, despite the patchiness of existing sources, at least some of the women involved and some of their stories have been restored to the overall picture. In the process of restoration, however, that picture has been substantially redrawn. An analysis that is sensitive to the gendered language of public media discourse can certainly illuminate policy questions around the organization, censorship, programming practices, and social function of a medium of mass communication such as radio. In short, I would argue that the history of radio cannot properly be understood if gender is absent as a category of analysis.

Throughout the preceding chapters the concept of the public and the private spheres has run as a leitmotif, providing the framework for a gendered analysis of German broadcasting in an age of crisis. But, historically and theoretically, the terms *public* and *private* are ambiguous and contested and require closer critical attention. In particular, the expression "public sphere," when used to denote that which lies outside the private, domestic realm, is prone to conflate distinct analytic entities like the state, the public waged economy, and the forum of public discourse. This concluding chapter seeks to attend to these ambiguities. It also explores how the particular constellation of factors that have been the object for this study can illuminate and are illuminated by the models of the public sphere delineated in the work and critiques of Hannah Arendt and Jürgen Habermas. The following discussion, then, seeks to draw out some of the historical and theoretical implications of the contemporaneous emergence of women as citizens with a political voice—that is to say, the emergence of mass politics—and radio as a mass medium, with its potential for reinvigorating the public sphere, and to trace the continuities and changes in the transition from a democratic to a totalitarian state.

## The Public and the Private

A key premise on which this study is based is that the perceived spatial and functional division of the sexes is not an inevitable consequence of biology but, rather, is an ideological construct that can be traced to specific historical conditions.[1] Yet, even when the divide between public and private is recognized as a culturally produced division between production and reproduction in the widest sense, there remain limitations to the explanatory weight that the public-private model can be made to bear.[2] Its simplicity renders it incapable of encompassing the subtlety and range of actual sociosexual arrangements. The two realms, public and private, have never been complete in their mutual exclusivity but are closely interrelated and systematically connected (see Gamarnikow et al. 1983). The productive system of society is a continuous process that reproduces the members of that society, their materials and instruments, and their social relations. Institutions in the public sphere, including the media, operate in socialization processes and the reproduction of ideology. By the same token domestic relations cannot be regarded as separate from the social sphere nor women's productive capacity within and without the home ignored.[3] If feminists are right in claiming that "the personal is political," then, as Joan Kelly pointed out in her essay "The Doubled Vision of Feminist Theory," it is no longer possible to maintain that there are two separate spheres of social reality, which is to say that "woman's place is not a separate sphere or domain of existence but a position within social existence generally" (1984, 57).

---

1. For example, Karin Hausen has demonstrated that only in the industrial capitalism of the nineteenth century could a sharper division of gender roles be developed, drawing on an eighteenth-century transformation in the definition of women in terms of innate characteristics rather than status which had coincided with a crisis of patriarchal authority and provided a new means of legitimizing the subordination of women (1983, 51–83; see also Frevert 1986, 15–25). *Essentialism,* rooted in biology, is a heatedly contested term in feminist debates. For useful elaborations of the various positions taken, see Alcoff 1988; Fuss 1989; Pateman 1989, 118–40; de Lauretis 1990.

2. For a useful discussion on the displacement of the paradigm of production in Marxist feminism, see Benhabib and Cornell 1987, 1–5. For a discussion of how the distinction has been contested within feminism, see Phillips 1991, 92–121.

3. The growth in "men's history" studies has heightened the awareness of male experience in the private sphere and the indistinct boundaries between the private and the public. See Filene 1987.

While bearing these reservations in mind, the concept of a gendered public-private divide nevertheless does represent a useful paradigm in considering the relationship between women and radio between the wars, not least because of the fact that contemporary debates were centered on the challenges to and defenses of the separate spheres that radio posed. It is in this sense that one can speak of radio "bridging the divide" between the public and the private. The nature of public broadcasting both highlighted the perceived division between the two spheres and redefined the boundary between them. The divide between those women who were active in the public sphere and those whose existence centered on the private was also diminished by the links that radio provided between the two worlds. The bridge, though, did not just carry one-way traffic, for the nature of public discourse that entered the home was redefined by the conditions of its reception in the domestic, feminine sphere. The point here is not to accept that separation as self-evident and reproduce it but problematize it so as to understand what was really at stake.

The separation of the "public" and the "private" has been of key importance in theories of modernity.[4] The modernizing processes of the uncoupling of household and economy, the increasing division of labor, the loosening of kinship ties, and so on, engendered the modern divide between public and private and the roles ascribed to the different spheres, the roles of citizen and worker in the public sphere, the client and nurturer in the private (Marshall 1994, 9–17). The gendered nature of those processes have been conventionally obscured by universalizing discourse. Feminist critiques of the public and private do not necessarily seek to abandon the notion of any distinction but to reformulate them in a nonexclusionary way.

There is an ambiguity evident in the delineation of the public and private in liberal theory (see Pateman 1989). The political theory of classic liberalism identifies the divide between public and private as that between the public realm of politics and the private realm of economics and the family, while liberal economic theory locates the distinction as lying between the public market place and the private, noneconomic home. At the heart of this worldview lie the rights and freedoms of the individual, yet the individual who moves in and between these realms is implicitly, yet undeniably, male (Eisenstein 1981; Elshtain 1981; Lloyd 1984). Classical Marxism abandoned the distinction between the political and the economic, recognized that the family was not separate from civil society, and rejected Hegel's claim that the state transcends particular interests to

---

4. Barbara Marshall has argued that the public-private dichotomy has been at the heart of modern social theory because it is an expression not simply of the gendered division of labor but also of the relationship between individual and society more generally (1994, 9–17).

express the universal and rational will.[5] In capitalist society the principle of impartiality serves to reproduce inequality (Young 1987, 65). In Engels's 1884 treatment of the "Woman Question" he located the origin of women's oppression in the emergence of private property under capitalism and the separation of the domestic from social production (1972, 137). However, Engels could only use the separation of these spheres as an explanation for the exclusion of women from public life because he naturalized women's performance of domestic labor. From this perspective the hope for liberation from oppression for women was ultimately dependent on socialist revolution, a position represented most forcefully in German social democracy by Klara Zetkin.

From a broadly liberal perspective feminists since Mary Wollstonecraft have argued that women's exclusion from the public sphere contradicts the democratic promise of universal emancipation and equality and have campaigned for entrance into the public sphere on an equal footing with men.[6] More recently, doubt has been cast on the recuperation of Enlightenment notions such as universality and equality which were formulated on the basis of structural exclusions, not least the exclusion of the feminine. Recent feminist political theory has therefore moved away from demanding parity within already existing social and political structures to demanding a reformulation of the concept of the public sphere that promotes plurality, heterogeneity, and multivocality (Fraser 1987, 1990; Young 1987; Dietz 1991, 1992). The feminist critique of the public-private divide therefore allows, or rather demands, a rethinking of citizenship, solidarity, and community "grounded in the interrelationship of the individual to collective life, or personal to political life, instead of their separation and opposition" (Pateman 1987, 135). This interrelationship between the public and the private, this blurring of the divide, is also a feature of broadcasting and the communicative ethos of broadcasting as it has developed, something to which I will return.

In her essay "Impartiality and the Civic Public" Iris Young (1987) offers a succinct account of feminist critiques of the unified, impartial, and rational male subject of the Enlightenment. This subject is a counterfactual construction impelled by what Adorno termed the "logic of identity," the principled reduction of the objects of thought to universal laws to a unity, a totality. But this process of reduction is a process of exclusion. Impartiality, for example, is defined by the exclusion of passion. As Young puts it, "only by expelling desire, affectivity and the body from reason can

---

5. Marx therefore abandoned Hegel's conception of the distinction between family, civil society, and state (Lloyd 1993, 74–85; Marshall 1994, 11).

6. The distinctions drawn are almost unbearably crude, but the focus here is on the different conceptualizations of the public-private divide rather than a history of feminism(s).

impartiality achieve its unity" (1987, 62). The excluded terms remain intimately bound up in the definition of categories, but the binary opposition is not one of equal parts; it is, instead, organized hierarchically. The rational (male) citizen must therefore rise above passion and sentiment. This dichotomy is reproduced in modern normative political theory in ascribing impartial reason to the universal, public realm of the state and ascribing desire, affectivity, and the body to the particular, private realm. It is reproduced in political practice by the exclusion of women from public life, a process that can be traced historically to the eighteenth century (Sennet 1974; Landes 1988). There is a spatial, as well as a historical, dimension to this process that is ignored by abstract universalism, with its placeless and nonreferential sense of identity that denies "the particular location of human lives in place and time" (Rustin 1987, 31). Since space and place are clearly important in the process of identity formation, then the confinement of women to the private realm of domesticity was, as Doreen Massey argues, "both a specifically spatial control and, through that, a social control of identity" (1994, 179).

Young has suggested that Habermas's theory of communicative action (1983) offers a potentially more fruitful framework for a normative reason that is not dependent on synthetic universal principles, based as it is on discussion, on being able to give reasons, to be reasonable, to talk, and to listen (1987, 68–73). In place of a transcendental ego as impartial arbiter of reason, Habermas claims that impartiality is presupposed by a normative discussion that seeks and expects to reach consensus. The move to identify the rational potential intrinsic in everyday communicative practices no longer restricts the search for normative potentials to a formation of the public sphere that was specific to a single epoch. Nevertheless, Habermas's discursive model of the public sphere falls back on universal principles in the contention that all particularized motives and interests are bracketed out in order for this discussion to take place, reproducing the dichotomy between reason and sentiment or interest, reinforced by the emphasis on verbal discourse to the exclusion of physical or emotional expression, rhetoric or gesture.

A model of the public realm that is similarly based on communicative action but that does not compromise its commitment to plurality in this way is the agonistic model of public space developed by Hannah Arendt.[7]

---

7. Margaret Canovan has argued that the concept of *plurality* is the major contribution which Arendt made to political thought. She cites Arendt's own remark that each of the key political thinkers of the past "has thrown one word into our world, has augmented it by this one word, because he responded rightly and thoughtfully to certain decisively new experiences of his time," and suggests that the word which Arendt threw into the world was "plurality" (1992, 280–81).

The "agonistic" view of public space is common to the "republican virtue" or "civic virtue" tradition of Western political thought, a tradition which Hannah Arendt in some way sought to recover. In her major theoretical work, *The Human Condition,* Arendt insists that the distinction between the public and private spheres is the distinction between the household and the political realm, a distinction which has been undermined by the "rise of the social" in the form of the modern nation-state (1958, 28). The public realm is properly the realm of "action" according to the triangular schema by which Arendt distinguished between fundamental human activities: *labor* (the activity corresponding to the biological processes of the human body); *work* (the activity corresponding to the unnaturalness of human existence—that which provides an artificial world of things); and *action* (the activity corresponding to the human condition of plurality) (1958, 7).

Now, as Nancy Fraser and many other critics point out, there are significant limitations for contemporary critical theory in any conception of the public sphere which requires a sharp separation between civil society and the state, a requirement which characterizes both the Habermasian and the Arendtian accounts of the decline of the public (1990, 76; Behabib 1992, 73–81); and clearly there are also problems for feminists in adopting a model which excludes the private sphere from its definition of politics (although it is important to realize that these activities are not represented as constructs of class or social relations but as properties of the human condition and therefore potentially within the range of every human being). Nevertheless, following Mary Dietz, I will argue that the concept of an agonistic politics with its emphasis on *action* and *plurality* remains a useful one and that it is possible to see Arendt's work a possible starting place for a feminist theory of politics, without accepting or endorsing her theory *tout court* (1991, 249–50). Plurality is the basic condition of both action and speech "because we are all the same, that is, human, in such a way that nobody is ever the same as anyone else who ever lived, lives, or will live" (1958, 175). Our ability to communicate is predicated on our equality as humans; the impetus to communicate is provided by our distinctiveness. The condition of plurality promotes the notion of a politics of shared differences (Dietz 1991, 236). Political speech, according to Arendt, is open discussion in which different citizens speak with one another, revealing themselves in what they say, enabling understanding, and establishing solidarity.[8] Mutual recognition depends not on a shared identity

8. Speech in Arendt's account is not necessary to the private sphere in which communication of "immediate identical needs and wants" can be done mimetically (1958, 179), nor are the "language games" that coordinate activity in the workplace or administration relevant for political speech (here labor is determined by natural necessity and so belongs in the private sphere).

but on the existence of actual physical spaces in which people can speak to one another in the world. The objects of that discussion are generated in that discussion, and, as Andrea Nye puts it, "they are objective only because they are things that are of 'inter-est.' literally 'between us,' constituted by relationships. They are not subjective because the relationships that constitute them are real; they are not fixed because the fact that there are objects between people creates new commonality and new objects of interest" (1994, 187). In times of crisis, Arendt argued, only renewed public discussion could formulate conceptualizations and therefore responses to events (1958, 58). No such response would be possible without the permanent and local public spaces in which such discussion could develop.

The public realm in Arendt's formulation, therefore, has a specifically *spatial* dimension. It is a space of appearances in which individuals gather in open discussion, a space in which freedom inheres, a space removed from the realm of the private. Its three-dimensionality is a feature of a plurality of perspectives, a space in which views are exchanged. Once private concerns colonize that space, as Arendt identified as happening in the modern world, the public realm founders. For example, the move to representative politics and welfare democracy transforms active citizens into passive, depoliticized clients, as spontaneous agonistic politics gives way to the routine of elections and the pursuit of private interests, while the public realm is deliberately demolished under totalitarian regimes, when the suppression of a plurality of opinion amounts to an elimination of the space between individuals, and the channels of communication between individuals are "replaced by a band of iron which holds them so tightly together that it is as though their plurality had disappeared into One Man of gigantic dimensions" (Arendt 1968, 164). In a situation in which the space for action is closed off, "resistance becomes the primary vehicle of spontaneity and agonistic subjectivity" (Villa 1992, 718).

Both Arendt and Habermas were concerned with the recovery of the public realm as a space for uncoerced deliberation and decision making among diverse equal citizens in the face of modern trends and processes which have distorted political life (Villa 1992, 412). The key difference in their formulation of the public and private spheres is that, in Arendt's model, the private is the realm of necessity, while freedom inheres only in the public realm. *Privacy,* as Arendt points out, is etymologically related to *privation* and *deprivation* (1958, 58). The privation of privacy for Arendt is to be that which is excluded from the public, hidden from view, shameful, and of no interest to others. For Habermas, in contrast, the private realm is a realm of freedom in which individuals are primarily formed and one that has to be defended against colonization by the state, and it is the gathering of *private* individuals in rational critical debate, which defines the public sphere (Calhoun 1992, 6–7). It is Habermas's discursive model of the public sphere that has been taken up much more widely by theorists of the media than Arendt's model, whose agonistic aspect he rejected.[9] Useful as the Habermasian model is, though, it has serious limitations from a feminist point of view and from the perspective of recent media theory. Although Arendt's model suffers from a similar gender blindness and a pessimism about modern mass culture and politics, it does seem to point to some new ways forward that are productive for a (feminist) critique of the media and the public sphere.[10] The discussion therefore now turns to look more closely at the value and limitations of Habermas's public sphere theory, particularly in light of its critical reception by feminist and media theorists, and seeks to suggest ways in which the Arendtian model offers a way out of some of the critical impasses in Habermas's formulation.

**Engendering the Public Sphere**

Some version of the "public sphere" has always been a part of democratic theory, that is to say, a forum of some sort where the governed can develop and express their political will to the government. Clearly, the dissemination of information and the free expression of opinion are prerequisites for an effective democracy. With the rise of mass politics the media of mass communication have increasingly taken on that role. How well the public sphere functions as the institutional site where citizens constitute themselves as active agents in the political process is a measure of the proper functioning of a democracy. It is in this sense that the concept of the public sphere, as defined by Habermas in *The Structural Transformation of the Public Sphere: An Enquiry into a Category of Bourgeois Society,* is so use-

---

9. Peter Dahlgren suggests that an Arendtian perspective can be "integrated with the orientation" which he develops in his recent book on television and the public sphere, which argues that the democratic character of the public sphere cannot simply be assumed but must be continually achieved. He therefore sets his analysis of television within a broader framework of social theory, in particular that which is concerned with civil society and citizenship. It is within this context that reference to Arendt is made, but he does not pursue it very far (1995, 144–45).

10. It is only this theoretical model of the public and private realms set out in *The Human Condition* with which the present discussion is concerned. Although there are problems associated with extracting this work from Arendt's wider oeuvre, taking this model as a departure for a feminist politics and analysis of the media does not necessarily imply a wholesale endorsement of her historical method or her analysis of totalitarianism and the Third Reich. These are questions which simply go beyond my present concerns and which have been widely debated elsewhere.

ful. Rather than being used in a simply descriptive sense, the public sphere should be understood as an analytic category, as an ideal type.[11]

In the tradition of critical theory Habermas sought to examine an actually existing social phenomenon and the conceptual categories which described it in order to reveal its historical conditions and limits for the sake of understanding and changing it. Habermas's premise was that public discussions about the exercise of political power that are both critical in intent and institutionally guaranteed have not always existed but grew out of a specific phase of bourgeois society. By the late eighteenth century the rising bourgeois classes in Western Europe, in struggling with the powers of the absolutist state, succeeded in generating a new social space between the public authority of the state and the private authority of civil society and the family, replacing the "representative publicity" of the medieval period with the creation of a public constituted by private people exercising their critical reason in public and unrestrained discussion about the regulation of civil society and the conduct of the state. As *private* citizens, the bourgeois public did not seek to rule but to oppose the principle of existing power with the principle of informal supervision, hence the demand to make proceedings public.

The literary salons, coffeehouses, an independent press concerned not only with news but with public opinion, and the rise of associational life were central to this process. These associations, constituted by the free (private) decisions of their founding members, based on voluntary membership, and characterized internally by egalitarian practices of sociability, free discussion, and decision by majority, though exclusively bourgeois and patriarchal, provided the lasting foundation for future norms of political equality, including the constitutional recognition of freedoms of expression and publication. As an institution, however, the bourgeois public sphere was short-lived, due to various overlapping trends having to do with the breakdown of the separation between the state and civil society. Not least among these was the "contamination" of rational debate by partisan interests, triggered by the example of the French Revolution, which meant the politicization of the public sphere. Moreover, the diffusion of the press allowed the public to expand beyond the bounds of the bour-

---

11. *Strukturwandel der Oeffentlichkeit* was first published in German in 1962 and not translated into English until 1989 (apparently because of an unfulfilled intention on Habermas's part to rework it [see Calhoun 1992, 5]), when it attracted renewed interest, not least given its new relevance to understanding the emergent democracies of Eastern Europe and the reinvigoration of civil society in the Republic of China. (The main thesis had appeared in English in *New German Critique* in 1974.) This renewed interest led Habermas to reflect again (see the essay in the 1992 collection edited by Craig Calhoun).

geoisie, meaning the public was no longer exclusive nor coherent. Its commercialization, furthermore, meant a shift from a "culture-debating" public to a "culture-consuming" public. The mass media in this formulation, therefore, control opinion rather than facilitating its formation and expression. The public sphere was further eroded, according to Habermas, by the expansion of the state and the collectivization of private interests in the welfare state, which blurred the distinction between public and private. In short, rational public discourse was supplanted by power politics between competing interested parties (between large organizations and the state excluding the public as private individuals) in a process that Habermas termed a "refeudalization," in which, instead of power being made public for scrutiny, it is made public for display, for re-presentation, and politics becomes a managed show put before a depoliticized population.

Although developments in the nineteenth and twentieth centuries have radically transformed the nature of public life, Habermas proposes that the bourgeois public sphere embodied certain ideas and principles which retain their relevance today as the indispensable basis of a free society (1992, 446). The key normative elements retained from the bourgeois model of the public sphere can be briefly summarized: a realm of social life in which public opinion can be formed and expressed, motivated by the search for norms and rational legitimations, to which there is universal access (social, political, and economic privileges are "bracketed out" to allow rational debate in the general interest) and freedom from constraint (so the consensus reached has binding force and is not simply an expression of insidious or overt violence), which is independent from the state (though the legitimation of the democratic state lies in its role of guarantor of the public sphere through law) and which mediates between society and state via a set of concrete institutions (including the media) within which public opinion is formed.

This analysis of the public sphere has been influential across a range of disciplines since it was first published in 1962, and especially since it finally appeared in an English version in 1989, and it has been critiqued, adapted, and refined from a variety of perspectives. The thrust of those critiques have primarily been to do with the questionable accuracy of the historical narrative, a neglect of the politics of gender, the idealization of universal principles and communicative rationality, and the pessimistic account of mass mediated culture. In various ways they point to the limitations of Habermas's normative model for the present study and for contemporary feminist media theory.

The question of the accuracy of Habermas's historical account is not of primary concern here, but it is worth noting the main charges made against it—namely, that, in setting up the bourgeois press as the embodiment of disinterested rational discourse, he adhered too closely to the self-image promoted by the players in the bourgeois public sphere, overstating its homogeneity and coherence, underplaying its vested class and gender interests, and underestimating both the challenge to that version of rationality as absolute mounted by the radical press and the ways in which possibilities for participation by counterpublics were intentionally obstructed and repressed by the bourgeois public sphere (Negt and Kluge 1973–93; Eley 1992; Curran 1993, 38–42).[12] In response to the criticisms that some of his historical material does not stand up to empirical scrutiny and that he confuses history and theory, Habermas (1992) argues that the overstylized nature of the golden past and the dystopian present, though in need of modification, does not falsify the larger outline of the process of transformation he initially identified. Nevertheless, his subsequent interest in developing a discourse-theory of democracy represents a move away from the search for normative potentials in a historically specific constellation. Although the same criticism might seem appropriate in Arendt's presentation of the classical Greek polis as a paradigm of public life, she does so, as Phillip Hansen has argued, in recognition of its importance to Western political history and philosophy, using it as a metaphor rather than intending it to provide empirically verifiable hypotheses about actual and possible political institutions (1993, 31; see also Isaac 1992, 230–31). For Arendt the public sphere (as the space of appearance) is a *potential* space which comes into being every time individuals gather together and act politically (to deliberate matters of public concern) and so "predates and precedes all formal constitution of the public realm and the various forms of government" (1958, 199).

Of more immediate concern than the general historical critiques are the feminist critiques that have reproved Habermas for accepting and reproducing the public-private divide without recognizing the subordination of women that this implies (Landes 1988; Pateman 1988; Ryan 1990; Eley 1992).[13] It was described earlier how the public sphere as the domain

---

12. Now in light of historical work that postdated his account, such as E. P. Thompson's study *The Making of the English Working Class* and Bakhtin's analysis of a plebeian culture in *Rabelais and His World,* as well as work that engages directly with *Structural Transformation* (e.g., Eley 1992), he concedes that the plebeian public sphere was more than a mere variant of the bourgeois model, because it develops its emancipatory potential in a new social context.

13. Habermas's more recent work provides a sophisticated account of the relations between public and private institutions in classical capitalist societies, suggesting that there are two distinct but interrelated public-private separations, one at the level of system (the separation of state from economy), the other at the level of the "lifeworld" (the separation of family from the space of political opinion formation). The two realms of privacy are linked

of reason and universality relies for its definition on its opposition to the private sphere of emotions and particularity. The bourgeois public sphere consequently recognizes men as uniquely well equipped as participants. In light of the feminist critique Habermas has come to accept that women were not excluded from the bourgeois public sphere *in the same fashion* as workers and peasants and others lacking "independence" but that women's exclusion had *structuring* significance (1992). He does not, however, follow through the consequences of that admission for the concept of a public sphere based on *reason.*

The premise of universal citizenship not only fails to take into account the prerequisites of property and gender, but, as Nancy Fraser has argued, the assumption that there can be a nonhierarchical, equal, and coercion-free public sphere in which interests are bracketed out and citizens deliberate as equals is simply naive in light of Foucault's work, which shows power in its modern form to be "local, continuous, productive, capillary and exhaustive" (Fraser 1989, 32). Moreover, the logical consequence of a political practice that rests on the bracketing out of social and economic differences must be that equality is not a necessary condition for political democracy (Fraser 1990, 65). But this surely has antidemocratic implications, as bracketing (ignoring) social inequalities works to further disadvantage the subordinate, since powerful informal pressures, not least having access to and competence in the vocabulary and grammar of the "common" language, can impede participatory parity even when everyone is formally licensed to participate.[14]

The characterization of the public sphere or spheres as an arena in which discussion should be restricted to the "common" good and not "private" interests is a distinction which serves to delegitimize or depoliticize certain points of view and interests, a recognition that, for instance, lay at the heart of the feminist assertion that "the personal is political." Clearly, there is a problem of assuming a "general interest" and "universal rationality," which demands that citizens internalize hegemonic conceptions of the public good and "the better argument." As Geoff Eley (1992) has suggested, a Gramscian notion of hegemony seems to describe more faithfully than a rational and consensual discursive public sphere the conflicts and contests over meaning within a society riven by class and gender inequali-

---

by the institutionalized roles of worker and consumer, while the two realms are linked by the institutionalized roles of citizen and later client. As Nancy Fraser has shown, Habermas fails to recognize the gendered identities of these roles and therefore to see that "male dominance is intrinsic rather than accidental to classical capitalism" (Fraser 1987, 45).

14. The criticisms of universal reason that I'm concentrating on here from a feminist point of view are also made from within a more broadly postmodern perspective (see Villa 1992).

ties in which the claim to rational discourse was simultaneously a claim to power. For Habermas, however, the universalist discourse of the bourgeois public sphere is not a hegemonic discourse in an exclusionary sense, because it provides areas of common ground for the excluded others and because contact with new social and cultural movements can transform these discourses and the structures of the public sphere itself from within. But such a position presupposes that there is a metadiscourse to which all speakers have access and to whose rules they universally consent, a presupposition that suppresses heterogeneity and plurality.

It also presupposes that the goal of dialogue is consensus, and it is here that the Arendtian model differentiates itself most clearly, in arguing for an agonistic politics. Plurality is not just a condition for political action and speech but also its *achievement* (Villa 1992, 717). Such performative action is an end in itself.[15] Once rules and regulations are imposed on public discourse, such as the requirement to seek consensus or to define the common good, then the space for active political individuals closes in, and the active citizen gives way to the passive subject. No topics can be ruled a priori not fitting for public deliberation.[16] Though it seems that Arendt is giving up the desirability of moral limits to political action, she argues that those limits ostensibly inherent in the philosophical definition of freedom have failed to prevent political atrocities, even in the name of freedom and reason, as Zygmunt Baumann has persuasively demonstrated in his analysis of modernity and the Holocaust (1989). What prevents this vision of politics from sliding into a kind of nihilism or postmodern relativism is, as Dana Villa points out, an appeal to the Kantian idea of a *sensus communis,* "a common feeling for the world, which provides a nontranscendental basis for judgements making a universal claim of validity" (1992, 719). However, in Arendt's narrative of the decline of the public sphere under the processes of modernity, she supposes that this "common feeling" for the world has been eroded away. In the discussion of radio and the reinvigoration of the public sphere that follows, I suggest that the development of the communicative ethos of broadcasting has acted as a brake to that

---

15. Culler describes the distinction between constative and performative utterances as defined by J. L. Austin (1975) as "a distinction between statements, or *constative* utterances, which describe a state of affairs and are true or false, and another class of utterances which are not true or false and which actually perform the action to which they refer (e.g., 'I promise to pay you tomorrow' accomplishes the act of promising). These he calls *performatives*" (1989, 112). The constative can therefore be understood as a special case of the performative.

16. For example, domestic violence was not considered a matter of public concern until feminists contested the view from the position of a subaltern counterpublic and "after sustained discursive contestation" succeeded in making it a common concern (see Fraser 1990, 71).

erosion. First, however, the discussion continues by following through some more general questions about the public sphere, media, and democracy.

## The Public Sphere, Media, and Democracy

Habermas's account of the decline of the public sphere painted a grimly pessimistic picture of the rise of the mass media that drew on the melancholy Frankfurt school critique, which viewed audiences as passive and impressionable, opening the way to the "engineering" of public opinion. Again, in the light of media scholarship in the intervening years, particularly around the concept of "active audiences," he accepts that his diagnosis of a "unilinear development from a politically active public to one withdrawn into a bad privacy, from a "culture-debating to a culture-consuming public," is too simplistic," and he recognizes the need to give more attention to the reception of media products in recent media theory (1992, 439).[17] His interpretation of the revolutions of 1989, for example, demonstrates a now much less pessimistic view of the role of the electronic mass media.

But a need to revise the pessimistic account of the role of the mass media in the structural transformation of the public sphere is not the only problem. The retention of a normative concept of the freedom of the press based on the category of the bourgeois public sphere is also problematic in light of the criticisms of universal reason previously discussed. As John Keane has argued, the various defenders of press freedom have historically trapped themselves in a performative contradiction, sanctioning "the open disputation of all except their own particular opinion on the nature of things," in seeking to legitimize the unrestricted clash of opinions by recourse to rational arguments that were "unchallengeable" (1991, 48–50). Keane makes a similar argument about how democracy itself should be understood (1984). Beginning from a position that casts doubt on the view "that argumentative reason can separate truth and falsity and produce a consensus among speaking and interacting subjects," Keane proposes that the philosophy of democracy can only be a particular language game in the plurality of contemporary language games, not a universal one nor a privileged one. Democracy, he suggests, can "survive and thrive without philosophical presuppositions, that it is best understood as an implied condition and practical consequence of the recognition that our modern

---

17. Habermas's argument that the public sphere in mass society had more to do with advertising than with rational-critical debate finds an echo in Andrew Wernick's analysis of contemporary "promotional culture" (1990).

world is marked (however imperfectly) by trends towards philosophical and political pluralism (1991, 172). The necessary conditions for a genuine plurality of expression for individuals and groups is therefore, he concludes, the separation of civil society from the state and the democratization of each, backed up and guaranteed by a plurality of (revised public service) communications media.

Although the connections are not made explicit, this nonfoundationalist conceptualization of democracy and the call for the democratization of institutions within civil society (including not least the media) seems to have more in common with Arendt's conception of politics and the idea of active citizenship than the model proposed by Habermas, guided as it is by the search for the common good and rational legitimations. Keane rejects the idea that consensus is the proper or likely outcome of democratic activity. Instead, there is "difference, openness and constant competition among power groups to produce and to control the definition of reality." The advantage of democracy over other systems is not that it guarantees "peace and quiet and good decisions, but that it offers citizens the right to judge (and to reconsider their judgements about) the quality of those decisions" (1991, 190). Even the question of the freedom of communication cannot be settled or realized but is, instead, constantly reformulated and regenerated in an ongoing project.

## Radio and the Reinvigoration of the Public Sphere

The concept of the public sphere has become increasingly important in media theory (Garnham 1986, 1993; Scannell 1989; Curran 1991, 1993; Dahlgren and Sparks 1993; Peters 1993). In line with this work, I will argue that the development of mass communication and broadcasting in particular, rather than being a nail in the coffin of the public sphere, represented its extension and reinvigoration. Paddy Scannell's influential essay "Public Service Broadcasting and Modern Public Life" offers a valuable model. Examining the experience of public service broadcasting in Great Britain, Scannell sees broadcasting "as a public good that has unobtrusively contributed to the democratization of everyday life, in public and private contexts, from its beginning through to today" (1989, 136). There are some differences in the German case, not least after 1933, but for the moment I will concentrate on the similarities. First of all, there was a service of mixed programs on nationwide channels available to all, engendering a common culture, reinventing a sense of national community, and generating a "shared public life of quite a new kind" (138). This feature of national public service broadcasting is surely a countervailing force to Arendt's pessimistic account of a decline of a "common feeling for the world" and Habermas's equally pessimistic account of the disintegration of the public sphere and the loss of common ground. Second, radio opened up access to a whole range of once exclusive or restricted events and activities to a wider and more varied public than ever before—a *general* public—an advantage that, I have argued, was felt most keenly by women traditionally restricted to the private sphere, particularly in rural and working-class communities. This entrance to another world was, for example, played up in a favorite advertising ploy by the RRG in the early 1930s, "Radiohören heißt doppelt leben" (To listen to radio is to live twice the life). Third, private life was resocialized and represented private persons in the public domain, creating "new communicative entitlements for excluded social groups" (142). Beyond the general implications of such a resocialization of the private sphere, it is remarkable how early women in Germany claimed this entitlement, albeit in an unsympathetic climate, with the carving out of a semiautonomous place in the schedules. Fourth, although broadcasting does not seem to allow for two-way discussions, a requisite of the Habermasian public sphere, Scannell argues that not only is this lack of reciprocity the case for most forms of public communication but that broadcasting offers an extra advantage in that the radio listener is not enthralled by the aura of presence, which creates a critical distance and a greater freedom of response (154). Habermas originally maintained that, in contrast to the appropriation of literature by group discussion and the critical discourse of literary publications, the mass media "removed the ground for a communication about what has been appropriated" (1989, 163). But, as many (usually television) audience studies have shown, the common knowledge of broadcast matter becomes the stuff of a whole range of social and critical interactions and a common cultural resource (Seiter 1989; Ang 1992; Morley 1993). In Raymond Williams's words, broadcasting was a way of "talking together about the processes of our common life" (cited in Curran 1993, 33). Finally, the widespread diffusion of broadcasting, together with the development of stylistic and scheduling forms that complement reception in the domestic sphere, has meant that the general public "has become familiar not simply with its modes of address, but with its performative styles" (Scannell 1989, 149). Broadcasting has therefore helped to bring about a real change in the communicative ethos of society by familiarizing performed forms of talk and helping to make performed talk generally more relaxed and spontaneous.

The significance of this becomes clear in Scannell's reworking of Habermas's ethics of communicative rationality in favor of an emphasis on *reasonableness,* which concentrates on the mechanisms of everyday social dialogue as opposed to the sterile precondition of the ideal speech situation of rational discourse (Scannell 1989, 158–60). These mechanisms include "tact, thoughtfulness and consideration for others, knowing how and when to listen," and they produce "agreements that are reasonable (as distinct from rational) and thus acceptable in the eyes of participants" (159). Since broadcasting's communicative ethos is grounded in its interconnection with private, daily life and the everyday communicative skills deployed in ordinary talk and mundane contexts, it serves to enhance "the reasonable . . . character of daily life in public and private contexts" (160). Here, then, in a different guise, there seems to be the possibility of a revived appeal to the *sensus communis* mourned by Arendt. It also seems to prepare the ground for a realization of her vision of politics based on the idea of active citizenship—that is to say, civic engagement and collective deliberation about all matters affecting the political community. Moreover, communicative rationality is not excluded from the Arendtian model of the public sphere, but it does not resort to a theorization of the ideal speech situation, instead prioritizing spontaneity, courage, and passion as indispensable moments in the revelation of the self that is political action (Dietz 1991, 248–49). In light of this discussion and the criticisms of Habermas's public sphere based on reason, a version of rationality like this which does not draw an impermeable distinction between reason and passion is clearly fruitful for a conceptualization of a feminist public sphere.

Clearly, Scannell's analysis of British public service broadcasting is set in the context of a broader democratic framework. The concept of "communicative entitlements," for example, presupposes communicative *rights,* which he regards as a "precondition of forms of democratic life in public and private" (160). What is striking, though, from the perspective of German radio, is how most of the conditions that are proposed as democratizing *prefigure and continue to inform* the broadcasting practices of a totalitarian regime. The description of a service of mixed programs on nationwide channels available to all, engendering a common culture, reinventing a sense of national community, and generating a "shared public life of quite a new kind," could serve equally well as a description of Nazi radio. The generalized access to public events, the socialization of the private sphere, the domestication of modes of address, and the provision of a common resource for social interaction were, as I have shown, all features of broadcasting in the Third Reich.

There are several things that could follow from this. Either the contribution of these aspects of broadcasting to democratization is overstated, or broadcasting continued in some way to provide a democratizing impulse within a profoundly antidemocratic regime. At this point I would tentatively suggest the latter. At the very least it follows that there are important implications for the question of continuity and change before and after 1933 and for the effectiveness of broadcast fascist propaganda. This is not to suggest a straightforward equivalence between public service broadcasting and Nazified radio, nor is it necessarily to privilege form over content, but it does suggest that an understanding of the democratizing potential of broadcasting goes some way to explaining some of the disjunctures between Nazi ideology, cultural practice, and the limited effectivity of broadcast propaganda.

Although these formal continuities are significant, another thing that certainly follows is the need to follow Scannell's example of a critical perspective that situates broadcasting forms in a broad social, political, and economic context. The transition to a totalitarian regime obviously has consequences for broadcasting that cannot be overlooked in the translation of Scannell's model to the German case of this period. During the Third Reich the reinvention of a sense of national community was one that was racially exclusive, access was opened up only to ideologically sanctioned public events, private life continued to be resocialized, but across a much narrower social spectrum, the destruction of aura may have continued to generate a critical distance, but the freedom of response and social interaction was forcefully curtailed, and the domesticated forms of address were employed in promoting a pernicious ideology.

However, the recourse to the language of rights and entitlements as the precondition of democratic life in public and private can be shown from an Arendtian perspective to be problematic; however, we have seen how plurality for Arendt is not a natural given but an *achievement* of political action. Political equality cannot rest on a theory of natural rights; it is, rather, an artificial, cultural attribute which is acquired when individuals enter the public realm and which is secured by democratic political institutions organized historically within the nation-state. As Arendt pointed out in *The Origins of Totalitarianism,* individuals stripped of civil and political rights during the Third Reich could not defend themselves by an appeal to their natural rights. To be excluded from the body politic is to have no rights at all (see Passerin d'Entrèves 1992, 150; Hansen 1993, 137–38). In fact she went further, in arguing that in an age of imperialism and war "the very phrase 'human rights' became for all concerned—victims, persecutors and onlookers alike—the evidence of hopeless idealism or fumbling feeble-mined hypocrisy." (1973, 269). Communicative rights and entitlements should therefore be understood as a product of action and speech that find actualization and recognition only within a democratic polity. In this respect, then, Arendt's model of the public sphere seems better able than the Habermasian version to accommodate Scannell's identification of new communicative entitlements being opened up by the socialization of the private sphere by a public service broadcasting system within a democratic state.

## Continuities, Changes, Contradictions

The theme of continuity and change is revisited if we turn now to consider the reinvigoration of the public sphere by broadcasting from a perspective that is sensitive to gender. Throughout the period, as I have demonstrated, the gendered division between the public and the private spheres provided the framework for the public discourse about the social function of radio and about the range and address of programming. Efforts to reestablish a "public" for the radio in the traditional sense in the form of listening groups or broadcasts in public places never really caught on. It was during the Weimar Republic that radio came to be defined as a public transmitter of privately received programs, an arrangement that, despite some half-hearted attempts to develop public reception, suited the Nazis' propagandistic aims in offering the chance to transmit political messages directly to a nationwide audience and literally to drive their message home. During the Weimar Republic this direct line to the home had represented a similar potential for the very different aims of feminist movements in the political education of newly enfranchised women. One of the primary incentives in setting up special programs for women was this vision of radio as a channel of democratic enlightenment, and certainly there was some acknowledgment of women's newly found place in the public sphere, even though it tended to be colored by a broadly bourgeois vision of women's role in work and politics. The other, more telling incentive came from conservative philosophies of the family and femininity. The domination of the resulting programs by the traditional concerns of women as housewives and consumers resulted from the general conservative bias in media policy in Weimar and from the participation of bourgeois housewives' unions in early program making.

The innovation of a separate service for women was one important part of the broadcasting inheritance that the Nazified system was proud to continue. Throughout the period women listening were constructed as a homogeneous group united in their maternal and domestic functions. During the Weimar period the audience was conceived and constructed as sectionalized not only by gender but also by age and profession, with a whole range of specifically targeted programs. After *Gleichschaltung* the schedules were uniformly presented to the homogeneously constructed audience that was the *Volksgemeinschaft*. Nevertheless, the tenet of complementary but separate spheres for the sexes was a broadly consistent theme in the Nazis' often inconsistent ideological schema, and so it was expedient to maintain separate programming and to keep the scheduling patterns designed to integrate women into the domestic sphere. The imperative for ideological consistency was strained as the pragmatic imperative to call on women to do war work became less and less resistible. Even then the language was often manipulated to obscure the contradictions between ideology and practice, as the German homeland became synonymous with the German homestead and women's maternal duty was conflated with their duty to the Fatherland.

How does this persistence of separate programs for women figure in the discussion about the public sphere? Useful insights can be gained by comparing the broadcast public sphere to the public sphere more generally, although there are also limitations to such an analogy. One of the democratizing conditions of broadcasting discussed earlier was its universality, that in principle every citizen has access to participate and costs are evenly spread. On one level, then, nationwide, mixed program broadcasting can be taken to be analogous to a unitary public sphere in which different voices are heard and different opinions formed and expressed both on the airwaves and in the social discussions initiated by the output (the material that is "put out" to the general public for such discussion).[18] Habermas maintains that a single comprehensive public sphere is preferable to a nexus of multiple publics (1992, 441), though he recognizes that the unresolved plurality of competing interests makes it doubtful whether there can ever emerge a general interest of the kind to which a public opinion could refer as a criterion. Yet, even in conceding the role of counterpublics, he still maintains that they must follow the same *rational* procedures of bracketing out differences and debating in the common interest and so on (466). Fraser has persuasively argued that multiple publics allow subaltern groups arenas for deliberation among themselves about their needs, objectives, and strategies that is not necessarily possible in a unitary sphere. A single sphere would mean filtering diverse rhetorical and stylistic norms through a single lens, and, since no lens is culturally neutral, it would privilege the expressive norms of one group over others (1990, 69). Counterpublics also help expand discursive space and in the long run militate against separatism in the sense that they aspire to disseminate their discourse to wider arenas.

On this level the value of counterpublics recognized by Fraser is confirmed from the perspective of this study. It was organization and debate within separate women's groups that helped pave the way for inclu-

18. It is interesting to note the potential for an international broadcast public sphere suggested by radio's disregard of national boundaries, something that was exploited in the oppositional broadcasting services throughout the period.

sion into the (broadcast) public sphere.[19] Moreover, the point about widening the discursive space and serving to redefine the unitary discourse is reaffirmed in light of the connections explored earlier between women finding their public voice and radio finding an institutional voice that could imitate private modes of speech (see chap. 8). But to suggest that the Frauenfunk, even in the Weimar Republic, in practice represented a counterpublic does rather stretch the analogy. It was too restricted by and too closely integrated into the radio system as a whole (which is not to suggest that counterpublics are necessarily progressive). Its democratic potential was foiled not only by the class bias which characterized the participation in and output from radio production across the board but also by the doctrine of nonpolitical radio and the structuring of schedules to match and maintain the domestic routine.

One of the main thrusts of the chapters on Weimar radio was to highlight the particular significance of gender politics to this policy of nonpolitical radio, and vice versa. The fractious political society into which public radio was launched in Germany was one that was still coming to terms with the bitterness of defeat and the tensions of modernization. A combination of pressures from within government and from commerce ensured that this most modern of media served the interests of the state and of the status quo. Thomas Childers has described how "public political discourse" in Weimar Germany was dominated by the print media and how "political mobilization strategies" by political parties "relied on the distribution of leaflets, pamphlets, and posters to saturate the public with their message, while their meetings, rallies, and other public events were given prime coverage in the partisan press" (1990, 338; see also Fritzsche 1990, 5–12, 75–80). According to a conventionally narrow definition of politics, the radio was clearly not an important player in this period. But the definition of politics was expanding during this period, and the radio's political influence should not be discounted. More to the point, since women were often implicitly, if not explicitly, excluded from conventional public politics (such as political meetings held in factories and public houses), it is arguable that women more readily recognized radio as a new forum for a kind of politics that did not put such a premium on public assembly and that could reach those sections of the population which had remained untouched by conventional means of mobilization and political participation. It is during periods of crisis, at moments of industrial, political, and social dislocation, that various social groups struggle to find a voice in the emergent new order—and, certainly, the successive phases of

19. For an account of the ways in which women of various classes and ethnicities in North America developed access to the official public sphere by a variety of routes in the last century, see Ryan 1990.

feminism can be linked to such moments (Alexander 1994, 275). What is interesting about the early twentieth century is that these social and political dislocations were attended by technological innovations that held out the possibility of new platforms from which such voices could be heard. At the same time, however, it is during periods of crisis when the media suffer most severely from political repression (Keane 1991, 96). In the light of a historical perspective that is sensitive to gender, it seems that for an extension of an active and participatory public sphere to be curtailed at this juncture was not simply a matter of short-term contingency but one that is closely bound up with the history of women's integration into the political process.

The analysis of public discourse about radio during the Weimar Republic has shown how this policy was designed to achieve more than simply keeping political extremism off the air. It was also designed to underline the sanctity of the home and family. Yet, at the same time, the pervasion of the private sphere by politics borne in the ether was constituted as another potential threat to the family—and, by association, to the state—at a time when it already seemed to be being undermined by the exodus of women from domestic responsibilities into more permanent forms of waged labor, into more active participation in the political sphere, and into expressions of a freer and more strident sexuality. The policy of nonpolitical radio, therefore, was a reaction both to women's transcendence of the public-private divide and to the challenge to that divide posed by the nature of public radio itself. It represented a denial of the democratic potential of a new public sphere and the redefinition of the private sphere that radio promised. Restriction of the democratic potential of radio by an ostensibly democratic regime in the name of protecting the interests of the state laid various foundations for the antidemocratic control of the media when Hitler came to power. It provided the focus for an antidemocratic movement to rail against the authoritarian nature of the existing regime. It did nothing to strengthen a fragile democratic culture, and it served to accustom listeners to the silencing of public criticism of political power and the promotion of cultural conformism.

If gender politics were influential in determining this policy, then the gag of nonpolitical radio in turn had implications for gender politics. It was a policy arguably most critical for women in domestic isolation deprived of an easily accessible and informal introduction to the political world. The conservative Weimar media policy of keeping public politics out of the private sphere in the years following the enfranchisement of women was in itself a political act. Nazi media policy, on the other hand, sought to politicize every aspect of the private sphere while denying women any real political agency. The second major foil to the liberating potential of radio for women was the interweaving of the schedules into the daily routine, consciously to accompany and alleviate the continual round of domestic family experience, from household chores through children's storytelling to the communal family listening of prime time. The traditional family was imagined at the heart of scheduling policy and was designed to forestall the perceived threat to stable family life, though the segmentation and routinization of domestic time and the translation of the rhythms of the factory into the home paradoxically also undermined the conventional image of domestic serenity.

But there is a third limitation to the democratizing potential of women's radio that has to do with the limitations of a consensus-bound model of the public sphere and the limitations of identity politics. This is to revisit one of the key dilemmas confronting feminist theory; in the words of Benhabib and Cornell, "how can feminist theory base itself upon the uniqueness of the female experience without reifying thereby one single definition of femaleness as the paradigmatic one—without succumbing, that is, to an essentialist discourse on gender?" (1987, 13). It is beyond the scope of this essay to engage head-on with these debates, though, once again, reference to the Arendtian model of the public sphere is constructive—despite its inattention to gender and feminism (Markus 1989)—partly because it emphasizes the weaknesses of identity politics but also not least because the conception of politics as collective action and the mutual engagement of peers in a public realm places an emphasis on speech, or "voice," that is central to feminist theory (Dietz 1991, 246–48) and, of course, to the radio.

As Honig has argued, Arendt's performative politics "can serve as a promising model for a feminist politics that seeks to contest (performatively and agonistically) the prevailing construction of sex and gender into binary and binding division of political space into a public and private realm" (1992, 216). Performative actions "do not express a prior, stable identity but presuppose an unstable, multiple self that seeks episodic self-realization in action and in the identity that is its reward" (220). The self, in other words, is fragmented, the site of a dialogic struggle between the public and the private. Following from this, Arendt rejects a politics of representation that imagines and projects a common identity based on gender, race, ethnicity, or nationality, because it closes down the space for pluralistic political action and obstructs "a politics of performativity that, instead of reproducing and re-presenting "what" we are, agonistically generates "who" we are by episodically producing new identities" (1963, 47; Butler 1990, 142–49; Honig 1992, 226). As long as gender—or ethnicity or nationality—is taken to be a constative, irresistible, noncontroversial given, then it belongs where Arendt left it, in the private, nonpolitical realm. Following Honig's reworking of Arendt's position, however, I would agree that a more powerful and empowering defense against identity politics is, "to resist the irresistible, not by privatizing it but by unmasking the would-be irresistible, homogeneous, constative and univocal identity in question as a performative production, fractured, fragmented, ill-fitting, and incomplete, the sedimented and not at all seamless product of a multitude of performances and behaviors, the naturalized product of innumerable repetitions" (1992, 231).

The contradiction of women's radio as it was practiced from 1923 to 1945 is that it both implicitly unmasked the univocal identity of most of the broadcast output while at the same time naturalizing the conventional gender relations by repeating them in a multitude of performances. The very constructedness of gender is made plain in the anxious repetitive reaffirmation of its "naturalized" social relations. At the same time, the limitations and perils of a cultural and political practice that is founded on gender identity become clear in the light of the appropriation of those practices to serve conservative and totalitarian designs. The carving out of a separate space within the public sphere for women as *citizens* would seem to be a pragmatic solution to the actually existing prejudices and institutional arrangements that had so long excluded women from political participation and denied the personal as political. But carving out a space for women as *women* closes down the space for a pluralistic performative politics. Although there were advocates of the former strategy in the establishment of women's radio in the Weimar Republic, for the various reasons already given, women's radio very quickly became predominantly a space for women as housewives, consumers, and mothers, categories derived from an understanding of women's intransient identity formation within the private sphere. That domesticated, maternalized space underscored the conventional gendered separation of the public-private divide in which women are excluded from the political and provided the model of a broadcasting practice that was perfectly suited to the ideological project of national socialism, a political theory and practice that fatefully located identity in the physiologies of race and gender.

To conclude, then, I hope to have demonstrated that a gendered history of radio in Germany during this period can act as a prism through which a whole range of historical and critical issues can be addressed. Not only does it restore women to the history of radio, but it also uncovers the gendered subtexts of broadcasting discourses, policies, and practices and highlights how radio is one of the sites where gender is produced, reproduced, and transformed. It also identifies some significant ways in which the cultural practice and propaganda of the Third Reich was anticipated in and enabled by the legacy of broadcasting in the Weimar Republic. It therefore relativizes and redefines the exploitation of the medium for Nazi propaganda and hopes to contribute to the growing understanding of fascism in its familiar, everyday guise. Moreover, in light of the evidence presented, I would repeat the claim made in the introduction that, if past constructions inform and illuminate the present, then the answers to the questions posed by this investigation would seem to have contemporary significance. This study has shown how gendered discourses helped determine the form of radio as a medium which straddles the domains of public and private and suggests that gender issues are always critical to and implicit in the relationship between the technological potential and the social application of a new medium. In particular, I hope to have contributed to the debates on the relationship between the media and democracy from a historical perspective which is forced to confront the consequences of a fatefully missed opportunity to promote mass democratic participation and a reinvigorated public sphere.

# Appendix 1

**Official Listening Figures in Germany 1924–43**

| | | | |
|---|---|---|---|
| 1.1.24 | 1,580 | 1.1.33 | 4,307,722 |
| 1.1.25 | 548,749 | 1.1.34 | 5,052,607 |
| 1.1.26 | 1,022,299 | 1.1.35 | 4,142,921 |
| 1.1.27 | 1,376,564 | 1.1.36 | 7,192,000 |
| 1.1.28 | 2,009,842 | 1.1.37 | 8,167,957 |
| 1.1.29 | 2,635,567 | 1.1.38 | 9,087,454 |
| 1.1.30 | 3,066,682 | 1.1.41 | 14,882,496 |
| 1.1.31 | 3,509,509 | 1.4.43 | 16,000,000 |
| 1.1.32 | 3,981,000 | | |

*Source:* Figures compiled from information in Fischer 1957, 14–37; and the statistics published by the RKK, BAK R56I/115:165.

*Note:* Fischer has no overall figures for 1932 but notes that in that crisis year of 1932, for every 100 new licenses, 74 were revoked. In 1937 Germany became the European nation with the highest listening figures. The United Kingdom followed, with 7,960,573. The 1941–43 figures are for the whole of the extended territory of the German Reich.

# Appendix 2

**A Composite Week of Programming for Women
and Young People, 1930**

In 1930 the magazine *Funk* began publishing a separate section devoted to
the week's broadcasting output for women and young people. In addition
to reports and articles about individual programs, a comprehensive schedule of all the specialist programs broadcast across the country was printed
week by week. This makes it possible to contrive a representative composite week of programming content for women and young people, by taking
a small sample from the schedules as a whole over the period. This is useful primarily in terms of seeing the volume of specialist coverage given to
these audience groups but also in gauging the range of topics covered. It is
also useful in giving an fuller indication of the picture in the regions, given
that other sources are relatively incomplete (see chaps. 1 and 2). The composite week is made up of a random selection of the seven weekdays across
the first five months of 1930. The year 1930 is a usefully representative year
for such an exercise, the patterns and principles of nonpolitical radio being
well established, the Frauen- und Jugendfunk being a firm pillar of the
overall schedule, further refined by the introduction of the Jungmädchen-
funk (see chap. 3). Bredow's guidelines had been in force for four years,
and there were still eighteen months to go before the next major reform of
the broadcasting system which paved the way for the Gleichschaltung of
radio in 1933 (see chap. 2).

Sunday, 5 January 1930

| Berlin | 11.00 | *Elternstunde* |
|---|---|---|
| | 14.00 | *Volksmärchen* |
| Breslau | 15.15 | *Die Wunderfahrt ins Maschinenland* |
| Frankfurt a.M. | 11.00 | *Elternstunde* |
| | 14.00 | *Kasperlstunde* |

| Hamburg | 9.00 | *Die Bedeutung der staatsbürgerlichen Erziehung der Jugend für unser Staatswesen* |
| | 14.00 | *Funkheinzelmann* |
| Königsberg | 15.10 | *Ein Kapitel Skitechnik* |
| Langenberg | 17.40 | *Dr Dolittles Abenteuer* |
| Leipzig | 16.00 | *Das Spiel von den Heiligen Drei Königen* |
| Munich | 15.30 | *Die praktische Frau* |
| Deutsche Welle | | as Berlin |

Monday, 26 January 1930

| Berlin | 15.20 | *Die Frau in der Angestelltenversicherung* |
| | 17.30 | *Jugendstunde: Naturwissenschaften* |
| Breslau | 16.00 | *Elternstunde* |
| Frankfurt a.M. | 15.15 | *Aus dem Leben der Indianer Nordamerikers* |
| | 16.00 | *Frauenstunde: Bratwurstvariationen; Mein Kind ist so schlecht.* |
| | 18.35 | *Die Bestimmungen der Schülerselbstverwaltung an den höheren Schulen in Preußen* |
| Hamburg | 16.15 | *Bastelstunde* |
| | 16.40 | *Jugendstunde* |
| | 19.00 | *Welcher Beruf ist aussichtsvoll?* |
| Königsberg | 15.30 | *Bastelstunde für unsere Kleinen* |
| | 18.45 | *Vermessungstechnik als Beruf* |
| Langenberg | 15.00 | *Was uns die Blumen erzählen* |
| | 16.05 | *Die jugendliche Arbeiterin auf der Arbeitssuche* |
| | 16.50 | *Jugendfunk* |
| Leipzig | 15.00 | *Gespräch mit einer Photographin* |
| | 20.30 | *"Mutter" Zyklus moderner Dichtungen von Stella Hay* |
| Munich | 17.35 | *Kinderbastelstunde* |
| Stuttgart | 18.35 | *Übertragung aus Frankfurt* |
| Deutsche Welle | 14.30 | *Eulenspiegel-Geschichten* |
| | 15.00 | *Neigung und Eignung der Berufswahl* |
| | 15.45 | *Die Frau als Komponistin* |

Tuesday, 18 February 1930

| Berlin | 9.00 | *Wie schutzt ihr euch vor Erkältungen* |
| | 15.20 | *Wohnungskultur und -unkultur im Orient* |

|  | 18.00 | *Das Cembalo* |
| Breslau | 16.00 | *Gibt es seelische Regungen im Säuglingsalter* |
|  | 17.30 | *Warum die Euler unter die Räuber gingen* |
|  | 18.40 | *Die geplagte Landarbeiterfrau* |
| Frankfurt a.M. | 15.15 | *Von der peruanischen Küste nach La Paz* |
|  | 16.00 | *Hausfrauennachmittag: Heringe* |
|  | 16.50 | *Wie erfahre ich, was in der politischen Welt vorgeht?* |
| Hamburg | 11.30 | *Kinderlieder* |
| Königsberg | 15.30 | *Rythmische Spielstunde* |
| Langenberg | 15.00 | *Russische Märchen und Lieder* |
|  | 16.50 | *Musikunterricht in der höheren Schule* |
|  | 17.30 | *Kinderchöre* |
| Leipzig | 18.05 | *Gabriele Reuter liest aus ihrne Erzählungen* |
| Munich | 14.45 | *Stunde der Hausfrau:1. Wir nähen eine Erstlingsausstattung. 2. Wie behandle ich Samt und Pelze? 3. Kartoffelspeisen* |
| Stuttgart | 15.30 | *Wohnung und Wohnungspflege* |
| Deutsche Welle | 9.00 | *Übertragung aus Berlin* |
|  | 14.30 | *Tanzturnen für Kinder* |
|  | 15.00 | *Jugend-Schachfunk* |
|  | 15.45 | *Handarbeiten: Tischkarte* |

Wednesday, 5 March 1930

| Berlin | 15.20 | *Wissenschaft in der Küche* |
|  | 15.40 | *Frühjahrsarbeiten im Obstgarten* |
|  | 17.30 | *Jugendstunde: Dichterstimmen* |
| Breslau | 17.30 | *Die Schule, eine Vorbereitung für das Leben* |
| Frankfurt a.M. | 15.15 | *Stunde der Jugend: Wie die Spanier und die Kroaten im 30-jährigen Kriege hausten* |
| Königsberg | 18.15 | *Wie in der Grundschule gearbeitet wird* |
|  | 18.45 | *Gesundheitsfürsorge für Tuberkulöse in Anstalten* |
| Langenberg | 14.30 | *Ratschläge fürs Haus* |
|  | 15.00 | *Handarbeitsstunde für junge Mädchen* |
| Leipzig | 10.50 | *Hausfrauenberuf und Gesundheit* |
|  | 14.30 | *"Humsti-Bumsti" Lustiges Hörspiel von Tilla Bunge* |
|  | 16.00 | *Mit den Schneeschuhen in die Berge* |
|  | 19.00 | *Sprechstunde für die reifere Jugend* |

| Munich | 16.55 | *Kleine Geschichten für Kinder* |
| | 18.15 | *Schachfunk für die Jugend* |
| | 18.45 | *Was soll ich werden? Schneiderin?* |
| Stuttgart | 15.00 | *Kinderstunde aus Frankfurt* |
| Deutsche Welle | 14.45 | *Kindertheater* |
| | 15.45 | *Die Nahrungsmittel in ihrem Verhältnis zu Ausnutzbarkeit der Nährwerte und Preis* |

Thursday, 27 March 1930

| Berlin | 17.55 | *Kinderlieder* |
| Breslau | 18.15 | *Studien- und Berufsfragen der Volkswirte* |
| Frankfurt a.M. | 15.15 | *Ein rheinischer Weberjunge erzählt* |
| | 18.35 | *Berufsneigung und Berufseignung* |
| Königsberg | 15.35 | *Jugendstunde: Zeit und moderne Weltum- seglung* |
| Langenberg | 14.30 | *Ratschläge fürs Haus* |
| | 15.00 | *Geschichte* |
| | 15.45 | *Bücher für die Jugendweihe* |
| Leipzig | 14.30 | *Von Fliegern und Flugzeugen* |
| Stuttgart | 15.30 | *Blumenstunde* |
| Deutsche Welle | 15.00 | *Die vermeintlichen Minderleistungen der Volksschule* |
| | 15.45 | *Aus der Praxis der Eheberatung* |
| | 18.20 | *Die Frau von heute und gestern* |

Friday, 11 April 1930

| Berlin | 15.20 | *Über Sachlichkeit und Führergeist der Frau* |
| | 17.45 | *Konzert für die Jugend* |
| Breslau | 16.00 | *Stunde der Frau: Brauchen wir Meisterin- nen der Hauswirtschaft?* |
| | 17.30 | *Kinderzeitung: Schnufftibus und der Zeitungsonkel* |
| Hamburg | 19.30 | *Vorschau auf die Tagungen der deutschen Jugendbünde* |
| Königsberg | 15.30 | *Wie die Märchenmutter Ostern vorbereitet* |
| | 16.00 | *Resteverwertung* |
| Langenberg | 14.30 | *Ratschläge fürs Haus* |
| | 15.00 | *Neue Kleider für unsere Anziehpuppe* |
| | 16.45 | *Jugendfunk* |
| Leipzig | 15.15 | *Die Aufgaben der deutschen Landfrau* |

| Munich | 14.45 | *Stunde der Frau: Frauen im Leben fremder Völker; Frauenrundschau; "Meine Damen, Ihre Männer beschweren sich"* |
|---|---|---|
| | 16.00 | *Rosenpflege* |
| | 18.15 | *Die Bedeutung der Milchzähne* |
| Deutsche Welle | 14.30 | Gertrud van Eyseren: *Kunterbunt* |
| | 15.00 | *Das kritische junge Mädchen* |

Saturday, 3 May 1930

| Berlin | 15.20 | *Jugendstunde: Auf Walfischfang* |
|---|---|---|
| | 16.00 | *Mietsallerlei* |
| | 18.00 | *Was jeder vom Sport wissen muß: Radsport* |
| Frankfurt a.M. | 17.55 | *Erziehung der Gruppe neben Erziehung des einzelnen* |
| Königsberg | 15.15 | *Der Schwinehirt: Hörspiel* |
| | 15.30 | *Literarische Jugendstunde* |
| Langenberg | 15.00 | *Von Negern und Negerlein* |
| Leipzig | 10.45 | *Blumen und Gärten im Mai* |
| | 14.30 | *Bastelstunde für die Jugend* |
| | 18.00 | *Funkbastelstunde* |
| Stuttgart | 14.00 | *Emilia Galotti* |
| | 18.35 | *Zahnpflege beim Kinde und bei Erwachsenen* |
| Deutsche Welle | 14.30 | Ursula Scherz: *Kinderbastelstunde* |
| | 15.00 | *Aus der pädagogischen Abteilung* |
| | 15.45 | Dr. Else Möbus: *Mutterschutz* |

# Appendix 3

**A Week of Women's Programs, 1937**

Each week the Press/Propaganda Department of the RFF would circulate details of the programs to be broadcast by the regional Frauenfunk departments to all of its branches. One of these circulars, for the week beginning Sunday, 21 March 1937, is reproduced (in edited form) here—again, simply to give some indication of the frequency and range of programs for women during this period.

Deutschlandsender

| | | |
|---|---|---|
| Tuesday, 23 March | 11.30–11.40 | *Gelee-Eier: eine schmackhafte Süßspeise für die Ostertage* |
| | 15.15–15.45 | *Spielzeug aus zwei Jahrhunderten* |
| Wednesday, 24 March | 09.40–10.00 | *Kleine Turnstunde für die Hausfrau* |
| Thursday, 25 March | 15.15.–15.45 | *Ein Frauenleben - der Tanzkunst gewidment* |
| Saturday, 27 March | 09.40–10.00 | *Kleine Turnstunde für die Hausfrau* |
| | 11.30–11.40 | *Deutsche Ostern in fremdem Land: Eine Mutter erzählt* |

Reichssender Berlin

| | | |
|---|---|---|
| Monday, 22 March | 09.30–10.00 | *Volkswirtschaftliche Kochen* |
| Tuesday, 23 March | 09.30–10.00 | *Kunterbunt für die Ganzleinen und ihre Mütter* |

| Wednesday, 24 March | 09.45–10.00 | *Schwestern in Übersee* |
| Thursday, 25 March | 16.30–17.00 | *Begegnungen mit großen Musikern* |
| Saturday, 27 March | 09.30–09.45 | *Mutter turnt mit dem Kind* |
| | 09.45–10.00 | *Verliebt-verlobt-verheiratet-geschieden* |

**Reichssender Breslau**

| Sunday, 21 March | 14.10–14.35 | *Handel und Wandel im Sowjetparadies: Aus dem Leben einer auslandsdeutschen Mutter* |
| Monday, 22 March | 08.20–08.30 | *Für die Landfrau* |
| Tuesday, 23 March | 16.30–16.50 | *Ostern ist vor der Tür: Zwiegespräch* |
| Thursday, 25 March | 08.15–08.30 | *Laß Dir auch mal eine Viertelstunde Zeit! Von Würz und Küchenkräutern* |
| | 16.00–16.20 | *Es schmeckt wie bei Mutter zu Haus* |

Tuesdays, Wednesdays, and Fridays    *Frauengymnastik*
from 08.00–08.20

**Reichssender Frankfurt**

| Sunday, 21 March | 11.15–11.30 | *Allerlei für den Ostertisch* |
| Tuesday, 23 March | 11.00–11.15 | *Ostergebäck* |
| Wednesday, 24 March | 11.15–11.30 | *Was kochen wir zu Ostern? Festlich und doch arbeitssparend* |
| Thursday, 25 March | 11.15–11.30 | *Deutsche Kräuter* |
| Saturday, 27 March | 11.15–11.30 | *Ich reise zu Verwandten!* |

**Reichssender Hamburg**

Daily from 08.00–08.15    *Allerlei Ratschläge*

**Reichssender Köln**

Daily at 08.00,    *Das Kalenderblatt,*
and from 08.10–08.30,    *Frauenturnen*

Reichssender Königsberg

| | | |
|---|---|---|
| Sunday, 21 March | 14.45–15.00 | *Hauslichkeit und Kultur: Die zweifachen Aufgaben der Frau* |
| Monday, 22 March | 14.15–14.25 | *Unsere Kleidung - zweck-mäßig und schön* |
| Tuesday, 23 March | 09.30–09.40 | *Die Hausfrau mitten in der Volkswirtschaft* |
| | 14.15–14.25 | *Zu neuen Frauenbüchern spricht Georg Neitzel* |
| Wednesday, 24 March | 11.05–11.30 | *Mütter und ihre Kinder: Vorbereitungen zum Schu-lanfang* |
| | 15.30–15.40 | *Praktische Winke und Erfahrungsaustausch von einer Hausfrau: Unser Ostertisch* |
| Thursday, 25 March | 09.30–09.40 | *Gemeinsame Arbeit mit jun-gen Hausfrauen: Wohin mit den Resten?* |
| | 15.25–15.45 | *Unser Kind lernt die Heimat kennen* |
| Saturday, 27 March | 09.30–09.40 | *Kürze berichte für die Küche: Verwertung der Glumse* |
| | 14.15–14.25 | *Sollen wir gesunde Kinder vorzeitig einschulen?* |
| Daily at 08.15, | | *Gymnastik für die Frau* |

Reichssender Leipzig

| | | |
|---|---|---|
| Sunday, 21 March | 14.10–14.40 | *Aus einem Arbeitsdienstlager für die weibliche Jugend* |
| Monday, 22 March | 15.00–15.15 | *Vom Honig zum Rüben-zucker* |
| Tuesday, 23 March | 15.00–15.20 | *Frauenberufe an der Zeitung* |
| Wednesday, 24 March | 09.30–09.45 | *Markt und Küche: Neues bil-liges Festtagsgebäck* |
| | 17.10–17.30 | *Verpflichtung und Aufgabe der Frau: Buchbericht* |

| Thursday, 25 March | 15.00–15.20 | *Sollen wir unseren Kindern bei den Schularbeiten helfen?* |
| Friday, 26 March | 09.30–09.55 | *Spielstunde für die Kleinsten und ihre Mütter* |
| | 10.00–10.30 | *Kinderszenen. Hörfolge mit Musik von Robert Schumann* |
| Saturday, 27 March | 09.30–09.45 | *Billig aber gut—der Küchenzettel der Woche* |

Reichssender München

| Monday, 22 March | 08.20–08.30 | *Neues billiges Festtagsgebäck* |
| Tuesday, 23 March | 16.10–16.50 | *Wenn's taut! Ein Münchener Hörbild: Kinderbildnisse ins deutsche Haus!* |
| Wednesday, 24 March | 08.20–08.30 | *Kleiner Marktbericht* |
| Thursday, 25 March | 08.20–08.30 | *Grüne Gemüse und Salate. Wie man sie zu Ostern auf den Tisch bringt* |
| Friday, 26 March | 08.20–08.30 | *Frische Flußfische* |
| | 16.10–16.50 | *Briefe an eine junge Frau. Hörfolge aus dem Werk und Leben von Rainer Maria Rilke* |
| Saturday, 27 March | 08.20–08.30 | *Hausfrauen aufgepaßt!* |
| Daily from 08.20–08.30, | | *Gymnastik für die Hausfrau* |

Reichssender Saarbrücken

| Monday, 22 March | 09.30–10.00 | *Was kochen wir? Überraschungen vom Osterhasen* |
| Tuesday, 23 March | 09.30–09.45 | *Plaudereien für die Hausfrau. Frau Finke sät Würzkräuter* |
| Thursday, 25 March | 11.30–11.45 | *Mutter und Kind, wir raten Dir! Wir malen Ostereier* |

Reichssender Stuttgart

| Monday, 22 March | 09.30–09.45 | *Ostern auf der Alb. Erinnerungen einer Schwäbin* |

| Tuesday, 23 March | 17.00–17.30 | *Blumen- und Pflanzenmarkt in der Osterwoche* |
| Wednesday, 24 March | 19.45–20.00 | *3 Stimmen zu einem österlichen Thema* |
| Thursday, 25 March | 09.30–09.45 | *Verwertung von Stoffresten* |
| | 17.10–17.40 | *Väter und Töchter* |
| Daily fifteen minutes, | | *Frauengymnastik* |

Taken from "Der Frauenfunk der Woche 21.3. - 27.3.37." RFF Rundschreiben F47/37 von Erika Kirmsse-Fillies, head of the Press/Propaganda dept., and Gertrud Kappesser, radio division, to all leaders, of the regional women's organisations and regional departmental heads in Press/Propaganda, BAK NS44/35.

# Bibliography

**Archives**

British Library
Bundesarchiv Koblenz (BA)
NS15        Der Beauftragte des Führers für die Überwachung der gesamten geisti-
            gen und weltanschaulichen Schulung und Erziehung des NSDAP
NS18        Reichspropagandaleiter der NSDAP
NS44        Reichsfrauenführung/NS Frauenschaft und Deutsches Frauenwerk
R32         Reichskunstwart (Film)
R34         Deutsches Nachrichtenbüro und Deutscher Kulturdienst
R43         Reichskanzlei
R48         Reichspostministerium
R55         Reichsministerium für Volksaufklärung und Propaganda
R56 I       Reichskulturkammer: Zentral
R56 IV      Reichskulturkammer: Presse und Rundfunk
R78         Reichsrundfunkgesellschaft
ZSg 1–5     Durchschriften von Organisationen und Verbänden

Bundesarchiv, Potsdam (BAP) (formerly the Zentrales Staatsarchiv der DDR)
15.01       Reichsministerium des Innern, 1879–45
            Bd. 49: Kultur, Kunst und Wissenschaft
47.01       Reichspostministerium, 1875–1945
50.01       Reichsministerium für Volksaufklärung und Propaganda
50.02       Reichsausschuß für Volkswirtschaftliche Aufklärung GmbH.
50.04       Reichsrundfunkgesellschaft
62DAF3      Deutsche Arbeitsfront
            Bd.4 F: Frauenfragen
            D660: Reichsrundfunkkammer
62Re1       Reichsfrauenführung
70Re2       Reichsgemeinschaft Deutscher Hausfrauen, 1915–35

Deutsches Filmmuseum, Frankfurt am Main
Deutsches Film- und Fernseh Institut, Berlin
Deutsches Rundfunkarchiv, Frankfurt am Main (DRA)
    Gedächtnisprokokolle 1: Frieda Magnus-Unzer
    Nachlaß Hersel
    Drei Jahre Berliner Rundfunkdarbietungen, 1923–26
    Das vierte Jahr. Berliner Rundfunkjahr, 15 August 1926–30 September 1927
    Fünf Jahre Berliner Rundfunk, 1923–28
    Das sechste Berliner Rundfunkjahr, 1 October 1928–30 September 1929
    Das Berliner Rundfunkjahr, 1930
    (Most of the radio journals consulted can be found at the DRA.)
Deutsches Rundfunkmuseum, Berlin
Filmarchiv der DDR, Berlin
Filmmuseum, Potsdam
German Historical Institute, London
Institut für Zeitgeschichte, Munich (IfZ)
Db40.02   Nachrichtendienst der Reichsfrauenführerin
Db40.09   Jahresberichte der NS Frauenschaft und des Deutschen Frauenwerks
MA441    Meldungen aus dem Reich: Bevölkerung, Stimmung und Frauenarbeitseinsatz im Kriege
Staatliches Filmarchiv der DDR
Staatsbibliothek, Berlin

## Books and Articles Published before 1945

Albrecht, Erna. 1926. "Welche Aufgaben haben die hauswirtschaftlichen und gewerblichen Fachschulen für die Mädchenbildung zu erfüllen?" *D. W. Funk* 5:195–96.
"Aus dem weiblichen Berufsleben: Ist Werbung Frauenberuf?" 1935. *Berliner Lokal-Anzeiger* 24 February.
Bäumer, Gertrud. 1928. "Zur Ausgestaltung des Programms." *Die Sendung* 39:50.
Bauer, Margarete. 1926. "Frau und Rundfunk." *Der Neue Rundfunk* 22:80.
Bauer, P. 1931. "Familie und Rundfunk." *Bayerische Radiozeitung,* 8 March.
"Die bayerische Frauenstunde." 1930. *Frauen und Jugendfunk: Beilage zum Funk* 9:35.
Behme, Theda. 1928. "Die praktische und schöne Einrichtung der Kleinwohnung." *Deutsche Welle* 43:405.
Bergmann, Ernst. 1932. *Erkenntnisgeist und Muttergeist: Eine Soziosophie der Geschlechter.* Breslau: F. Hirt.
———. 1933. *Deutschland, das Bildungsland der neuen Menschheit.* Breslau: F. Hirt.
"Berufslenkung 1938 durch den Rundfunk." 1938. *Nachrichtendienst der Reichsfrauenführung* (February): 9.
Beyer, Karl. 1936. *Familie und Frau im neuen Deutschland.* Langensalze: Julius Beltz.

Brady, Robert A. 1933. *The Rationalization Movement in German Industry: A Study in the Evolution of Economic Planning.* Berkeley: University of California Press.

Bremen-Hirschkendt, Gerda von. 1933a. "Frauenschulung für den Rundfunk." *Die Deutsche Frauenfront* 1:119.

———. 1933b. "Weshalb sind wir Nationalsozialisten? Frauen sprechen über ihren Weg zur deutschen Volksgemeinschaft." *Der Angriff,* 15 March.

"Briefe an den Funk." 1925. *Funk* 6:76.

Brix, Meta. 1930a. "Was bringt der Rundfunk den Frauen?" *Frauen und Jugendfunk: Beilage zum Funk* 34:134.

———. 1930b. "Frauenstunde—Jungmädchenstunde: Eine nachdenkliche Betrachtung." *Frauen und Jugendfunk: Beilage zum Funk* 12:45.

———. 1931. "Der männliche Sprecher in der Frauenstunde." *Funk* 27:216.

———. 1932. "Eine neue deutsche Ansagerin." *Funk* 27:106.

Buczkowska, Maria. 1931–32. "Der Rundfunk und die Frau." *Rufer und Hörer,* 1:561.

Burger, [?]. 1931b. "Das berufstätige junge Mädchen und ihr männlicher Vorgesetzter." *Deutsche Welle* 50:481.

———. 1931a. "Jugend hilft der Jugend." *Deutsche Welle* 33:312–13.

Burghöfer, Friedrich. 1927. "Bedeutung der Geburtenbeschränkung für Volk und Familie." *D.W. Funk* 22:654–56.

———. 1928. "Bevölkerungsentwicklung und Wirtschaft." *Deutsche Welle* 27: 500–501.

Coler, Luise, and Emmy Pfannstiehl. 1940. *Frau und Mutter,* 4th ed. Düsseldorf: A. Bagel.

Delius, K. 1927. "Land- und hauswirtschaftliche Frauenberufe." *D.W. Funk* 10:299–301.

Dery, Dora. 1928. "Ich spreche Funk." *Der Deutsche Rundfunk* 49:3317.

Deutscher Textilarbeiterverband, ed. 1930. *Mein Arbeitstag, Mein Wochenende: 150 Berichte von Textilarbeiterinnen.* Berlin: Textilpraxis Verlag.

"Deutschlandsender: Frauenfunk einschalten." 1935. *Die Sendung* 23:374.

Diel, Louise. 1927. "Wie lebt die Berufsfrau in Amerika?" *D.W. Funk* 20:589–90.

———. 1928. "Selbstbedienung ist Trumpf!" *Deutsche Welle* 32:572–73.

———. 1930. "Was die verheiratete Frau über die berufstätige denkt und umgekehrt." *Deutsche Welle* 12:229.

Drewitz, Anna. 1930. "Die Hausfrau in ihrer Berufsorganisation." *Deutsche Welle* 26:511.

———. 1931. "Wenn meine Tochter heiratet." *Deutsche Welle* 14:122.

Dreyer, Ernst Adolf. 1934. *Deutsche Kultur im neuen Reich: Wesen, Aufgabe und Ziel der Reichskulturkammer.* Berlin: Schlielfen-Verlag.

Dürre, Konrad. 1927. "Der Kinderfunk der deutschen Welle." *Deutsche Welle* 23:685–86.

Eckert, Gerhard. 1940. *Der Rundfunk als Führungsmittel.* Heidelberg: Vowinkel.

"Einlaß während der Wochenschau: Der Präsident der RFK gibt mit Zustimmung des RMVP bekannt." 1943. *Kultur Informationen* 6, no. 272 (1 April): 19.

E. M. 1930. "Rundfunkpläne der Dorotheenschule zu Cöpenick." *Frauen und Jugendfunk: Beilage zum Funk* 3:9–10.

Engelmann, Susanne. 1927. "Probleme der deutschen Mädchenerziehung." *D.W. Funk* 15:134–35.

*Entwicklung des deutschen Rundfunks in Zahlen 1923–30.* 1931. Berlin: RRG.

E. S. 1930. "Die Frau und ihr Rundfunkkoffer." *Frauen und Jugendfunk: Beilage zum Funk* 18:71.

F. M. 1934–35. "Die festgelegten Sendungen." *Rufer und Hörer* 4:47.

F. R. 1928. "Pflichten und Freuden der Mutterschaft." *Deutsche Welle* 28:510.

———. 1929. "Ehereformen im Spiegel neuzeitlicher Literatur." *Deutsche Welle* 1:14–15.

———. 1930. "Die Wohnungsfrage als volkswirtschaftliches Problem." *Deutsche Welle* 29:556.

———. 1931. "Erwerbstätigkeit und Mutterschaft." *Deutsche Welle* 20:182.

Flesch, Hans. 1926. "Die kulturellen Aufgaben des Rundfunks." *Tagung des RRG am 26. & 27.Februar 1926 in Stuttgart,* 24–27. Berlin: Reichsdruckerei.

———. 1930. "Der Kampf um die Rundfunkzensur." *Funk* 5:18.

Fliegel, Alice. 1927a. "Frauen Schaffen des XX. Jahrhunderts." *Die Norag* 37:21.

———. 1927b. "Die Frau im Rundfunk." *Die Norag* 57.

———. 1929. "Die Frau im Rundfunk." *Die Norag* 105.

Fournier-Olden, Christine. 1931. "Die Nerven der Mutter." *Deutsche Welle* 45:432.

Frankl-Hutterer, Anna. 1931. "Die Frau und der Rundfunk." *Arbeiterfunk* 38:455.

Franzen-Hellersberg, Lisbeth. 1927. "Die jugendliche Arbeiterin in Büro und Werkstatt." *DW Funk* 24:722–23.

"Die Frau als Persönlichkeit." 1929. *Deutsche Welle* 43:724.

"Die Frau als Verbraucherin." 1931. *Der Deutsche,* 9 May.

"Frau im Funk: Presse-Revue nach Gandersheim." 1929. *Norag. Das 5. Jahr, 78.* Hamburg: Rufu Verlag.

"Frau und Kind in Münchener Rundfunk." 1926. *Der Deutsche Rundfunk* 38:2667.

"Frauenamt der DAF: Rundfunk-Meldungen des Frauenamtes." 1937. *Nachrichtendienst der Reichsfrauenführung* (February): 61.

"Frauen-fragen." 1928. *Der Deutsche Rundfunk* 35:2330.

"Frauenfunk." 1928. *Deutsche Welle* 27:489.

"Frauenschaffen des 20. Jahrhunderts." 1927. *Funk* 45:374.

"Frauenstunden im Westdeutschen Rundfunk." 1930a. *Frauen und Jugendfunk: Beilage zum Funk* 37:146.

"Frauenstunden im Westdeutschen Rundfunk." 1930b. *Frauen und Jugendfunk: Beilage zum Funk* 40:160.

"Frauenstunde in wirtschaftlicher Notzeit." 1932. *Funk* 13:51.

"Frauenwirtschaftskammer." 1934. *Hamburger Tageblatt,* 23 December.

"Frauenwerk und Rundfunk." 1935. *Kreuz-Zeitung,* 22 March.

"Frauen helfen sich untereinander." 1931. *Deutsche Welle* 31:291–92.

Freytag, Hilde. 1935. "Unsere Rundfunkarbeit." In *Mädel im Dritten Reich,* ed. Hilde Munske, 39–42. Berlin: Freiheitsverlag.

Frobenius, Else. 1931. "Väter und Töchter." *Deutsche Welle* 39:368.

"Der Führer spricht zu den deutschen Frauen." 1935–36. *NS Frauen-Warte* 8:238.

*Fünf Jahre Berliner Rundfunk: ein Rückblick, 1923–28.* 1928. Berlin: Funk-Stunde.

Funck, Hertha Maria. 1927. "Fünf Minuten der Hausfrau." *Der Neue Rundfunk* 24:793.

———. 1931. "Die Frau und der Rundfunk." *Arbeiterfunk* 9:1.

Giese, Fritz, *Girlkultur: Vergleiche zwischen Amerikanischem und europäischem Rhythmus und Lebensgefühl.* 1925. Munich: Delphin.

Gins, H. A., and T. Gins. 1930. "Zwiegespräch eines Arztes mit einer besorgten Mutter wegen der Impfung ihres Kindes." *Deutsche Welle* 10:188.

Gottschewski, Lydia. 1934. *Männerbund und Frauenfrage.* Munich: Lehmann.

Grünbaum, M. 1927. "Frauenfragen und Frauensorgen im Rundfunk." *Der Neue Rundfunk* 14:374.

"Gruß an die Kinderreichen: Eine Neuerung der Hitlerjugend im Rundfunk." 1936. *Der Deutsche Rundfunk* 44.

H. R. 1931. "Die Frau als Ansager." *Die Werag: Das Ansageblatt des West-deutschen Rundfunks* 3:59.

Hadamovsky, Eugen. 1934a. *Der Rundfunk im Dienste der Volksführung.* Leipzig: n.p.

———. 1934b. *Dein Rundfunk: Das Rundfunkbuch für alle Volksgenossen.* Munich: Zentralverlag der NSDAP, F. Eher.

Hagemann, Walter. 1938. *Handbuch des deutschen Rundfunks.* Heidelberg and Berlin: n.p.

Hanna, Gertrud. 1931. "Fünf Jahre Frauenfunk." *Gewerkschaftliche Frauen-zeitung* 1:6–7.

Heinrich Hansen. 1936. *Die Festtage des Dritten Reiches,* ed. NS Lehrerbund. Bayreuth: Gauverlag Bayerische Ostmark.

Hensel, Werner, and Kessler, Erich. 1935. *1000 Hörer Antworten.* Berlin: n.p.

Hersel, Carola. 1928. "Hilf zu Haus und bleibe schön." *Deutsche Welle* 38:700–701.

———. 1930. "Das junge Mädchen und der Rundfunk." *Frauen und Jugendfunk: Beilage zum Funk* 26:101.

———. 1933. "Wie der Rundfunk Hilfe von Jugend zu Jugend mobilisierte." *Freie Wohlfahrtspflege* 2:86.

Herzog, Paul. 1930. "Die Frau im Rundfunk." *Die Sendung* 8:125–27.

Hessig, Edith. 1938. "Die 'politische Haltung' der Frau." *Frauenstunde: Zeitungs-dienst des Reichsnährstandes* 19.

Heuß-Knapp, Elly. 1931. "Bestand und Erschütterung der Familie." *Deutsche Welle* 16:141.

Hitler, Adolf. 1938. *My Struggle.* London: Hurst and Blackett.

Homeyer, A. 1940. *Die Neuordnung des höheren Schulwesens im Dritten Reich.* Berlin: H. Klokow.

Honekamp, Anne. 1930. "Hausfrau und Rundfunk." *Frauen und Jugendfunk: Beilage zum Funk* 25:97.

J. B. 1927. "Frauenfunk." *Der Neue Rundfunk* 27:811.

*Jahresbericht vom Frankfurter Hausfrauenverein e.V.* 1924. Frankfurt a.M.: n.p.

Janssen, Magda. 1935. "Aus dem Tagwerk 'Stunde der Frau' im Reichssender München." *Völkischer Beobachter,* 7 February.

Jason, Alexander. 1935–36. *Handbuch des Films.* Berlin: Hoppenstedt.

Jennings, Hilda and Winifred Gill. 1939. *Broadcasting in Everyday Life: A Survey of the Social Effects of the Coming of Broadcasting.* London: BBC.

John, Alfred. 1930. "Frauen- und Jugendstunden im Breslauer Sender." *Frauen und Jugendfunk: Beilage zum Funk* 12:67.

Jokl, Margarete. 1930. "Umgangsformen junger Menschen untereinander." *Deutsche Welle* 29:564.

Jolockwicz, E. 1932. *Der Rundfunk: Eine psychologische Untersuchung.* Berlin: Max Hesses.

"Die Jugendlichen müssen selbst vor das Mikrophon. 1930. *Neue Berliner Zeitung,* 7 March.

"Jungmädchen-Stunde." 1929. *Deutsche Welle* 52:891.

Kappstein,Theodor. 1930. "Das Jungmädchen als Objekt und Subjekt." *Frauen und Jugendfunk: Beilage zum Funk* 30:117.

Kardorff, Katharina. 1929. "Die Frau und der politische Rundfunk: für Unparteilichkeit und Aufklärung." *Der Deutsche Rundfunk* 46, 15 November.

Kirkpatrick, Clifford. 1939. *Women in Nazi Germany.* London: Jarrolds.

Kleinschmitt, Edmund. 1931. "Nationale Disziplin beim Einkauf: Ein Wort an unsere Frauen." *Deutsche Handels Wacht,* 24 December, 361–62.

Knupffer, Paula. 1935. "Frauenfunk." *Der Deutsche Rundfunk* 20:1.

Köhler-Irrgang, Ruth. 1940. *Die Sendung der Frau in der deutschen Geschichte.* Leipzig: Hase and Kochler.

Kolb, Richard, and Heinrich Stiekmeier. eds. 1933. *Rundfunk und Film im Dienste Nationaler Kultur.* Düsseldorf: Friedrich Floeder.

Kris, E., and H. Speier. 1944. *German Radio Propaganda: Report on Home Broadcasts during the War.* London: Oxford University Press.

Krüger, E. 1928. "Gesundheitsschutz der gewerbstätigen Frau." *Deutsche Welle* 20:369.

Kuhlmann, Hertha. 1942. "Die Frau und der Rundfunk unter besonderer Berücksichtigung des Frauenfunks." Ph.D. diss., Friedrich Wilhelm University, Berlin.

"Der Kurszettel der Hausfrau; Ein interessanter Versuch der Berliner 'Funk-Stunde.'" 1924. *Funk* 5:83.

L.Bd. 1930. "Schaffende Frauen im Rundfunk." *Frauen und Jugendfunk: Beilage zum Funk* 8:30.

Landsberg, Erich. 1929. "Die Frau von heute und gestern." *Deutsche Welle* 9:174.

Mann, Hans. 1931. "Schulfunk in Zahlen." *Der Schulfunk,* 509.

Matz, Elsa. 1931. "Der Staat und die Kinderreichen." *Deutsche Welle* 43:412.

Mendzee, Margret. 1930a. "Die deutsche Ansagerin." *Frauen und Jugendfunk: Beilage zum Funk* 12:46.

———. 1930b. "Deutsche Ansagerinnen." *Frauen und Jugendfunk: Beilage zum Funk* 23:72.

———. 1930c. "Der weibliche Ansager." *Frauen und Jugendfunk: Beilage zum Funk* 8:31.

———. 1930d. "Zeitung, Rundfunk, Kind." *Frauen und Jugendfunk: Beilage zum Funk* 4:14.

Menzerath, Magda. 1944. *Kampffeld Heimat: Deutsche Frauenleistung im Kriege.* Allemannen: Albert Jauss.

Menzel, Werner. 1930. "Laßt Jugend und Frauen sprechen." *Frauen und Jugendfunk: Beilage zum Funk* 11:441.

Meyer, Erna. 1926. *Der Neue Haushalt: Ein Wegweiser zur Wissenschaftlichen Hausführung.* Stuttgart: Frank'sche Verlagshandlung.

Meyer, Maria. 1933. "Die Frau muß mitwirken: Aufbau und Aufgaben der FWK." *Hamburger Tageblatt,* 7 August.

"Mitverantwortung für Deutschlands Nahrungsfreiheit." 1936. *Kurzberichte für die Frau,* 2 April.

Möbus, Else. 1931. "Die Frau des Arbeitslosen." *Deutsche Welle* 27:253.

"Mutter und Kind: Eine neue Gesprächsfolge des Westdeutschen Rundfunks." 1930. *Frauen und Jugendfunk: Beilage zum Funk* 20:78.

Munske, Hilde. 1935. "Das Mädel in der Presse-und Propagandaarbeit." In *Mädel im Dritten Reich,* ed. Hilde Munske, 43–45. Berlin: Freiheitsverlag.

"Nachrichtendienst: Rundfunkstunden für die Frau." 1933. *Amtliche Frauenkorrespondenz,* 1 December, 578.

"Neue Sendereihe des Frauenfunks im Reichssender Leipzig." [1924?] *RRG Presse-Mitteilungen,* 489. Berlin: Reichsrundfunkgesellschaft:8.

"Neuregelung des Frauenfunks in Leipzig." 1935. *Der Deutsche Rundfunk* 40:10.

Peakok, Mary. 1926. "Rundfunk und Frauen." *Der Deutsche Rundfunk* 46:3248.

Peck, Lisa. 1933–34a. "Die Frau und der Rundfunk!" *Rufer und Hörer* 3:243–51.

———. 1933–34b. "Frauenfunk in Deutschland und im Ausland." *Rufer und Hörer* 3:359–66.

———. 1934. "Was wünschen sich die Frauen vom Rundfunk?" *Völkischer Beobachter,* 6 September.

———. 1934–35a. "Die Frau und der Rundfunk—in Zahlen!" *Rufer und Hörer* 4:65–74.

———. 1934–35b. "Notwendigkeit der Zusammenarbeit im Frauenfunk." *Rufer und Hörer* 4:427— -30.

Pelz-Langenscheidt, Else. "Die Ausstellung 'Heim und Technik' in München." *Deutsche Welle* 24 (1928): 434–35.

Potthoff, Heinz. 1928. *Hauswirtschaft und Volkswirtschaft: Zugleich ein Wegweiser für die Ausstellung, "Heim und Technik" Sommer 1928 in München.* Düsseldorf: Verlag der Wermeister- Buchhandlung.

"Das Problem der Ansagerin: Stimmcharakter und Klangfarbe." 1933. *Funk* 32:125.

Prüfer, [?]. 1930. "Volkswirtschaftliche Viertelstunde für die Hausfrau." *Deutsche Welle* 19:379.

Rabe, Sofia. 1932. *Die Frau im National-Sozialistischen Staat.* Munich: Broschurenreihe der Reichspropagandaleitung der NSDAP.

Radel, Frieda. 1926. "Die Schule der Frau." In *Norag Jahrbuch 1926,* 49–51. Hamburg: Rufu Verlag.

Radel, Frieda. 1928. "Die Schule der Frau: Hans Bredow Schule im Nordischen Rundfunk." In *Die Norag 3. Jahrbuch 1927: Frauenschaffen der Gegenwart.* Hamburg: Rufu Verlag.

Reichenau, Irmgard. 1933. *Deutsche Frauen an Adolf Hitler.* Leipzig: Klein.

"Reichseinheitliche Aufklärungs- und Werbeaktion für das Deutsche Frauenwerk." 1937. *Nachrichtendienst der Reichsfrauenführung* (May): 132–34.

Reiners, Käte. 1942–43. "Wir hören in Kürze eine Sondermeldung." *NS-Frauenwarte* 1:3.

Rengier, P. 1929. "Hausfrauenaufgaben in der Gegenwart und hauswirtschaftliche Berufsbildung." *Deutsche Welle* 11:211.

Rodt, Ellen. 1933. "Rundfunk-Hörkultur." *Amtliche Frauenkorrespondenz,* 13 January, 924– 25.

Rosenberg, Alfred. 1930. *Der Mythos des 20. Jahrhunderts: Eine Wertung der seelisch-geistigen Gestaltenkämpfe unserer Zeit.* Munich: Hoheneichen.

"Der Rundfunk im Dienste der Hausfrau." 1925. *Königsberger Rundfunk* 24.

"Rundfunk von Einzelwerbung befreit." 1935. *Der Angriff,* 20 March.

Sauter-Kindler, Eugenie. 1928. "Zwei Jahre Frauenstunde." *Südfunk* 10:6.

Scherrel, Felix. 1926. "Frauensorgen im Rundfunk." *Der Neue Rundfunk* 38:891.

Scherz, Ursula. 1932. "Frauenstunde in wirtschaftlicher Notzeit." *Funk* 13:51.

Scheumann, F.K. Leiter der Eheberatungsstelle Berlin, Prenzlauer Berg. 1927. "Sinn und Wesen der Eheberatung." *D.W. Funk* 22:654.

Schirach, Baldur von. 1934. *Die Hitler-Jugend: Idee und Gestalt.* Leipzig: n.p.

Schmalfuß, Hannes. 1938. "Rundfunk und Bevölkerungspolitik." *Der Rundfunk: Blätter für nationalsozialistische Kulturgestaltung* 1:9.

Scholtz-Klink, Gertrud. 1934. "Die Frau als Mitarbeiterin an der Nationalwirtschaft." *Deutsche Wochenschau* 38.

———. 1936. *Verpflichtung und Aufgabe der Frau im nationalsozialistischen Staat.* Berlin: Junker und Dünnhaupt.

———. 1944. "Die Reichsfrauenführerin zum Muttertag 'Mütter, ihr tragt das Vaterland,' Ansprache im Deutschen Rundfunk am 20.5.44." *Völkischer Beobachter,* 22 May.

Schott, Andreas. 1927. "Die Hans-Bredow-Schule für Volkswissenschaft." In *Norag Jahrbuch 1926.* Hamburg: Rufu Verlag: n.p.

Schreiber, Adele. 1927a. "Bahnbrechende Frauen." *Der Deutsche Rundfunk* 6, February.

———. 1927b. "Bahnbrechende Frauen: 2. Vortragsreihe der Berliner Funk-Stunde." *Der Deutsche Rundfunk* 50:3435.

———. 1928. "Dein Rundfunk—sei Deine Welt!" *Die Sendung* 12:131.

Schubotz, H. 1928. "Zwei Jahre Deutsche Welle." *D.W. Funk* 1:2.

Schwabach, Erik Ernst. 1928. *Revolutionierung der Frau.* Leipzig: Der neue Geistverlag.

Schwarz, Hedwig. 1929. "Die Hausfrau und der Rundfunk." *Die Sendung* 24:437.

Semmelroth, Ellen, and Erika Kirmsse. 1938. *Frauen schaffen für Deutschland.* Munich: Lehmann.

Simons, Gerda. 1929. "Eheliche Auseinandersetzung." *Deutsche Welle* 14:220–21.

Sprengel, [?]. 1929. "Die gegenwärtige Lage des bäuerlichen Haushalts." *Deutsche Welle* 31:496.

Staepfele, Kurt. 1929. "Wer will, kann wissen!" *Norag: Das fünfte Jahr.* Hamburg: Rufu Verlag.

Statistisches Reichsamt, ed. 1925. *Zahlen zur Geldentwertung in Deutschland 1914 bis 1923.* Berlin: Statistisches Reichsamt.

Stege, Fritz. 1943. "Das Ohr der Welt." *Leipziger Neueste Nachrichten,* 28 October.

"Der Stellvertreter des Führers zur Werbeaktion des Deutschen Frauenwerkes: Rundschreiben 58/37 vom 11.5.37." 1937. *Nachrichtendienst der Reichsfrauenführung* (June): 153.

Sternberg, Edith. 1931. "Die Hausfrau als Verwalterin des Volksvermögens." *Deutsche Welle:* 387–89.

Steup, Else. 1931. "Frauen helfen sich untereinander." *Deutsche Welle* 36:842.

Suhr, Werner. 1933. "Rundfunk und weibliche Jugend." *Rufer und Hörer* 11:502.

———. 1934. "Frauen am Mikrofon." *Die Sendung* 16:299–300.

Theurer, Elsbeth. 1930. "Winke zur Arbeitserleichterung der Landfrau." *Deutsche Welle* 34:648.

Thomas, Katherine. 1943. *Women in Nazi Germany.* London: Gollancz.

Tschauner, Ellie. 1932. "Frauen im Rundfunk." *Der Deutsche Rundfunk* 3:4–5.

"Unsere Meinung: Die am Lautsprecher." 1933. *Der Deutsche Rundfunk (Sonderheft: Die Frau).* 12:2.

"Unterhaltungsrundfunk in Deutschland: Entwicklung der Gesamt-Teilnehmerzahl des Reiches." 1926. *Mitteilungen des Reichspostministeriums,* n.p.

Varges, Kurt. 1941. "Sprachrohr des Führers: Der deutsche Rundfunk in großen Zeiten." *Deutscher Kulturdienst* 108: n.p.

"Verbrauchslenkung und Vorratswirtschaft Notwendig: Darré an die Frauen." 1936. *Westfälische Landeszeitung,* 5 February.

Voigt, Bruno. 1929. "5 Jahre ARK." *Arbeiterfunk* 3:227.

Vormeyer, E. 1927. "Der Rundfunk und die Psyche des Jugendlichen." *Der Neue Rundfunk* 20:565.

Vorwerck, Else. 1941. "Die Hausfrau als Wirtschaftsfaktor." *Deutsche Allgemeine Zeitung,* 1 June.

W. J. 1930. "Münchener Stunde des Jungen Mädchens." *Frauen und Jugendfunk: Beilage zum Funk* 44:174.

Wagner, Emmy. 1936. "Auf die Hausfrau kommt es an: Die wirtschaftspolitische Bedeutung der Konsumgewohnheiten der Frauen." *Völkischer Beobachter,* 16 February.

Weber, Max. 1930. *The Protestant Ethic and the Spirit of Capitalism.* London: Unwin Hyman.

"Wechsel in der Leitung der Münchener Jugendstunde." 1930. *Frauen und Jugendfunk: Beilage zum Funk* 51:202.

Weigel, Hilde. 1926. "Das ländlich hauswirtschaftliche Lehrlingswesen als Grundlage zu den wichtigsten landwirtschaftlichen Berufen." *D.W.Funk* 5:225–27.

Weiland, R. 1933. *Die Kinder der Arbeitslosen.* Berlin: R. Müller.

Weinberg, Margarete. 1931. "Überspannung der Hausfrauentugend." *Deutsche Welle* 29:272.

Weininger, Otto. 1903. *Geschlecht und Charakter.* Vienna and Leipeig: W. Braumuller.

Weiß, Ilse. 1930. "Die Ausgestaltung der Frauenstunde im Rundfunk." *Die Sendung* 52:838.

Wendelmuth, Gerda. 1930. "Wie paßt die Landfrau im Sommer ihren Küchenzettel den Forderungen der neuzeitlichen Ernährungsweise an?" *Deutsche Welle* 28:545.

"Wert der Familie." 1930. *Deutsche Welle* 19:366.

"Wie kommt das Programm der Deutschen Welle zustande?" 1927. *D.W. Funk* 7:174.

"Wie werde ich Rundfunksprecher?" 1930. *Die Schlesische Volkszeitung,* 4 February.

"Wirtschaftspolitik in der Küche." 1931. *Die Kölnische Zeitung,* 25 February.

Würzburger, Karl. 1928. "Die berufstätige Frau als Hausfrau." *Deutsche Welle* 26:474–75.

Zobeltilz, Feodor von. 1928. "Die Gesamtheit der Vorträge." In *Fünf Jahre Berliner Rundfunk: ein Rückblick, 1923–28.* Berlin: Funk-Stunde, 209–10.

"Zu dem Hilfswerk von Carola Hersel." 1931. *Deutsche Welle* 51:489.

Zuar, Ralph. 1926. "Die Stellung der Frau zum Rundfunk." *Die Sendung* 11:3.

## Books and Articles Published after 1945

Aberle, Gerhard. 1982. *Rundfunk und Rundfunkhören im Dritten Reich.* Munich: Bayerischer Rundfunk.

Adam, B. 1990. *Time and Social Theory.* Cambridge: Polity.

Albrecht, Gerd. 1969. *Nazi Filmpolitik: Eine soziologische Untersuchung über die Spielfilme des Dritten Reiches.* Stuttgart: Enke.

Alcoff, Linda. 1988. "Cultural Feminism versus Post-Structuralism: The Identity Crisis in Feminist Theory." *Signs: Journal of Women in Culture and Society* 13(3): 406–36.

Alexander, Sally. 1994. "Women, Class and Sexual Differences in the 1830s and 1840s: Some Reflections on the Writing of a Feminist History." In *Culture/Power/History,* ed. Nicholas B. Dirks, Geoff Eley, and Sherry B. Ortner, 269–96. New Jersey: Princeton.

Althusser, Louis. 1984. *Essays on Ideology.* London: Verso.

Anderson, Benedict. 1983. *Imagined Communities: Reflections on the Origin and Spread of Nationalism.* London: Verso.

Ang, Ien. 1991. *Desperately Seeking the Audience.* London: Routledge.

Arendt, Hannah. 1958. *The Human Condition.* Chicago: University of Chicago Press.

———. 1963. *On Revolution.* New York: Penguin Books.

———. 1968. *The Origins of Totalitarianism.* New York: Harcourt Brace Jovanovich.

———. 1973. *The Origins of Totalitarianism.* Rev. ed. New York: Harcourt Brace Jovanovich.

Arendt, Hans-Jürgen, and Siegfried Scholze. 1983. *Zur Rolle der Frau in der Geschichte des Deutschen Volkes, 1830 bis 1945: Eine Chronik.* Leipzig: Verlag für die Frau.

Arnheim, Rudolf. 1979a. *Kritiken und Aufsätze zum Film.* Frankfurt a.M.: Fischer.

———. 1979b. *Rundfunk als Hörkunst.* Munich: Carl Hanser.

Arnold, Erik, and Lesley Burr. 1985. "Housework and the Appliance of Science." In *Smothered by Invention: Technology in Women's Lives,* ed. Wendy Faulkner and Erik Arnold, 144–62. London: Pluto.

August, Eugene. 1985. *Men's Studies: A Selected and Annotated Interdisciplinary Bibliography.* Littleton, Colo.: Libraries Unlimited.

Austin, J. L. 1975. *How to Do Things with Words.* Cambridge, Mass.: Harvard University Press.

Baird, J. W. 1974. *The Mythical World of Nazi War Propaganda, 1939–1945.* Minneapolis: University of Minnesota Press.

Bajohr, Stefan. 1979. *Die Hälfte der Fabrik: Geschichte der Frauenarbeit in Deutschland, 1914–1945.* Marburg: Verlag Arbeiterbewegung und Gesellschaftswissenschaft.

Balser, Christof. 1986. "Das Frauenbild im deutschen Spielfilm 1933–1945." Master's thesis, University of Cologne.

Barrett, Michèle, et al., eds. 1979. *Ideology and Cultural Production.* London: Croom Helm.

Barthes, Roland. 1973. *Mythologies.* Trans. Annette Lavers. London: Paladin.

———. 1975. *S/Z.* London: Jonathan Cape.

———. 1980. *Writing Degree Zero.* New York: Hill and Wang.

Bastowski, Friedrun, Christa Linder, and Ulrike Prokop, eds. 1981. *Frauenalltag und Frauenbewegung im 20. Jahrhundert.* 5 vols. Frankfurt a.M.: Historisches Museum.

Bauer, Thomas. 1993. *Deutsche Programmpresse 1923 bis 1941. Entstehung, Entwicklung und Kontinuität der Rundfunkzeitschriften.* Munich: Rundfunkstudien 6.

Bauman, Zygmunt. 1989. *Modernity and the Holocaust.* Ithaca: Cornell University Press.

Bausch, Hans. 1956. *Der Rundfunk im politischen Kräftespiel der Weimarer Republik, 1923–1933.* Tübingen: Mohr.

———, ed. 1980. *Rundfunk in Deutschland.* 5 vols. Frankfurt a.M.: dtv.

Beauvoir, Simone de. 1972. *The Second Sex.* Trans. H. M. Parshley. Harmondsworth: Penguin.

Behnken, Klaus, and Frank Wagner, eds. 1989. *Inszenierung der Macht: Aesthetische Fascination im Faschismus.* Kreuzberg: Dirk Nishen.

Behrens, Tobias. 1986. *Die Entstehung der Massenmedien in Deutschland. Ein Vergleich von Film, Hörfunk und Fernsehen und ein Ausblick auf die neuen Medien.* Frankfurt a.M.: Peter Lang.

Belach, Helga. 1979. *Wir tanzen um die Welt: Deutsche Revuefilme, 1933–1945.* Munich: Hanser.

Benhabib, Seyla. 1992. "Models of Public Space: Hannah Arendt, the Liberal Tradition, and Jürgen Habermas." In *Habermas and the Public Sphere,* ed. Craig Calhoun, 73–98. Cambridge, Mass.: MIT Press.

Benhabib, Seyla, and Drucilla Cornell, eds. 1987. *Feminism as Critique: On the Politics of Gender.* Minneapolis: University of Minnesota Press.

Benjamin, Louise M. 1992. "Defining the Public Interest and Protecting the Public Welfare in the 1920s: Parallels between Radio and Movie Regulation." *Historical Journal of Film, Radio and Television* 12(1): 87–101.

Benjamin, Walter. 1982. *Gesammelte Schriften.* Ed. R. Tiedemann. Frankfurt a.M.: Suhrkamp.

———. 1984. *Allegorien kultureller Erfahrung: Ausgewählte Schriften, 1920–1940.* Leipzig: Reclam.

———. 1992. "The Work of Art in the Age of Mechanical Reproduction." In Mast, Cohen, and Braudy, *Film Theory,* 665–82.

Bennett, Judith. 1989. "Feminism and History." *Gender and History* 1(3): 251–72.

Bennett, Tony, ed. 1990. *Popular Fiction: Technology, Ideology, Production, Reading.* London: Routledge.

Bereano, Philip, Christine Bose, and Erik Arnold. 1985. "Kitchen Technology and the Liberation of Women from Housework." In *Smothered by Invention: Technology in Women's Lives,* ed. Wendy Faulkner and Erik Arnold, 162–81. London: Pluto.

Berelson, Bernard. 1952. *Content Analysis in Communication Research.* New York: Free Press.

Berman, Marshall. 1988. *All That Is Solid Melts into Air: The Experience of Modernity.* New York: Penguin.

Bessel, Richard, and Edgar J. Feuchtwanger, eds. 1981. *Social Change and Political Development in Weimar Germany.* London: Croom Helm.

Bessel, Richard. 1993. *Germany after the First World War.* Oxford: Clarendon Press.

———, ed. 1987. *Life in the Third Reich.* Oxford: Oxford University Press.

Bessler, Hansjörg. 1980. *Hörer und Zuschauerforschung,* ed. Hans Bausch. *Rundfunk in Deutschland,* vol. 5. Munich: dtv.

Boak, Helen. 1981. "Women in Weimar Germany: The 'Frauenfrage' and the Female Vote." In *Social Change and Political Development in Weimar Germany,* ed. Richard Bessel and Edgar J. Feuchtwanger, 155–73. London: Croom Helm.

Boberach, Hans. 1984. *Meldungen aus dem Reich, 1938–45.* Herrsching: Pawlak.

Bock, Gisela. 1984. "Racism and Sexism in Nazi Germany: Motherhood, Compulsory Sterilization, and the State." In *When Biology Became Destiny: Women in Weimar and Nazi Germany,* ed. Renate Bridenthal et al., 271–96. New York: Monthly Review Press.

Bock, Gisela. 1989. Women's History and Gender History: Aspects of an International Debate." *Gender and History* 1(1): 7–30.

Boelcke, Willi, ed. 1966. *Kriegspropaganda 1939–1941: Geheime Ministerkonferenzen im Reichspropagandaministerium.* Stuttgart: Deutsche Verlags-Anstalt.

Bose, Christine, Philip Bereano, and M. Malloy. 1984. "Household Technology and the Social Construction of Housework." *Techology and Culture* 25:53–82.

Bowlby, Rachel. 1987. "Modes of Modern Shopping: Mallarmé at the *Bon Marché.*" In *The Ideology of Conduct: Essays in Literature and the History of Sexuality,* ed. Nancy Armstrong and Leonard Tennenhouse, 185–205. London: Methuen.

Bracher, Karl Dietrich, Manfred Funke, and Hans-Adolf Jacobsen, eds. 1987. *Die Weimarer Republik, 1918–1933: Politik, Wirtschaft, Gesellschaft.* Bonn: Droste.

Bramsted, E. K. 1965. *Goebbels and National Socialist Propaganda.* East Lansing: Michigan State University Press.

Braun, Christina von. 1992. "'Der Jude' und 'Das Weib': Zwei Stereotypen des 'Anderen' in der Moderne." *Metis* 2:6–28.

Brecht, Bertolt. 1967. "Radiotheorie 1927–1932." In "Schriften zur Literatur und Kunst," 1:119–29. *Gesammelte Werke,* 20 vols. Frankfurt a.M.: Peter Suhrkamp.

Bredow, Hans. 1960. *Im Banne der Aetherwellen,* 2 vols. 2d ed. Stuttgart: Mundus.

Brennicke, Ilona, and Joe Hembus. 1983. *Klassiker des deutschen Stummfilms, 1910–1930.* Munich: Goldmann.

Bridenthal, Renate. 1984. "'Professional' Housewives: Stepsisters of the Women's Movement." In *When Biology Became Destiny: Women in Weimar and Nazi Germany,* ed. Renate Bridenthal et al., 153–73. New York: Monthly Review Press.

Bridenthal, Renate, and Claudia Koonz. 1984. "Beyond Kinder, Küche, Kirche: Weimar Women in Politics and Work." In *When Biology Became Destiny: Women in Weimar and Nazi Germany,* ed. Renate Bridenthal et al., 33–65. New York: Monthly Review Press.

———, eds. 1977. *Becoming Visible: Women in European History.* Boston: Houghton Mifflin.

Bridenthal, Renate, Atina Grossmann, and Marion Kaplan, eds. 1984. *When Biology Became Destiny: Women in Weimar and Nazi Germany.* New York: Monthly Review Press.

Briggs, Asa. *The Golden Age of Wireless.* London: Oxford University Press, 1965.

Brockmann, Stephen. 1994. "Weimar Sexual Cynicism." In *Dancing on the Volcano: Essays on the Culture of the Weimar Republic,* ed. Thomas Kniesche and Stephen Brockman, 165–80. Columbia: Camden House.

Brod, Harry, ed. 1987. *The Making of Masculinities: The New Men's Studies.* Boston: Allen and Unwin.

Broszat, Martin. 1981. *The Hitler State: The Foundation and Development of the Internal Structure of the Third Reich.* London: Longman.

Brown, Mary. 1990. "Motley Moments: Soap Opera, Carnival, Gossip and the Power of the Utterance." *Television and Women's Culture: The Politics of the Popular,* 183–200. London: Sage.

Butler, Judith. 1990. *Gender Trouble: Feminism and the Subversion of Identity.* London: Routledge.

Canoran, Margaret. 1992. *Hannah Arendt: A Reinterpretation of Her Political Thought.* Cambridge: Cambridge University Press.

Cardiff, David. 1986. "The Serious and the Popular: Aspects of the Evolution of Style in the Radio Talk, 1928–1939." In *Media, Culture and Society: A Critical Reader,* ed. Richard Collins, 228–46. London: Sage.

Carr, William. 1987. "Nazi Policy against the Jews." In *Life in the Third Reich,* ed. Richard Bessel, 69–82. Oxford: Oxford University Press.

Carroll, Bernice. 1968. *Design for Total War, Arms and Economics in the Third Reich.* The Hague: Mouton.

Charman Tony. 1989. *The German Home Front, 1939–1945.* London: Barrier Jenkins.

Childers, Thomas. 1990. "The Social Language of Politics in Germany: The Sociology of Political Discourse in the Weimar Republic." *American Historical Review* 95:331–58.

Cooke, Philip. 1990. *Back to the Future.* London: Unwin Hyman.

Cowan, Ruth Schwartz. 1989. *More Work for Mother: The Ironies of Household Technology from the Open Hearth to the Microwave.* London: Free Association Books.

Cramer, Judith. 1989. "Radio: A Woman's Place Is on the Air." In *Women in Mass Communication: Challenging Gender Values,* ed. Pamela Creedon, 214–26. London: Sage.

Crisell, Andrew. 1986. *Understanding Radio.* London: Methuen.

Cubitt, Sean. 1985. "The Politics of the Living Room." In *Television Mythologies,* ed. Len Masterman, 1–23. London: Comedia.

Culler, Jonathan. 1989. *On Deconstruction: Theory and Criticism after Structuralism.* London: Routledge.

Cumberbatch, Guy, and Dennis Howitt. 1989. *A Measure of Uncertainty: The Effects of the Mass Media.* London: John Libbey.

Curran, James. 1991. "Mass Media and Democracy: A Reappraisal." In *Mass Media and Society,* ed. James Curran and Michael Gurevitch, 82–117. London: Routledge.

Curran, James. 1993. "Rethinking the Media as a Public Sphere." In *Communication and Citizenship: Journalism and the Public Sphere in the New Media Age,* ed. Peter Dahlgren and Colin Sparks, 28–57. London: Routledge.

Curran, James, and Michael Gurevitch, eds. 1991. *Mass Media and Society.* London: Edward Arnold.

Curran, James, and Jean Seaton. 1981. *Power without Responsibility: The Press and Broadcasting in Britain.* Glasgow: Fontana.

Dahl, Peter. 1978. *Arbeitersender und Volksempfänger: Proletarische Radio-Bewegung und bürgerlicher Rundfunk bis 1945.* Frankfurt a.M.: Syndikat.

———. 1983. *Radio: Sozialgeschichte des Rundfunks für Sender und Empfänger.* Reinbek: Rowohlt.

Dahlgren, Peter. 1995. *Television and the Public Sphere: Citizenship, Democracy and the Media.* London: Sage.

Dahlgren, Peter, and Colin Sparks, eds. 1993. *Communication and Citizenship: Journalism and the Public Sphere in the New Media Age.* London: Routledge.

Dahms, Maria. 1967. "Vom Wirken der Frauenfunk-Redaktion Leipzig." *Beiträge zur Geschichte des Deutschen Rundfunks* 1:68–100.

Davis, Robert E. 1976. *Response to Innovation: A Study of Popular Argument about New Mass Media.* New York: Arno.

Dietz, Mary. 1991. "Hannah Arendt and Feminist Politics." In *Feminist Interpretations and Political Theory,* ed. Mary Lyndon Shanley and Carole Pateman, 232–52. Cambridge: Polity.

———. 1992. "Context Is All: Feminism and Theories of Citizenship." In *Dimensions of Radical Democracy,* ed. Chantal Mouffe, 63–85. London: Verso.

Diller, Ansgar. 1980. *Rundfunkpolitik im Dritten Reich,* ed. Hans Bausch. *Rundfunk in Deutschland,* vol. 2. Munich: dtv.

———. 1985. *Rundfunk und Fernsehen in Deutschland: Texte zur Rundfunkpolitik von der Weimarer Republik bis zur Gegenwart.* Stuttgart: Reclam.

Domansky, Elisabeth. 1990. "Der Erste Weltkrieg." In *Bürgerliche Gesellschaft in Deutschland: Historische Einblicke, Fragen, Perspektiven,* ed. Lutz Niethammer et al., 285–319. Frankfurt a.M.: Fischer.

Domarus, Wolfgang. 1977. *Nationalsozialismus, Krieg und Bevölkerung: Untersuchungen: zur Lage, Volksstimmung und Struktur in Augsburg während des dritten Reiches.* Munich: Miscellanea Bavarica Monacensia.

Donzelot, Jacques. 1979. *The Policing of Families.* New York: Pantheon.

DuBois, E. 1978. *Feminism and Suffrage.* Ithaca, N.Y.: Cornell University Press.

Duchrow, Lucie. 1967. "Erinnerungen an den ersten Frauenfunk im Berliner Rundfunk nach 1945." *Beiträge zur Geschichte des Deutschen Rundfunks* 1:55–67.

———. 1975. "'Denken Sie an die Kinder!': Der erste Frauenfunk nach 1945." In *Erinnerungen sozialistischer Rundfunkpioniere: Ausgewählte Erlebnisberichte zum 30. Rundfunkjubiläum,* ed. Manfred Scholz et al., 63–70. Berlin: Staatliches Komitee für Rundfunk beim Ministerrat der DDR, Eigener Verlag.

During, Simon, ed. 1993. *The Cultural Studies Reader.* London: Routledge.

Eberle, M. 1985. *World War One and the Weimar Artists: Dix, Grosz, Beckmann, Schlemmer.* New Haven: Yale University Press.

Ehrenreich, Barbara, and Deirdre English. 1988. *For Her Own Good: 150 Years of the Experts' Advice to Women.* 2d ed. London: Pluto.

Eisenstein, Zilla. 1981. *The Radical Future of Liberal Feminism.* New York: Longman.

Eley, Geoff. 1992. "Nations, Publics, and Political Cultures: Placing Habermas in the Nineteenth Century." In *Habermas and the Public Sphere,* ed. Craig Calhoun, 289–339. Cambridge, Mass.: Harvard University Press.

Elliott, Philipp. 1986. "Intellectuals, the 'Information Society' and the Disappearance of the Public Sphere." In *Media, Culture and Society: A Critical Reader,* ed. Richard Collins, 104–15. London: Sage.

Ellul, James. 1973. *Propaganda: The Formation of Men's Attitudes.* New York: Vintage Books.

Ellwanger, Karen. 1989. "Frau nach Maß: Der Frauentyp der 40er Jahre im Zeichensystem des Filmkostüms." In *Inszenierung der Macht: Aesthetische Fascination im Faschismus,* ed. Klaus Behnken and Frank Wagner, 119–25. Kreuzberg: Dirk Nishen.

Elshtain, Jean Bethke. 1974. "Moral Woman and Immoral Man: A Consideration of the Public and Private Split and its Political Ramifications." *Politics and Society* 4:453–61.

———. 1981. *Public Man, Private Woman.* Princeton: Princeton University Press.

Engels, Friedrich. 1972. *The Origin of the Family, Private Property and the State.* New York: International Publishers.

Evans, Richard J. 1976. *The Feminist Movement in Germany, 1894–1933.* London: Sage.

Evans, Richard J., and Dick Geary. 1987. *The German Unemployed: Experiences and Consequences of Mass Unemployment from the Weimar Republic to the Third Reich,* 1–22. London: Croom Helm.

Evans, Richard J., and W. R. Lee, eds. 1981. *The German Family. Essays on the Social History of the Family in 19th and 20th Century Germany.* London: Croom Helm.

Faulkner, Wendy, and Erik Arnold, eds. 1985. *Smothered by Invention: Technology in Women's Lives.* London: Pluto.

Feldman, Gerald. 1986. "The Weimar Republic: A Problem of Modernisation?" *Archiv für Sozialgeschichte* 26:1–26.

Fessmann, I. 1973. "Rundfunk und Rundfunkrecht in der Weimarer Republik." *Beiträge zur Geschichte des Rundfunks* 4:129–39.

Fest, Joachim. 1970. *The Face of the Third Reich: Portraits of the Nazi Leadership.* Trans. Micheal Bullock. New York: Ace Books.

———. 1984. *Hitler.* New York: Harcourt Brace Jovanovich.

Filene, Peter. 1987. "The Secrets of Men's History." In *The Making of Masculinities: The New Men's Studies,* ed. Harry Brod, 103–19. Boston: Allen and Unwin.

Fischer, Erwin. 1957. *Dokumente zur Geschichte des deutschen Rundfunks und Fernsehens.* Göttingen: Musterschmidt.

Först, Walter. 1972. "Zur Quellenlage der Rundfunkgeschichte in Deutschland." *Rundfunk und Fernsehen* 3:46–56.

Foucault, Michel. 1972. *The Archaeology of Knowledge.* Trans. A. M. Sheridan Smith. New York: Pantheon.

———. 1980a. *The History of Sexuality,* vol. 1: *An Introduction.* Trans. Robert Hurley. New York: Vintage Books.

———. 1980b. *Power/Knowledge: Selected Interviews and Other Writings.* Brighton: Harvester.

Fraser, Nancy. 1987. "What's Critical about Critical Theory? The Case of Habermas and Gender." In *Feminism as Critique: On the Politics of Gender,* ed.

Seyla Benhabib and Drucilla Cornell, 31–56. Minneapolis: University of Minnesota Press.

———. 1989. *Unruly Practices: Power, Discourse and Gener in Contemporary Social Theory.* Cambridge: Polity.

———. 1990. "Rethinking the Public Sphere: A Contribution to the Critique of Actually Existing Democracy." *Social Text* 8–9:56–80.

———. 1992. "Sex, Lies, and the Public Sphere: Some Reflections on the Confirmation of Clarence Thomas." *Critical Inquiry* 18(3): 132–34.

Frauengruppe Faschismusforschung. eds. 1981. *Mutterkreuz und Arbeitsbuch: zur Geschichte der Frauen in der Weimarer Republik und im Nationalsozialismus.* Frankfurt a.M.: Fischer.

Frevert, Ute. 1986. *Frauen-Geschichte: Zwischen Bürgerlicher Verbesserung und Neuer Weiblichkeit.* Frankfurt a.M.: Suhrkamp.

———. 1988. "Kunstseidener Glanz: Weibliche Angestellte." In *Neue Frauen: Die zwanziger Jahre,* ed. Kristine von Soden and Maruta Schmidt, 25–30. Berlin: Elefanten Press.

Friedlander, Judith, Blanche Wiesen Cook, Alice Kessler-Harris, and Carroll Smith Rosenberg, eds. 1986. *Women in Culture and Politics: A Century of Change.* Bloomington: Indiana University Press.

Frisby, David. 1985. *Fragments of Modernity: Theories of Modernity in the Work of Simmel, Kracauer and Benjamin.* Cambridge: Polity.

Fritzsche, Peter. 1994. "Landscape of Danger, Landscape of Design: Crisis and Modernism in Weimar Germany." In *Dancing on the Volcano: Essays on the Culture of the Weimar Republic,* ed. Thomas Kniesche and Stephen Brockman, 29–46. Columbia: Camden House.

Fuss, Diana. 1989. *Essentially Speaking: Feminism, Nature and Difference.* London: Routledge.

Gamarnikow, Eva, et al., eds. 1983. *The Public and the Private.* London: Heinemann.

Garnham, Nicholas. 1986. "The Media and the Public Sphere." In *Communicating Politics: Mass Communications and the Political Process,* ed. Peter Golding, Graham Murdoch, and Nicholas Garnham, 37–54. Leicester: Leicester University Press.

———. 1993. "The Mass Media, Cultural Identity and the Public Sphere in the Modern World." *Public Culture* 5(2): 251–65.

Gay, Peter. 1978. *Weimar Culture: The Outsider as Insider.* 3d ed. London: Penguin.

Gerhard, Ute. 1978. *Verhältnisse und Verhinderungen. Frauenarbeit, Familie und Rechte der Frauen im 19. Jahrhundert.* Frankfurt a.M.: Suhrkamp.

Gersdorff, Ursula von. 1969. *Frauen im Kriegsdienst.* Stuttgart: Deutsche Verlags-Anstalt.

Gessner, Dieter. 1981. "The Dilemma of German Agriculture during the Weimar Republic." In *Social Change and Political Development in Weimar Germany,* ed. Richard Bessel and Edgar J. Feuchtwanger, 134–54. London: Croom Helm.

Giddens, Anthony. 1990. *The Consequences of Modernity.* Cambridge: Polity.
———. 1991. *Modernity and Self-Identity.* Cambridge: Polity.
Golding, Peter, and Graham Murdock. 1991. "Culture, Communications, and Political Economy." In *Mass Media and Society,* ed. James Curran and Michael Gurevitch, 15–32. London: Routledge.
Gottschalk, Louis. 1950. *Understanding History.* New York: Knopf.
Grossmann, Atina. 1984a. "Abortion and Economic Crisis: The 1931 Campaign against Paragraph 218." In *When Biology Became Destiny: Women in Weimar and Nazi Germany,* ed. Renate Bridenthal et al., 66–86. New York: Monthly Review Press.
———. 1984b. "The New Woman and the Rationalisation of Sexuality in Weimar Germany." In *Desire: The Politics of Sexuality,* ed. Ann Snitow et al., 190–211. London: Virago.
———. 1986. "*Girlkultur* or Thoroughly Rationalized Female: A New Woman in Weimar Germany?" In *Women in Culture and Politics: A Century of Change,* ed. Judith Friedlander et al., 62–80. Bloomington: Indiana University Press.
Groth, Michael. 1980. "Hans Fritzsche—Karriere eines Publizisten." *Rundfunk und Geschichte: Mitteilungen* 1:42–50.
Grunberger, Richard. 1971. *A Social History of the Third Reich.* London: Weidenfeld and Nicholson.
Guttsman, W. L. 1990. *Workers' Culture in Weimar Germany: Between Tradition and Commitment.* Oxford: Berg.
Habermas, Jürgen. 1974a. "Hannah Arendt's Communications Concept of Power." *Social Research* 44(1).
———. 1974b. "The Public Sphere: An Encyclopedia Article." *New German Critique* 1(3): 49–55.
———. 1983. *The Theory of Communicative Action,* vol. 1: *Reason and the Rationalisation of Society.* Cambridge: Polity.
———. 1989. *The Structural Transformation of the Public Sphere: An Enquiry into a Category of Bourgeois Society.* Trans. Thomas Burger. Cambridge: Polity.
———. 1992. "Further Reflections on the Public Sphere." Trans. Thomas Burger. In *Habermas and the Public Sphere,* ed. Craig Calhoun, 422–61. Cambridge, Mass.: Harvard University Press.
Hagemann, Karen. 1990. *Frauenalltag und Männerpolitik: Alltagsleben und gesellschaftliches Handeln von Arbeiterfrauen in der Weimarer Republik.* Bonn: Dietz.
Hagemann, Walter. 1948. *Publizistik im Dritten Reich.* Hamburg: n.p.
Hahn, C. 1981. "Der öffentliche Dienst und die Frauen: Beamtinnen in der Weimarer Republik." In *Mutterkreuz und Arbeitsbuch: zur Geschichte der Frauen in der Weimarer Republik und im Nationalsozialismus,* ed. Frauengruppe Faschismusforschung, 49–78. Frankfurt a.M.: Fischer.
Hake, Sabine. 1987. "Girls and Crisis: The Other Side of Diversion." *New German Critique* 40:147–64.
Hall, Stuart. 1993. "Encoding, Decoding." In *The Cultural Studies Reader,* ed. Simon During, 90–103. London: Routledge.

Hansen, Miriam. 1983. "Early Silent Cinema: Whose Public Sphere?" *New German Critique* 29:147–84.

———. 1991. *Babel and Babylon: Spectatorship in American Silent Film.* Cambridge, Mass.: Harvard University Press.

———. 1993. "Early Cinema, Late Cinema, Permutations of the Public Sphere." *Screen* 34(3): 197–210.

———. 1995. "America, Paris, The Alps: Kracauer, and Benjamin. On Cinema and Modernity." In *Cinema and the Invention of Modern Life,* ed. Leo Charney and Vanessa R. Schwarz. Berkeley: University of California Press.

Hansen, Phillip. 1993. *Hannah Arendt: Politics, History and Citizenship* Cambridge: Polity.

Hardt, Hanno. 1976. "The Rise and Problems of Media Research in Germany." *Journal of Communication* 26(3): 90–95.

Harvey, David. 1992. *The Condition of Postmodernity.* Oxford: Blackwell.

Hausen, Karin. 1981. "Family and Role Division: The Polarisation of Sexual Stereotypes in the 19th Century—An Aspect of the Dissociation of Work and Family Life." In *The German Family. Essays on the Social History of the Family in 19th and 20th Century Germany,* ed. Richard J. Evans and W. R. Lee, 51–83. London: Croom Helm.

———. 1984a. "Mother's Day in the Weimar Republic." In *When Biology Became Destiny: Women in Weimar and Nazi Germany,* ed. Renate Bridenthal et al., 131–52. New York: Monthly Review Press.

———. 1984b. "Mütter, Söhne und der Markt der Symbole und Waren: Der deutsche Muttertag 1923–1933." In *Emotionen und materielle Interessen,* ed. Hans Medick and David Sabean, 473- —523. Göttingen: Vandenhoech and Ruprecht.

———. 1987. "The German Nation's Obligation to the Heroes' Widows of World War I." In *Behind the Lines: Gender and the Two World Wars,* ed. Margaret Randolph Higonnet et al., 126–40. New Haven and London: Yale University Press.

———, ed. 1983. *Frauen suchen ihre Geschichte: historische Studien zum 19. und 20. Jahrhundert.* Munich: Beck.

Heiber, Helmut. 1993. *The Weimar Republic.* Trans. W. E. Yuill. Oxford: Blackwell.

Hermand, Jost. 1994. "*Neue Sachlickeit:* Ideology, Lifestyle, or Artistic Movement." In *Dancing on the Volcano: Essays on the Culture of the Weimar Republic,* ed. Thomas Kniesche and Stephen Brockman, 57–67. Columbia: Camden House.

Herzstein, R. E. 1978. *The War That Hitler Won: The Most Infamous Propaganda Campaign in History.* London: Putnam.

Heydeck, Horst. 1975. "Aufschlussreiche Vergleichserlebnisse: Rundfunkjournalist vor 1933 und nach 1945." In *Erinnerungen sozialistischer Rundfunkpioniere: Ausgewählte Erlebnisberichte zum 30. Rundfunkjubiläum,* ed. Manfred Scholz et al., 133–37. Berlin: Staatliches Komitee für Rundfunk beim Ministerrat der DDR, Eigener Verlag.

Higonnet, Margaret, et al., eds. 1987. *Behind the Lines: Gender and the Two World Wars.* New Haven: Yale University Press.

Hirschfeld, Gerhard, ed. 1986. *The Policies of Genocide: Jews and Soviet Prisoners of War in Nazi Germany.* London: German Historical Institute.

Hobsbawm, Eric, and Terence Ranger. 1983. *The Invention of Tradition.* Cambridge: Cambridge University Press.

Hofer, Walther. 1972. *Der Nationalsozialismus Dokumente, 1933–1945.* Frankfurt a.M.: Fischer.

Holland, Patricia. 1987. "When a Woman Reads the News." In *Boxed In: Women and Television,* ed. Helen Baehr and Gillian Dyer, 133–51. London: Pandora.

Honey, Maureen. 1983. "The Working Class Woman and Recruitment Propaganda during World War Two: Class Differences in the Portrayal of War Work." *Signs: Journal of Women in Culture and Society* 8(4): 672–87.

Honig, B. 1992. "Toward an Agonistic Feminism: Hannah Arendt and the Politics of Identity." In *Feminists Theorise the Political,* ed. Judith Butler and Joan W. Scott, 215–35. London: Routledge.

Hood, Stuart. 1979–80. "Brecht on Radio." *Screen* 20(3–4): 16–28.

Hörburger, Christian. 1975. *Das Hörspiel der Weimarer Republik: Versuch einer kritischen Analyse.* Stuttgart: Akademischer Verlag Hans-Dieter Heinz.

Horkheimer, Max, and Theodor Adorno. 1985. *Dialektik der Aufklärung: Philosophische Fragmente.* 2d ed. Frankfurt a.M.: Fischer.

Hull, David S. 1969. *Film in the Third Reich.* Berkeley: University of California Press.

Huyssen, Andreas. 1986. *After The Great Divide: Modernism, Mass Culture, Postmodernism.* Bloomington: Indiana University Press.

Isaac, Jeffrey. 1992. *Arendt, Camus and Modern Rebellion.* New Haven and London: Yale University Press.

Jensen, Joli. 1990. *Redeeming Modernity: Contradictions in Media Criticism.* London: Sage.

Johnson, Lesley. 1981. "Radio and Everyday Life. The Early Years of Broadcasting in Australia, 1922–1945." *Media Culture and Society* 3:167–78.

———. 1990. *The Unseen Voice: A Cultural Study of Early Australian Radio.* London: Routledge.

Kaes, Anton, Martin Jay, and Edward Dimendberg, eds. 1994. *The Weimar Republic Sourcebook.* Berkeley: University of California Press.

Kaplan, Gisela T., and Clive S. Kessler. 1989. *Hannah Arendt: Thinking, Judging, Freedom.* Sydney: Allen and Unwin.

Karpf, Anne. 1987. "Radio Times—Private Women and Public Men." In *Out of Focus: Writings on Women and the Media,* ed. Kate Davies et al., 168–77. London: The Women's Press.

Keane, John. 1984. *Public Life and Late Capitalism.* Cambridge: Polity.

———. 1991. *The Media and Democracy.* Cambridge: Polity.

Kelly, Joan. 1984. *Women, History and Theory: The Essays of Joan Kelly.* Chicago and London: University of Chicago Press.

Kershaw, Ian. 1983. "How Effective Was Nazi Propaganda?" In *Nazi Propaganda:*

*The Power and the Limitations,* ed. David Welch, 180–205. London: Croom Helm.

———. 1987. *The "Hitler Myth": Image and Reality in the Third Reich.* Oxford: Clarendon.

———. 1989. *The Nazi Dictatorship: Problems and Perspectives of Interpretation.* London: Arnold.

———, ed. 1990. *Weimar. Why did German Democracy Fail?* London: Weidenfeld and Nicholson.

Kessler, Hannelore. 1981. *Die Deutsche Frau: NS Frauenpropaganda im Völkischen Beobachter.* Köln: Pahl-Rugenstein.

King, Josephine, and Mary Stott, eds. 1977. *Is This Your Life? Images of Women in the Media.* London: Virago.

Klaus, Martin. 1983. *Mädchen im Dritten Reich: Der Bund Deutscher Mädel.* Cologne: Pahl- Rugenstein.

Klein, Burton. 1959. *Germany's Economic Preparations for War.* Cambridge, Mass.: Harvard University Press.

Klingler, Walter. 1980. "Die Rolle des Unterhaltungsrundfunks im Kriegswinter, 1941–42: Zur Vorgeschichte der Umorganisation in der Rundfunkführung im Februar 1942." *Rundfunk und Geschichte: Mitteilungen* 1:50–62.

Klinksiek, Dorothea. 1982. *Die Frau im NS Staat.* Stuttgart: Deutsche Verlags Anstalt.

Kniesche, Thomas W., and Stephen Brockmann, eds. 1994. *Dancing on the Volcano: Essays on the Culture of the Weimar Republic.* Columbia: Camden House.

Koch, Christine. 1988. "Schreibmaschine, Bügeleisen und Muttertagssträuße; Der bescheidene Frauenalltag in den zwanziger Jahren." In *Neue Frauen: Die zwanziger Jahre,* ed. Kristine von Soden and Maruta Schmidt, 89–102. Berlin: Elefanten Press.

Kocka, Jürgen. 1984. *Facing Total War: German Society, 1914–1918* Cambridge, Mass: Harvard University Press.

Kolb, Eberhard. 1984. *Die Weimarer Republik.* Munich: Oldenbourg.

Koonz, Claudia. 1984. "The Competition for Women's *Lebensraum.*" In *When Biology Became Destiny: Women in Weimar and Nazi Germany,* ed. Renate Bridenthal et al., 199–236. New York: Monthly Review Press.

———. 1986. "Some Political Implications of Separatism: German Women between Democracy and Nazism, 1928–1934." In *Women in Culture and Politics: A Century of Change,* ed. Judith Friedlander et al., 269–85. Bloomington: Indiana University Press.

———. 1988. *Mothers in the Fatherland: Women, the Family and Nazi Politics.* London: Methuen.

Kracauer, Siegfried. 1975. "The Mass Ornament. 1927." *New German Critique* 5:67–76.

———. 1977. *Das Ornament der Masse.* Frankfurt a.M.: Fischer.

Kramarae, Cheris, ed. 1988. *Technology and Women's Voices: Keeping in Touch.* London: Routledge and Kegan Paul.

Kramer, Helgard. 1987. "Frankfurt's Working Women: Scapegoats or Winners of the Great Depression?" In *The German Unemployed,* ed. Richard J. Evans and Dick Geary, 108–41. London: Croom Helm.

Kristeva, Julia. 1984. *Revolution in Poetic Language.* New York: Columbia University Press.

Kuhn, Annette. 1988. *Cinema, Censorship and Sexuality, 1909–1925.* London: Routledge.

———. 1990. "Der Antifeminismus als verborgene Theoriebasis des deutschen Faschismus." In *Frauen und Faschismus in Europa: Der faschistische Körper,* ed. Leonore Siegele- Wenschkewitz and Gerda Stuchlik, 38–50. Pfaffenweiler: Centaurus.

Kuhn, Annette, and Valentina Rothe. 1982. *Frauen im Deutschen Faschismus: Eine Quellensammlung mit Fachwissenschaftlichen und Fachdidaktischen Kommentaren.* Düsseldorf: Schwann.

Kutsch, Arnulf. 1985. *Rundfunkwissenschaft im Dritten Reich.* Munich: Rundfunkstudien 2.

Labanyi, Peter. 1989. "Visualisation and Aestheticization in the Third Reich." In *The Burden of German History, 1919–1945,* ed. Michael Laffan, 151–77. London: Methuen.

Landes, Joan B. 1987. "Women and the Public Sphere: A Modern Perspective." *Social Analysis* 15:20–31.

———. 1988. *Women and the Public Sphere in the Age of the French Revolution.* Ithaca: Cornell University Press.

Lihotzky, Grete. 1994. "Rationalization in the Household." In *The Weimar Republic Sourcebook,* ed. Anton Kaes, Martin Jay, and Edward Dimendberg, 462–65. Berkeley: University of California Press.

Lang, Rudolf, ed. 1977. *Rundfunkgeschichte: Ein Literaturverzeichnis.* Cologne: Westdeutscher Rundfunk.

Langer, Hermann. 1978. "Die imperialistische Verführung der Jugend durch den faschistischen Rundfunk in den Jahren 1939–1941." *Beiträge zur Geschichte des Rundfunks* 3:49–66.

Lash, Scott, and John Urry. 1994. *Economies of Signs and Space.* London: Sage.

Lauretis, Teresa de. 1987. *Technologies of Gender: Essays on Theory, Film, and Fiction.* London: Macmillan.

———. 1990. "Uppping the anti [*sic*] in feminist theory." In *Conflicts in Feminism,* ed. Marianne Hirsch and Evelyn Fox Keller, 255–70. New York: Routledge.

Lehker, Marianne. 1984. *Frauen im Nationalsozialismus.* Frankfurt a.M.: Materialis Verlag.

Leiser, Erwin. 1974. *Nazi Cinema.* London: Secker and Warburg.

Lerg, Winfried B. 1970. *Die Entstehung des Rundfunks in Deutschland.* 2d ed. Frankfurt a.M.: Josef Knecht.

———. 1980. *Rundfunk in der Weimarer Republik,* ed. Hans Bausch. *Rundfunk in Deutschland,* vol. 1. Munich: dtv.

Lewis, Beth Irwin. 1990. "*Lustmord:* Inside the Window of the Metropolis." In *Berlin: Culture and Metropolis,* ed. Charles, W. Haxthausen and Heidrun Suhr, 111–40. Oxford: University of Minnesota Press.

Lewis, Peter, and Jeremy Booth. 1989. *The Invisible Medium: Public, Commercial and Community Radio.* London: Macmillan.

Lloyd, Genevieve. 1993–84. *The Man of Reason: "Male" and "Female" in Western Philosophy.* 2d ed. London: Routledge.

Lück, Margret. 1979. *Die Frau im Männerstaat: Die gesellschaftliche Stellung der Frau im Nationalsozialismus: Eine Analyse aus pädagogischer Sicht.* Frankfurt a.M.: Lang.

Macciocchi, Maria-Antonietta. 1976. *Jungfrauen, Mütter und ein Führer: Frauen im Faschismus.* Berlin: Klaus Wagenbach.

Macdonald, Myra. 1995. *Representing Women: Myths of Femininity in the Popular Media.* London: Edward Arnold.

Macdonald, Sharon, et al., eds. 1987. *Images of Women in Peace and War: Cross-Cultural and Historical Perspectives.* London: Macmillan Education.

Markus, Maria. 1989. "The 'Anti-Feminism' of Hannah Arendt." In *Hannah Arendt: Thinking, Judging, Freedom,* ed. Gisela T. Kaplan and Clive S. Kessler, 119–32. Sydney: Allen and Unwin.

Marshall, Barbara L. 1994. *Engendering Modernity: Feminism, Social Theory and Social Change.* Cambridge: Polity.

Marßolek, Inge, et al. 1995. "Zuhören und Gehörtwerden: Radiogeschichte und Geschlecterordnung im Dritten Reich und der DDR der fünziger Jahre," *Zwischenbericht,* History seminar, University of Hannover, February.

Maschmann, Melita. 1963. *Fazit—Kein Rechtfertigungsversuch.* Stuttgart: Deutsche Verlagsanstalt.

Mason, Tim. 1976a. "Women in Germany, 1925–1940: Family, Welfare and Work." *History Workshop* 2:5–32.

Mason, Tim. 1976b. "Women in Nazi Germany." *History Workshop* 1:74–113.

Massey, Doreen. 1994. *Space, Place and Gender.* Cambridge: Polity.

Mast, Gerald, Marshall Cohen, and Leo Braudy, eds. 1992. *Film Theory and Criticism.* 4th ed. Oxford: Oxford University Press.

Mattelart, Michèle. 1986. "Women in the Cultural Industries." In *Media, Culture and Society: A Critical Reader,* ed. Richard Collins, 63–81. London: Sage.

———. 1986. *Women, Media, Crisis: Femininity and Disorder.* London: Comedia.

McKay, Anne. 1988. "Speaking Up: Voice Amplification and Women's Struggle for Public Expression." In *Technology and Women's Voices: Keeping in Touch,* ed. Chris Kramarae, 188– 200. London: Routledge and Kegan Paul.

McLaughlin, Lisa. 1993. "Feminism, the Public Sphere, Media and Democracy." *Media, Culture and Society* 5(3):599–620.

Miller, Daniel. 1995. "Consumption as the Vanguard of History." In *Acknowledging Consumption: A Review of New Studies,* ed. Daniel Miller, 1–57. London: Routledge.

Milward, Alan. 1965. *The German Economy at War.* London: Athlone.

———. 1976. "Fascism and the Economy." In *Fascism: A Reader's Guide,* ed. Walter Laqueur, 379–412. Cambridge: Cambridge University Press.

Mizejewski, Linda. 1992. *Divine Decadence: Fascism, Female Spectacle, and the Making of Sally Bowles.* Princeton: Princeton University Press.

Mommsen, Walter. 1986. "The Realisation of the Unthinkable." In *The Policies of*

*Genocide: Jews and Soviet Prisoners of War in Nazi Germany,* ed. Gerald Hirschfeld, 93–144. London: German Historical Institute.

Moores, Sean. 1988. "'The Box on the Dresser': Memories of Early Radio and Everyday Life." *Media, Culture and Society* 10:23–40.

Morley, David. 1989. "Changing Paradigms in Audience Research." In *Remote Control: Television, Audiences and Cultural Power,* ed. Ellen Seiter et al., 16–43. London: Routledge.

———. 1993. *Television, Audiences and Cultural Studies.* London: Routledge.

Morley, David, and Roger Silverstone. 1990. "Domestic Communication: Technologies and Meanings." *Media, Culture and Society* 12:31–55.

Mosse, George L. 1968. *Nazi Culture: Intellectual, Cultural and Social Life in the Third Reich.* New York: Gosset and Dunkley.

———. 1975. *The Nationalisation of the Masses: Political Symbolism and Mass Movements in Germany from the Napoleonic Wars through the Third Reich.* New York: Fertig.

Mumford, Lewis. 1962. *Technics and Civilisation.* London: Routledge and Kegan Paul.

Namier, Lewis B. 1952. *In the Nazi Era.* London: Macmillan.

Negt, Oskar, and Alexander Kluge. 1993. *Public Sphere and Experience.* Minneapolis: University of Minnesota Press.

Newton, Judith, and Deborah Rosenfelt, eds. 1985. *Feminist Criticism and Social Change.* London: Methuen.

Nochimson, Martha. 1992. *No End to Her: Soap Opera and the Female Subject.* Berkeley: University of California Press.

Nolan, Mary. 1990. "'Housework Made Easy': The Taylorized Housewife in Weimar Germany's Rationalised Economy." *Feminist Studies* 16(3): 549–77.

———. 1994a. "Imagining America, Modernizing Germany." In *Dancing on the Volcano: Essays on the Culture of the Weimar Republic,* ed. Thomas Kniesche and Stephen Brockman, 72–84. Columbia: Camden House.

———. 1994b. Visions of Modernity: American Business and the Modernization of Germany. Oxford: Oxford University Press.

Nye, Andrea. 1994. *Philosophia: The Thought of Rosa Luxembourg, Simone Weil and Hannah Arendt.* London: Routledge.

Overy, Richard J. 1982. *The Nazi Recovery.* London: Macmillan.

———. 1989. "Hitler's War and the German Economy: A Reinterpretation." In *War, Peace and Social Change in 20th Century Europe,* ed. Clive Emsley Arthur Marwick and Wendy Simpson, 208–25. Milton Keynes: Open University Press.

Pateman, Carole. 1988. "The Fraternal Social Contract." In *Civil Society and the State: New European Perspectives,* ed. John Keane, 34–57. London: Verso.

———. 1989. "Feminist Critiques of the Public/Private Dichotomy." *The Disorder of Women: Democracy, Feminism and Political Theory,* 118–40. Cambridge: Polity.

Passerin d'Entrèves, Maurizio. 1992. "Hannah Arendt and the Idea of Citizenship." In *Dimensions of Radical Democracy,* ed. Chantal Mouffe, 145–68. London: Verso.

Paterson, Richard. 1990. "A Suitable Schedule for the Family." In *Understanding Television,* ed. Andrew Goodwin and Garry Whannel, 30–41. London: Routledge.

Pegg, Mark. 1983. *Broadcasting and Society, 1918–1939.* London: Croom Helm.

Peters, J. D. 1993. "Distrust of Representation: Habermas on the Public Sphere." *Media, Culture and Society* 15(4): 541–71.

Petro, Patrice. 1987. "Modernity and Mass Culture in Weimar: Contours of a Discourse on Sexuality in Early Theories of Perception and Representation." *New German Critique* 40:115–46.

———. 1989. *Joyless Streets: Women and Melodramatic Representation in Weimar Germany.* Princeton: Princeton University Press.

Petzina, Dieter. 1968. *Autarkiepolitik im Dritten Reich.* Stuttgart: Deutsche Verlagsanstalt.

Peukert, Detlev J. K. 1987. *Inside Nazi Germany: Conformity, Opposition and Racism in Everyday Life.* London: Batsford.

———. 1991. *The Weimar Republic: The Crisis of Classical Modernity.* Trans. Richard Deveson. London: Penguin.

Phillips, Anne. 1991. *Engendering Democracy.* Cambridge: Polity.

Pohle, Heinz. 1955. *Der Rundfunk als Instrument der Politik 1923–1938.* Hamburg: Verlag Hans Bredow-Institut.

Probyn, Elspeth. 1993. "Technologizing the Self." *Sexing the Self: Gendered Positions in Cultural Studies,* 108–37. London: Routledge.

Raboy, Marc, and Bernard Dagenais, eds. 1992. *Media, Crisis and Democracy: Mass Communication and the Disruption of Social Order.* London: Sage.

Richieri, G. 1988. "Italian Broadcasting and Fascism." *Media, Culture and Society* 2:49–56.

Riedel, Heide. 1987. *60 Jahre Radio: Von der Rarität zum Massenmedium.* 2d ed. Berlin: Deutsches Rundfunk-Museum.

Rifkin, J. 1987. *Time Wars: The Primary Conflict in Human History.* New York: Henry Holt.

Rosenhaft, Eve. 1987. "The Unemployed in the Neighbourhood: Social Dislocation and Political Mobilisation in Germany 1929–1933." In *The German Unemployed,* ed. Richard J. Evans and Dick Geary, 194–227. London: Croom Helm.

———. 1992. "Women, Gender, and the Limits of Political History in the Age of 'Mass' Politics." In *Elections, Mass Politics, and Social Change in Modern Germany,* ed. Larry Eugene Jones and James Retallack, 149–73. Cambridge: Cambridge University Press.

Rosenhaft, Eve, and W. L. Lee. 1990. *State and Society in Modern Germany.* Oxford: Berg.

Rüdiger, Jütta, ed. 1983. *Die HJ und ihr Selbstverständnis im Spiegel ihrer Aufgabengebiete.* Lindhurst: Askania.

Rupp, Leila J. 1977. "Mother of the Volk: The Image of Women in Nazi Ideology." *Signs: Journal of Women in Culture and Society* 3(2): 362–75.

———. 1978. *Mobilising Women for War: German and American Propaganda, 1939–1945.* Princeton: Princeton University Press.

Rürup, Reinhard, ed. 1989. *Topography of Terror: Gestapo, SS and Reichssicher-heitshauptamt on the "Prince Albrecht-Terrain." A Documentation.* Berlin: Arenhövel.

Rustin, Michael. 1987. "Place and Time in Socialist Theory." *Radical Philosophy* 47:30–36.

Ryan, Mary. 1990. *Women in Public: Between Banners and Ballots, 1825–1880.* Baltimore: Johns Hopkins University Press.

Sachs, Jacqueline, Philip Liebermann, and Donna Erikson. 1973. "Anatomical and Cultural Determinants of Male and Female Speech." *Language Attitudes: Current Trends and Prospects.* Washington, D.C.: George Washington University Press.

Sachse, Carola. 1982. "Hausarbeit im Betrieb, Betriebliche Sozialarbeit unter dem Nationalsozialismus." In *Angst, Belohnung, Zucht und Ordnung: Herrschaftsmechanismen und Nationalsozialismus,* ed. Carola Sachse et al., 218–41. Opladen: Westdeutscher Verlag.

Saldern, Adelheid von. 1990. "The Workers' Movement and Cultural Patterns on Urban Housing Estates and in Rural Settlements in Germany and Austria During the 1920s." *Social History* 15(3):333–76.

Sandford, John. 1976. *The Mass Media of the German-Speaking Countries.* London: Oswald Wolf.

Sauer, Wolfgang. 1972. "Weimar Culture: Experiments in Modernism." *Social Research* 39:254–84.

Sayers, Janet. 1987. "Science, Sexual Difference, and Feminism." In *Analyzing Gender: A Handbook of Social Science Research,* ed. Beth B. Hess and Myra Marx Ferree, 68–91. Newbury Park, Ca.: Sage.

Scannell, Paddy. 1984. "Editorial." *Media, Culture and Society* 4:333–35.

———. 1988. "Radio Times: The Temporal Arrangements of Broadcasting in the Modern World." In *TV and Its Audience: International Research Perspectives,* ed. Phillip Drummond and Richard Paterson, 15–31. London: BFI.

———. 1989. "Public Service Broadcasting and Modern Public Life." *Media, Culture and Society* 11(1): 135–66.

———, ed. 1991. *Broadcast Talk.* London: Sage.

Schäfer, Hans Dieter. 1981. *Das gespaltene Bewußtsein. Über Deutsche Kultur und Lebenswirklichkeit, 1933–1945.* Munich: Hanser.

Schiller-Lerg, Sabine. 1984. *Walter Benjamin und der Rundfunk.* Munich: K. G. Saur.

Schmidt, Maruta, and Gabi Dietz, eds. 1983. *Frauen unterm Hakenkreuz.* Berlin: Elefanten Press.

Schoenbaum, David. 1966. *Hitler's Social Revolution: Class and Status in Nazi Germany 1933–1939.* New York: Doubleday.

Scholtz-Klink, Gertrud. 1978. *Die Frau im Dritten Reich.* Tübingen: Grabert.

Scholz, Manfred, et al., eds. 1975. *Erinnerungen sozialistischer Rundfunkpioniere: Ausgewählte Erlebnisberichte zum 30. Rundfunkjubiläum.* Berlin: Staatliches Komitee für Rundfunk beim Ministerrat der DDR, Eigener Verlag.

Schrader, Bärbel, and Jürgen Schebera. 1987. *Kunstmetropole Berlin, 1918–1933.* Berlin: Aufbau-Verlag.

Schröter, Heinz. 1973. *Unterhaltung für Millionen: Vom Wunschkonzert zur Schlagerparade.* Düsseldorf: Econ.

Schütte, Wolfgang. 1971. *Regionalität und Föderalismus im Rundfunk: Die geschichtliche Entwicklung in Deutschland, 1923–45.* Berlin: Knecht.

Scott, Joan W. 1986. "Gender: A Useful Category of Historical Analysis." *American Historical Review* 91(5): 1053–75.

———. 1988. *Gender and the Politics of History.* New York: Columbia University Press.

Seiter, Ellen, Hans Borchers, Gabriele Kreutzner, and Eva-Maria Warth, eds. 1989. *Remote Control: Television, Audiences and Cultural Power.* London: Routledge.

Sennett, Richard. 1974. *The Fall of Public Man.* New York: Random House.

Shirer, William. 1977. *The Rise and Fall of the Third Reich,* 2d ed. Trowbridge: Book Club Associates.

Short, K. R. M., ed. 1983. *Film and Radio Propaganda in World War II.* Knoxville: University of Tennessee Press.

Slattery, J. F. 1992. "Oskar Zuversichtlich: A German's Response to British Radio Propaganda during World War II." *Historical Journal of Film, Radio and Television* 12(1): 69–85.

Smith, Barbara Clark, and Kathy Peiss. 1989. *Men and Women: A History of Costume, Gender and Power.* Washington, D.C.: National Museum of American History.

Snitow, Ann, Christine Stansell, and Sharon Thompson, eds. 1984. *Desire: The Politics of Sexuality.* London: Virago.

Soden, Kristine von, and Maruta Schmidt, eds. 1988. *Neue Frauen: Die zwanziger Jahre.* Berlin: Elefanten Press.

Soley, Lawrence. 1989. *Radio Warfare: OSS and CIA Subversive Propaganda.* New York and London: Praeger.

Sontheimer Kurt. 1987. "Die politische Kultur der Gegensätze." In *Die Weimarer Republik, 1918–1933: Politik, Wirtschaft, Gesellschaft,* ed. Karl Dietrich Bracher et al., 454–64. Bonn: Droste.

Spacks, Patricia Meyer. 1986. *Gossip.* London: University of Chicago Press.

Spender, Dale. 1980. *Man Made Language.* London: Routledge and Kegan Paul.

Spigel, Lynn. 1992. *Make Room for TV: TV and the Family Ideal in Postwar America.* Chicago: University of Chicago Press.

Stachura, Peter. 1987. *Inside Nazi Germany: Conformity, Opposition and Racism in Everyday Life.* London: Batsford.

———. 1989. *The Weimar Republic and the Younger Proletariat.* London: Macmillan.

Steinert, Marlis. 1970. *Hitlers Krieg und die Deutschen. Stimmung und Haltung der deutschen Bevölkerung im Zweiten Weltkrieg.* Düsseldorf: Econ.

———. 1981–82. "Notes on Nazi Propaganda." *Screen Education* 40:34–47.

Stephenson, Jill. 1975. *Women in Nazi Society.* London: Croom Helm.

———. 1981. *The Nazi Organisation of Women.* London: Croom Helm.

———. 1983. "Propaganda, Autarky and the German Housewife." In *Nazi Pro-*

*paganda: The Power and the Limitations,* ed. David Welch, 117–42. London: Croom Helm.

Stern, J. P. 1975. *Hitler, the Führer and the People.* Berkeley: University of California Press.

Stürmer, Micheal. 1967. *Koalition und Opposition in der Weimarer Republik, 1924–1930.* Düsseldorf: Droste.

———. 1985. *Die Weimarer Republik. Belagerte Civitas.* 2d ed. Königstein: Verlagsgruppe Athenaum.

Szepanksy, Gerda. 1983. *Frauen leisten Widerstand: 1933–1945.* Frankfurt a.m.: Fischer.

———. 1987. *Blitzmädel, Heldenmutter, Kriegerwitwe: Frauenleben im zweiten Weltkrieg.* Frankfurt a.M.: Fischer.

Taylor, A. J. P. 1961. *The Course of German History.* London: Methuen.

Taylor, Brandon, and Wilfried van der Will, eds. 1990. *The Nazification of Art: Art, Design, Music, Architecture and Film in the Third Reich.* Winchester: Winchester Press.

Thalmann, Rita. 1984. *Frausein im dritten Reich.* Frankfurt: Ullstein.

Theweleit, Klaus. 1989. *Männerphantasien: Frauen, Fluten, Körper, Geschichte.* Reinbek: Rowohlt.

Thompson, E. P. 1967. "Time, Work-Discipline and Industrial Capitalism." *Past and Present* 38:56–97.

Thrift, Nigel. 1990. "The Making of A Capitalist Time Consciousness." In *The Sociology of Time,* ed. John Hassard, 105–9. London: Macmillan.

Tidl, George. 1984. *Die Frau im Nationalsozialismus.* Vienna: Europa.

Tröger, Annemarie. 1984. "The Creation of a Female Assembly Line Proletariat." In *When Biology Became Destiny: Women in Weimar and Nazi Germany,* ed. Renate Bridenthal et al., 237–70. New York: Monthly Review Press.

Tucholsky, Kurt. 1994. "Radio Censorship." In *The Weimar Republic Sourcebook,* ed. Anton Kaes, Martin Jay, and Edward Dimendberg, 603–4. Berkeley: University of California Press.

Turner, Bryan. 1992. "Ideology, and Utopia in the Formation of an Intelligentsia: Reflections on the English Cultural Conduit." *Theory, Culture and Society* 9:183–210.

Usborne, Cornelie. 1992. *The Politics of the Body in Weimar Germany: Women's Reproductive Rights and Duties.* Basingstoke: Macmillan.

Vanek, Joann. 1974. "Time Spent on Housework." *Scientific American* 231(5):116–20.

Villa, Dana. 1992. "Postmodernism and the Public Sphere." *American Political Science Review* 86(3): 714–21.

Vorwerck, Else. 1948. *Hauswirtschaft in Selbstverwaltung: Ein erster großer Versuch, 1934–1945.* Hannover: Rotenburg.

Wajcman, Judy. 1991. *Feminism Confronts Technology.* Cambridge: Polity.

Walker, Alexander. 1984. *Dietrich.* London: Thames and Hudson.

Waller, Jane, and Michael Vaughan-Rees. 1987. *Women in Wartime: The Role of Women's Magazines, 1939–45.* London: Optima.

Warner, Marina. 1985. *Monuments and Maidens: The Allegory of the Female Form.* London: Picador.

Warth, Eva-Maria. 1990. "The Reconceptualisation of Women's Roles in Wartime National Socialism: An Analysis of 'Die Frau meiner Träume.' " In *The Nazification of Art: Art, Design, Music, Architecture and Film in the Third Reich,* ed. Brandon Taylor and Wilfried van der Will, 219–30. Winchester: Winchester Press.

Welch, David, A. 1983. *Propaganda and the German Cinema, 1933–1945.* Oxford: Clarendon.

———. 1993. "Manufacturing a Consensus: Nazi Propaganda and the Building of a 'National Community' *Volksgemeinschaft." Contemporary European History* 2(1): 1–15.

———, ed. 1983. *Nazi Propaganda: The Power and the Limitations.* London: Croom Helm.

Wernick, Andrew. 1990. *Promotional Culture.* London: Sage.

Wickham, James. 1983. "Working-Class Movement and Working-Class Life: Frankfurt am Main during the Weimar Republic." *Social History* 8:315–43.

Willett, John. 1978. *The New Sobriety, 1917–1933: Art and Politics in the Weimar Period.* London: Thames and Hudson.

———. 1984. *The Weimar Years: A Culture Cut Short.* London: Thames and Hudson.

Williams, Raymond. 1976. *Keywords: A Vocabulary of Culture and Society.* Glasgow: Fontana / Croom Helm.

———. 1990. *Television:Technology and Cultural Form.* 2d ed. London: Routledge.

Willier, Hartmut. 1977. "Die Kultur- und Medienpolitischen Auffassungen in der Arbeiter-Radio-Presse von Anbeginn bis zur Spaltung des Arbeiterradiobundes im Jahre 1929." Master's thesis, Technische Universität Berlin.

Winkler, Dörte. 1977. *Frauenarbeit im "Dritten Reich."* Hamburg: Hoffmann.

Winkler, Heinrich A. 1984. *Von der Revolution zur Stabilisierung: Arbeiter und Arbeiterbewegung in der Weimarer Republik 1918 bis 1924.* Bonn: Dietz.

———. 1985. *Der Schein der Normalität. Arbeiter und Arbeiterbewegung in der Weimarer Republik 1924 bis 1930.* Bonn: Dietz.

———. 1987. *Der Weg in der Katastrophe. Arbeiter und Arbeiterbewegung in der Weimarer Republik 1930 bis 1933.* Bonn: Dietz.

Witte, Karsten. 1981–82. "Visual Pleasure Inhibited: Aspects of the German Revue Film." *New German Critique* 24(5): 238–63.

Wittrock, Christine. 1983. *Weiblichkeitsmythen: das Frauenbild im Faschismus und seine Vorläufer in der Frauenbewegung der 20er Jahre.* Frankfurt a.M.: Seidler.

Wollen, Peter. 1993. *Raiding the Icebox: Reflections on Twentieth Century Culture.* London: Verso.

Wulf, Joseph. 1983. *Presse und Funk im Dritten Reich: Eine Dokumentation.* Frankfurt a.M.: Ullstein.

Young, Iris. 1987. "Impartiality and the Civic Public: Some Implications of Feminist Critiques of Moral and Political Theory." In *Feminism as Critique: On the Politics of Gender,* ed. Seyla Benhabib and Drucilla Cornell, 57–76. Minneapolis: University of Minnesota Press.

Zeman, Z. A. B. 1978. *Nazi Propaganda.* Oxford: Oxford University Press.

Ziege, Eva-Maria. 1995. "Gottesmörder—Mörder der Göttinnen?" In *Antisemitismus. Vorurteile und Mythen,* ed. Julius H. Schoeps, 180–95. Munich: Piper.

Zinna, Hedda. 1975. "Mit dem Blick nach Deutschland." *Beiträge zur Geschichte des Rundfunks* 4:36–40.

Zoonan, Liesbet van. 1988. "Rethinking Women and the News." *European Journal of Communication* 3:25–53.

———. 1993. "A Tyranny of Intimacy? Women, Femininity and Television News." In *Communication and Citizenship: Journalism and the Public Sphere in the New Media Age,* ed. Peter Dahlgren and Colin Sparks, 217–35. London: Routledge.

# Index

abortion, 19, 67–68, 162
Adorno, Theodor, 6n, 224
advertising, 41, 62–64, 72, 114, 181, 183n, 234n
aestheticization of politics, 7n, 100n
agonistic public sphere, 225–28, 243
amateur radio, 32, 33, 39, 136
Americanization, 4, 170–72
Anlinger, Else, 118
announcers, 199–206. *See also* presenters
Annuske, Edith, 135
anti-Semitism, 20, 95, 98, 117, 128, 179–80
   in radio policy, 100–101, 128, 209
*Arbeiterfunk,* 37, 58
Arbeiterradiobund (ARBD), 37, 58
Arbeiterradioklubs (ARK), 35, 37, 61
*Arbeitersender,* 38, 68
Arendt, Hannah, 15, 221, 225–28, 233–35, 237–38, 243–44
audience. *See* listeners; reception
audience research, 11, 104–9, 132, 236

Baake, Curt, 37
Barthes, Roland, 211, 212n
Baumann, Zygmunt, 179n, 233
BBC, 9, 74, 137–38, 140
Benjamin, Walter, 5n, 7n, 100n
Bergmann, Ernst, 98
Berlin, 23, 157
birth control, 19, 124, 162–63
   Nazi sterilization policy, 98
*Blaue Engel, Der,* 87
Bock, Gisela, 10, 125
Bodenstedt, Hans, 64, 77
Borkmann, Ewis, 70

Brecht, Bertolt, 6, 35
Bredow, Hans, 29–35 passim, 44, 47, 50, 64, 90, 100, 197
Bremen-Hirschkendt, Gerda von, 110, 112–13
Bretschneider, Anneliese, 167
Brix, Meta, 195
broadcasting as public sphere, 3, 25–28, 34, 240, 242
broadcasting companies, 30–32, 31n
   Berliner Funkstunde, 31, 63, 66, 100, 176, 194, 197, 200
   British Broadcasting Company, 30
   Deutsche Stunde (DS), 30, 31
   Drahtloser Dienst (Dradag), 30, 31, 50, 132n
   Funkdienst GmbH, 63
   Westdeutscher Rundfunk, 197
Brose, Hans, 186
Bund Deutscher Frauen (BDF), 60n, 76, 111, 164
Bund Deutscher Mädel (BDM), 94, 120–23
Buoncampagni, Luisa, 199, 200

Caemmerer, Margaret, 67
campaigns
   boycott of Jewish trade, 179–80
   direction of consumption, 178–92, 216
   Frauen helfen siegen, 142
   health policy, 162
   Kampf dem Verderb, 182, 185
   Mädel, wir brauchen Euch, 119
   Sachgemäßes Waschen, 186–91
   Winterhilfe, 91, 118, 182
Canovan, Margaret, 225n

catholic women's organizations, 111
censorship
    Nazi radio, 94, 101, 208
    Weimar cinema, 27
    Weimar radio, 6, 28, 50, 100, 196–97
    *See also* propaganda
centralization
    of Nazi radio, 99, 101
    of Weimar radio, 50–52
children's radio. *See* Kinderfunk
citizenship, 19, 223, 227–28, 233
civil society, 151, 226, 235
class
    audiences, 102, 107, 138
    critiques of middle class output, 35–38,
        61–63, 69, 81, 85, 90, 202, 241
    middle class critiques of radio, 38–46
    middle class women, 19, 23, 58–59, 86,
        144, 155–56, 168
    in Nazi ideology, 101, 111–12, 119
    and the public sphere, 226, 229, 231, 236
    working class women, 19, 86, 144,
        155–56, 170
    *See also* housewives' unions; trade
        unions; workers' radio movement
communicative action, 225
communicative entitlements, 236, 238
communicative ethos of broadcasting, 224,
    233, 237
communicative rationality, 236–37
consumer power, 84, 176, 178, 190–92
consumerism
    Third Reich, 173–92 passim
    Weimar, 168–72
continuity and change, 58, 94, 115–20, 165,
    175–76, 237, 239–45
counterpublics, 14, 240–41
crisis, 4–5, 17–18, 53, 227, 241–42
    economic (*see* Depression)
    of the family, 5, 21, 22, 163, 166
    and the media, 18
    of modernity, 157, 161
critical theory, 229, 234

Dahlgren, Peter, 228n
*D. W. Funk,* 80, 150
democratization, 156, 235, 237–39
    women's radio, 240–43
Depression, 25, 41, 49, 67, 68, 81, 83, 91–93,
    122, 164, 169, 178, 182, 200
Dery, Dora, 194

Deutsche Arbeitsfront (DAF), 183, 188
    women's office, 111, 114, 182, 190
Deutsche Frauenfront (DFF), 111–13
Deutscher Frauen-Kampfbund, 76
Deutscher Kurzwellensender. *See* short-
    wave
Deutsches Frauenwerk (DFW), 111–13,
    177, 183, 188, 214
    Reichsreferentin für Waschfragen,
        186
    V/H department, 112, 178, 182
*Deutsche Rundfunk, Der,* 39, 46, 116, 194,
    202, 203
Deutsches Nachrichtenbüro, 204
Deutsches Rundfunkarchiv, 8n, 86, 150
Deutsche Welle, 13, 31, 36, 59, 150–72, 166,
    176, 177
    Frauenfunk, 79–85, 153–72
*Deutsche Welle,* 150
Deutschlandsender, 50, 93, 94, 112, 117,
    120, 131, 135, 178, 204, 206
    Frauenfunk, 95, 116, 185
Diehl, Guida, 76
Diel, Louise, 170–71
Dietz, Mary, 226
divorce, 19, 21
DNVP, 41, 46, 48
domestic science. See home economics
domestic void, 152
double burden (for working women), 22,
    25n, 153, 155, 165, 168
drama, 79, 117, 120
Dreßler-Andreß, Horst, 100
Drewitz, Anna, 66, 80
Dreyer, Ernst, 97
Durkheim, Emile, 159n
Duske, Carl Friedrich, 100
DVP, 76

Eckert, Gerd, 204
education
    Berliner Funkstunde, 66
    Deutsche Welle, 79–85, 150
    Hans Bredow Schule, 74–79
    *See also* political education; Schulfunk
effects, 11, 12n, 52, 140, 178
Einödshofer, Maria, 201
electronics industry, 26, 30. *See also* radio
    sets
Eley, Geoff, 232
Elternfunk (parents' radio), 68

employment
Third Reich, 140–45
Weimar Republic, 20, 23–25, 47
Engels, Friedrich, 154n, 224
Enlightenment, 151, 224
entertainment
as morale booster, 132, 141
Nazi radio, 102–3
as propaganda, 130
wartime, 138
Weimar cinema, 27
Weimar radio, 29–30, 50, 62
*Erkenntnisgeist,* 97–99
eugenics, 163, 169
exhibitions, 77, 79, 153, 180
exiles, 111, 143–45
experts, 40, 149, 151–53, 156, 216
Eyseren, Gertrud van, 200

fascism. *See* Nazi ideology
feminism on the radio, 44–47, 60, 66, 77,
    239, 241–42, 244
Fillies-Kirmsse, Erika, 105, 114, 115n
film
Aufklärungsfilme, 21n, 27
*Die Stimme aus dem Äther,* 206–7
history, 7
influence on radio, 79
as new medium, 26–27, 60, 161
as propaganda, 101, 121, 123, 129, 131,
    178, 188
regulation, 26–27
as shop window, 170
street films, 23
in wartime, 128
See also *Wochenschauen*
Flesch, Hans, 197, 201
Fliegel, Alice, 45, 77, 79, 158
Fordism, 23n, 154
foreign broadcasts:
BBC, 141–43
German anti-fascists, 143–45
illegal reception, 38, 102, 105, 128, 131n,
    134, 141–45
Italy, 199
monitoring, 148
Soviet Union, 37–38, 143
Foucault, Michel, 5n, 9, 11n, 232
Four Year Plans, 124, 174, 181, 183–86, 189
Frankfurt Kitchen, 157
Frankl-Hutterer, Anna, 58

Fraser, Nancy, 15n, 226, 231n, 232, 240
Frauenfunk, 7, 9, 49, 57
and democracy, 240–41
Frauenfunk (Nazi):
aims, 112, 124
Deutschlandsender, 95, 116, 185
newsgathering, 135
organization, 113–14, 132
personnel, 112
politics, 124
propaganda, 132
racism, 180
regions: Berlin, 116, 120; Breslau, 116–17;
    Cologne, 116–17; Danzig, 188; Frank-
    furt, 116–17; Hamburg, 116, 177–78;
    Königsberg, 117, 208–16; Leipzig, 116,
    185; Munich, 118, 120; Saarbrücken,
    120; Stuttgart, 116; war effort, 132;
    wartime, 145
Frauenfunk (Weimar):
Deutsche Welle, 79–85, 153–72
influences, 57–59
introduction of, 57, 60–65
marginalization of, 59, 71
organization, 58–85
regions: 65–79; Berlin, 58, 60–61, 65–68;
    Breslau, 60–61; Cologne, 70–72;
    Frankfurt, 60–61, 72; Hamburg, 73–79;
    Königsberg, 61; Leipzig, 61, 62, 72–73;
    Munich, 60, 68–70; Münster, 60;
    Stuttgart, 73
Frauenfunksprechstunde, 70
*Frauenspiegel,* 145
Frauenwirtschaftskammer (FWK), 177
freedom of the press, 27, 229, 234
Freier Radiobund (FRB), 37–38
Freytag, Hilde, 121
Frick, Wilhelm, 100, 112
Fritzsche, Hans, 132
*Frontberichte,* 132, 145
*Führerprinzip,* 99
Funck, Hertha Maria, 37, 48, 71
*Funk,* 42, 65, 200, 204, 206
*Funk und Bewegung,* 100
*Funk-Woche,* 206

Gayl, Wilhelm von, 50
gender
as category of analysis, 10, 221
technology of, 10–11
*See also* public and private

generation gap, 86, 88
Gestapo, 105
Giddens, Anthony, 5–6, 159n
Girl–Kultur, 171
*Gleichschaltung,* 53, 94, 99, 209, 239
  of consumption, 175
  of radio, 116
  of women's organizations, 111
  of youth radio, 94, 122
Gödecke, Heinz, 135, 206
Goebbels, Joseph, 20, 100–102, 127,
    129–30, 132, 136, 137n, 144, 220n
Goebbels, Magda, 93
Göring, Hermann, 101n, 175n, 186
gossip, 80, 131, 194, 217
Gottschewski, Lydia, 111–13
Gramsci, Antonio, 232
gymnastics, 117

Haase, Annamarie, 143
Habermas, Jürgen
  public sphere theory, 14, 25, 221, 234–40
  theory of communicative action, 225
Hadamovsky, Eugen, 100n, 113, 114
Haentzschel, Kurt, 30, 33
Hamburg, 157
Hanna, Gertrud, 83
Hans Bredow Schule, 74–79
Hansen, Miriam, 26
Hansen, Phillip, 231
Hardt, Ernst, 197
Hausen, Karin, 164–65, 222n
Hauswirtschafts-Rundfunk (home economy
    radio). *See* home economics
Hegel, Georg, 45n, 223
Heilmann, Ernst, 29–30
Hersel, Carola, 85–95
Hess, Rudolf, 184
Heuß-Knapp, Elly, 89, 187–88
Hinkel, Hans, 129–30, 206
Hitler State, 114
Hitler, Adolf, 20, 101n, 138, 197–98, 211,
    217, 242
Hitler-Stalin pact, 138
Hitlerjugend (HJ), 120–22
hobby programs (Bastelstunden), 81, 169
Holocaust, 179n, 233
home economics, 41, 65, 76, 151, 171,
    176–77. *See also* rationalization of the
    home; Volkswirtschaft/Hauswirtschaft
*Hörerstreik,* 102

*Hörkultur,* 103–4
housewives' unions, 57, 60–62, 72, 80,
    111
housework
  as profession, 40, 152–53
  rationalization of, 151–55
housing policy, 156–57

identity politics, 243–45
imagined community, 45n, 202, 235
industrialization, 150, 158, 161
inflation, 22–23, 32–33, 170

Jäger-Jessen, Elfriede, 69
Jewish women's organizations, 111
*Jugend hilft der Jugend,* 91–93
Jugendstunde, 87–89, 92
Jungmädchenstunde, 89–94, 120–21

*Kameradschaftsdienst,* 136
Kamnitzer, Ilse, 201
*Kampfzeit,* 110–11
Kapp Putsch, 33
Kappesser, Gertrud, 114, 115n, 131n
Kardorff-Oheimb, Katharina, 46, 48
Keane, John, 18, 234–35, 242
Kelly, Joan, 222
Kinderfunk (children's radio), 37, 59, 69,
    84, 86–87, 117, 120–23, 136, 200,
    209–10
Kisch, Egon Erwin, 38
Knupffer, Paula, 116
Köhn-Behrens, Charlotte, 207–8
Kollontai, Alexandra, 154n
Koonz, Claudia, 124–25
KPD, 36–37, 67, 111, 156
Kracauer, Siegfried, 7n, 169n, 170
Kristallnacht, 179
Kristeva, Julia, 218–19
Krummacher, Gottfried, 111
Kuhlmann, Herta, 8, 107–9
Kuhn, Eva, 136
*Kulturbeiräte,* 28, 197

Landsberg, Erich, 167
*Lebensraum,* 124n, 125–26
leisure time, 59, 86, 102, 117, 161
Ley, Robert, 113, 183
licenses
  Third Reich, 128
  Weimar, 32, 33, 42

listeners
  as citizens, 34, 244–45
  as community, 212, 216
  as consumers, 63, 65, 169–73, 174–92
  as housewives, 39, 42–44, 103–4
  as mothers, 39, 127, 162–65
  as soldiers' wives, 135, 136
  survey, 106–9
  as widows, 133–34; as wives, 39–40, 104, 127
  as working women, 66, 69, 118, 166–69
  *See also* reception
listeners' letters, 65, 69, 71, 90–93, 119, 131, 144n, 201, 208
listening as collective experience, 45, 119, 157, 161, 174
listening figures
  anti–fascist stations, 138, 140
  Third Reich, 102
  Weimar, 32, 42, 50, 64
listening groups, 37, 113, 209, 239
live broadcasts, 44, 197, 208
loudspeakers, 102–3
Lüders, Marie Elisabeth, 76, 77

*Machtübernahme,* 100
Mädelfunk, 121
magazines, 187
Magnus-Unzer, Frieda, 209–16
marriage, 19, 86, 162
  on the air, 136
Marx, Karl, 158, 159, 223
masculinity
  Nazi ideology, 111, 122, 127
  youth radio, 87
mass culture, 156, 169, 177
Massey, Doreen, 225
mass society, 19–20, 174
Matz, Else, 76
melodrama, 79
Mende, Clara, 76
Mendzee, Margret, 195n
men's radio, 59
Meyer, Erna, 154n
military broadcasts, 102, 107, 129, 133, 137
Miller, Daniel, 176n
mobile privatization, 160
mobilization
  of female labour, 140–45
  feminist, 44–47

political, 36n, 42, 44–47, 241
  of women in Third Reich, 126
Möbus, Else, 95, 166, 187
modernity, 5–6, 41, 53, 149–72 passim, 223, 233
modernization, 18n, 150, 153, 173, 223, 241
Mommsen, Walter, 179n
morale, 128–35, 137, 185
motherhood
  in Nazi ideology, 117, 124–26, 145–46
  scientific, 41, 151, 162, 165
  social motherliness, 19
  *See also* listeners; *Muttergeist;* programs (Nazi); programs (Weimar)
Mothers' Day
  Third Reich, 112, 114, 116, 138, 139, 144n, 184
  Weimar, 164–65
musical programs
  Nazi radio, 102, 106–7, 130, 137, 139, 191, 197
  Weimar radio, 32–33, 60, 63, 73, 78, 161
*Muttergeist,* 97–99, 118, 150, 203
Mütterschulen, 112, 118

National Federation, 111
Nazi economy, 173–75, 179
nazification. See *Gleichschaltung*
Nazi ideology
  family, 124
  fascism, 174
  gender, 97–99
  identity, 244
  masculinity, 111
  on radio, 205
  women, 117, 125, 127, 145–46, 150–51, 211, 240
Nebuschka, Toni, 201
*Neue Rundfunk, Der,* 35, 46, 47, 58, 61, 63, 67, 71, 77, 155
New Plan (1934), 175
news
  Nazi radio, 114, 123
  wartime, 127, 135, 137
  Weimar radio, 34, 50
newsreels. See *Wochenschauen*
New Woman, 21–22, 171
Nolan, Mary, 153, 155, 171
nonpolitical radio, 28, 29, 33–35, 44, 47–48, 58, 61, 68, 85, 92, 100, 125, 196, 202, 241

Norag, 48, 64, 93
November revolution 1919, 33
NS Frauenschaft (NSF), 93, 103, 111, 113,
    118, 143, 177–79, 188, 209
*NS Frauen-Warte,* 137
NS Volkswohlstand (NSV), 112
*NS-Funk,* 100, 206
NSDAP, 25, 110
    banned from Weimar radio, 100
    membership, 111

organization
    of Weimar Frauenfunk, 58–85
    of Weimar radio, 27–35
    of Nazi Frauenfunk, 113–15;
    of Nazi radio, 99–101, 120–23

Papen, Franz von, 50
Pateman, Carole, 223
Paulsen, Harald, 206
Peakok, Mary, 39–40
Peck, Lisa, 7n, 97, 106
performative action, 233, 243
Perkins Gilman, Charlotte, 154n
Peukert, Detlef, 5n, 21, 23n
photography, 161
pirate radio, 37
*Plauderei* (chitchat). *See* presentation
plurality, 233, 235, 238, 244
    in Arendt, 225–28
    in feminist theory, 224
political education:
    Nazi radio, 123, 239
    Weimar radio, 44, 46, 48, 76, 84
politicization
    of the private sphere, 49, 124–26, 156,
        242
    of the public sphere, 229
    of radio, 47–52, 123
postmodernism, 159n, 233
presentation, 193–220
    anti-Semitic, 180, 216
    development of, 99
    dialogue, 64, 72, 78, 162, 207
    double articulation, 210
    experts, 203
    Hersel, 94
    innovations, 64
    mode of address, 127, 144–45, 211, 217,
        220

*Muttergeist,* 203
Nazi propaganda, 197–98
Plauderei, 65, 67, 69, 89, 141, 193, 208
resistance broadcasts, 144–45
presenters
    men, 65, 72, 194–96
    Nazi radio, 132, 204–6
    Weimar radio, 65, 69
press
    comparison with radio, 34, 42, 48, 67, 77,
        92
    in competition with radio, 64
    freedom of, 27, 229, 234
    influence on Frauenfunk, 57, 60
    nazification, 100
    political mobilization, 241
    as social need, 161
privacy, 227
programs (Nazi)
    on careers for women, 119
    current affairs, 135, 149, 150
    discussion, 208
    fashion, 119
    gymnastics, 116–17, 124
    motherhood, 116, 119, 150
    press reviews, 135
    recipes, 116, 211
    for relatives of fallen soldiers, 137–38
    for rural women, 116
    V/H, 116–17, 173–92 passim
    for women abroad, 116
    for working women, 116
    wartime requests, 138–40
    on women and war, 149
    women in the arts, 118
programs (Weimar)
    on careers for women, 66, 75, 80, 83, 90,
        166–69
    current affairs, 49
    direction of consumption, 81–82, 176–
        77
    discussion, 66; fashion, 63, 68, 73
    government broadcasts, 50
    household tips, 60–75 passim, 80, 171
    interview, 196
    Jungmädchenstunde, 89–90
    marriage, 67, 75, 162–63
    for men, 59
    motherhood, 67–68, 72, 81–83, 162–66
    press reviews, 48

rationalization, 154
recipes, 66, 73, 80, 83
romance, 63
for rural women, 165
talks, 68, 73, 75, 77, 78, 195
V/H, 81
women in the arts, 75, 77, 79, 81
women in politics, 66, 72, 75
propaganda, 20, 97, 102, 239, 245
anti-Semitic, 129
anti-Soviet, 38, 128
direction of consumption, 127, 150,
174–92, 174
entertainment, 132
international, 140
Jugendfunk, 120–23
other media, 180, 184, 191
Nazi Frauenfunk, 120, 125, 132, 173–92
passim
Nazi propaganda pre-1933, 100, 110
Nazi racist policies, 104
presentation, 210–20
rationalization, 155–56
for relatives of fallen soldiers, 137–38
repetition, 220
resistance, 140–45
wartime, 127–28
prostitution, 21, 23
protestant women's organizations, 111
public and private, 59, 85, 124, 151, 173,
221, 222–35
in Arendt, 226–28
gendered spheres, 3, 12, 19, 20n, 222n
identity politics, 243–44
in liberal theory, 17n, 223, 224
in Marxist theory, 223
in Nazi ideology, 98
spatial dimension, 225
public opinion, 234
wartime, 128–35
public service broadcasting, 33, 70, 74, 97,
235–39
public sphere, 44, 151, 171, 221–45
broadcast, 125, 240
as category of analysis, 229
cinema, 27
Habermas, 14, 25, 234–39
media and democracy, 234
spatial dimension, 227, 231
and women's radio, 240–43

Radel, Frieda, 75–77
radio
as collective experience, 45, 119, 157, 161,
174
as companion, 41, 45, 130
as consumer good, 149, 170
first broadcast, 32, 62
as link to outside world, 32, 40, 42, 43,
99, 158, 236
as modernizer, 150
as new medium, 3, 6, 10, 11, 26, 29, 153,
159, 245
as secondary medium, 40, 43, 103
as social need, 161
spatial dimension, 157
as technology of gender, 10–11
as voice of the nation, 113–14, 199,
204
in the workplace, 161
in USA, 29, 62
radio journals, 11, 37n, 35–47 passim, 137n,
150
radio policy
1923–26, 27–31
1926 guidelines, 34, 47–48
1932 reforms, 37, 49–52, 99
Third Reich, 99–104, 130–32
radio sets
homemade, 36, 37, 88
introduction of, 26
production in Third Reich, 103
requisition of, 128
technophobia, 42–43
Volksempfänger, 101–3, 137, 177
radio wardens, 105
Rahl, Mady, 206
rationality, 225, 231–35, 236–37
rationalization
of architecture, 153, 156–57
of agriculture, 158
of the home, 73
of housework, 80, 149, 153,
154–55
of labour, 23, 168
of listening, 158
propaganda about, 155
of reproduction, 162
Third Reich, 177
working class experience of, 156
rationing, 188, 216–19

reception
  family, 39, 193
  illegal, 32, 102, 105, 128, 131n, 134, 137n, 136–40
  private, 28, 30, 174
  public, 25, 30, 37, 102, 161
regional stations
  Weimar, 30n, 31, 60–79, 197, 201
  Third Reich, 101, 116–20, 132, 137, 185, 189, 208–16
  *See also* Frauenfunk
Reichsausschuß für Volkswirtschaftliche Aufklärung (RVA), 180–91, 216
Reichsfrauenführerin. *See* Scholtz–Klink
Reichsfrauenführung (RFF), 105, 111–12, 119, 132, 136, 184
Reichsjugendführung (RJF), 121–22
Reichskulturkammer (RKK), 95, 97, 101, 206
Reichsministerium des Innern (RMI), 29, 35, 48, 50, 52, 100, 112
Reichsministerium für Volksaufklärung und Propaganda (RMVP), 101, 130, 134, 188
  employment policy, 142–43
Reichsministerium für Wissenschaft, Erziehung und Volksbildung, 121
Reichsmütterdienst (RMD), 112
Reichsnährstand, 112, 118, 177
Reichspostministerium (RPM), 29, 30, 31, 32, 50
Reichspropagandaleitung (RPL), 105, 131n
Reichsrundfunkgesellschaft (RRG), 32, 41, 50, 62, 201, 209, 236
Reichsrundfunkkammer (RRK), 101
Reichssendeleitung (RSL), 105, 113, 121, 130, 205
Reichsverband Deutscher Hausfrauen (RDH), 60–61, 112
Reicke, Ilse, 89
Reiners, Käte, 137
resistance, 136–40, 191, 227
Rodt, Ellen, 103
Rosenberg, Alfred, 98, 130n
*Rufer und Hörer,* 106, 122, 209
Ruhr occupation, 70
rural programming, 165

Saldern, Adelheid von, 7n
Sauckel, Fritz, 141

Scannell, Paddy, 219, 235–39
Schacht, Hjalmar, 173
schedules, 52, 57, 81, 158–59, 243
  calendrical role, 164
  Nazi radio, 104, 119, 132, 150
Schirach, Baldur von, 122n
Schmidt, Grete, 139
Schmidt, Johanna, 190
Scholtz-Klink, Gertrud, 111, 113, 138, 178, 184, 189
Scholz, Edith, 201
Scholz, Erich, 49, 50–51, 93
Schreiber, Adele, 45–46, 66
Schubotz, Hermann, 92
Schule der Frau, 75–79, 99, 116, 118
Schulfunk (school radio):
  Third Reich, 120, 209; Weimar, 37, 79, 87
Schütte-Lihotzky, Grete, 157
*Schwarzhörer,* 32. *See also* reception, illegal
Scott, Joan, 10
scripts
  Bunter Nachmittag, 208–16
  direction of consumption, 219
  on rationing, 216–19
*Sendung, Die,* 40, 43, 45, 49, 202, 203, 206
*sensus communis,* 233, 235, 237
service broadcasting, 65
Severing, Carl, 48, 49
sex crime, 21
sex reform, 162
sexuality, 87, 162, 167
shopping, 169n, 170–71, 175
short-wave, 134, 136
Siber, Paula, 111–12
Sicherheitsdienst (SD), 105
  reports, 128, 130, 132, 135, 137
Simons, Gerda, 80
soap opera, 62, 75
*Sonderweg,* 4
Spanish Civil War, 138
SPD, 36, 37, 45, 49, 66, 111, 154n, 156
sponsorship, 62–64, 70
Steup, Else, 92
*Stimme aus dem Äther, Die,* 206–7
Stoffregen, Götz, 204
suburbs, 161
suffrage, 19–20, 44
Suhr, Werner, 123, 203

targeted programming, 36, 57, 79, 123, 138. *See also* schedules

Taylorization, 23n, 154, 169–71
Teetzmann, Martha–Elisabeth, 201
telegraphy, 23n, 161
telephone, 6n, 23n, 90n, 161
television, 144n
Thewelweit, Klaus, 21n
time
  checks, 62, 159
  social organization of, 158–61
  *See also* schedules
trade unions, 83, 111, 153, 156, 168
training, 113, 200, 203

*Überwachungsausschüsse,* 28, 37, 197
Uhlig, Anneliese, 206
unemployment, 23, 82, 86, 166, 168n, 169,
  182, 200
universalism, 224–25, 230
Unterhaltungsrundfunk (entertainment
  radio), 29, 62. *See also* entertainment
urban/rural divide, 68, 80, 150, 157–58

*Verbrauchslenkung* (direction of consumption). *See* propaganda
Villa, Dana, 233
voices
  of authority, 199
  disembodied, 206, 218–19
  in feminist theory, 243
  transmission of, 198–99
*Völkischer Beobachter,* 135, 151, 179, 208
Volksempfänger. *See* radio sets
*Volksgemeinschaft,* 14, 94, 101, 114, 120,
  126, 173, 239
Volkswirtschaft/Hauswirtschaft (V/H), 81,
  173–92 passim. *See also* propaganda,
  direction of consumption
Vorwerck, Else, 178, 182
Voss, Ernst Ludwig, 30

Wagner, Emmy, 179
Waitzmann, Ernst, 206
Waldow, Ernst, 206
war. *See* World War One; World War
  Two
Wauer, William, 81
Weimar Republic
  constitution, 19, 27, 44, 164
  demography, 21n, 86n

political extremism, 25, 33
position of women, 18–25
Weiß, Ilse, 69
Wessel, Karl, 200, 206
Williams, Raymond, 159–60, 236
*Wochenschauen* (newsreels), 127, 128,
  132
Wolf, Margarete, 201
Wollstonecraft, Mary, 224
Woman Question, 151, 152, 224
women's history, 9–11
women's organizations
  Third Reich, 110–12.
  *See also* Bund Deutscher Frauen,
  Deutsches Frauenwerk, NS Frauenschaft, Reichsfrauenführung, Reichsverband Deutscher Hausfrauen, Zentralstelle der deutschen Hausfrauenvereine
women's radio. *See* Frauenfunk.
workers' radio movement, 35–38, 50, 58,
  138, 155, 161
  aims, 36
  membership, 36–38
World War One:
  aftermath, 3, 18–22, 86, 163, 241
  mobilization, 19
World War Two, 127–48 passim
  bereavement, 133–34
  Eastern front, 128, 143
  war economy, 173–74
  morale, 128–35, 205–6
  outbreak, 127–28, 185
  preparation, 128
  propaganda, 216–20
  reports, 127–34
  Total War, 144–46
  war effort, 127, 140–45, 189, 217
*Wunschkonzert,* 135
Würzburger, Karl, 168

Young, Iris, 224–26
youth radio, 87–95, 120–23

*Zeitspiegel,* 132, 144, 145
Zeitungs-und Rundfunkschau, 132
Zentralstelle der deutschen Hausfrauen-
  vereine (ZdH), 66, 81, 176
Zetkin, Klara, 224
Zuar, Ralph E., 40